# SUPERMAN
## ACTION COMICS
### VOL. 5 THE HOUSE OF KENT

# SUPERMAN
## ACTION COMICS
### VOL. 5 THE HOUSE OF KENT

**BRIAN MICHAEL BENDIS**
writer

**JOHN ROMITA JR.**
penciller

**KLAUS JANSON** and **DANNY MIKI**
inkers

**BRAD ANDERSON**
colorist

**DAVE SHARPE**
letterer

**JOHN ROMITA JR., KLAUS JANSON,** and **BRAD ANDERSON**
collection cover artists

**SUPERMAN** created by **JERRY SIEGEL** and **JOE SHUSTER**
**SUPERGIRL** based on the characters created by **JERRY SIEGEL** and **JOE SHUSTER**
**SUPERBOY** created by **JERRY SIEGEL**
By special arrangement with the Jerry Siegel family

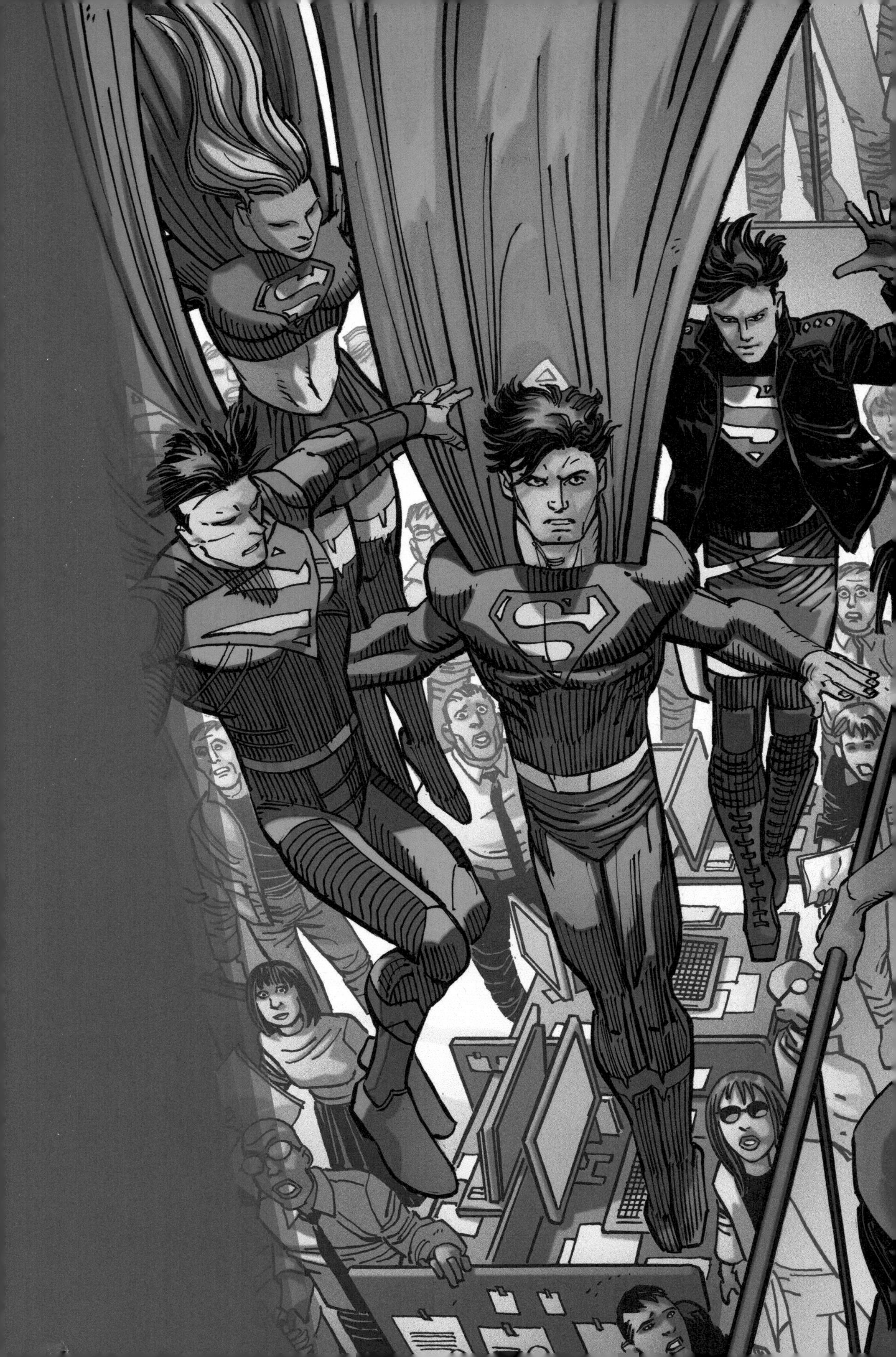

JAMIE S. RICH  Editor – Original Series

BRITTANY HOLZHERR  Associate Editor – Original Series & Editor – Collected Edition

BIXIE MATHIEU  Assistant Editor – Original Series

STEVE COOK  Design Director – Books

CURTIS KING JR.  Publication Design

ERIN VANOVER  Publication Production

MARIE JAVINS  Editor-in-Chief, DC Comics

DANIEL CHERRY III  Senior VP – General Manager

JIM LEE  Publisher & Chief Creative Officer

JOEN CHOE  VP – Global Brand & Creative Services

DON FALLETTI  VP – Manufacturing Operations & Workflow Management

LAWRENCE GANEM  VP – Talent Services

ALISON GILL  Senior VP – Manufacturing & Operations

NICK J. NAPOLITANO  VP – Manufacturing Administration & Design

NANCY SPEARS  VP – Revenue

SUPERMAN: ACTION COMICS VOL. 5: THE HOUSE OF KENT

DC Comics, 2900 West Alameda Ave., Burbank, CA 91505

Printed by LSC Communications, Owensville, MO, USA. 8/20/21. First Printing.

ISBN: 978-1-77951-271-0

Library of Congress Cataloging-in-Publication Data is available.

PEFC Certified

This product is from
sustainably managed
forests and controlled
sources

PEFC/29-31-337     www.pefc.org

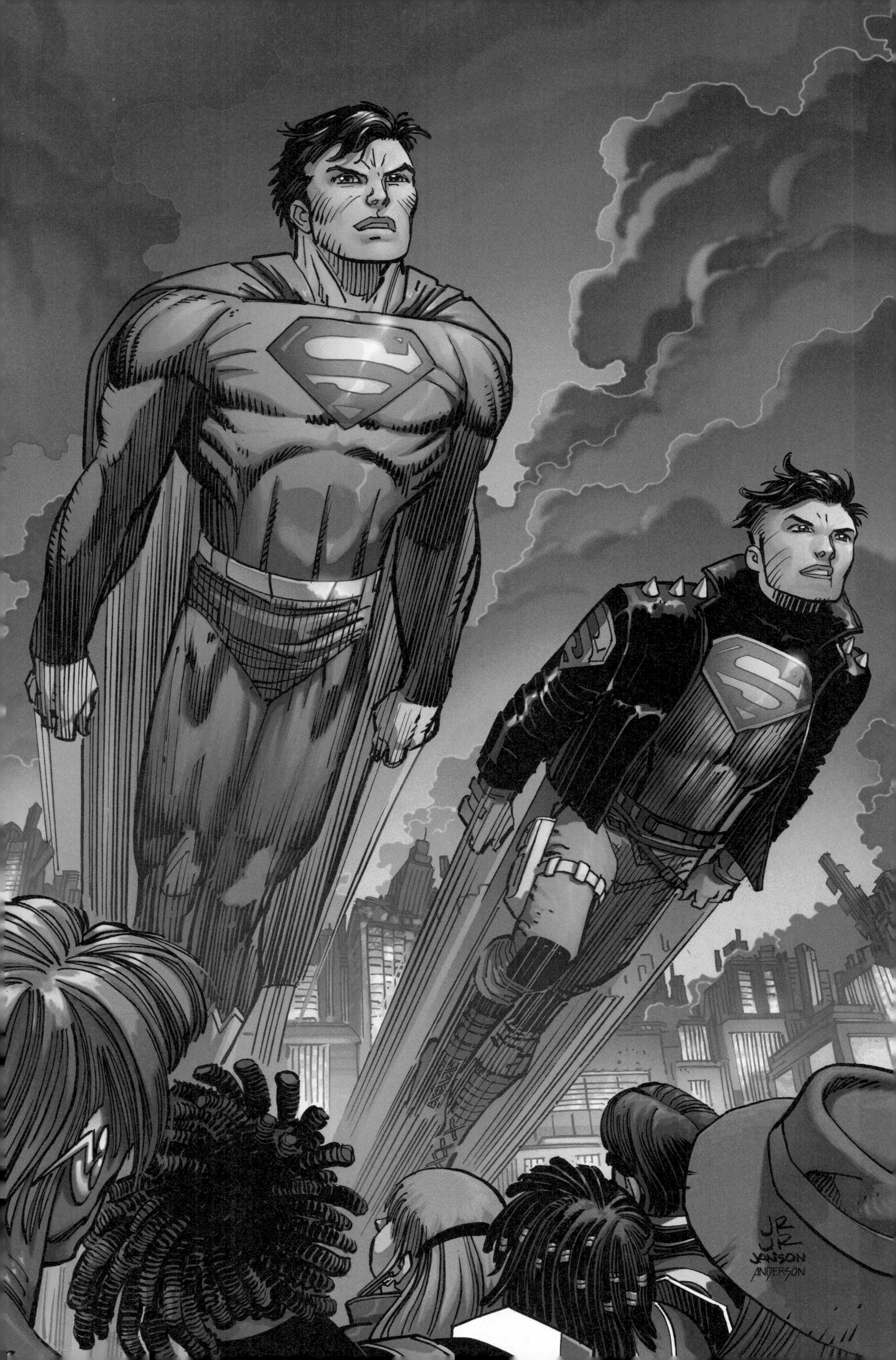
JR JR
JANSON
ANDERSON

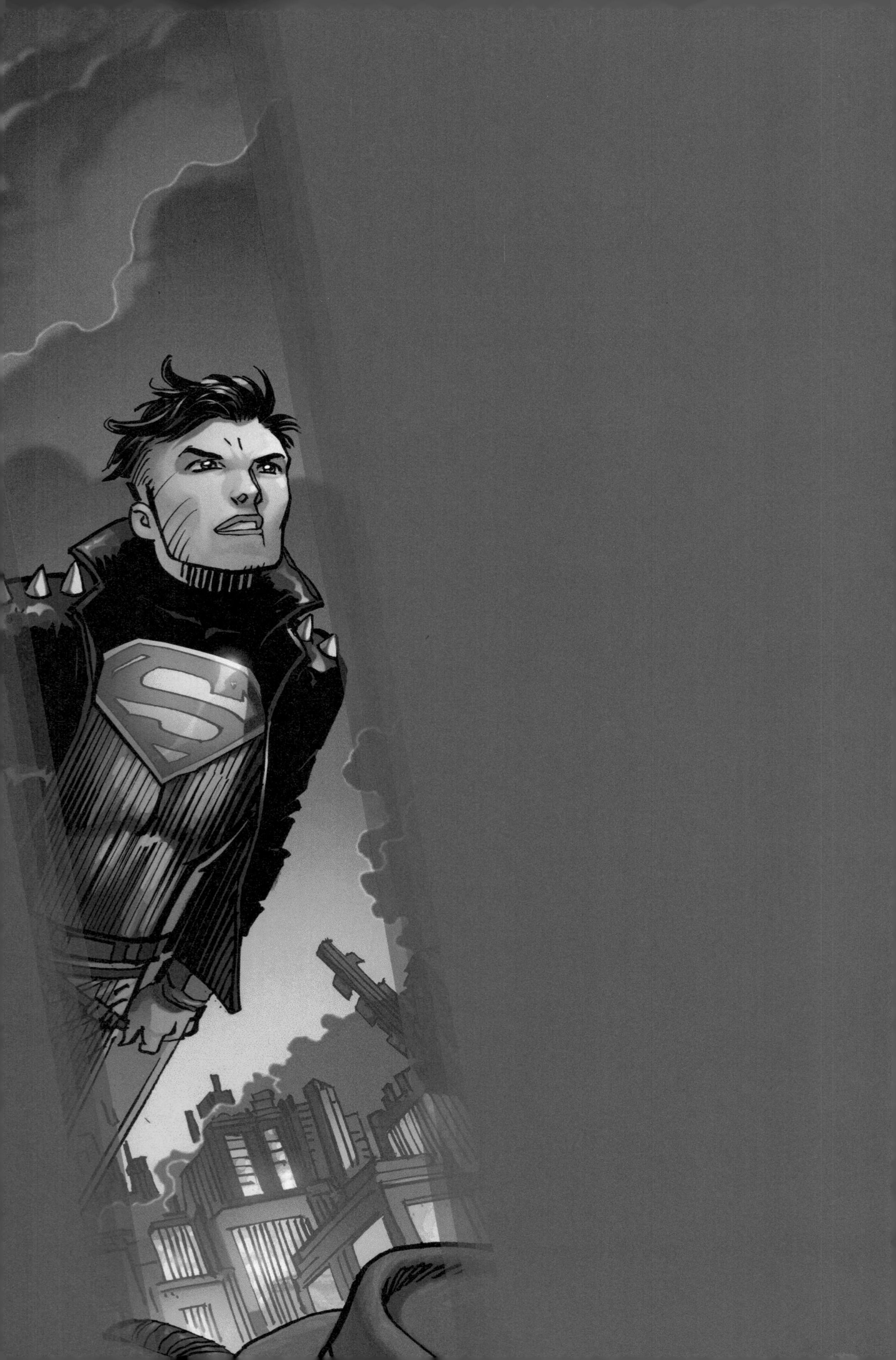

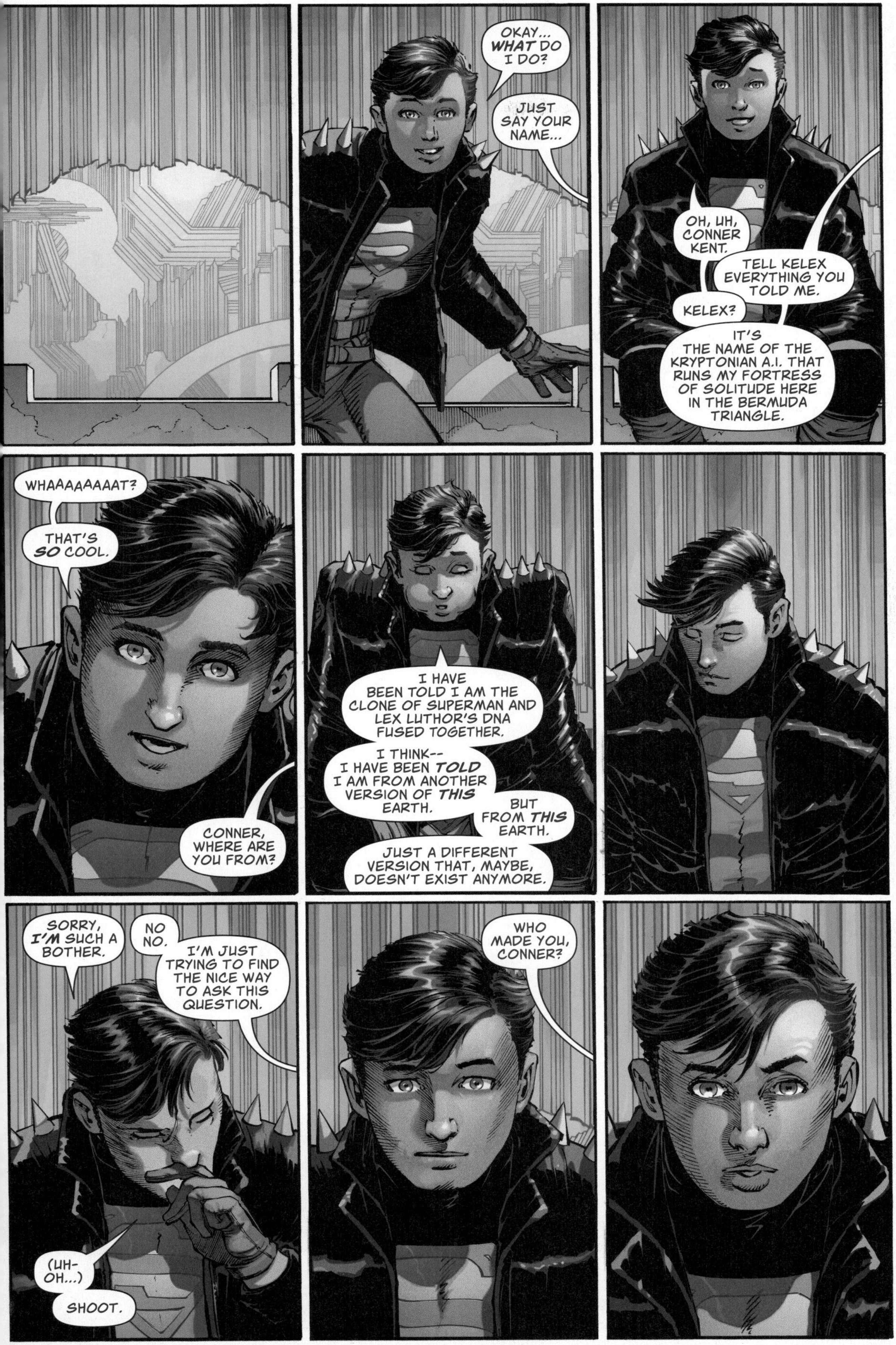
OKAY... WHAT DO I DO?
JUST SAY YOUR NAME...
OH, UH, CONNER KENT.
TELL KELEX EVERYTHING YOU TOLD ME.
KELEX?
IT'S THE NAME OF THE KRYPTONIAN A.I. THAT RUNS MY FORTRESS OF SOLITUDE HERE IN THE BERMUDA TRIANGLE.
WHAAAAAAAAT?
THAT'S SO COOL.
CONNER, WHERE ARE YOU FROM?
I HAVE BEEN TOLD I AM THE CLONE OF SUPERMAN AND LEX LUTHOR'S DNA FUSED TOGETHER.
I THINK-- I HAVE BEEN TOLD I AM FROM ANOTHER VERSION OF THIS EARTH.
BUT FROM THIS EARTH.
JUST A DIFFERENT VERSION THAT, MAYBE, DOESN'T EXIST ANYMORE.
SORRY, I'M SUCH A BOTHER.
NO NO.
I'M JUST TRYING TO FIND THE NICE WAY TO ASK THIS QUESTION.
(UH-OH...)
SHOOT.
WHO MADE YOU, CONNER?

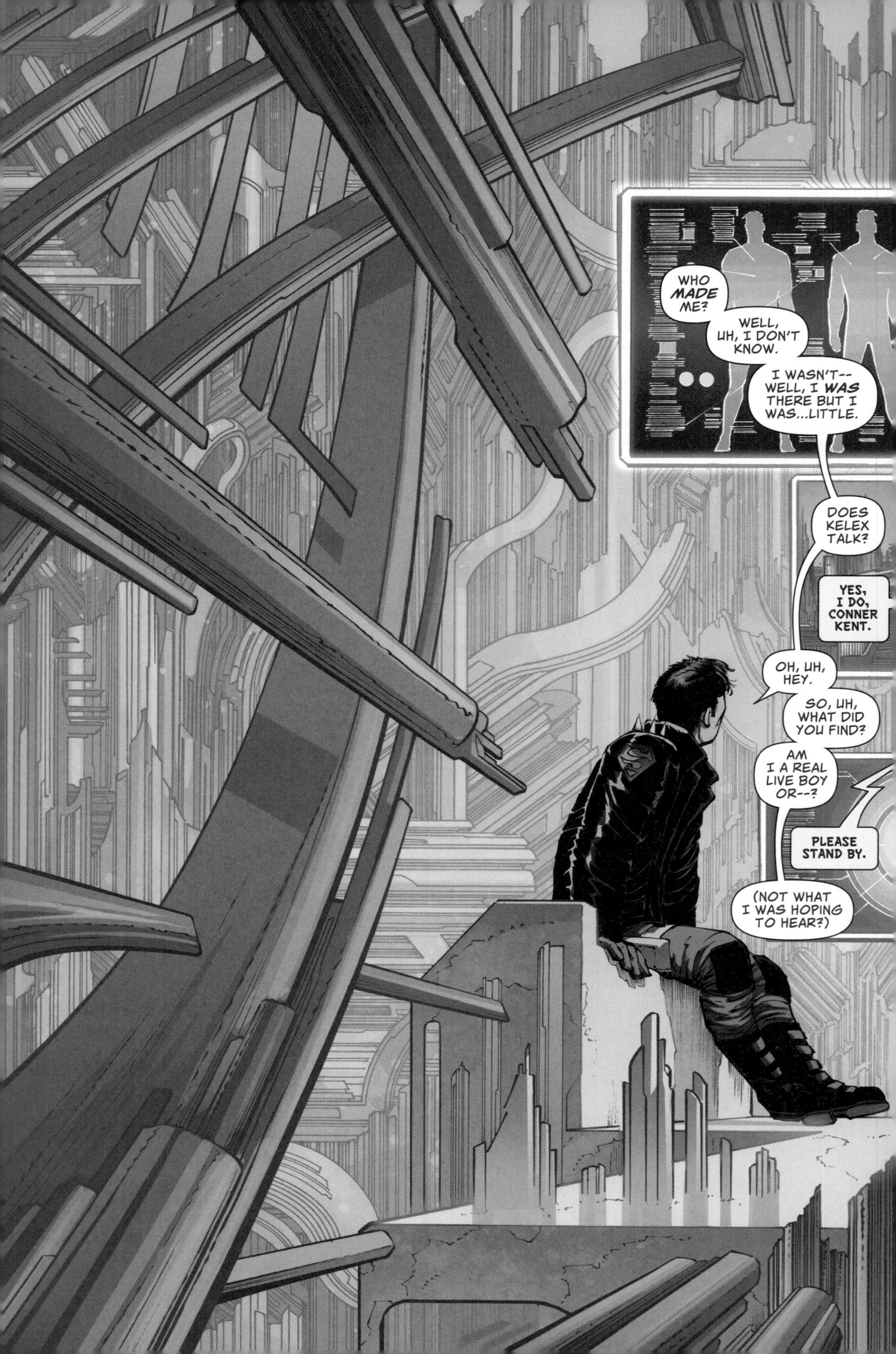
WHO MADE ME?
WELL, UH, I DON'T KNOW.
I WASN'T-- WELL, I WAS THERE BUT I WAS...LITTLE.
DOES KELEX TALK?
YES, I DO, CONNER KENT.
OH, UH, HEY.
SO, UH, WHAT DID YOU FIND?
AM I A REAL LIVE BOY OR--?
PLEASE STAND BY.
(NOT WHAT I WAS HOPING TO HEAR?)

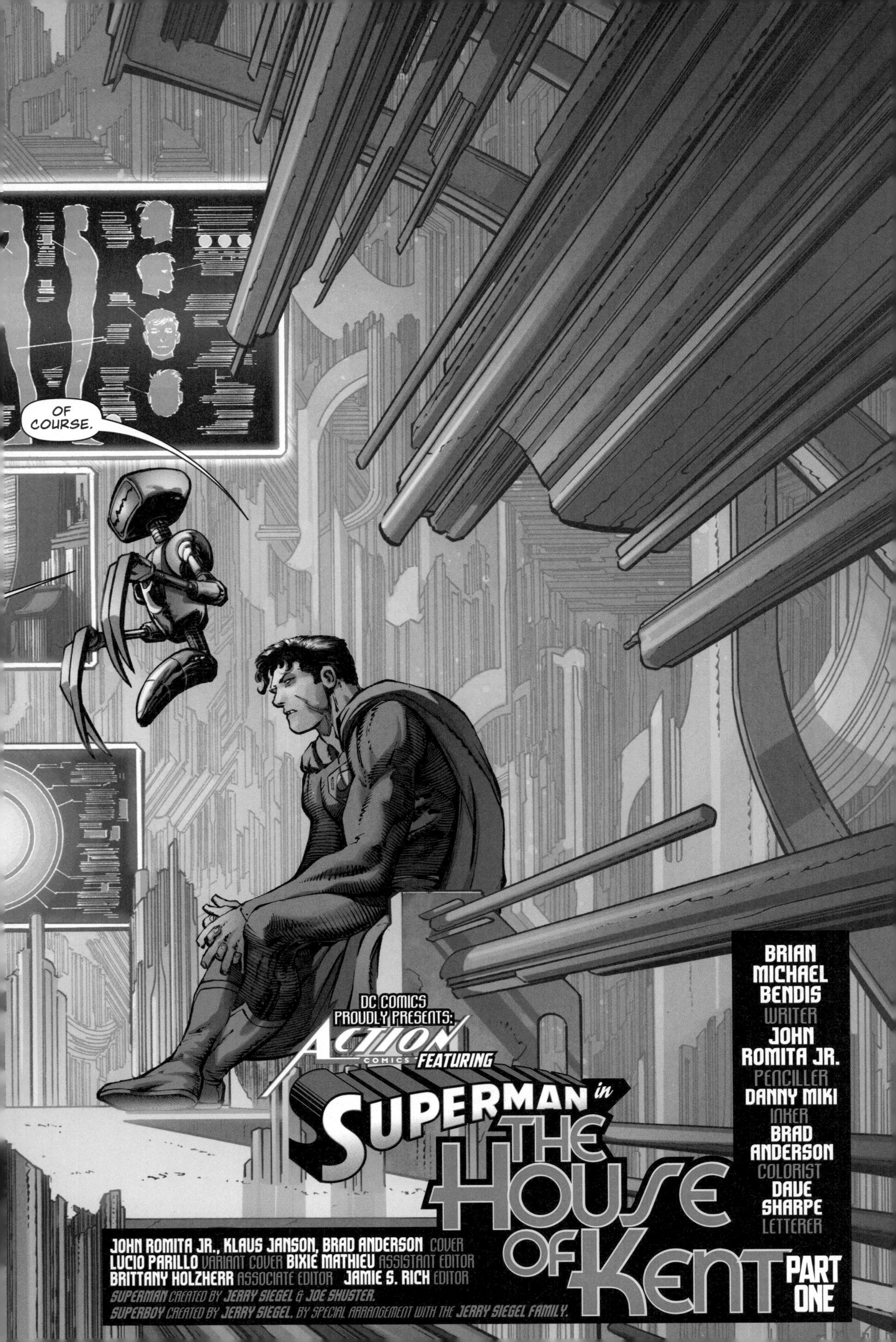

OF COURSE.
DC COMICS PROUDLY PRESENTS:
ACTION COMICS FEATURING
SUPERMAN in
THE HOUSE OF KENT
PART ONE
BRIAN MICHAEL BENDIS WRITER
JOHN ROMITA JR. PENCILLER
DANNY MIKI INKER
BRAD ANDERSON COLORIST
DAVE SHARPE LETTERER
JOHN ROMITA JR., KLAUS JANSON, BRAD ANDERSON COVER
LUCIO PARILLO VARIANT COVER BIXIE MATHIEU ASSISTANT EDITOR
BRITTANY HOLZHERR ASSOCIATE EDITOR JAMIE S. RICH EDITOR
SUPERMAN CREATED BY JERRY SIEGEL & JOE SHUSTER.
SUPERBOY CREATED BY JERRY SIEGEL. BY SPECIAL ARRANGEMENT WITH THE JERRY SIEGEL FAMILY.

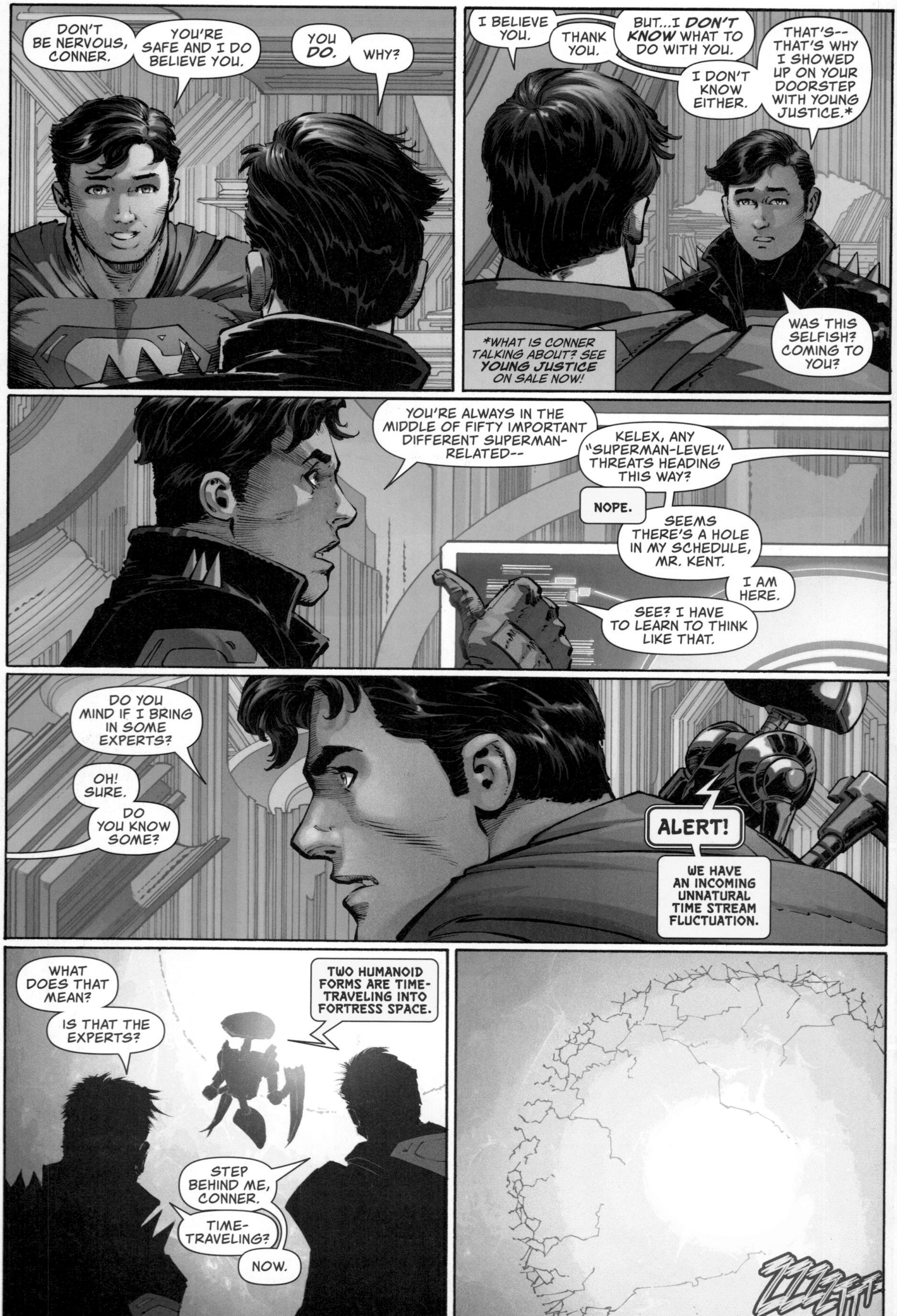

DON'T BE NERVOUS, CONNER.
YOU'RE SAFE AND I DO BELIEVE YOU.
YOU DO.
WHY?
I BELIEVE YOU.
THANK YOU.
BUT...I DON'T KNOW WHAT TO DO WITH YOU.
I DON'T KNOW EITHER.
THAT'S-- THAT'S WHY I SHOWED UP ON YOUR DOORSTEP WITH YOUNG JUSTICE.*
*WHAT IS CONNER TALKING ABOUT? SEE YOUNG JUSTICE ON SALE NOW!
WAS THIS SELFISH? COMING TO YOU?
YOU'RE ALWAYS IN THE MIDDLE OF FIFTY IMPORTANT DIFFERENT SUPERMAN-RELATED--
KELEX, ANY "SUPERMAN-LEVEL" THREATS HEADING THIS WAY?
NOPE.
SEEMS THERE'S A HOLE IN MY SCHEDULE, MR. KENT.
I AM HERE.
SEE? I HAVE TO LEARN TO THINK LIKE THAT.
DO YOU MIND IF I BRING IN SOME EXPERTS?
OH! SURE.
DO YOU KNOW SOME?
ALERT!
WE HAVE AN INCOMING UNNATURAL TIME STREAM FLUCTUATION.
WHAT DOES THAT MEAN?
IS THAT THE EXPERTS?
TWO HUMANOID FORMS ARE TIME-TRAVELING INTO FORTRESS SPACE.
STEP BEHIND ME, CONNER.
TIME-TRAVELING?
NOW.
ZZZZZFFF

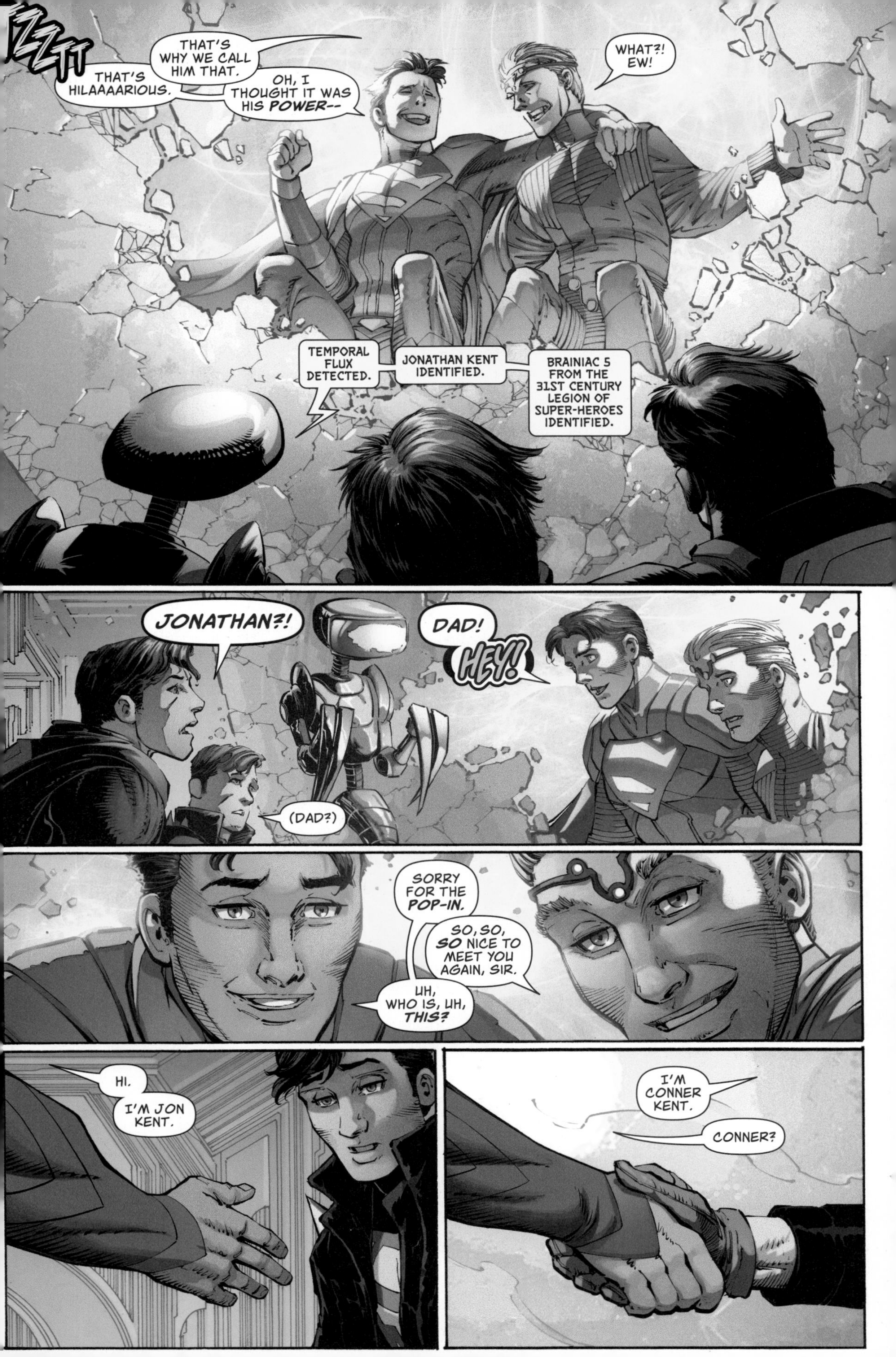
ZZTT
THAT'S HILAAAARIOUS.
THAT'S WHY WE CALL HIM THAT.
OH, I THOUGHT IT WAS HIS POWER--
WHAT?! EW!
TEMPORAL FLUX DETECTED.
JONATHAN KENT IDENTIFIED.
BRAINIAC 5 FROM THE 31ST CENTURY LEGION OF SUPER-HEROES IDENTIFIED.
JONATHAN?!
DAD!
HEY!
(DAD?)
SORRY FOR THE POP-IN.
SO, SO, SO NICE TO MEET YOU AGAIN, SIR.
UH, WHO IS, UH, THIS?
HI.
I'M JON KENT.
I'M CONNER KENT.
CONNER?

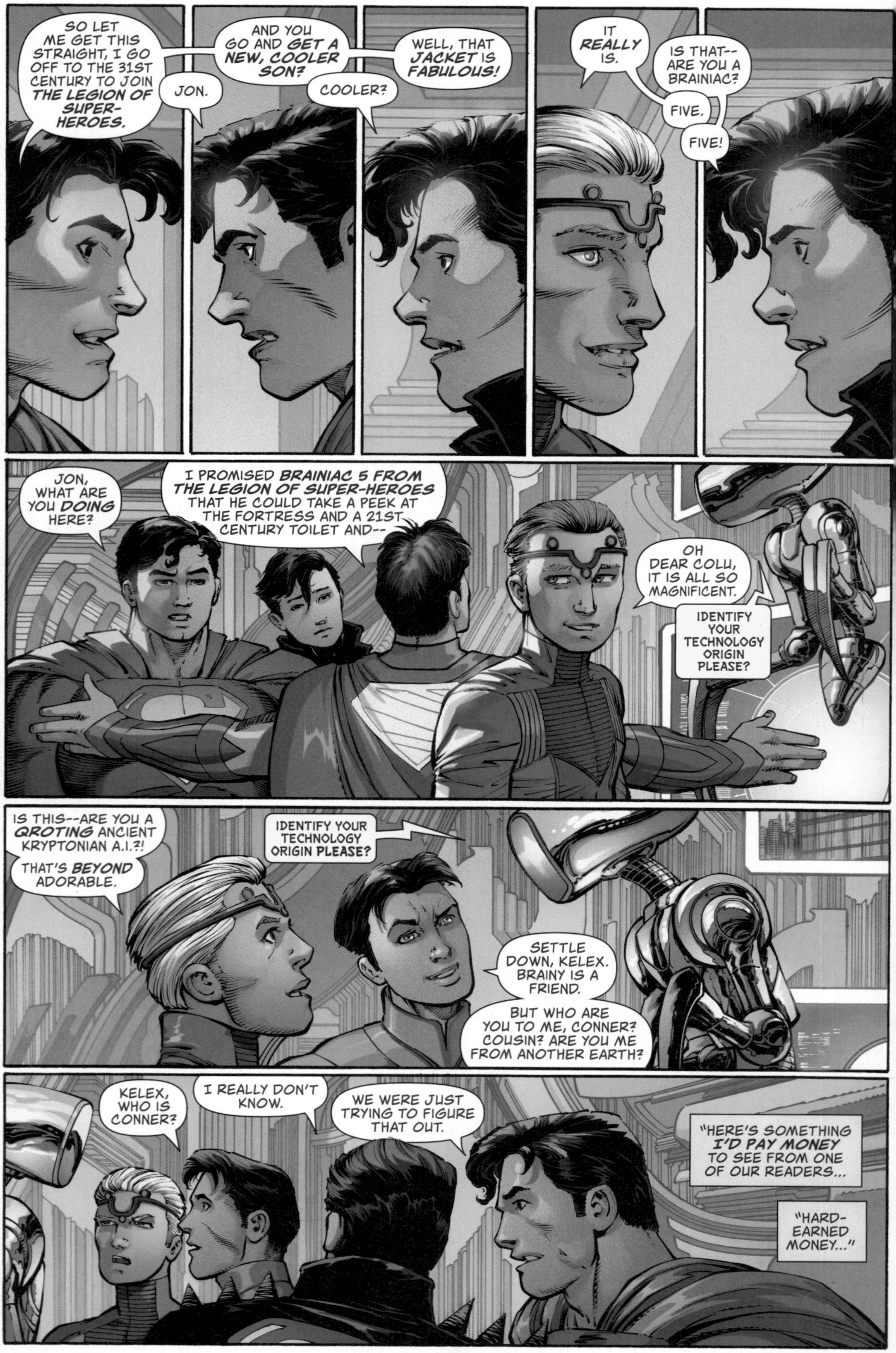
SO LET ME GET THIS STRAIGHT, I GO OFF TO THE 31ST CENTURY TO JOIN THE LEGION OF SUPER-HEROES.
AND YOU GO AND GET A NEW, COOLER SON?
JON.
WELL, THAT JACKET IS FABULOUS!
COOLER?
IT REALLY IS.
IS THAT-- ARE YOU A BRAINIAC?
FIVE.
FIVE!
JON, WHAT ARE YOU DOING HERE?
I PROMISED BRAINIAC 5 FROM THE LEGION OF SUPER-HEROES THAT HE COULD TAKE A PEEK AT THE FORTRESS AND A 21ST CENTURY TOILET AND--
OH DEAR COLU, IT IS ALL SO MAGNIFICENT.
IDENTIFY YOUR TECHNOLOGY ORIGIN PLEASE?
IS THIS--ARE YOU A QROTING ANCIENT KRYPTONIAN A.I.?!
THAT'S BEYOND ADORABLE.
IDENTIFY YOUR TECHNOLOGY ORIGIN PLEASE?
SETTLE DOWN, KELEX. BRAINY IS A FRIEND.
BUT WHO ARE YOU TO ME, CONNER? COUSIN? ARE YOU ME FROM ANOTHER EARTH?
KELEX, WHO IS CONNER?
I REALLY DON'T KNOW.
WE WERE JUST TRYING TO FIGURE THAT OUT.
"HERE'S SOMETHING I'D PAY MONEY TO SEE FROM ONE OF OUR READERS...
"HARD-EARNED MONEY..."

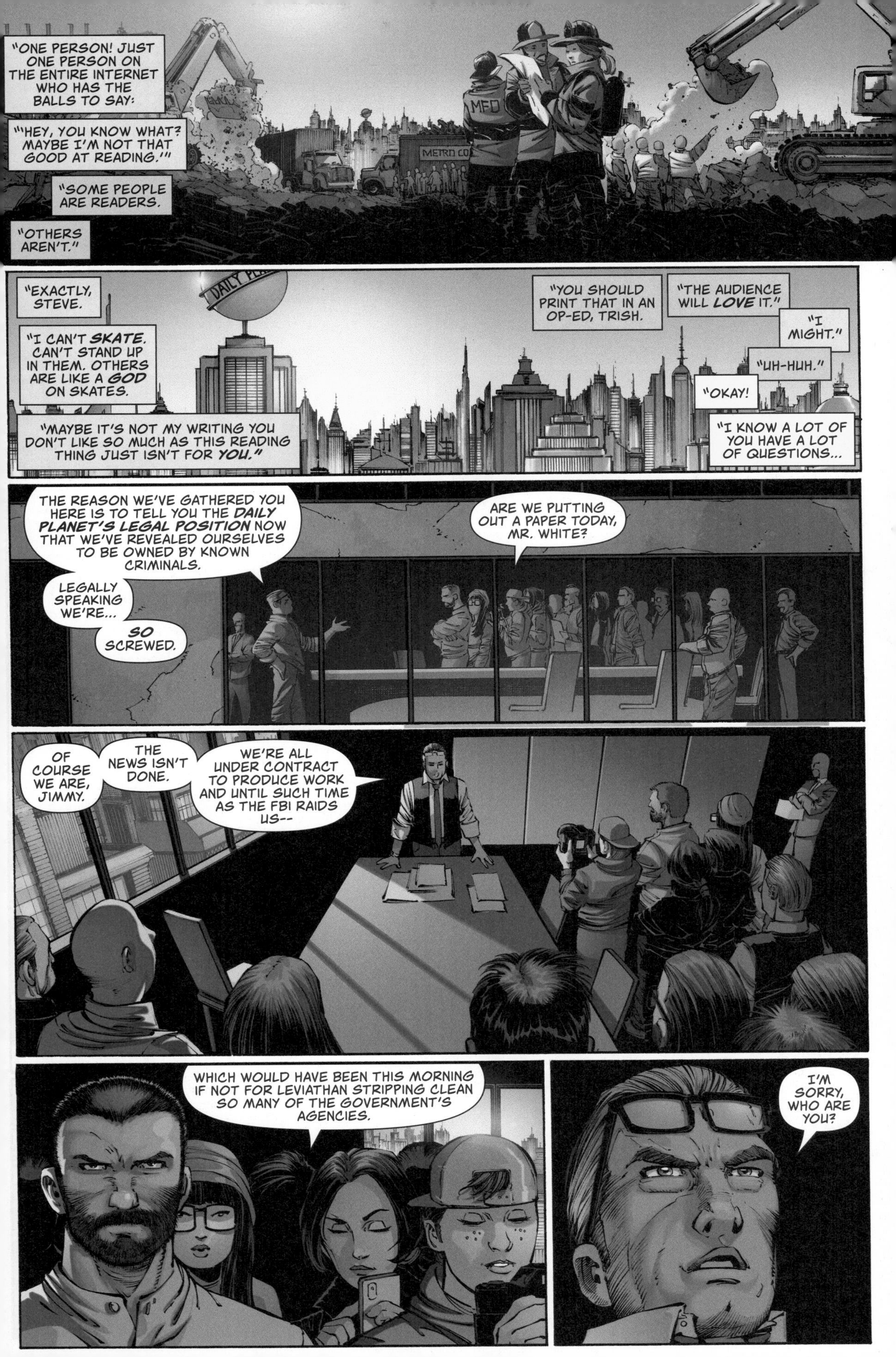

"ONE PERSON! JUST ONE PERSON ON THE ENTIRE INTERNET WHO HAS THE BALLS TO SAY:
"'HEY, YOU KNOW WHAT? MAYBE I'M NOT THAT GOOD AT READING.'"
"SOME PEOPLE ARE READERS.
"OTHERS AREN'T."
MFD
METRO CO
DAILY PL
"EXACTLY, STEVE.
"I CAN'T SKATE. CAN'T STAND UP IN THEM. OTHERS ARE LIKE A GOD ON SKATES.
"MAYBE IT'S NOT MY WRITING YOU DON'T LIKE SO MUCH AS THIS READING THING JUST ISN'T FOR YOU."
"YOU SHOULD PRINT THAT IN AN OP-ED, TRISH.
"THE AUDIENCE WILL LOVE IT."
"I MIGHT."
"UH-HUH."
"OKAY!
"I KNOW A LOT OF YOU HAVE A LOT OF QUESTIONS...
THE REASON WE'VE GATHERED YOU HERE IS TO TELL YOU THE DAILY PLANET'S LEGAL POSITION NOW THAT WE'VE REVEALED OURSELVES TO BE OWNED BY KNOWN CRIMINALS.
LEGALLY SPEAKING WE'RE...
SO SCREWED.
ARE WE PUTTING OUT A PAPER TODAY, MR. WHITE?
OF COURSE WE ARE, JIMMY.
THE NEWS ISN'T DONE.
WE'RE ALL UNDER CONTRACT TO PRODUCE WORK AND UNTIL SUCH TIME AS THE FBI RAIDS US--
WHICH WOULD HAVE BEEN THIS MORNING IF NOT FOR LEVIATHAN STRIPPING CLEAN SO MANY OF THE GOVERNMENT'S AGENCIES.
I'M SORRY, WHO ARE YOU?

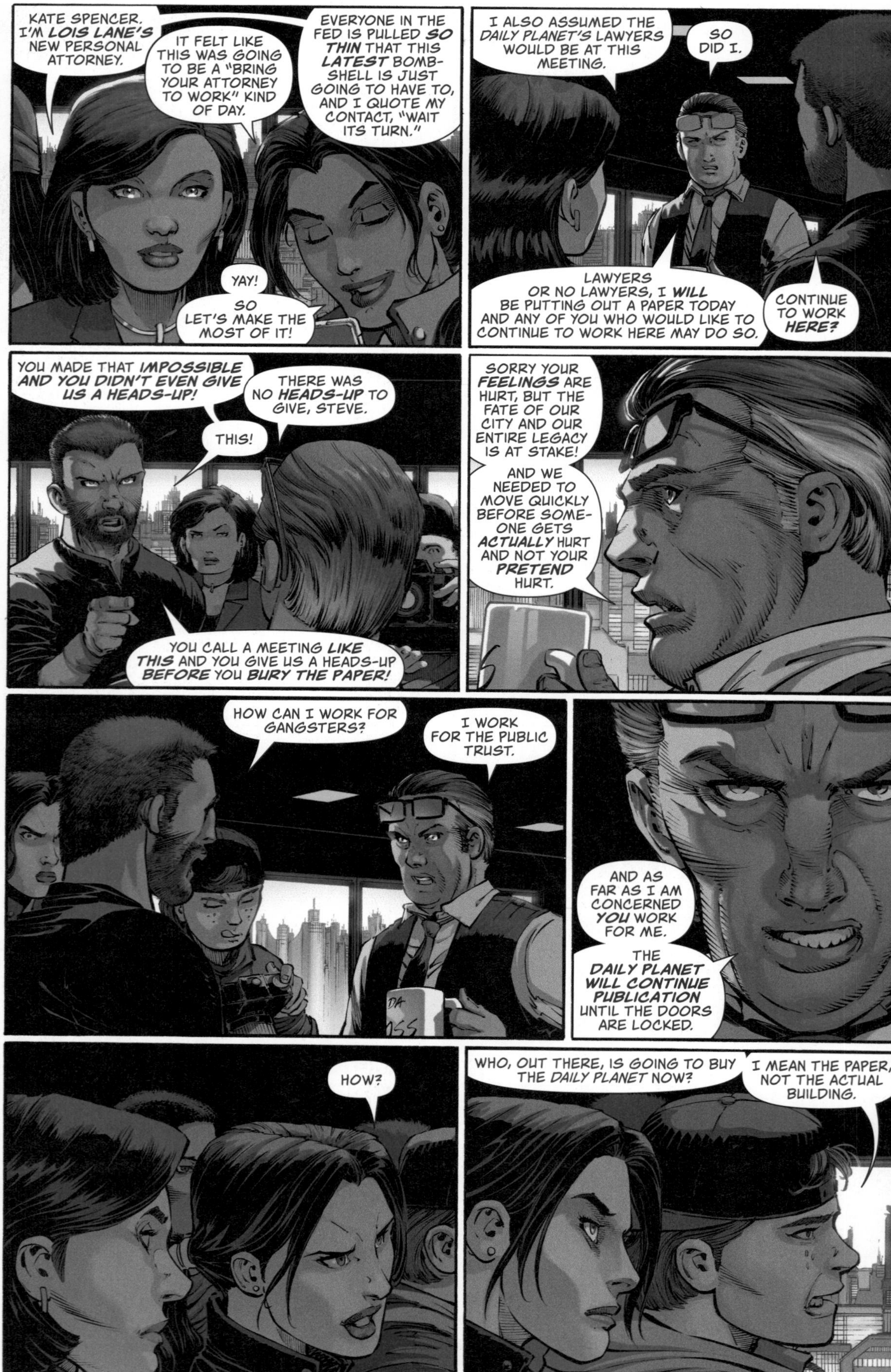
KATE SPENCER. I'M LOIS LANE'S NEW PERSONAL ATTORNEY.
IT FELT LIKE THIS WAS GOING TO BE A "BRING YOUR ATTORNEY TO WORK" KIND OF DAY.
EVERYONE IN THE FED IS PULLED SO THIN THAT THIS LATEST BOMBSHELL IS JUST GOING TO HAVE TO, AND I QUOTE MY CONTACT, "WAIT ITS TURN."
YAY!
SO LET'S MAKE THE MOST OF IT!
I ALSO ASSUMED THE DAILY PLANET'S LAWYERS WOULD BE AT THIS MEETING.
SO DID I.
LAWYERS OR NO LAWYERS, I WILL BE PUTTING OUT A PAPER TODAY AND ANY OF YOU WHO WOULD LIKE TO CONTINUE TO WORK HERE MAY DO SO.
CONTINUE TO WORK HERE?
YOU MADE THAT IMPOSSIBLE AND YOU DIDN'T EVEN GIVE US A HEADS-UP!
THERE WAS NO HEADS-UP TO GIVE, STEVE.
THIS!
YOU CALL A MEETING LIKE THIS AND YOU GIVE US A HEADS-UP BEFORE YOU BURY THE PAPER!
SORRY YOUR FEELINGS ARE HURT, BUT THE FATE OF OUR CITY AND OUR ENTIRE LEGACY IS AT STAKE!
AND WE NEEDED TO MOVE QUICKLY BEFORE SOMEONE GETS ACTUALLY HURT AND NOT YOUR PRETEND HURT.
HOW CAN I WORK FOR GANGSTERS?
I WORK FOR THE PUBLIC TRUST.
AND AS FAR AS I AM CONCERNED YOU WORK FOR ME.
THE DAILY PLANET WILL CONTINUE PUBLICATION UNTIL THE DOORS ARE LOCKED.
HOW?
WHO, OUT THERE, IS GOING TO BUY THE DAILY PLANET NOW?
I MEAN THE PAPER, NOT THE ACTUAL BUILDING.

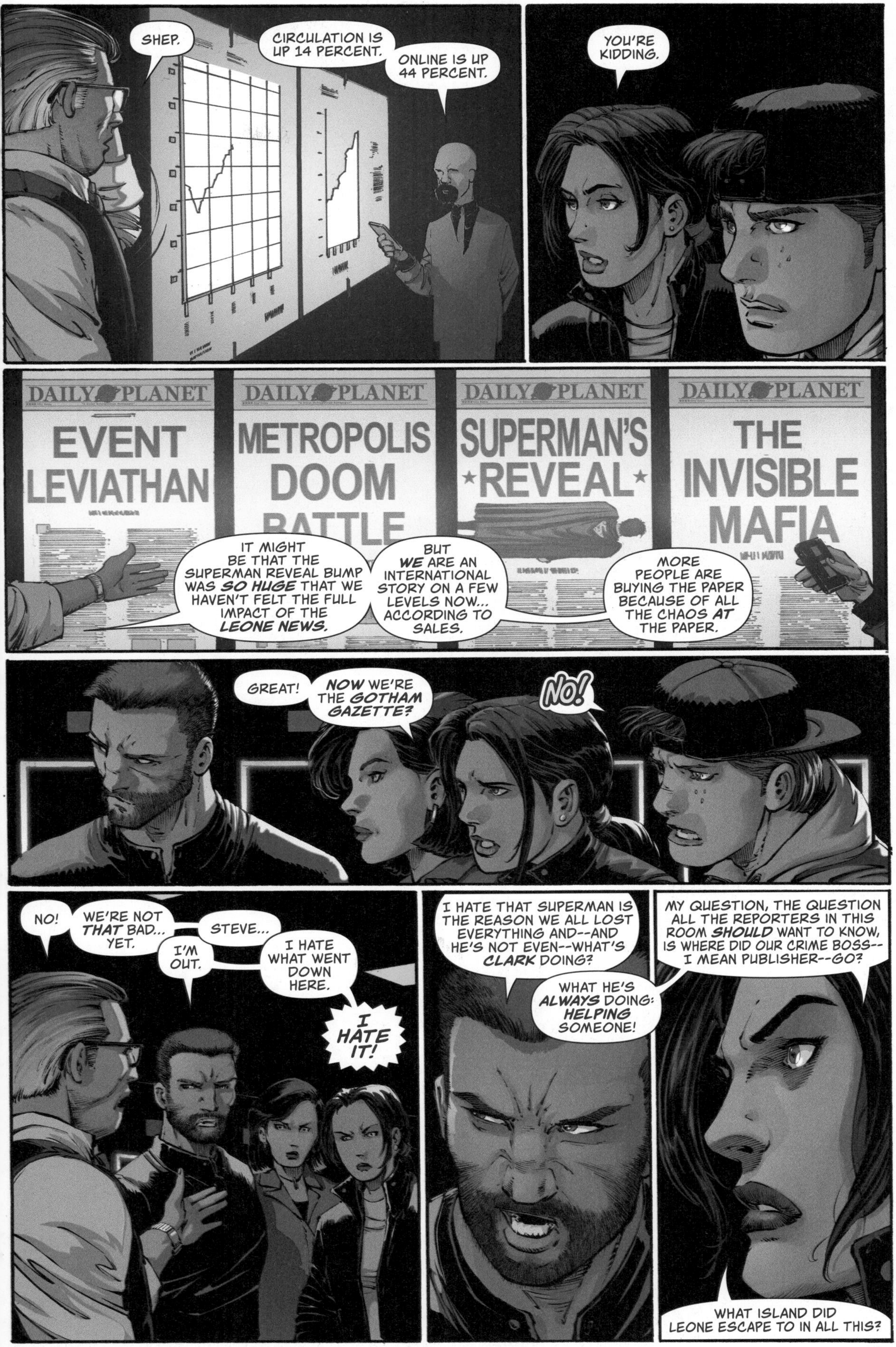
SHEP.
CIRCULATION IS UP 14 PERCENT.
ONLINE IS UP 44 PERCENT.
YOU'RE KIDDING.
DAILY PLANET
EVENT LEVIATHAN
DAILY PLANET
METROPOLIS DOOM BATTLE
DAILY PLANET
SUPERMAN'S REVEAL
DAILY PLANET
THE INVISIBLE MAFIA
IT MIGHT BE THAT THE SUPERMAN REVEAL BUMP WAS SO HUGE THAT WE HAVEN'T FELT THE FULL IMPACT OF THE LEONE NEWS.
BUT WE ARE AN INTERNATIONAL STORY ON A FEW LEVELS NOW... ACCORDING TO SALES.
MORE PEOPLE ARE BUYING THE PAPER BECAUSE OF ALL THE CHAOS AT THE PAPER.
GREAT!
NOW WE'RE THE GOTHAM GAZETTE?
NO!
NO!
WE'RE NOT THAT BAD... YET.
STEVE...
I'M OUT.
I HATE WHAT WENT DOWN HERE.
I HATE IT!
I HATE THAT SUPERMAN IS THE REASON WE ALL LOST EVERYTHING AND--AND HE'S NOT EVEN--WHAT'S CLARK DOING?
WHAT HE'S ALWAYS DOING: HELPING SOMEONE!
MY QUESTION, THE QUESTION ALL THE REPORTERS IN THIS ROOM SHOULD WANT TO KNOW, IS WHERE DID OUR CRIME BOSS--I MEAN PUBLISHER--GO?
WHAT ISLAND DID LEONE ESCAPE TO IN ALL THIS?

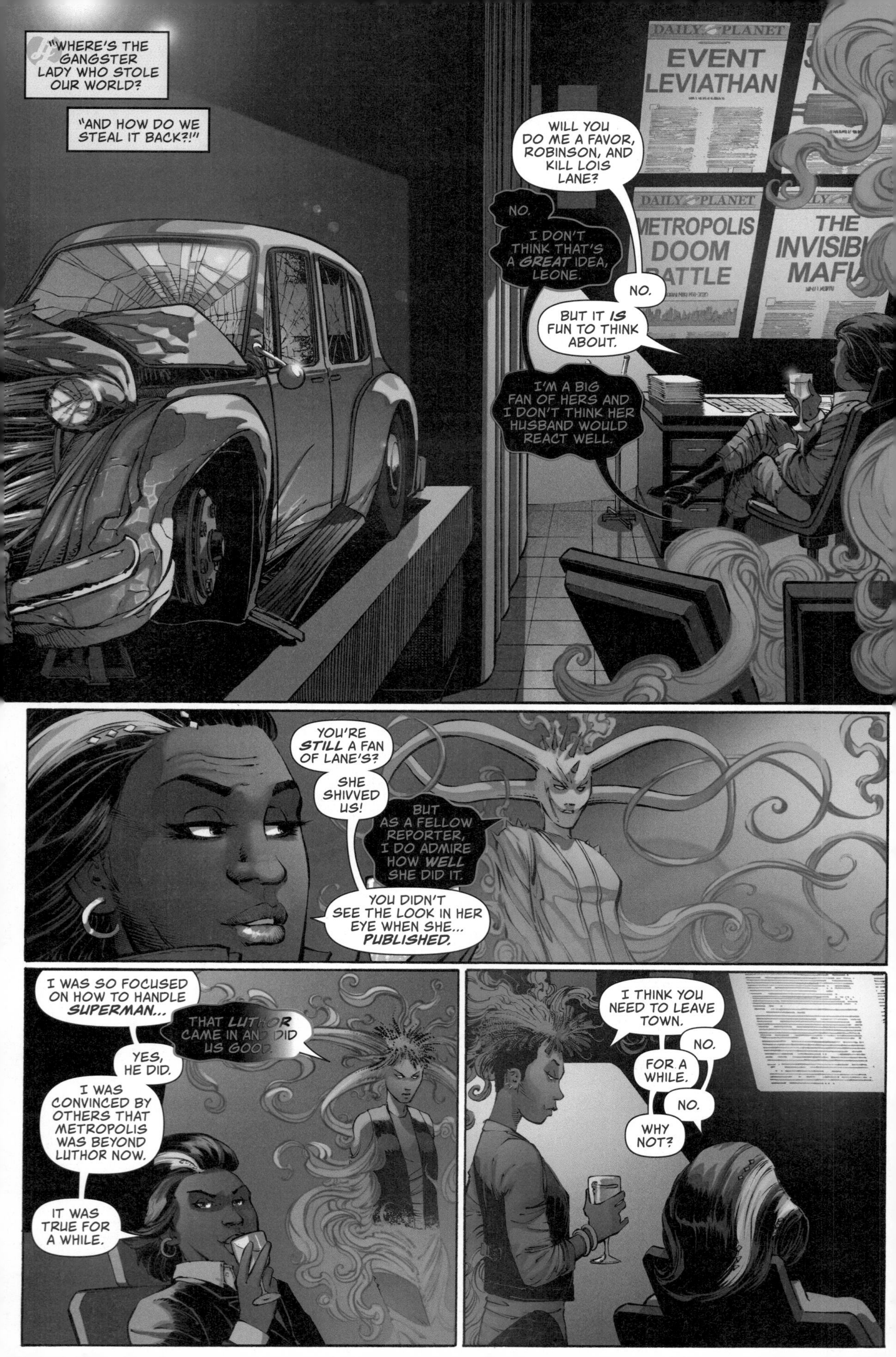
"WHERE'S THE GANGSTER LADY WHO STOLE OUR WORLD?
"AND HOW DO WE STEAL IT BACK?!"
DAILY PLANET
EVENT LEVIATHAN
WILL YOU DO ME A FAVOR, ROBINSON, AND KILL LOIS LANE?
NO.
I DON'T THINK THAT'S A *GREAT* IDEA, LEONE.
NO.
BUT IT *IS* FUN TO THINK ABOUT.
I'M A BIG FAN OF HERS AND I DON'T THINK HER HUSBAND WOULD REACT WELL.
DAILY PLANET
METROPOLIS DOOM BATTLE
THE INVISIB MAFI
YOU'RE *STILL* A FAN OF LANE'S?
SHE SHIVVED US!
BUT AS A FELLOW REPORTER, I DO ADMIRE HOW *WELL* SHE DID IT.
YOU DIDN'T SEE THE LOOK IN HER EYE WHEN SHE... *PUBLISHED.*
I WAS SO FOCUSED ON HOW TO HANDLE *SUPERMAN...*
THAT *LUTHOR* CAME IN AND DID US GOOD.
YES, HE DID.
I WAS CONVINCED BY OTHERS THAT METROPOLIS WAS BEYOND LUTHOR NOW.
IT WAS TRUE FOR A WHILE.
I THINK YOU NEED TO LEAVE TOWN.
NO.
FOR A WHILE.
NO.
WHY NOT?

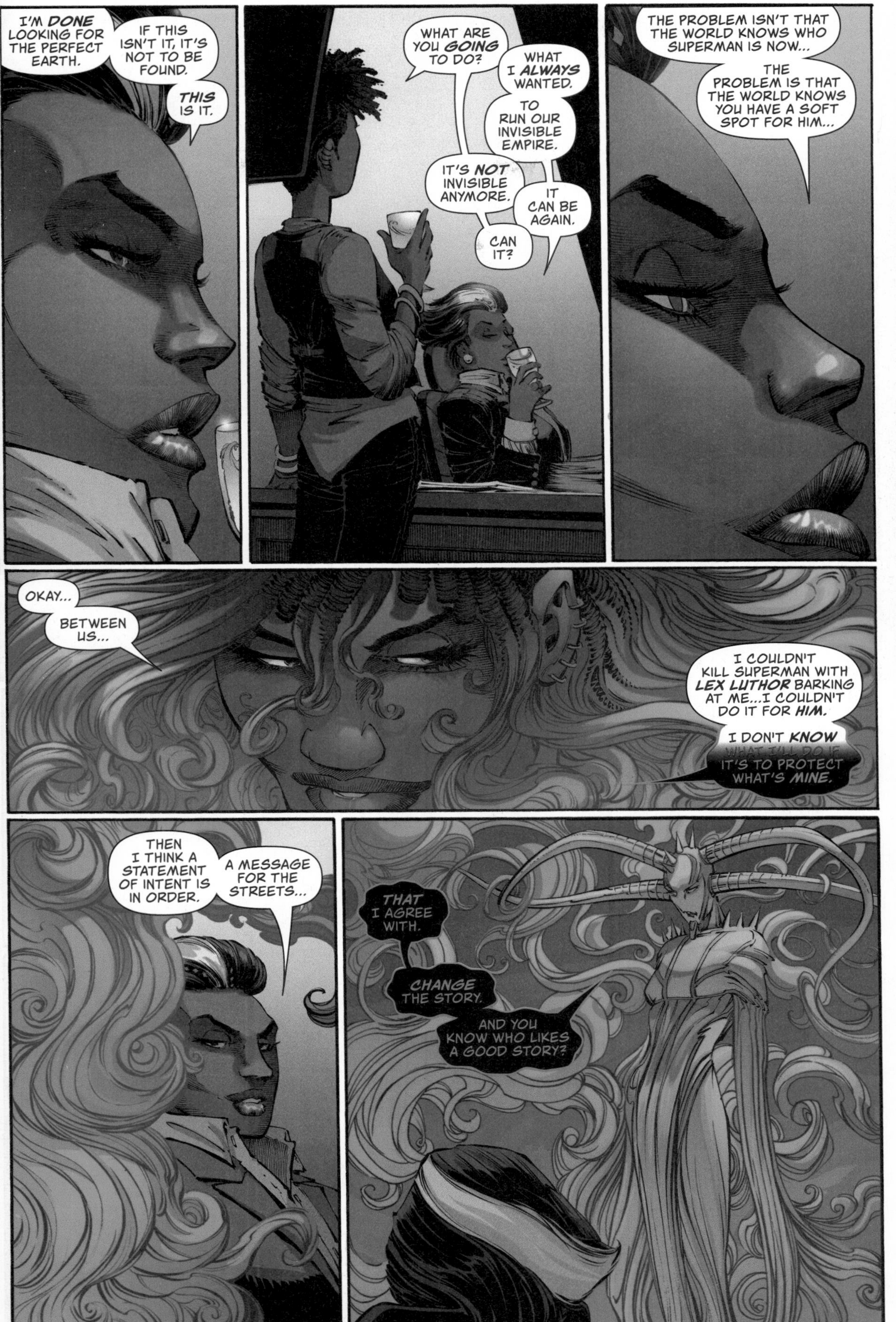
I'M DONE LOOKING FOR THE PERFECT EARTH.
IF THIS ISN'T IT, IT'S NOT TO BE FOUND.
THIS IS IT.
WHAT ARE YOU GOING TO DO?
WHAT I ALWAYS WANTED.
TO RUN OUR INVISIBLE EMPIRE.
IT'S NOT INVISIBLE ANYMORE.
IT CAN BE AGAIN.
CAN IT?
THE PROBLEM ISN'T THAT THE WORLD KNOWS WHO SUPERMAN IS NOW...
THE PROBLEM IS THAT THE WORLD KNOWS YOU HAVE A SOFT SPOT FOR HIM...
OKAY...
BETWEEN US...
I COULDN'T KILL SUPERMAN WITH LEX LUTHOR BARKING AT ME...I COULDN'T DO IT FOR HIM.
I DON'T KNOW WHAT I'LL DO IF IT'S TO PROTECT WHAT'S MINE.
THEN I THINK A STATEMENT OF INTENT IS IN ORDER.
A MESSAGE FOR THE STREETS...
THAT I AGREE WITH.
CHANGE THE STORY.
AND YOU KNOW WHO LIKES A GOOD STORY?

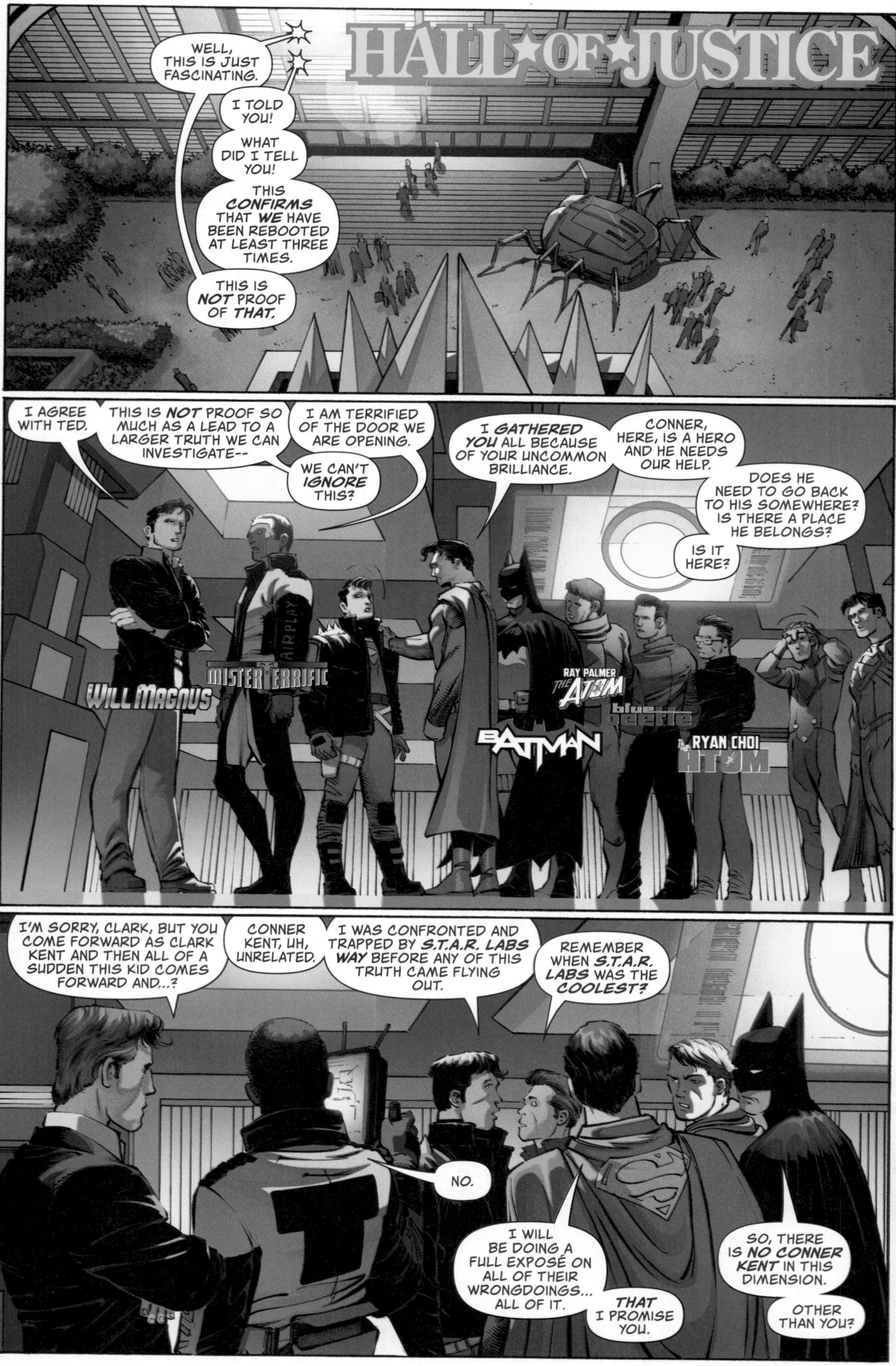
HALL OF JUSTICE
WELL, THIS IS JUST FASCINATING.
I TOLD YOU!
WHAT DID I TELL YOU!
THIS CONFIRMS THAT WE HAVE BEEN REBOOTED AT LEAST THREE TIMES.
THIS IS NOT PROOF OF THAT.
I AGREE WITH TED.
THIS IS NOT PROOF SO MUCH AS A LEAD TO A LARGER TRUTH WE CAN INVESTIGATE--
I AM TERRIFIED OF THE DOOR WE ARE OPENING.
WE CAN'T IGNORE THIS?
I GATHERED YOU ALL BECAUSE OF YOUR UNCOMMON BRILLIANCE.
CONNER, HERE, IS A HERO AND HE NEEDS OUR HELP.
DOES HE NEED TO GO BACK TO HIS SOMEWHERE? IS THERE A PLACE HE BELONGS?
IS IT HERE?
WILL MAGNUS
MISTER TERRIFIC
RAY PALMER THE ATOM
BATMAN
blue beetle
RYAN CHOI THE ATOM
I'M SORRY, CLARK, BUT YOU COME FORWARD AS CLARK KENT AND THEN ALL OF A SUDDEN THIS KID COMES FORWARD AND...?
CONNER KENT, UH, UNRELATED.
I WAS CONFRONTED AND TRAPPED BY S.T.A.R. LABS WAY BEFORE ANY OF THIS TRUTH CAME FLYING OUT.
REMEMBER WHEN S.T.A.R. LABS WAS THE COOLEST?
NO.
I WILL BE DOING A FULL EXPOSÉ ON ALL OF THEIR WRONGDOINGS... ALL OF IT.
THAT I PROMISE YOU.
SO, THERE IS NO CONNER KENT IN THIS DIMENSION.
OTHER THAN YOU?

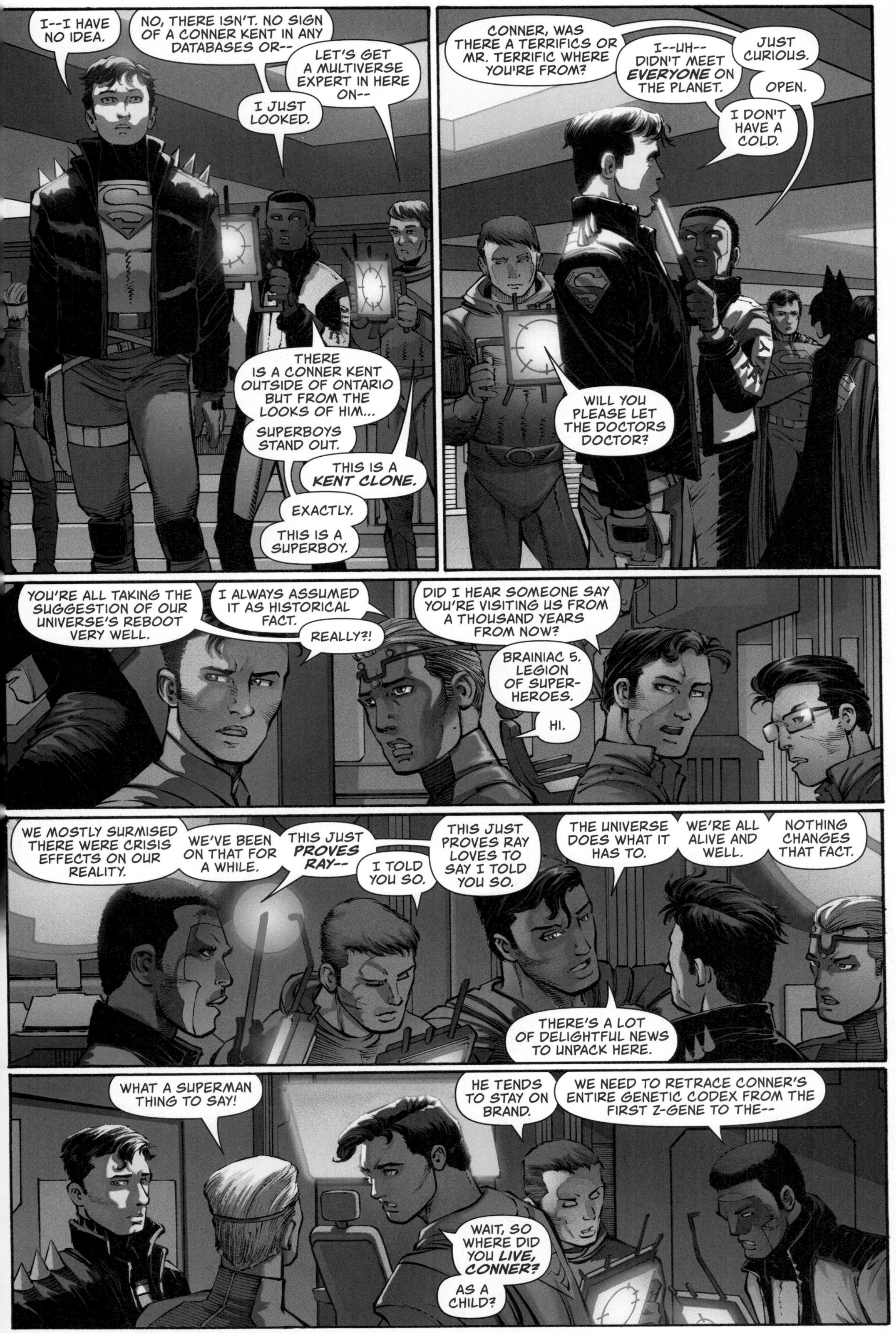
I--I HAVE NO IDEA.
NO, THERE ISN'T. NO SIGN OF A CONNER KENT IN ANY DATABASES OR--
LET'S GET A MULTIVERSE EXPERT IN HERE ON--
I JUST LOOKED.
THERE IS A CONNER KENT OUTSIDE OF ONTARIO BUT FROM THE LOOKS OF HIM...
SUPERBOYS STAND OUT.
THIS IS A KENT CLONE.
EXACTLY.
THIS IS A SUPERBOY.
CONNER, WAS THERE A TERRIFICS OR MR. TERRIFIC WHERE YOU'RE FROM?
I--UH-- DIDN'T MEET EVERYONE ON THE PLANET.
JUST CURIOUS.
OPEN.
I DON'T HAVE A COLD.
WILL YOU PLEASE LET THE DOCTORS DOCTOR?
YOU'RE ALL TAKING THE SUGGESTION OF OUR UNIVERSE'S REBOOT VERY WELL.
I ALWAYS ASSUMED IT AS HISTORICAL FACT.
REALLY?!
DID I HEAR SOMEONE SAY YOU'RE VISITING US FROM A THOUSAND YEARS FROM NOW?
BRAINIAC 5. LEGION OF SUPER-HEROES.
HI.
WE MOSTLY SURMISED THERE WERE CRISIS EFFECTS ON OUR REALITY.
WE'VE BEEN ON THAT FOR A WHILE.
THIS JUST PROVES RAY--
I TOLD YOU SO.
THIS JUST PROVES RAY LOVES TO SAY I TOLD YOU SO.
THE UNIVERSE DOES WHAT IT HAS TO.
WE'RE ALL ALIVE AND WELL.
NOTHING CHANGES THAT FACT.
THERE'S A LOT OF DELIGHTFUL NEWS TO UNPACK HERE.
WHAT A SUPERMAN THING TO SAY!
HE TENDS TO STAY ON BRAND.
WE NEED TO RETRACE CONNER'S ENTIRE GENETIC CODEX FROM THE FIRST Z-GENE TO THE--
WAIT, SO WHERE DID YOU LIVE, CONNER?
AS A CHILD?

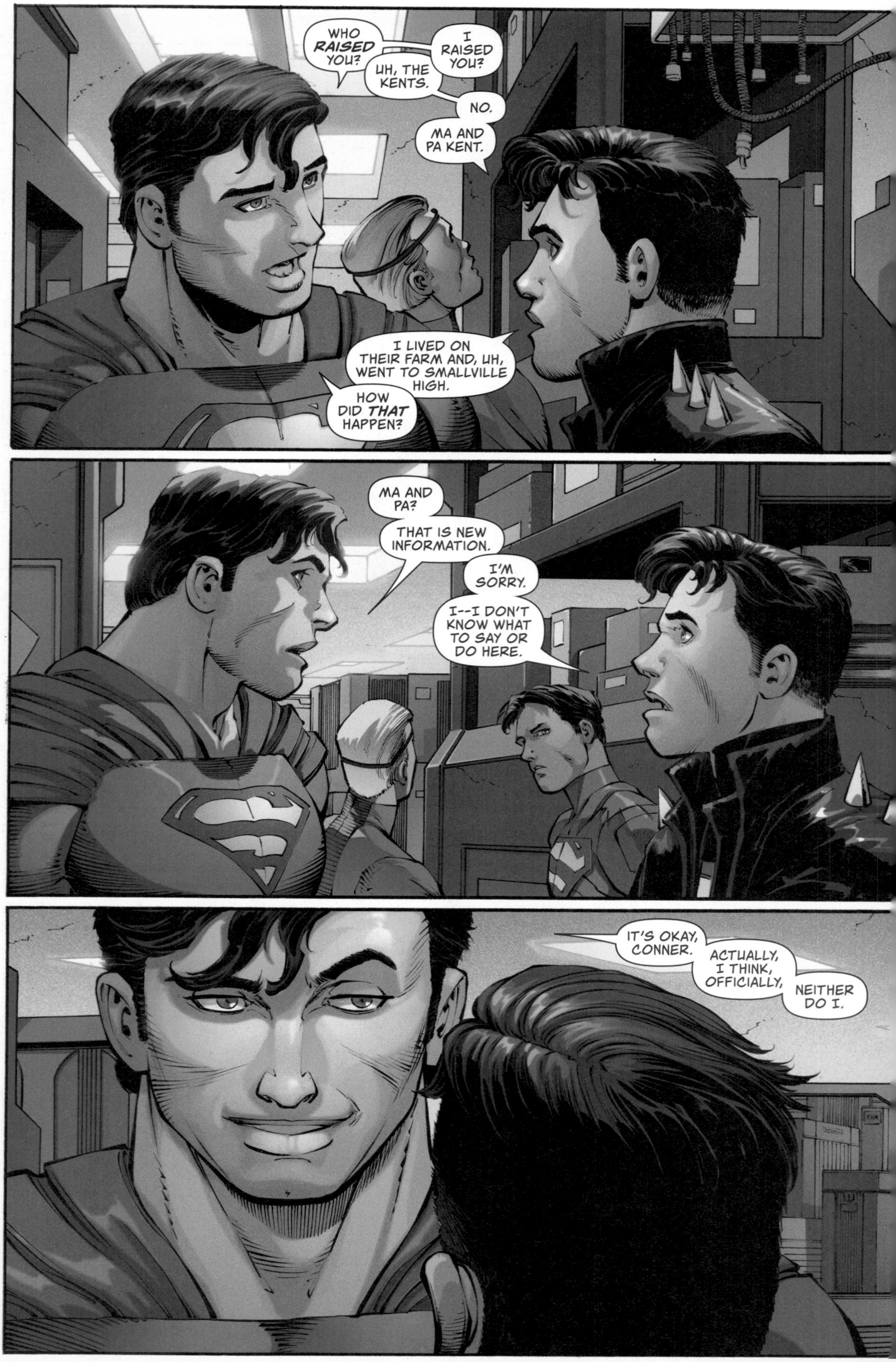
WHO RAISED YOU?
I RAISED YOU?
UH, THE KENTS.
NO.
MA AND PA KENT.
I LIVED ON THEIR FARM AND, UH, WENT TO SMALLVILLE HIGH.
HOW DID THAT HAPPEN?
MA AND PA?
THAT IS NEW INFORMATION.
I'M SORRY.
I--I DON'T KNOW WHAT TO SAY OR DO HERE.
IT'S OKAY, CONNER.
ACTUALLY, I THINK, OFFICIALLY,
NEITHER DO I.

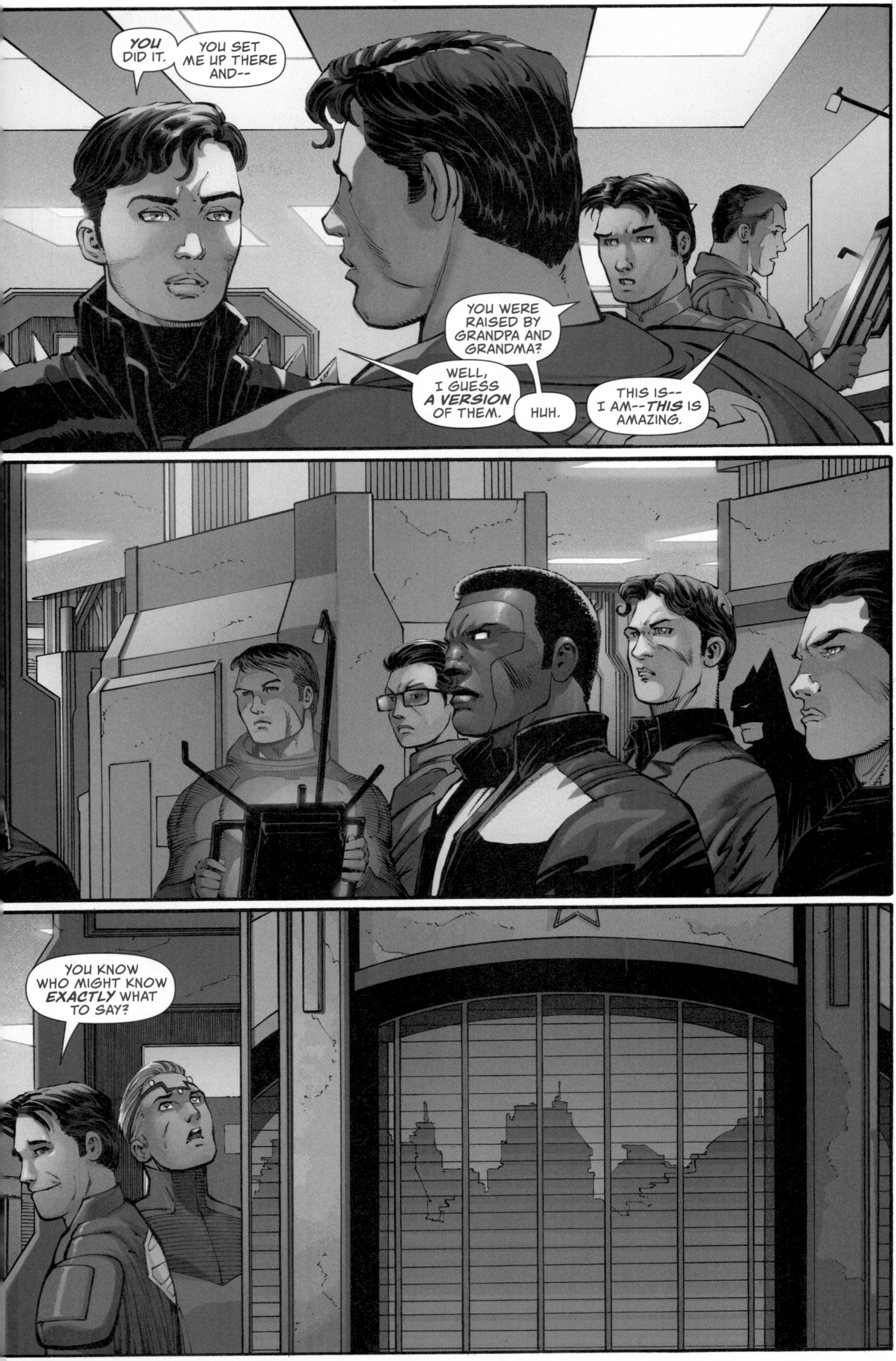
YOU DID IT.
YOU SET ME UP THERE AND--
YOU WERE RAISED BY GRANDPA AND GRANDMA?
WELL, I GUESS A VERSION OF THEM.
HUH.
THIS IS-- I AM--THIS IS AMAZING.
YOU KNOW WHO MIGHT KNOW EXACTLY WHAT TO SAY?

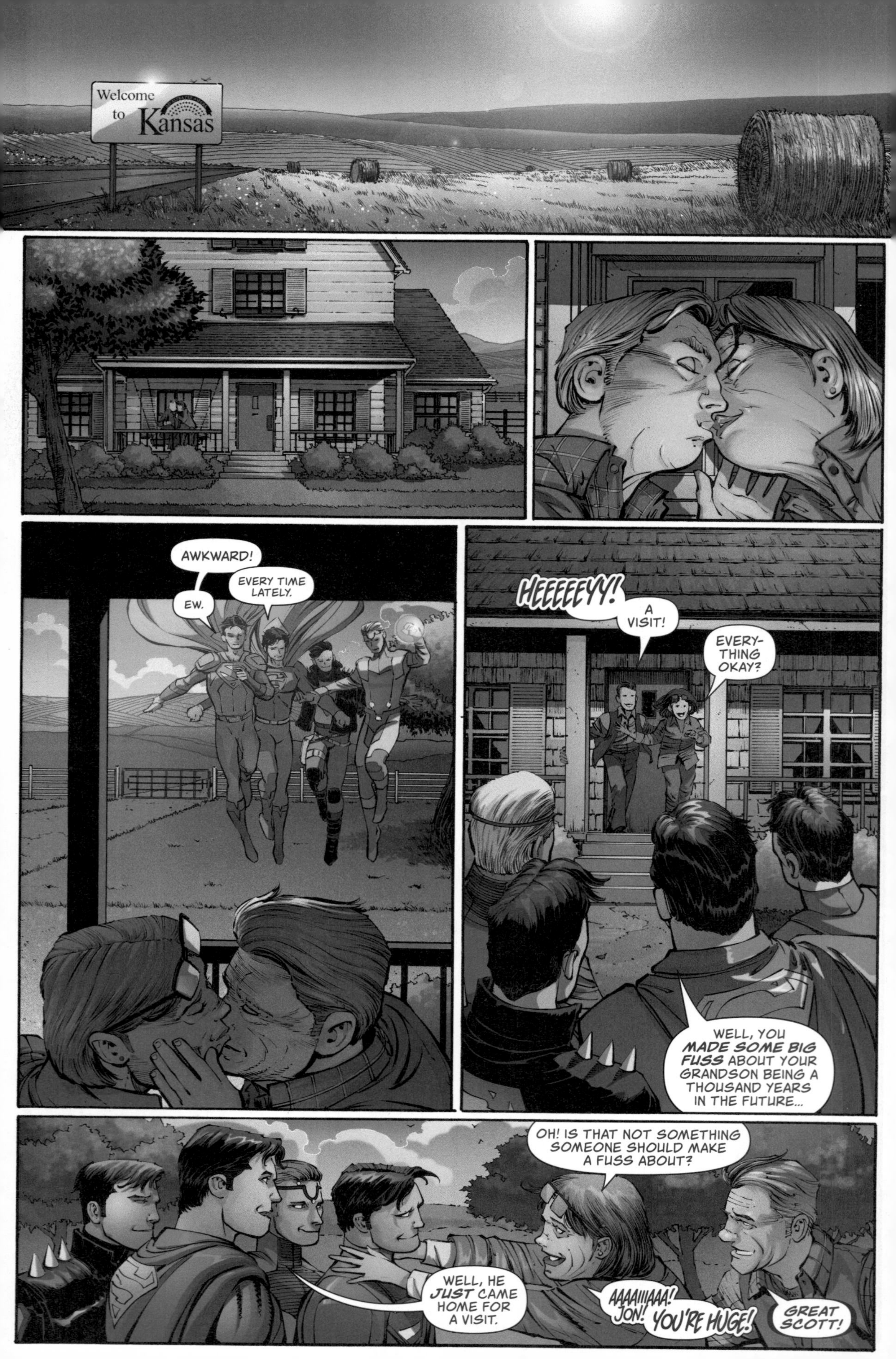
Welcome to Kansas
AWKWARD!
EW.
EVERY TIME LATELY.
HEEEEEYY!
A VISIT!
EVERY-THING OKAY?
WELL, YOU MADE SOME BIG FUSS ABOUT YOUR GRANDSON BEING A THOUSAND YEARS IN THE FUTURE...
OH! IS THAT NOT SOMETHING SOMEONE SHOULD MAKE A FUSS ABOUT?
WELL, HE JUST CAME HOME FOR A VISIT.
AAAAIIIAAA! JON! YOU'RE HUGE!
GREAT SCOTT!

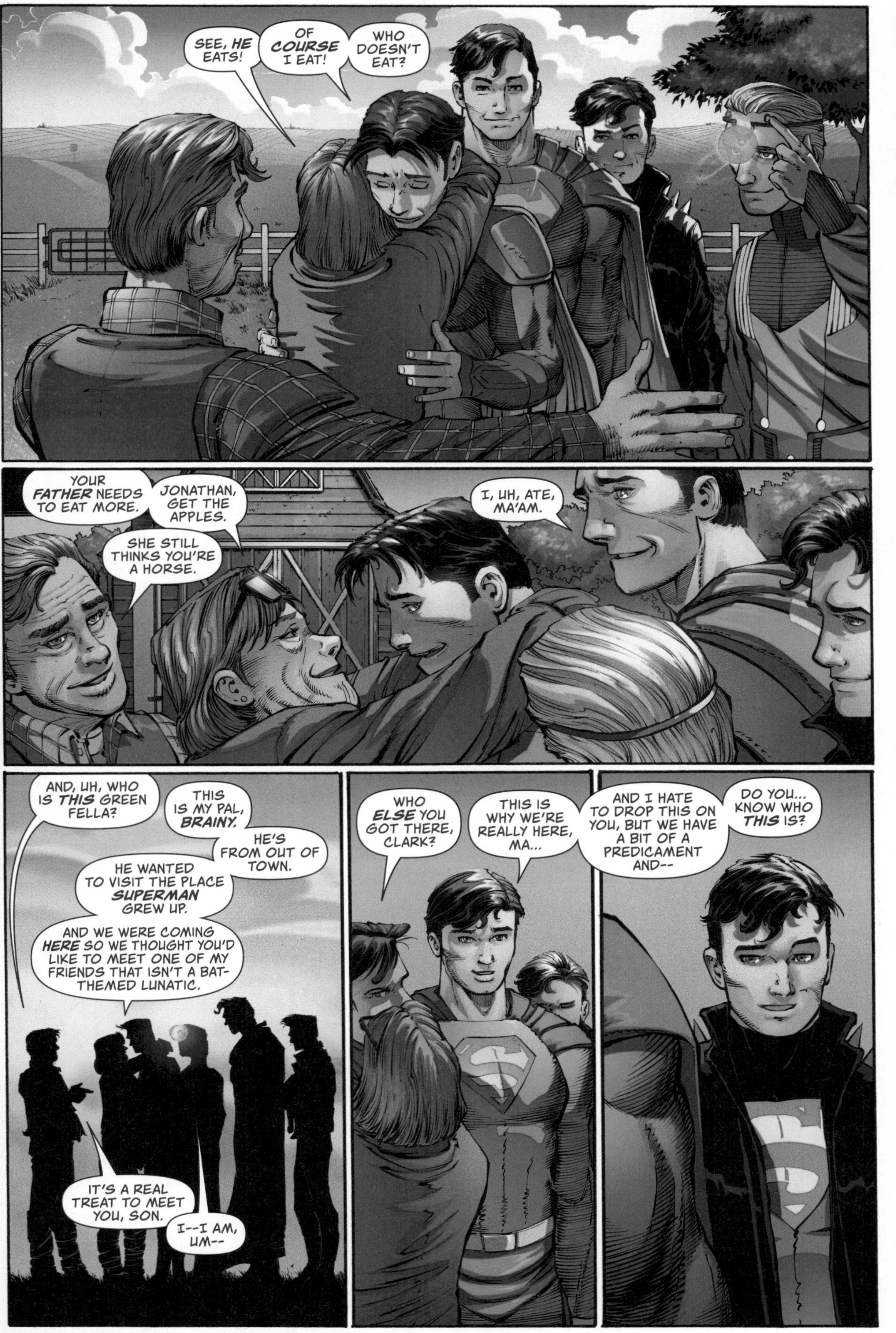
SEE, HE EATS!
OF COURSE I EAT!
WHO DOESN'T EAT?
YOUR FATHER NEEDS TO EAT MORE.
JONATHAN, GET THE APPLES.
SHE STILL THINKS YOU'RE A HORSE.
I, UH, ATE, MA'AM.
AND, UH, WHO IS THIS GREEN FELLA?
THIS IS MY PAL, BRAINY.
HE'S FROM OUT OF TOWN.
HE WANTED TO VISIT THE PLACE SUPERMAN GREW UP.
AND WE WERE COMING HERE SO WE THOUGHT YOU'D LIKE TO MEET ONE OF MY FRIENDS THAT ISN'T A BAT-THEMED LUNATIC.
IT'S A REAL TREAT TO MEET YOU, SON.
I--I AM, UM--
WHO ELSE YOU GOT THERE, CLARK?
THIS IS WHY WE'RE REALLY HERE, MA...
AND I HATE TO DROP THIS ON YOU, BUT WE HAVE A BIT OF A PREDICAMENT AND--
DO YOU... KNOW WHO THIS IS?

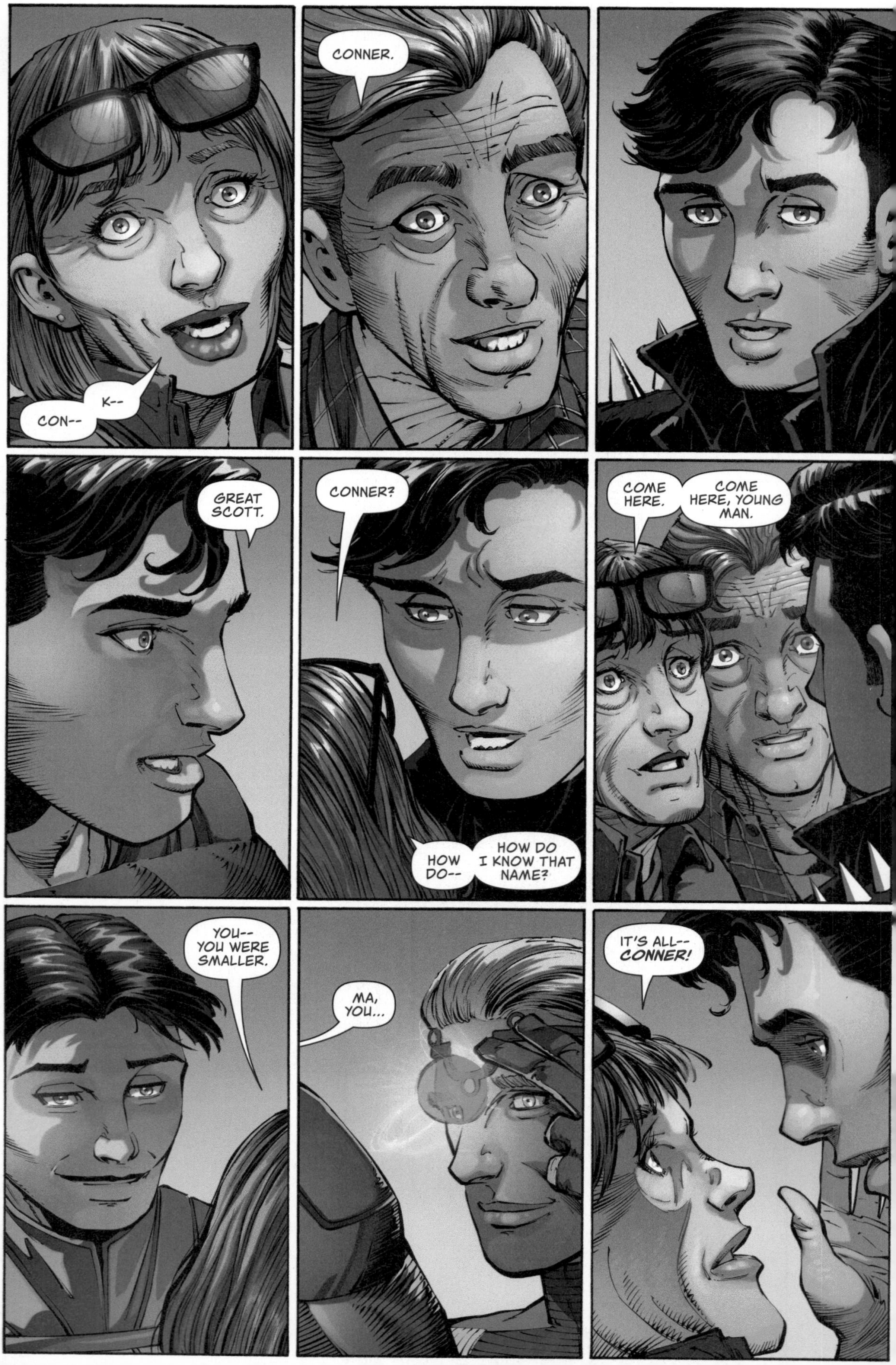
K--
CON--
CONNER.
GREAT SCOTT.
CONNER?
HOW DO--
HOW DO I KNOW THAT NAME?
COME HERE.
COME HERE, YOUNG MAN.
YOU-- YOU WERE SMALLER.
MA, YOU...
IT'S ALL-- CONNER!

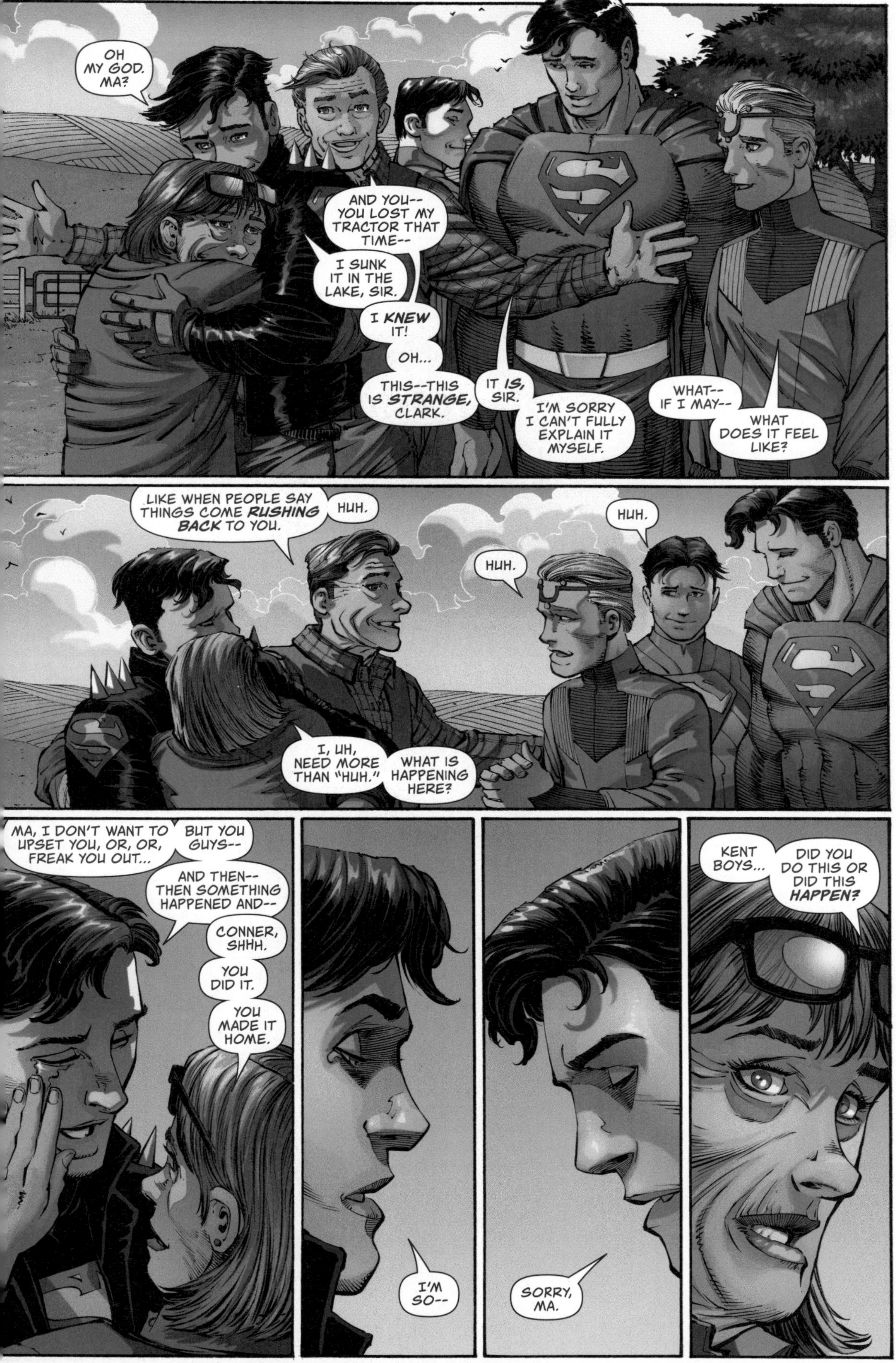
OH MY GOD. MA?
AND YOU-- YOU LOST MY TRACTOR THAT TIME--
I SUNK IT IN THE LAKE, SIR.
I KNEW IT!
OH...
THIS--THIS IS STRANGE, CLARK.
IT IS, SIR.
I'M SORRY I CAN'T FULLY EXPLAIN IT MYSELF.
WHAT-- IF I MAY--
WHAT DOES IT FEEL LIKE?
LIKE WHEN PEOPLE SAY THINGS COME RUSHING BACK TO YOU.
HUH.
HUH.
HUH.
I, UH, NEED MORE THAN "HUH."
WHAT IS HAPPENING HERE?
MA, I DON'T WANT TO UPSET YOU, OR, OR, FREAK YOU OUT...
BUT YOU GUYS--
AND THEN-- THEN SOMETHING HAPPENED AND--
CONNER, SHHH.
YOU DID IT.
YOU MADE IT HOME.
I'M SO--
SORRY, MA.
KENT BOYS...
DID YOU DO THIS OR DID THIS HAPPEN?

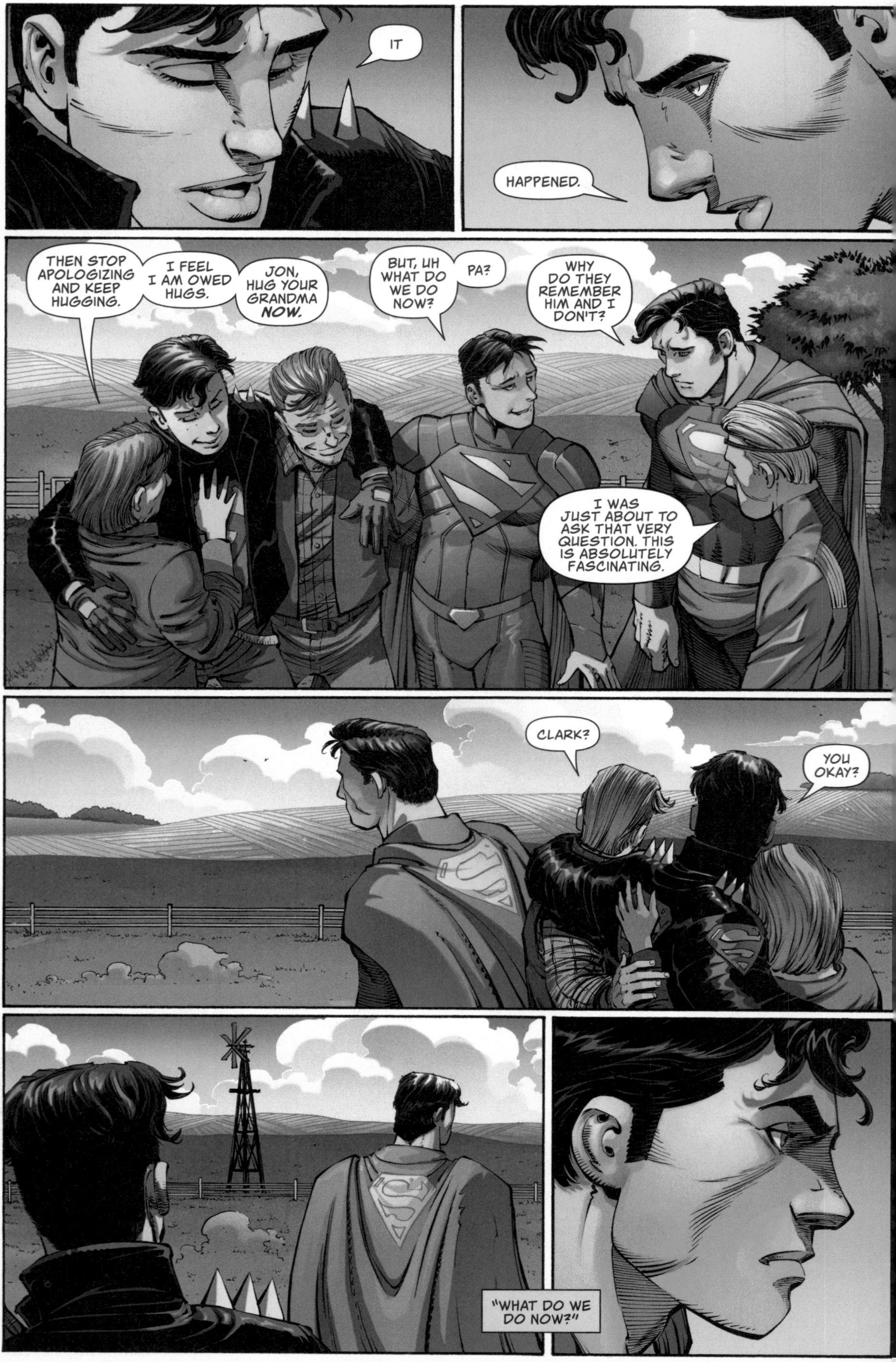
IT
HAPPENED.
THEN STOP APOLOGIZING AND KEEP HUGGING.
I FEEL I AM OWED HUGS.
JON, HUG YOUR GRANDMA NOW.
BUT, UH WHAT DO WE DO NOW?
PA?
WHY DO THEY REMEMBER HIM AND I DON'T?
I WAS JUST ABOUT TO ASK THAT VERY QUESTION. THIS IS ABSOLUTELY FASCINATING.
CLARK?
YOU OKAY?
"WHAT DO WE DO NOW?"

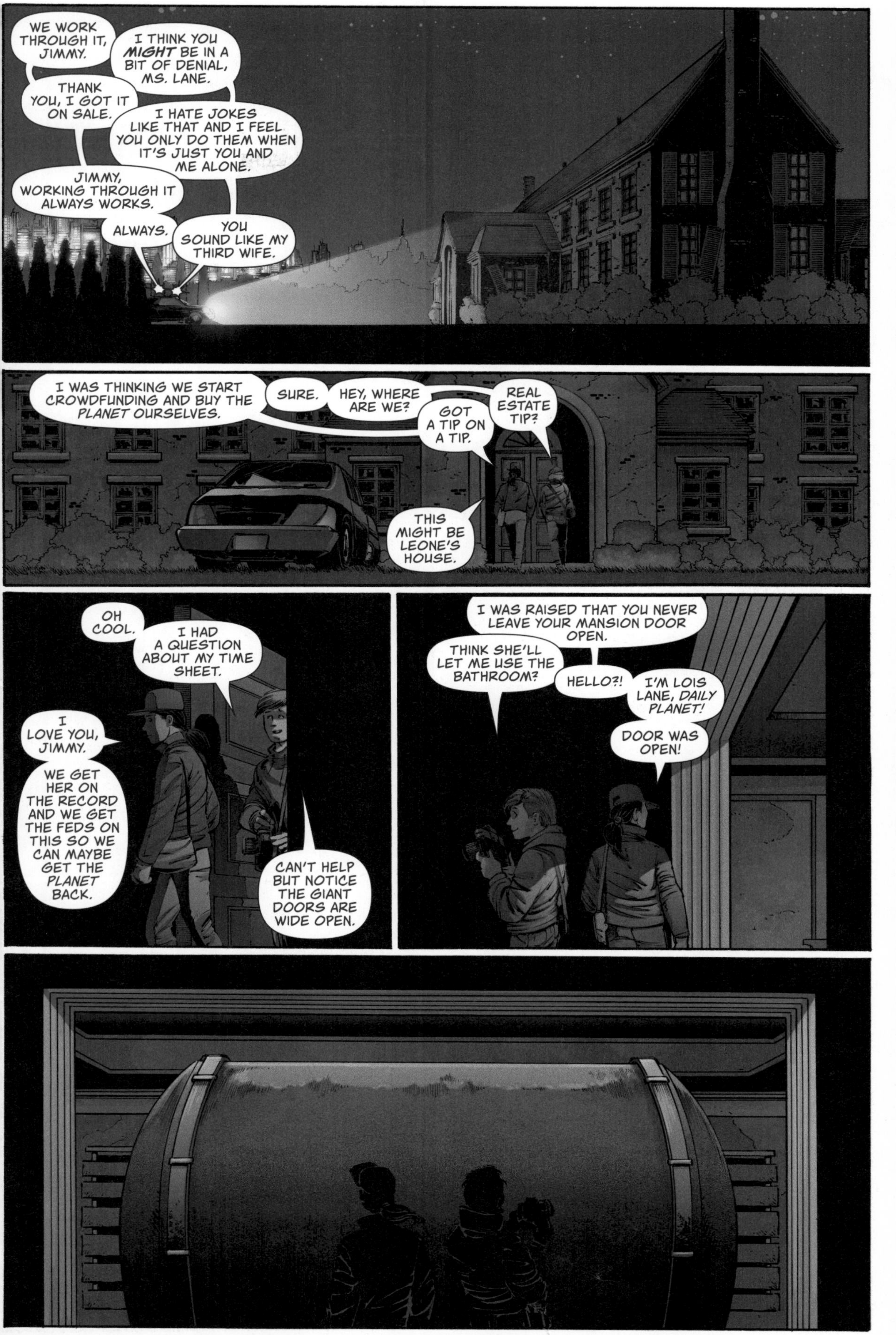
WE WORK THROUGH IT, JIMMY.
I THINK YOU *MIGHT* BE IN A BIT OF DENIAL, MS. LANE.
THANK YOU, I GOT IT ON SALE.
I HATE JOKES LIKE THAT AND I FEEL YOU ONLY DO THEM WHEN IT'S JUST YOU AND ME ALONE.
JIMMY, WORKING THROUGH IT ALWAYS WORKS.
ALWAYS.
YOU SOUND LIKE MY THIRD WIFE.
I WAS THINKING WE START CROWDFUNDING AND BUY THE *PLANET* OURSELVES.
SURE.
HEY, WHERE ARE WE?
REAL ESTATE TIP?
GOT A TIP ON A TIP.
THIS MIGHT BE LEONE'S HOUSE.
OH COOL.
I HAD A QUESTION ABOUT MY TIME SHEET.
I LOVE YOU, JIMMY.
WE GET HER ON THE RECORD AND WE GET THE FEDS ON THIS SO WE CAN MAYBE GET THE *PLANET* BACK.
CAN'T HELP BUT NOTICE THE GIANT DOORS ARE WIDE OPEN.
I WAS RAISED THAT YOU NEVER LEAVE YOUR MANSION DOOR OPEN.
THINK SHE'LL LET ME USE THE BATHROOM?
HELLO?!
I'M LOIS LANE, *DAILY PLANET!*
DOOR WAS OPEN!

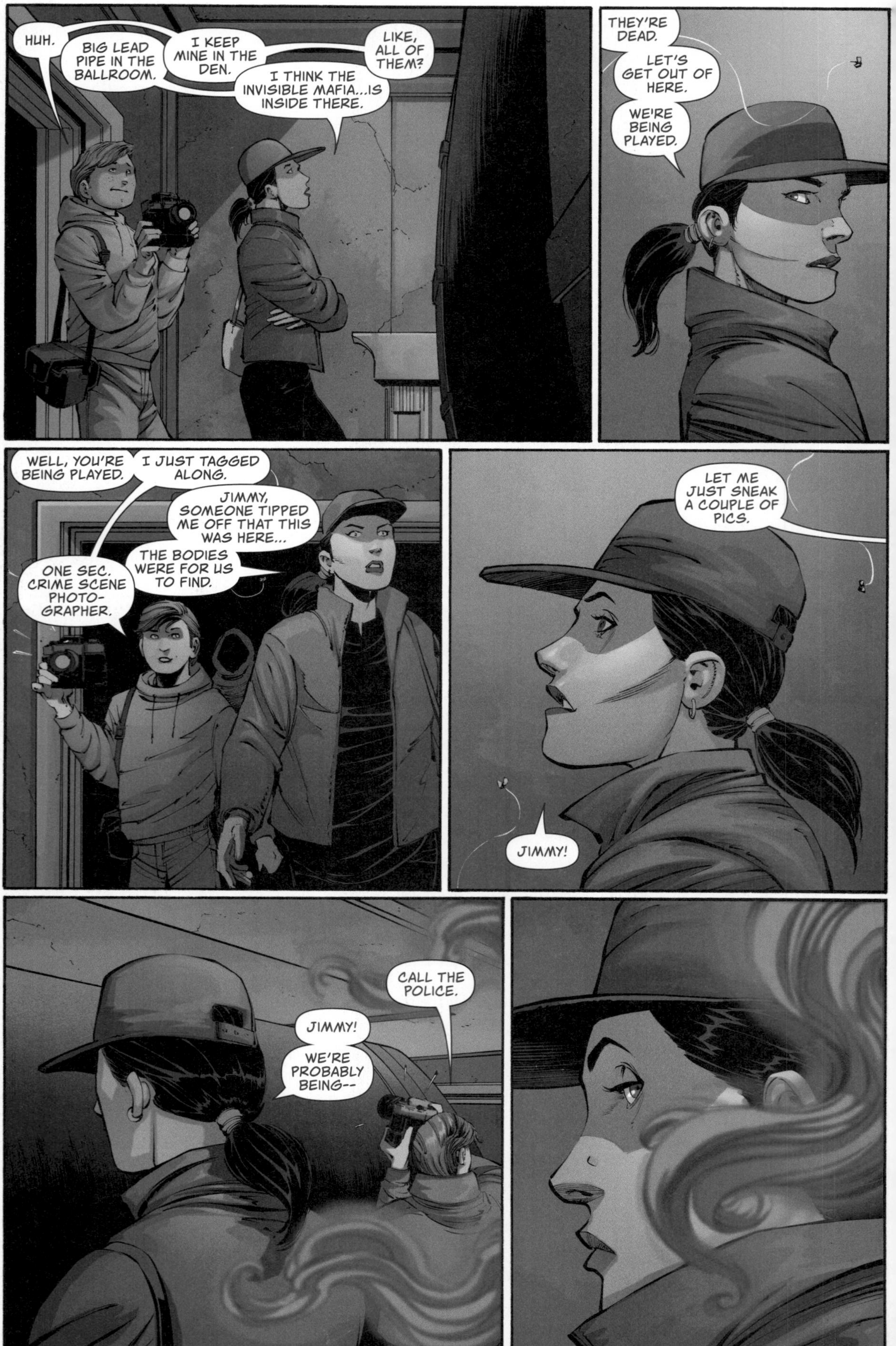
HUH.
BIG LEAD PIPE IN THE BALLROOM.
I KEEP MINE IN THE DEN.
LIKE, ALL OF THEM?
I THINK THE INVISIBLE MAFIA...IS INSIDE THERE.
THEY'RE DEAD.
LET'S GET OUT OF HERE.
WE'RE BEING PLAYED.
WELL, YOU'RE BEING PLAYED.
I JUST TAGGED ALONG.
JIMMY, SOMEONE TIPPED ME OFF THAT THIS WAS HERE...
THE BODIES WERE FOR US TO FIND.
ONE SEC. CRIME SCENE PHOTO-GRAPHER.
LET ME JUST SNEAK A COUPLE OF PICS.
JIMMY!
CALL THE POLICE.
JIMMY!
WE'RE PROBABLY BEING--

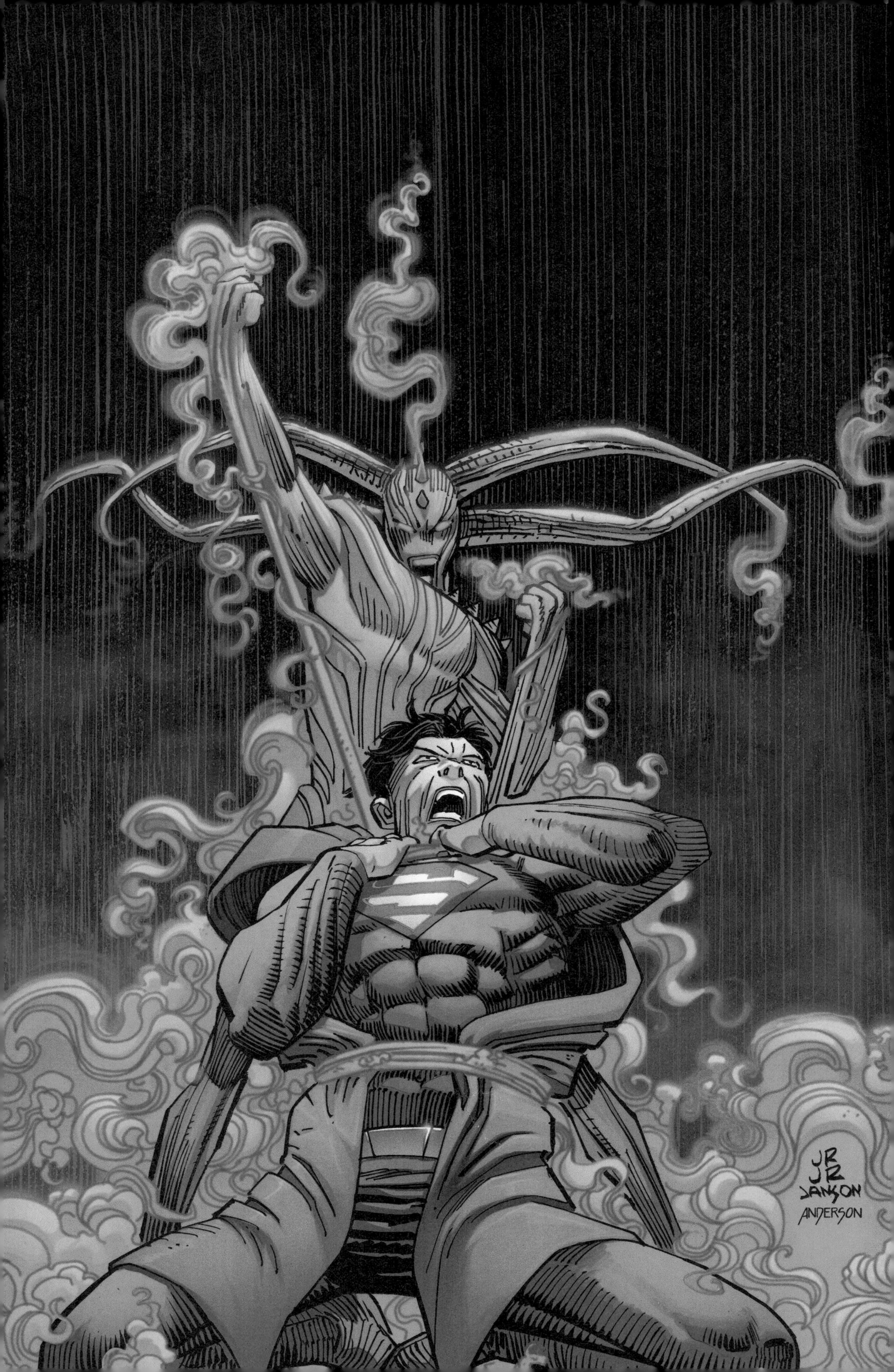
JR JR
JANSON
ANDERSON

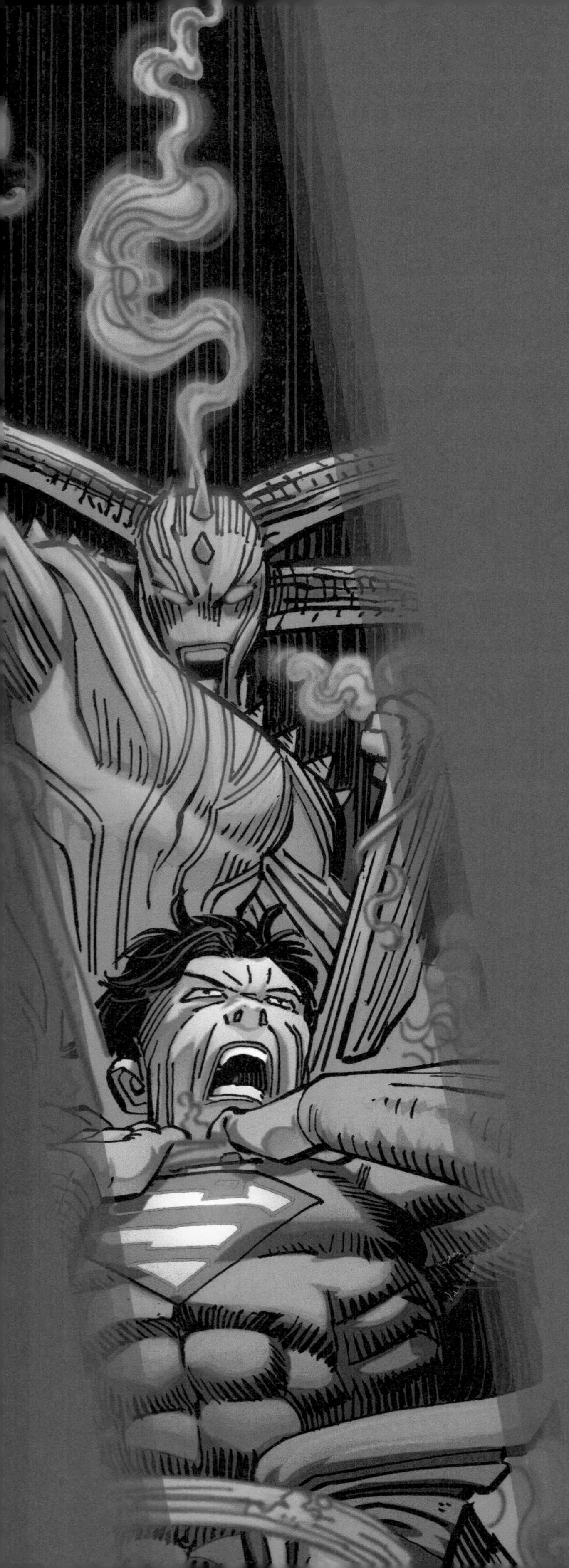

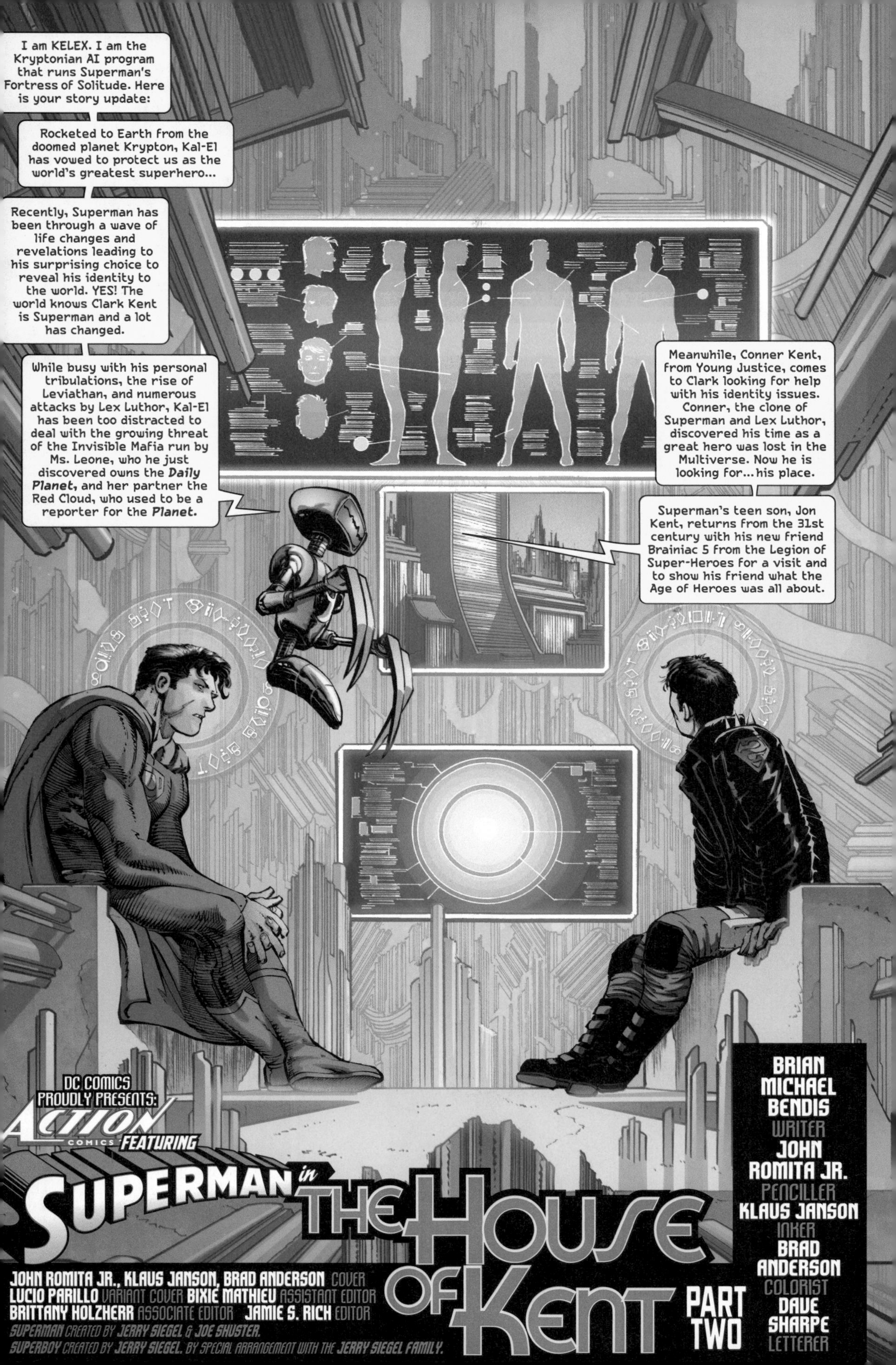
I am KELEX. I am the Kryptonian AI program that runs Superman's Fortress of Solitude. Here is your story update:
Rocketed to Earth from the doomed planet Krypton, Kal-El has vowed to protect us as the world's greatest superhero...
Recently, Superman has been through a wave of life changes and revelations leading to his surprising choice to reveal his identity to the world. YES! The world knows Clark Kent is Superman and a lot has changed.
While busy with his personal tribulations, the rise of Leviathan, and numerous attacks by Lex Luthor, Kal-El has been too distracted to deal with the growing threat of the Invisible Mafia run by Ms. Leone, who he just discovered owns the *Daily Planet*, and her partner the Red Cloud, who used to be a reporter for the *Planet*.
Meanwhile, Conner Kent, from Young Justice, comes to Clark looking for help with his identity issues. Conner, the clone of Superman and Lex Luthor, discovered his time as a great hero was lost in the Multiverse. Now he is looking for... his place.
Superman's teen son, Jon Kent, returns from the 31st century with his new friend Brainiac 5 from the Legion of Super-Heroes for a visit and to show his friend what the Age of Heroes was all about.
DC COMICS PROUDLY PRESENTS: ACTION COMICS FEATURING
SUPERMAN in THE HOUSE OF KENT PART TWO
BRIAN MICHAEL BENDIS WRITER
JOHN ROMITA JR. PENCILLER
KLAUS JANSON INKER
BRAD ANDERSON COLORIST
DAVE SHARPE LETTERER
JOHN ROMITA JR., KLAUS JANSON, BRAD ANDERSON COVER
LUCIO PARILLO VARIANT COVER BIXIE MATHIEU ASSISTANT EDITOR
BRITTANY HOLZHERR ASSOCIATE EDITOR JAMIE S. RICH EDITOR
SUPERMAN CREATED BY JERRY SIEGEL & JOE SHUSTER.
SUPERBOY CREATED BY JERRY SIEGEL. BY SPECIAL ARRANGEMENT WITH THE JERRY SIEGEL FAMILY.

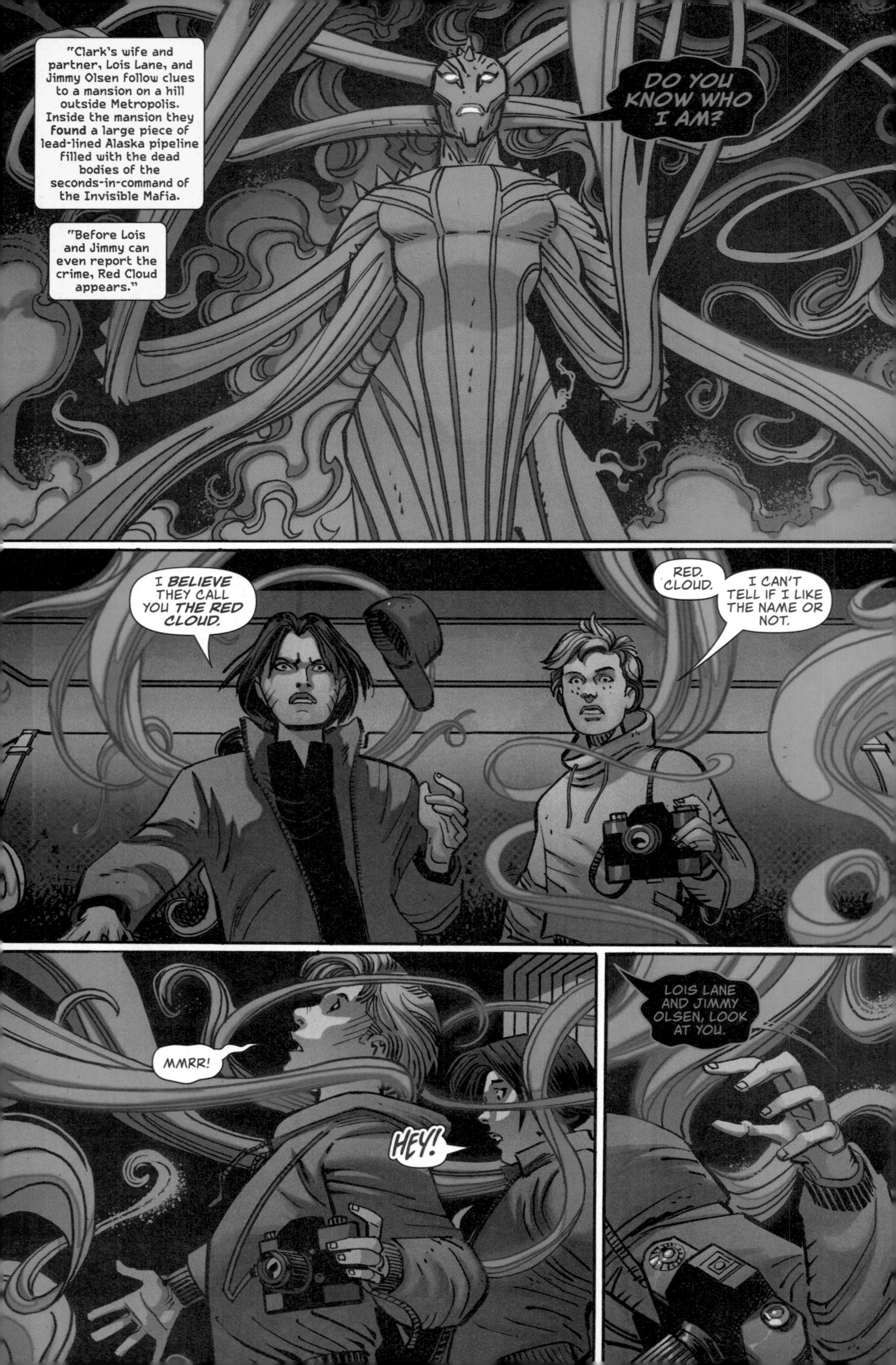
"Clark's wife and partner, Lois Lane, and Jimmy Olsen follow clues to a mansion on a hill outside Metropolis. Inside the mansion they **found** a large piece of lead-lined Alaska pipeline filled with the dead bodies of the seconds-in-command of the Invisible Mafia.
"Before Lois and Jimmy can even report the crime, Red Cloud appears."
DO YOU KNOW WHO I AM?
I *BELIEVE* THEY CALL YOU *THE RED CLOUD.*
RED. CLOUD.
I CAN'T TELL IF I LIKE THE NAME OR NOT.
MMRR!
HEY!
LOIS LANE AND JIMMY OLSEN, LOOK AT YOU.

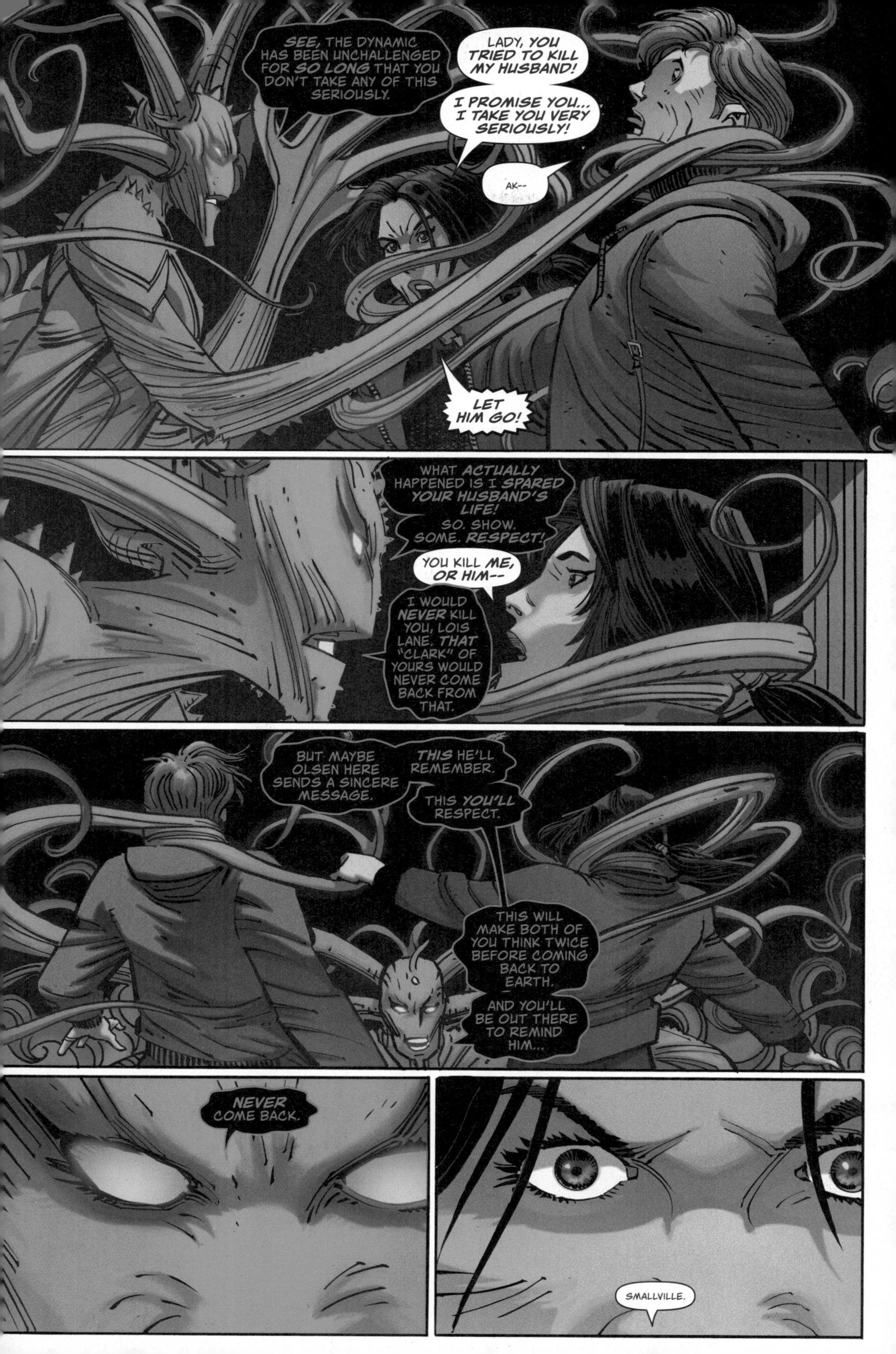
SEE, THE DYNAMIC HAS BEEN UNCHALLENGED FOR SO LONG THAT YOU DON'T TAKE ANY OF THIS SERIOUSLY.
LADY, YOU TRIED TO KILL MY HUSBAND!
I PROMISE YOU... I TAKE YOU VERY SERIOUSLY!
AK--
LET HIM GO!
WHAT ACTUALLY HAPPENED IS I SPARED YOUR HUSBAND'S LIFE!
SO. SHOW. SOME. RESPECT!
YOU KILL ME, OR HIM--
I WOULD NEVER KILL YOU, LOIS LANE. THAT "CLARK" OF YOURS WOULD NEVER COME BACK FROM THAT.
BUT MAYBE OLSEN HERE SENDS A SINCERE MESSAGE.
THIS HE'LL REMEMBER.
THIS YOU'LL RESPECT.
THIS WILL MAKE BOTH OF YOU THINK TWICE BEFORE COMING BACK TO EARTH.
AND YOU'LL BE OUT THERE TO REMIND HIM...
NEVER COME BACK.
SMALLVILLE.

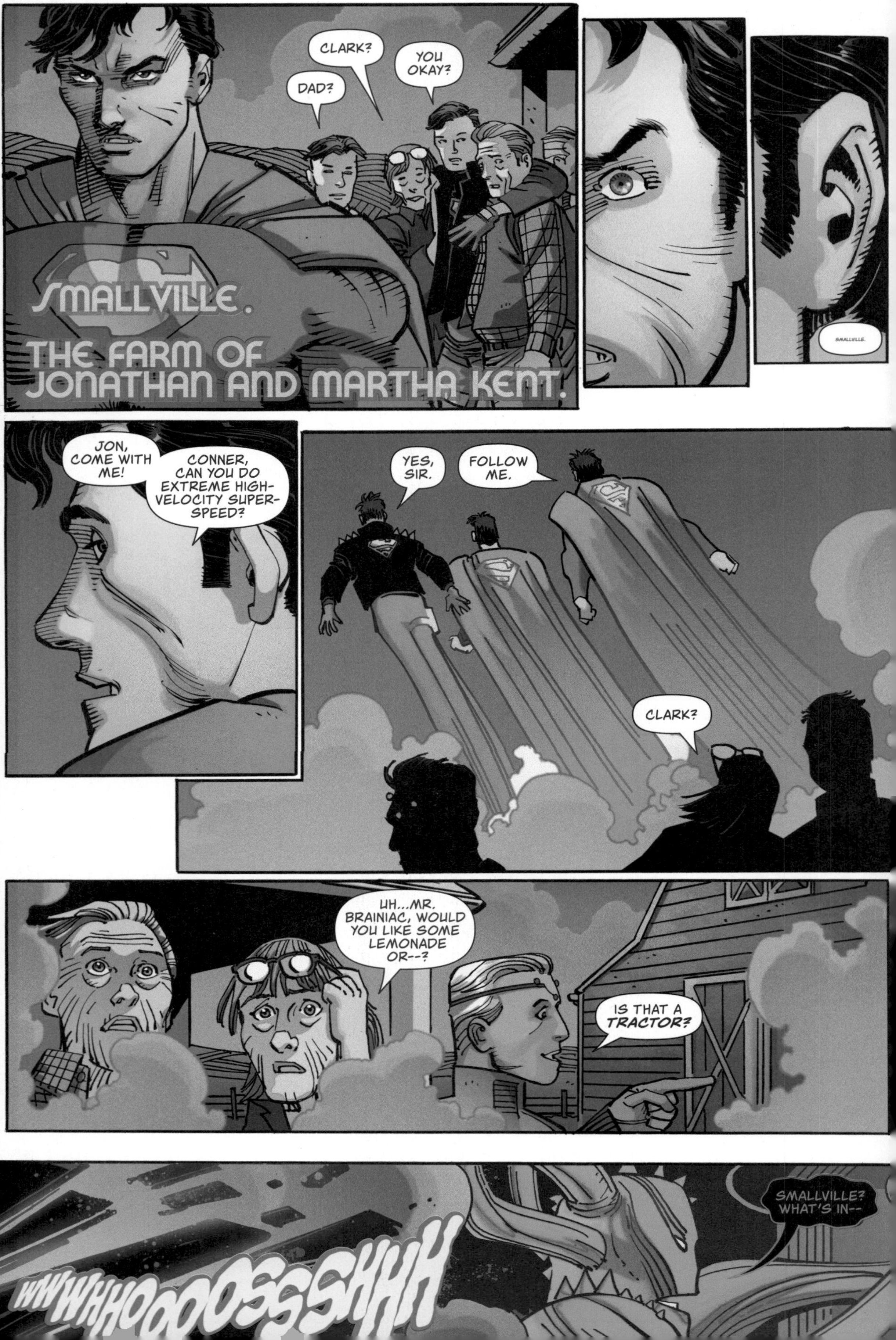

SMALLVILLE.
THE FARM OF JONATHAN AND MARTHA KENT.
DAD?
CLARK?
YOU OKAY?
SMALLVILLE.
JON, COME WITH ME!
CONNER, CAN YOU DO EXTREME HIGH-VELOCITY SUPER-SPEED?
YES, SIR.
FOLLOW ME.
CLARK?
UH...MR. BRAINIAC, WOULD YOU LIKE SOME LEMONADE OR--?
IS THAT A *TRACTOR*?
WWWHHOOOOOSSSHHH
SMALLVILLE? WHAT'S IN--

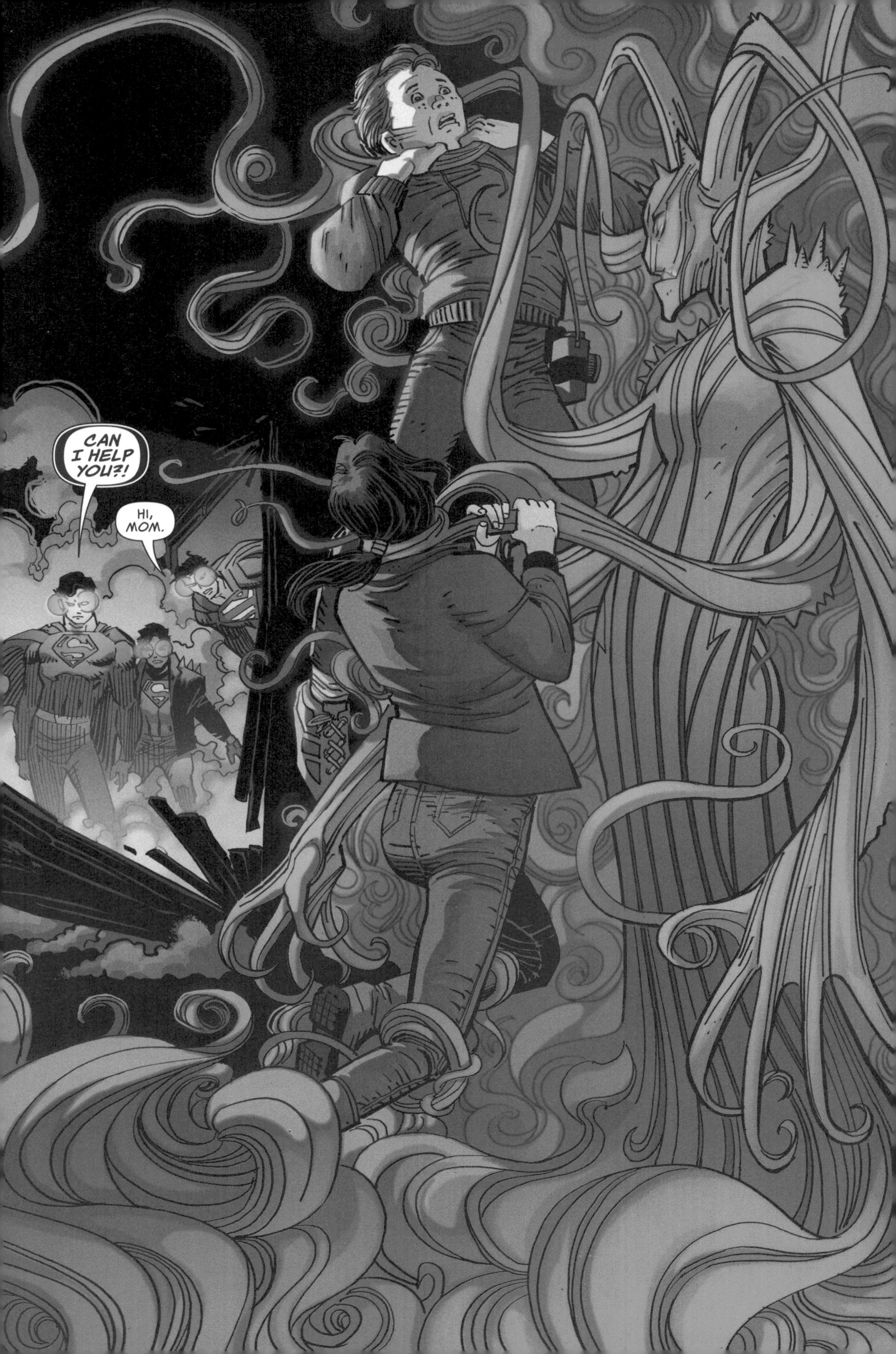
CAN I HELP YOU?!
HI, MOM.

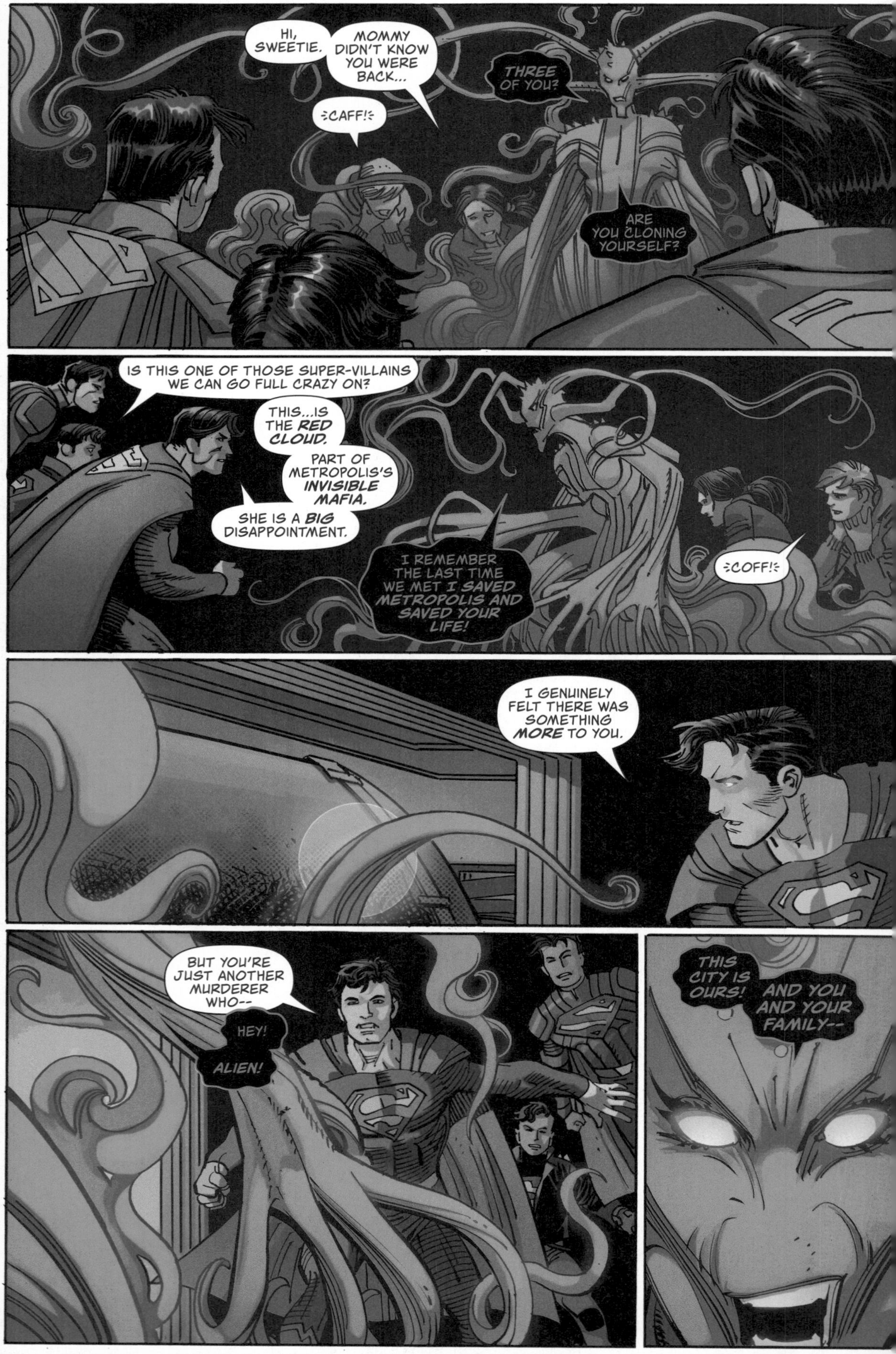
HI, SWEETIE.
MOMMY DIDN'T KNOW YOU WERE BACK...
CAFF!
THREE OF YOU?
ARE YOU CLONING YOURSELF?
IS THIS ONE OF THOSE SUPER-VILLAINS WE CAN GO FULL CRAZY ON?
THIS...IS THE RED CLOUD.
PART OF METROPOLIS'S INVISIBLE MAFIA.
SHE IS A BIG DISAPPOINTMENT.
I REMEMBER THE LAST TIME WE MET I SAVED METROPOLIS AND SAVED YOUR LIFE!
COFF!
I GENUINELY FELT THERE WAS SOMETHING MORE TO YOU.
BUT YOU'RE JUST ANOTHER MURDERER WHO--
HEY!
ALIEN!
THIS CITY IS OURS!
AND YOU AND YOUR FAMILY--

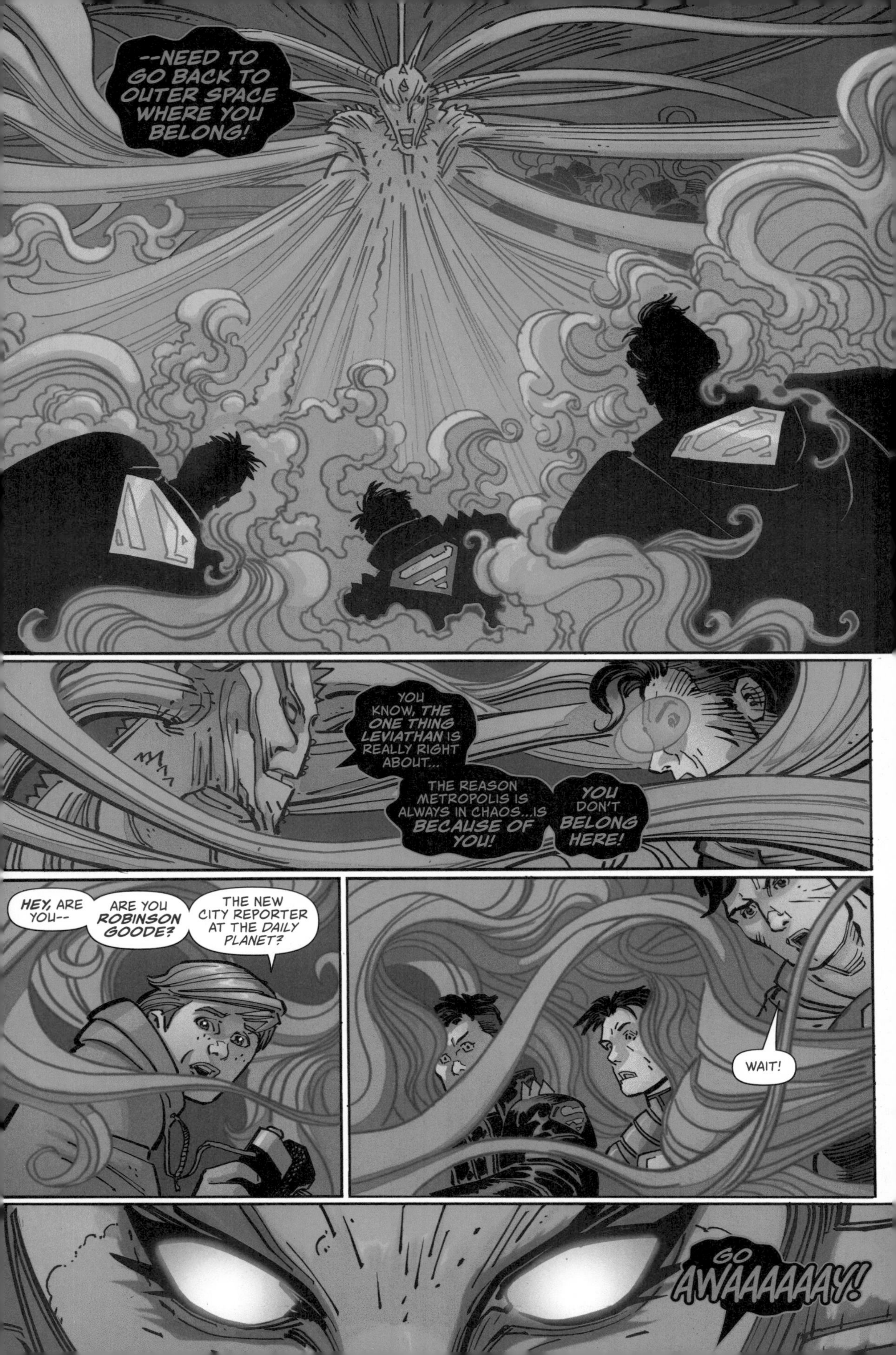
--NEED TO GO BACK TO OUTER SPACE WHERE YOU BELONG!
YOU KNOW, THE ONE THING LEVIATHAN IS REALLY RIGHT ABOUT...
THE REASON METROPOLIS IS ALWAYS IN CHAOS...IS BECAUSE OF YOU!
YOU DON'T BELONG HERE!
HEY, ARE YOU--
ARE YOU ROBINSON GOODE?
THE NEW CITY REPORTER AT THE DAILY PLANET?
WAIT!
GO AWAAAAAAY!

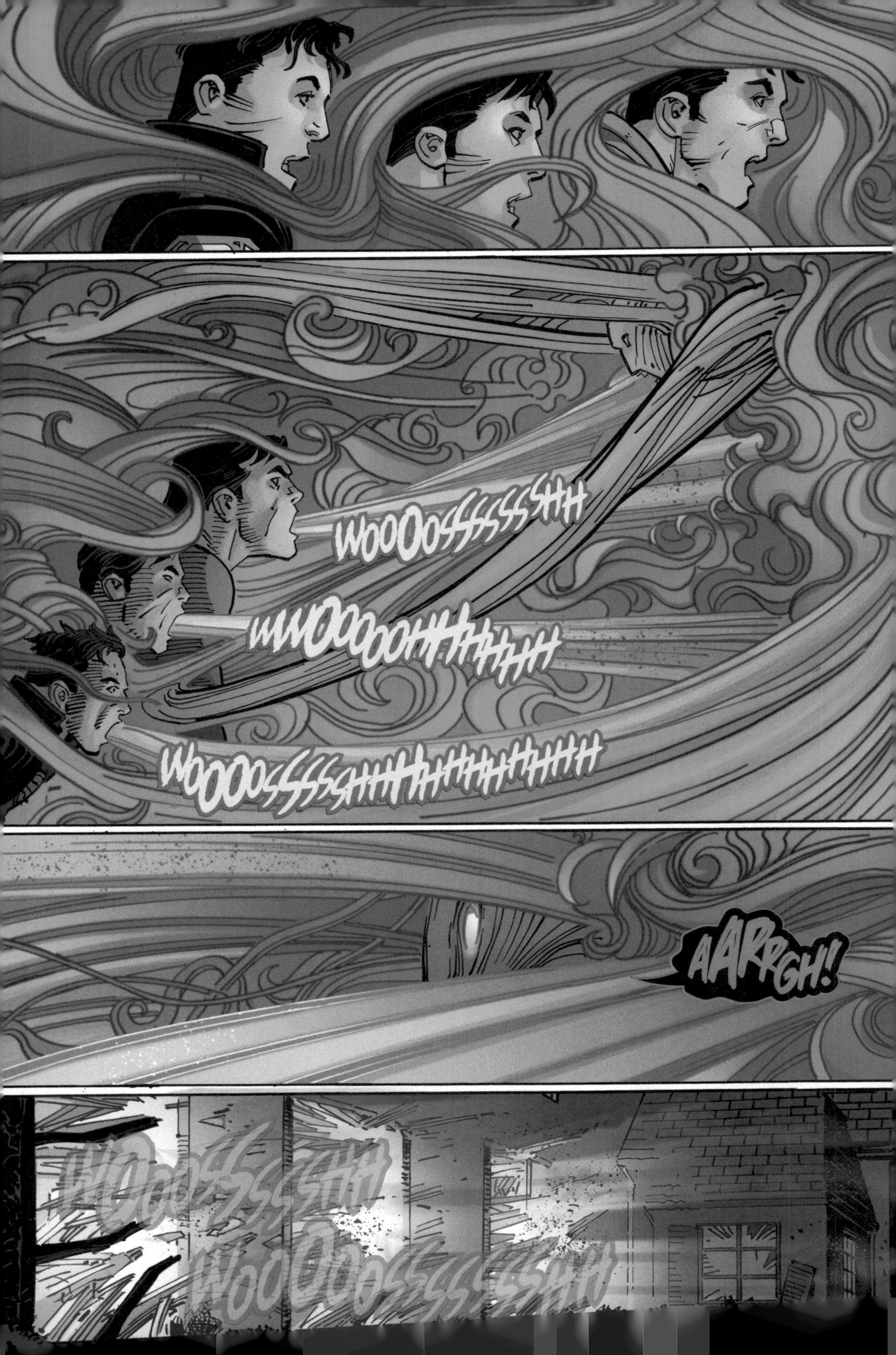
WOOOOSSSSSSSHH
WWOOOOOHHHHHHHH
WOOOOSSSSHHHHHHHHHHHHH
AARRGH!
WOOOSSSHH
WOOOOOSSSSSSHH

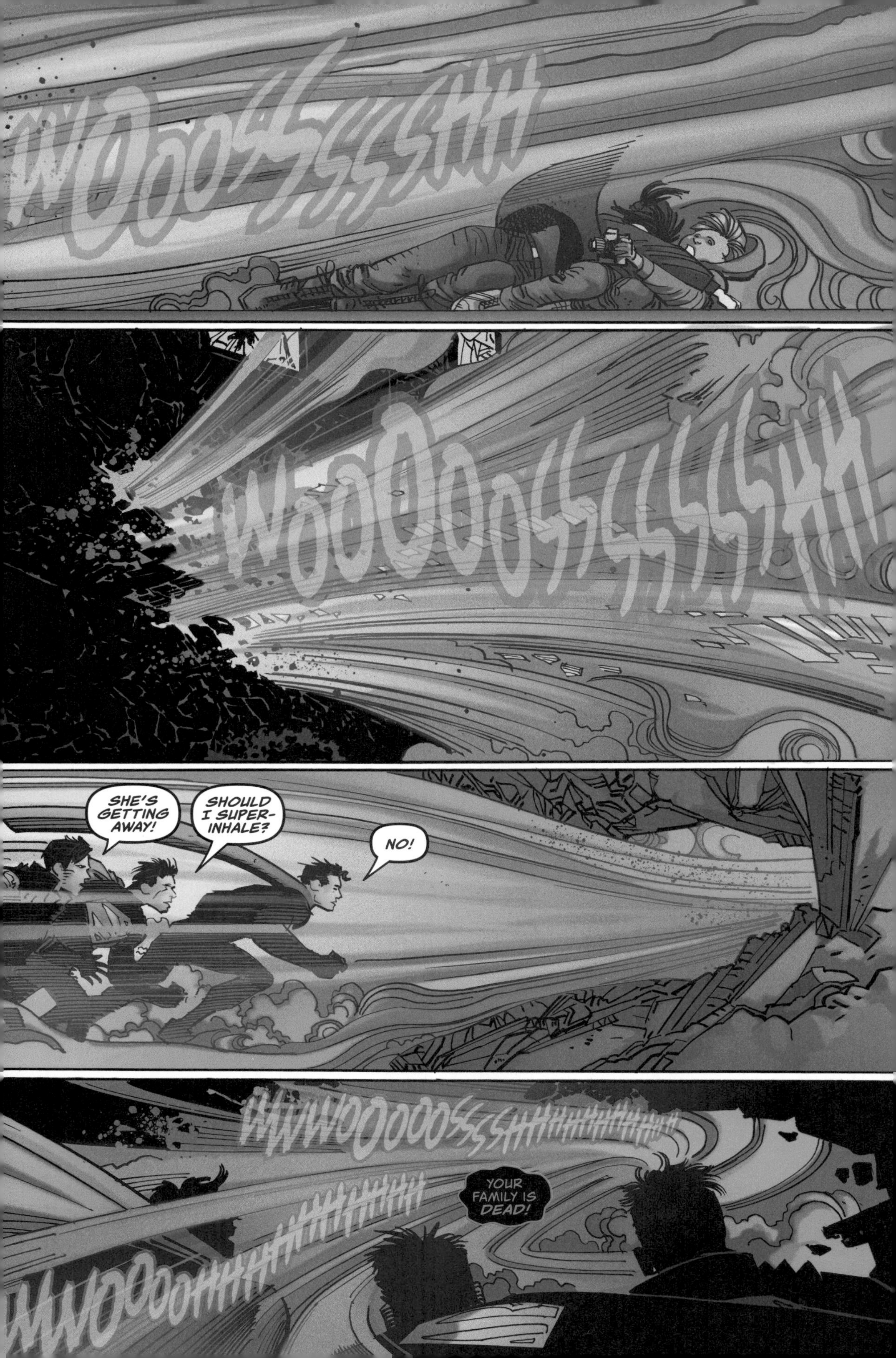
SHE'S GETTING AWAY!
SHOULD I SUPER-INHALE?
NO!
YOUR FAMILY IS DEAD!

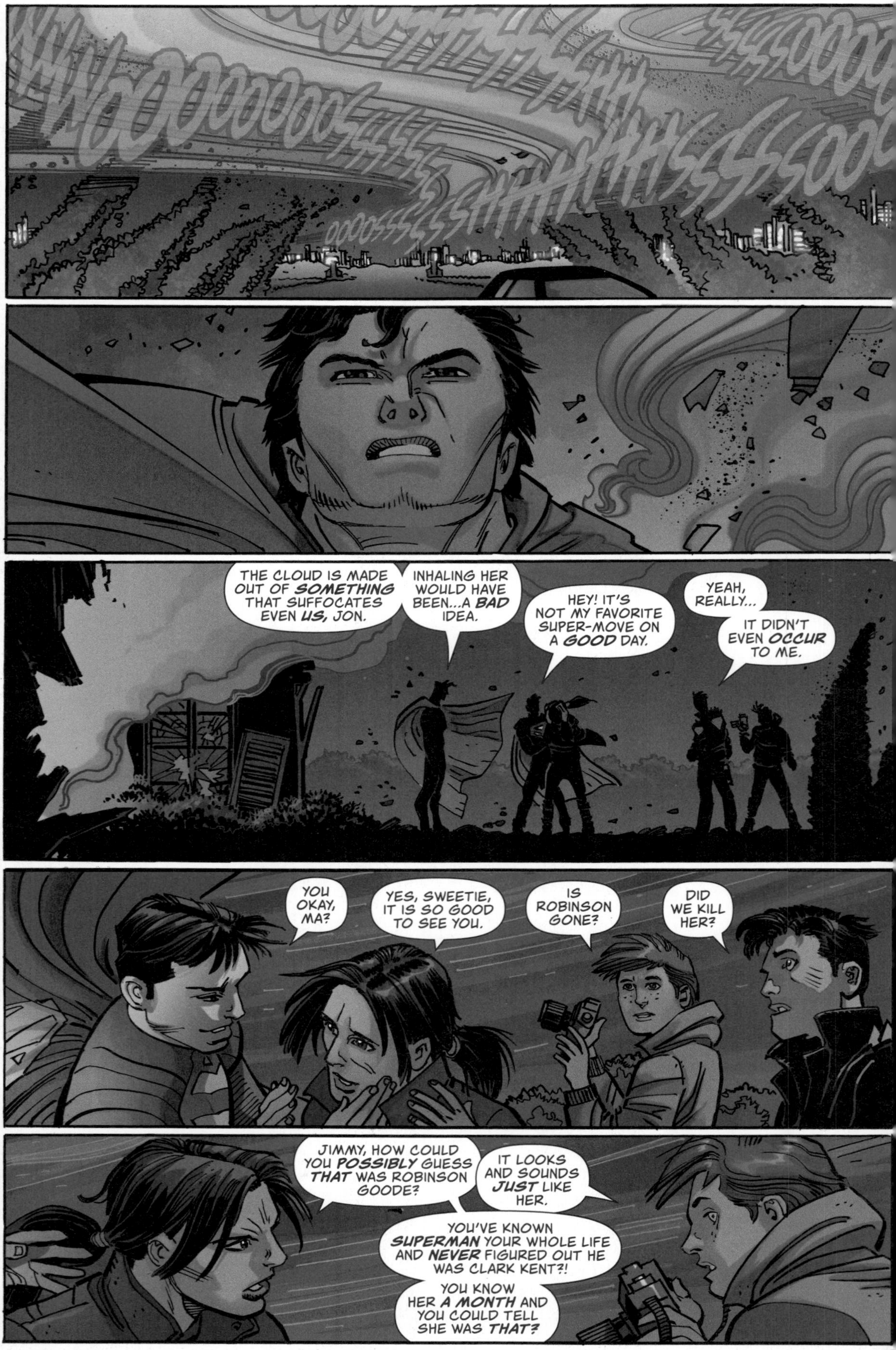
WHOOOOOOOOSSSSS
OOOOSSSSSHHHHHHSSSSOOO
THE CLOUD IS MADE OUT OF SOMETHING THAT SUFFOCATES EVEN US, JON.
INHALING HER WOULD HAVE BEEN...A BAD IDEA.
HEY! IT'S NOT MY FAVORITE SUPER-MOVE ON A GOOD DAY.
YEAH, REALLY...
IT DIDN'T EVEN OCCUR TO ME.
YOU OKAY, MA?
YES, SWEETIE, IT IS SO GOOD TO SEE YOU.
IS ROBINSON GONE?
DID WE KILL HER?
JIMMY, HOW COULD YOU POSSIBLY GUESS THAT WAS ROBINSON GOODE?
IT LOOKS AND SOUNDS JUST LIKE HER.
YOU'VE KNOWN SUPERMAN YOUR WHOLE LIFE AND NEVER FIGURED OUT HE WAS CLARK KENT?!
YOU KNOW HER A MONTH AND YOU COULD TELL SHE WAS THAT?

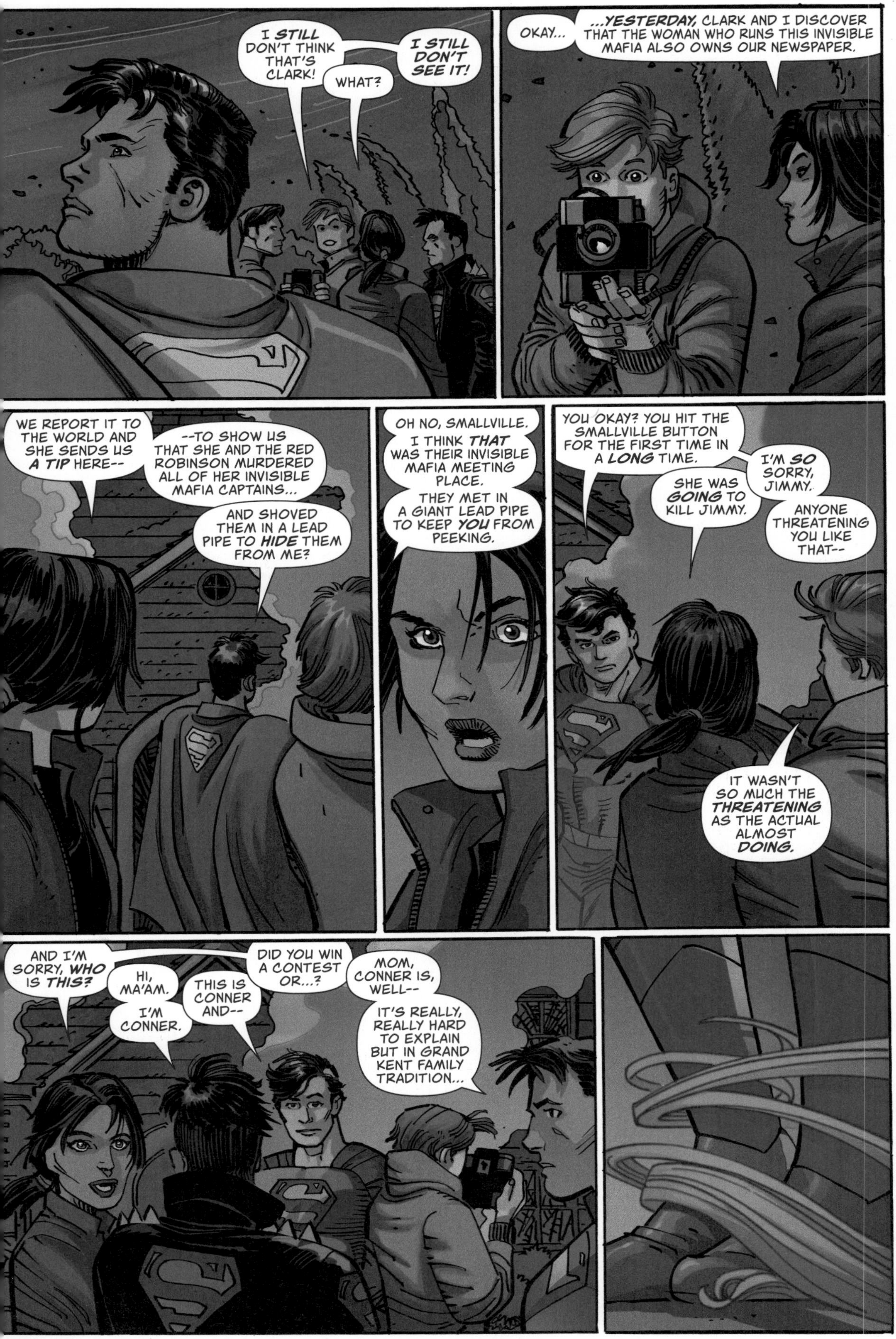
I STILL DON'T THINK THAT'S CLARK!
WHAT?
I STILL DON'T SEE IT!
OKAY...
...YESTERDAY, CLARK AND I DISCOVER THAT THE WOMAN WHO RUNS THIS INVISIBLE MAFIA ALSO OWNS OUR NEWSPAPER.
WE REPORT IT TO THE WORLD AND SHE SENDS US A TIP HERE--
--TO SHOW US THAT SHE AND THE RED ROBINSON MURDERED ALL OF HER INVISIBLE MAFIA CAPTAINS...
AND SHOVED THEM IN A LEAD PIPE TO HIDE THEM FROM ME?
OH NO, SMALLVILLE. I THINK THAT WAS THEIR INVISIBLE MAFIA MEETING PLACE.
THEY MET IN A GIANT LEAD PIPE TO KEEP YOU FROM PEEKING.
YOU OKAY? YOU HIT THE SMALLVILLE BUTTON FOR THE FIRST TIME IN A LONG TIME.
SHE WAS GOING TO KILL JIMMY.
I'M SO SORRY, JIMMY.
ANYONE THREATENING YOU LIKE THAT--
IT WASN'T SO MUCH THE THREATENING AS THE ACTUAL ALMOST DOING.
AND I'M SORRY, WHO IS THIS?
HI, MA'AM.
I'M CONNER.
THIS IS CONNER AND--
DID YOU WIN A CONTEST OR...?
MOM, CONNER IS, WELL--
IT'S REALLY, REALLY HARD TO EXPLAIN BUT IN GRAND KENT FAMILY TRADITION...

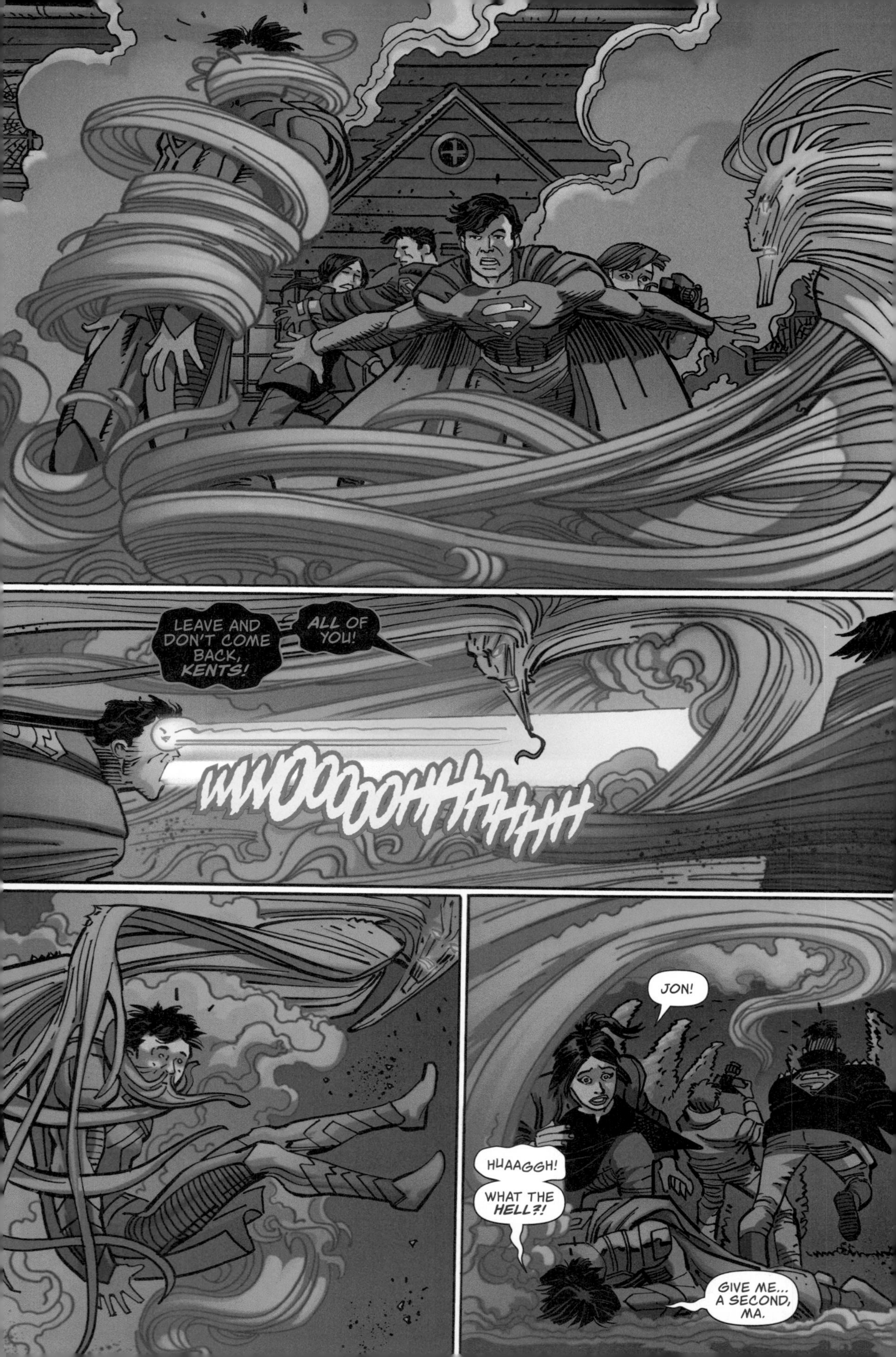
LEAVE AND DON'T COME BACK, KENTS!
ALL OF YOU!
WHOOOOOOHHHHHHH
JON!
HUAAGGH!
WHAT THE HELL?!
GIVE ME... A SECOND, MA.

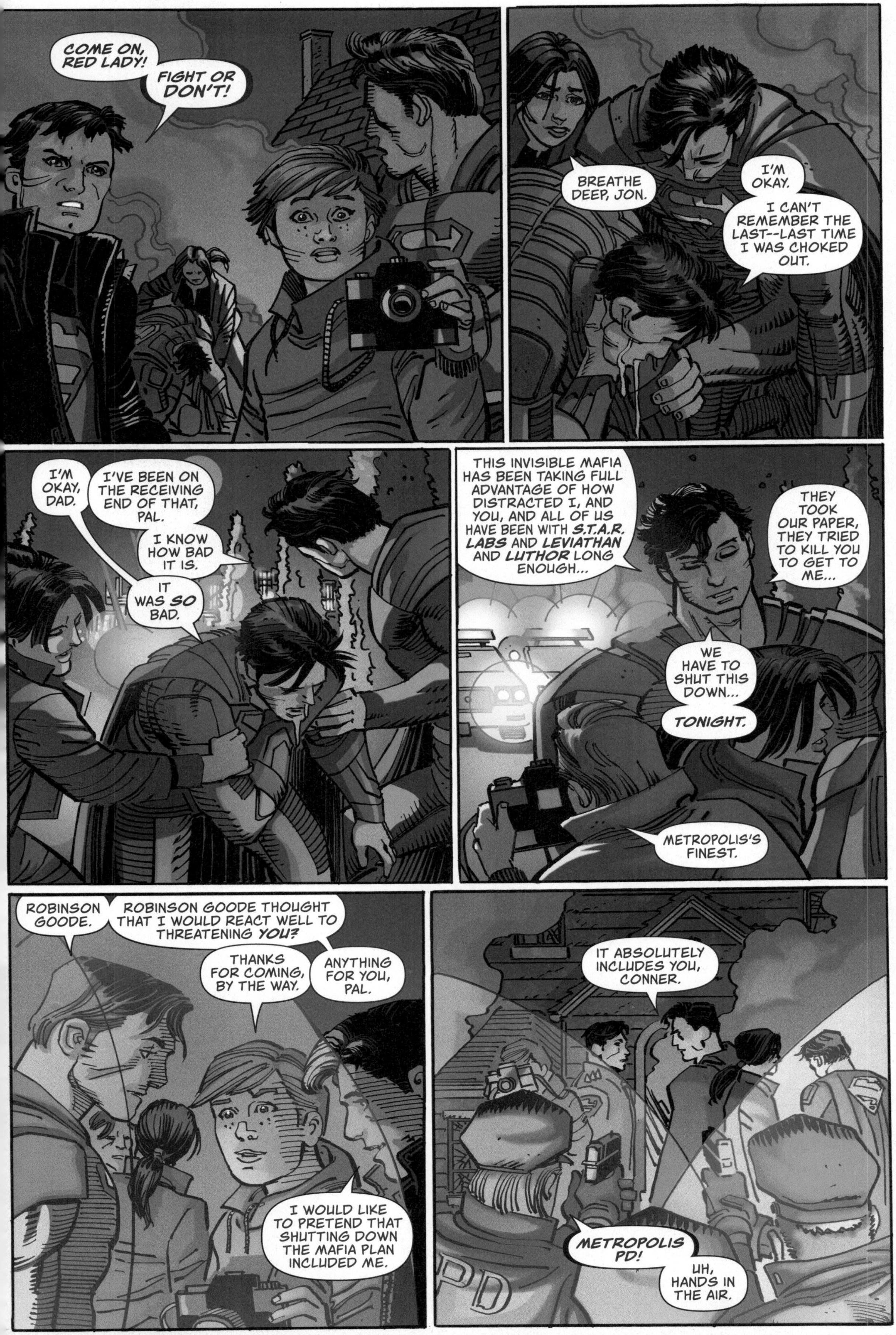

COME ON, RED LADY!
FIGHT OR DON'T!
BREATHE DEEP, JON.
I'M OKAY.
I CAN'T REMEMBER THE LAST--LAST TIME I WAS CHOKED OUT.
I'M OKAY, DAD.
I'VE BEEN ON THE RECEIVING END OF THAT, PAL.
I KNOW HOW BAD IT IS.
IT WAS SO BAD.
THIS INVISIBLE MAFIA HAS BEEN TAKING FULL ADVANTAGE OF HOW DISTRACTED I, AND YOU, AND ALL OF US HAVE BEEN WITH S.T.A.R. LABS AND LEVIATHAN AND LUTHOR LONG ENOUGH...
THEY TOOK OUR PAPER, THEY TRIED TO KILL YOU TO GET TO ME...
WE HAVE TO SHUT THIS DOWN...
TONIGHT.
METROPOLIS'S FINEST.
ROBINSON GOODE.
ROBINSON GOODE THOUGHT THAT I WOULD REACT WELL TO THREATENING YOU?
THANKS FOR COMING, BY THE WAY.
ANYTHING FOR YOU, PAL.
I WOULD LIKE TO PRETEND THAT SHUTTING DOWN THE MAFIA PLAN INCLUDED ME.
IT ABSOLUTELY INCLUDES YOU, CONNER.
METROPOLIS PD!
UH, HANDS IN THE AIR.

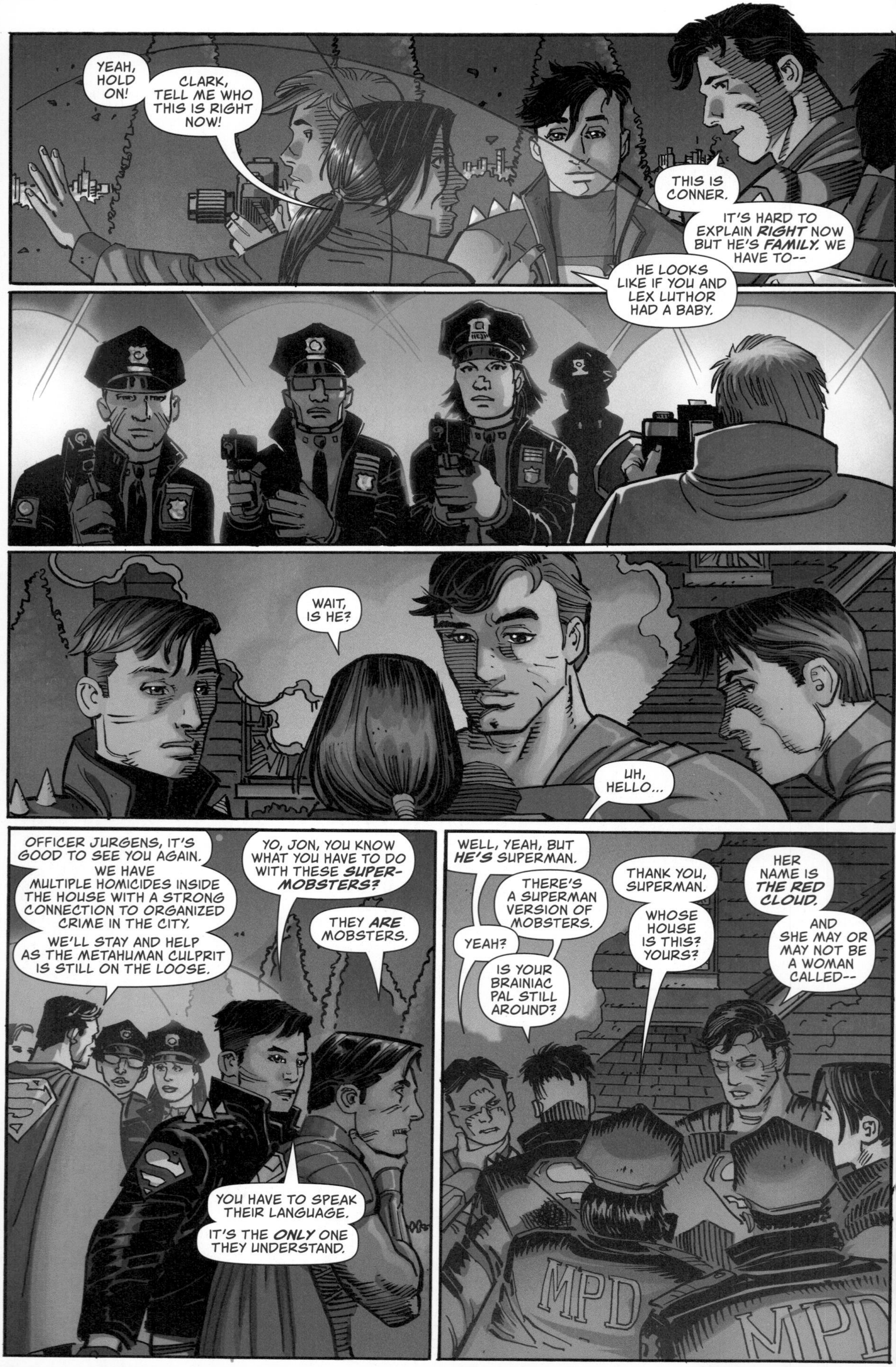
YEAH, HOLD ON!
CLARK, TELL ME WHO THIS IS RIGHT NOW!
THIS IS CONNER.
IT'S HARD TO EXPLAIN *RIGHT* NOW BUT HE'S *FAMILY.* WE HAVE TO--
HE LOOKS LIKE IF YOU AND LEX LUTHOR HAD A BABY.
WAIT, IS HE?
UH, HELLO...
OFFICER JURGENS, IT'S GOOD TO SEE YOU AGAIN.
WE HAVE MULTIPLE HOMICIDES INSIDE THE HOUSE WITH A STRONG CONNECTION TO ORGANIZED CRIME IN THE CITY.
WE'LL STAY AND HELP AS THE METAHUMAN CULPRIT IS STILL ON THE LOOSE.
YO, JON, YOU KNOW WHAT YOU HAVE TO DO WITH THESE *SUPER-MOBSTERS?*
THEY *ARE* MOBSTERS.
YOU HAVE TO SPEAK THEIR LANGUAGE.
IT'S THE *ONLY* ONE THEY UNDERSTAND.
WELL, YEAH, BUT *HE'S* SUPERMAN.
THERE'S A SUPERMAN VERSION OF MOBSTERS.
YEAH?
IS YOUR BRAINIAC PAL STILL AROUND?
THANK YOU, SUPERMAN.
WHOSE HOUSE IS THIS? YOURS?
HER NAME IS *THE RED CLOUD.*
AND SHE MAY OR MAY NOT BE A WOMAN CALLED--
MPD
MPD

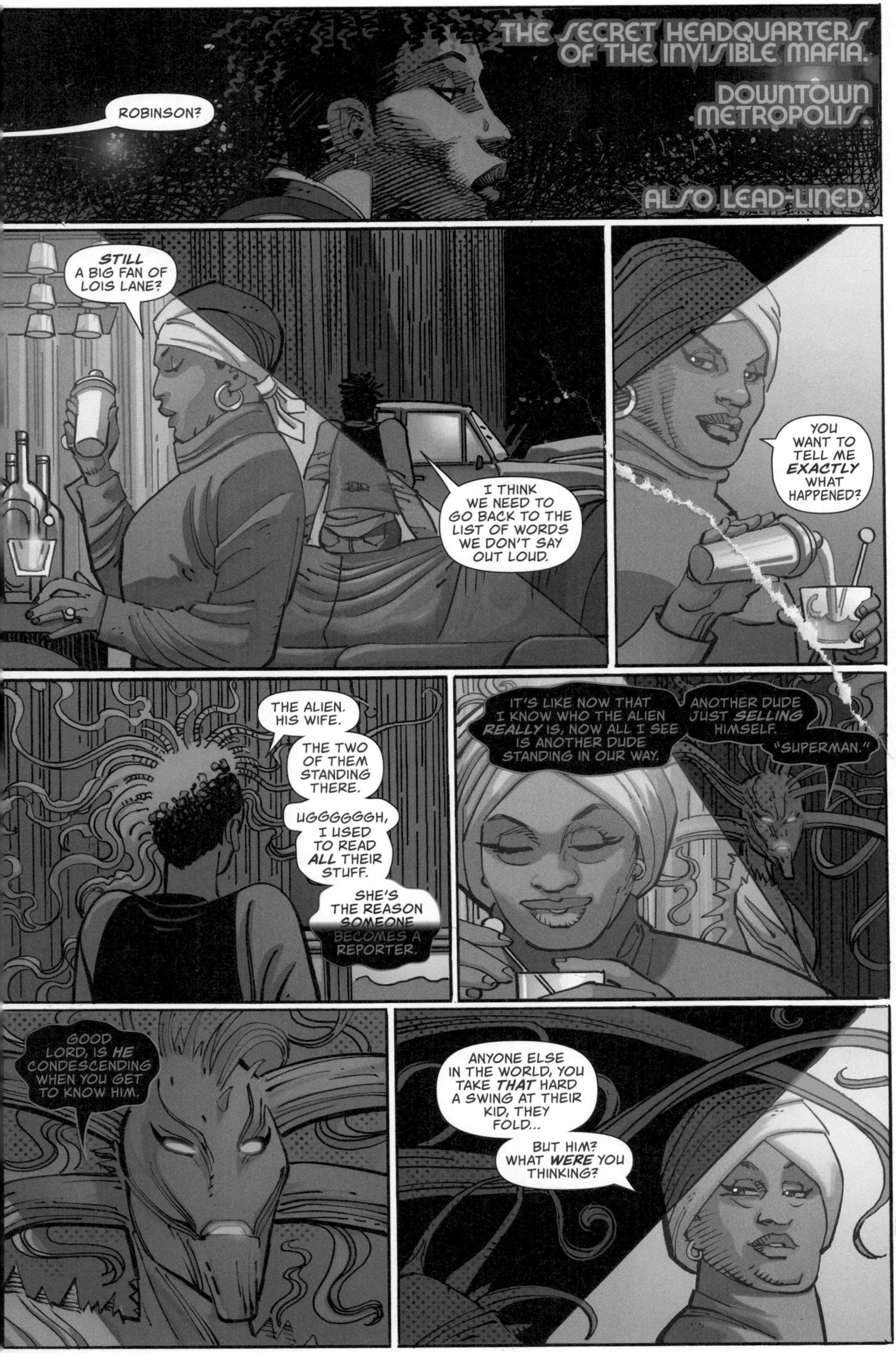
THE SECRET HEADQUARTERS OF THE INVISIBLE MAFIA.
DOWNTOWN METROPOLIS.
ALSO LEAD-LINED.
ROBINSON?
STILL A BIG FAN OF LOIS LANE?
I THINK WE NEED TO GO BACK TO THE LIST OF WORDS WE DON'T SAY OUT LOUD.
YOU WANT TO TELL ME EXACTLY WHAT HAPPENED?
THE ALIEN. HIS WIFE.
THE TWO OF THEM STANDING THERE.
UGGGGGGH, I USED TO READ ALL THEIR STUFF.
SHE'S THE REASON SOMEONE BECOMES A REPORTER.
IT'S LIKE NOW THAT I KNOW WHO THE ALIEN REALLY IS, NOW ALL I SEE IS ANOTHER DUDE STANDING IN OUR WAY.
ANOTHER DUDE JUST SELLING HIMSELF.
"SUPERMAN."
GOOD LORD, IS HE CONDESCENDING WHEN YOU GET TO KNOW HIM.
ANYONE ELSE IN THE WORLD, YOU TAKE THAT HARD A SWING AT THEIR KID, THEY FOLD...
BUT HIM? WHAT WERE YOU THINKING?

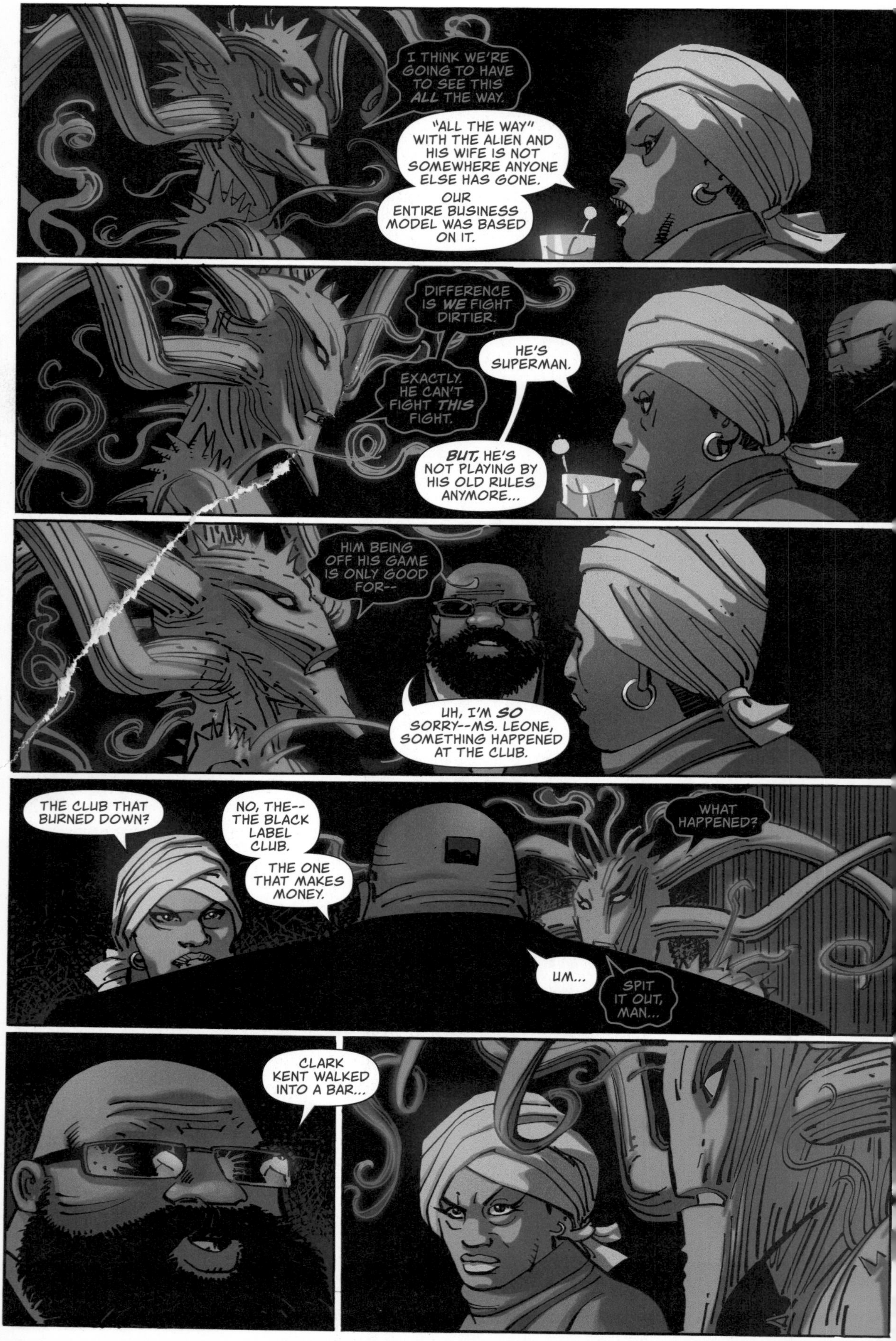
I THINK WE'RE GOING TO HAVE TO SEE THIS ALL THE WAY.
"ALL THE WAY" WITH THE ALIEN AND HIS WIFE IS NOT SOMEWHERE ANYONE ELSE HAS GONE.
OUR ENTIRE BUSINESS MODEL WAS BASED ON IT.
DIFFERENCE IS WE FIGHT DIRTIER.
HE'S SUPERMAN.
EXACTLY. HE CAN'T FIGHT THIS FIGHT.
BUT, HE'S NOT PLAYING BY HIS OLD RULES ANYMORE...
HIM BEING OFF HIS GAME IS ONLY GOOD FOR--
UH, I'M SO SORRY--MS. LEONE, SOMETHING HAPPENED AT THE CLUB.
THE CLUB THAT BURNED DOWN?
NO, THE-- THE BLACK LABEL CLUB.
THE ONE THAT MAKES MONEY.
WHAT HAPPENED?
UM...
SPIT IT OUT, MAN...
CLARK KENT WALKED INTO A BAR...

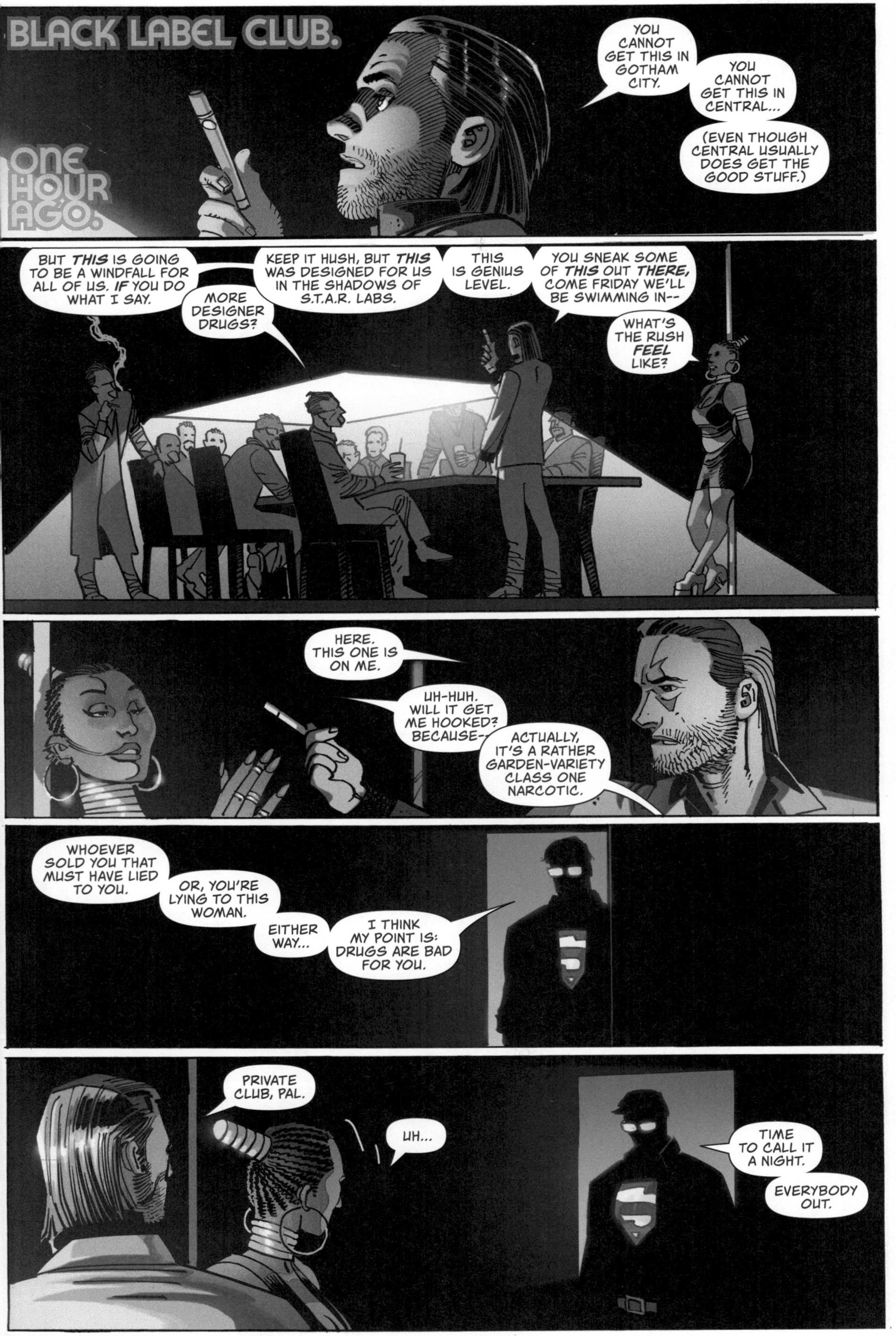
BLACK LABEL CLUB.
ONE HOUR AGO.
YOU CANNOT GET THIS IN GOTHAM CITY.
YOU CANNOT GET THIS IN CENTRAL...
(EVEN THOUGH CENTRAL USUALLY DOES GET THE GOOD STUFF.)
BUT THIS IS GOING TO BE A WINDFALL FOR ALL OF US. IF YOU DO WHAT I SAY.
MORE DESIGNER DRUGS?
KEEP IT HUSH, BUT THIS WAS DESIGNED FOR US IN THE SHADOWS OF S.T.A.R. LABS.
THIS IS GENIUS LEVEL.
YOU SNEAK SOME OF THIS OUT THERE, COME FRIDAY WE'LL BE SWIMMING IN--
WHAT'S THE RUSH FEEL LIKE?
HERE. THIS ONE IS ON ME.
UH-HUH. WILL IT GET ME HOOKED? BECAUSE--
ACTUALLY, IT'S A RATHER GARDEN-VARIETY CLASS ONE NARCOTIC.
WHOEVER SOLD YOU THAT MUST HAVE LIED TO YOU.
OR, YOU'RE LYING TO THIS WOMAN.
EITHER WAY...
I THINK MY POINT IS: DRUGS ARE BAD FOR YOU.
PRIVATE CLUB, PAL.
UH...
TIME TO CALL IT A NIGHT.
EVERYBODY OUT.

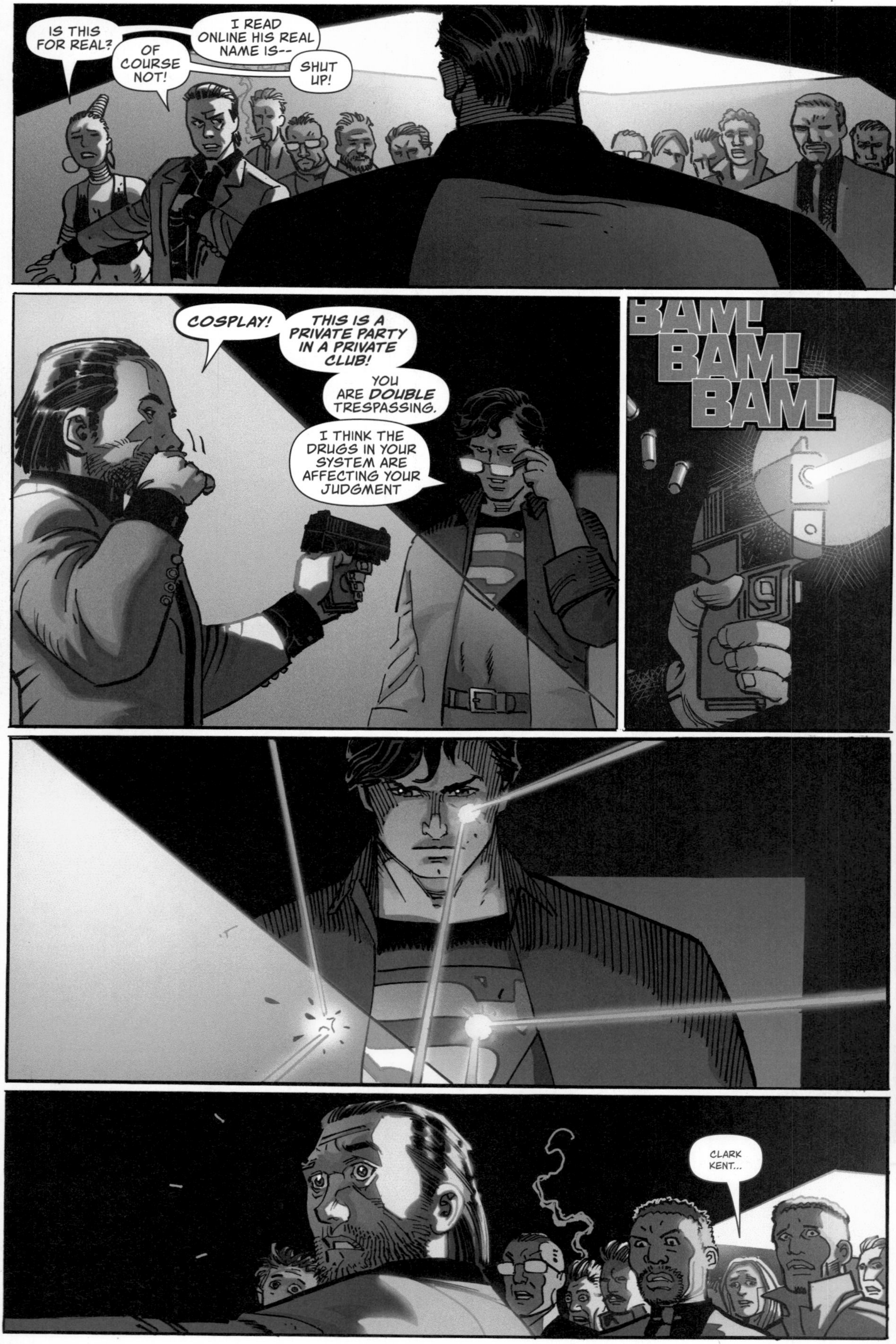
IS THIS FOR REAL?
I READ ONLINE HIS REAL NAME IS--
OF COURSE NOT!
SHUT UP!
COSPLAY!
THIS IS A PRIVATE PARTY IN A PRIVATE CLUB!
YOU ARE DOUBLE TRESPASSING.
I THINK THE DRUGS IN YOUR SYSTEM ARE AFFECTING YOUR JUDGMENT
BAM! BAM! BAM!
CLARK KENT...

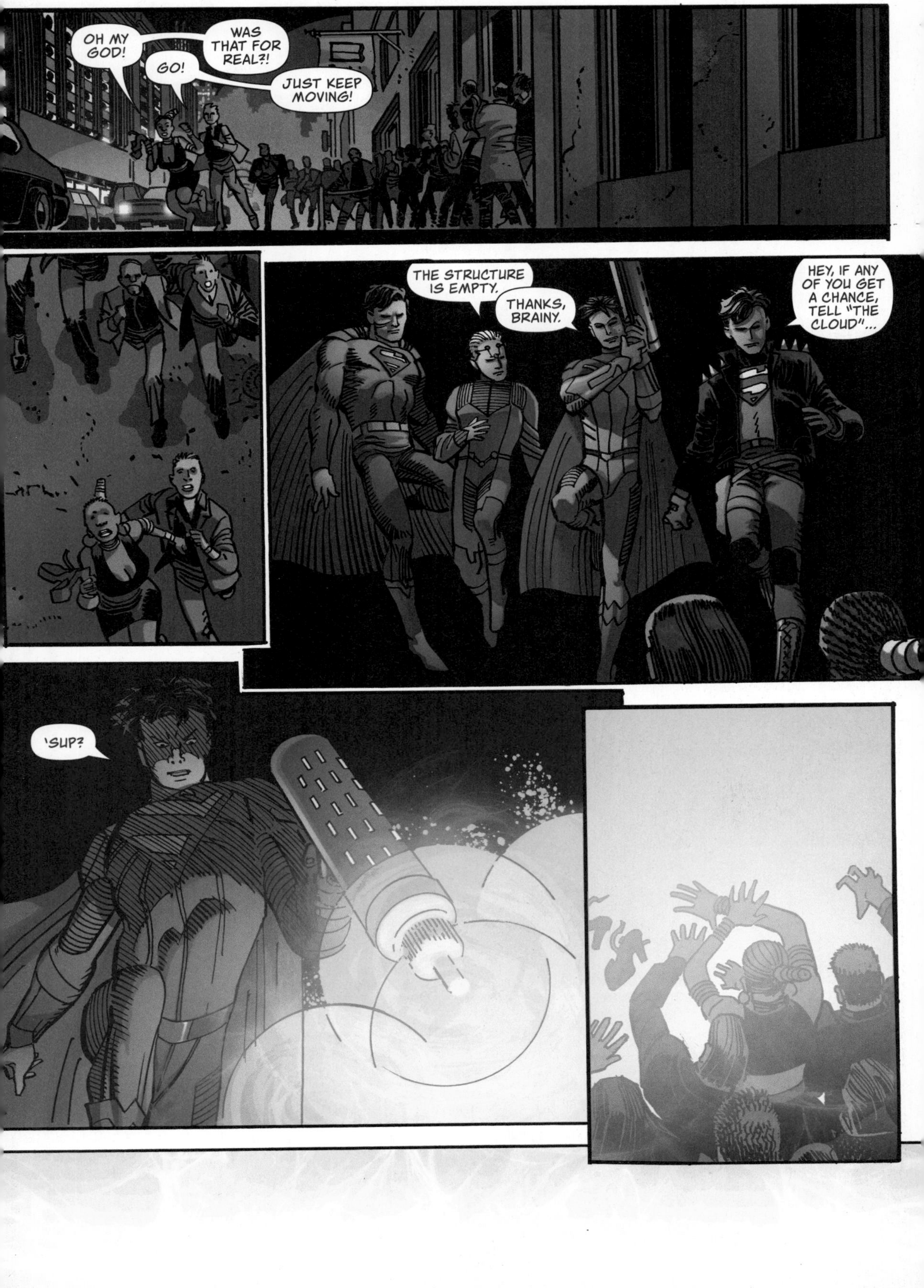
OH MY GOD!
WAS THAT FOR REAL?!
GO!
JUST KEEP MOVING!
THE STRUCTURE IS EMPTY.
THANKS, BRAINY.
HEY, IF ANY OF YOU GET A CHANCE, TELL "THE CLOUD"...
'SUP?

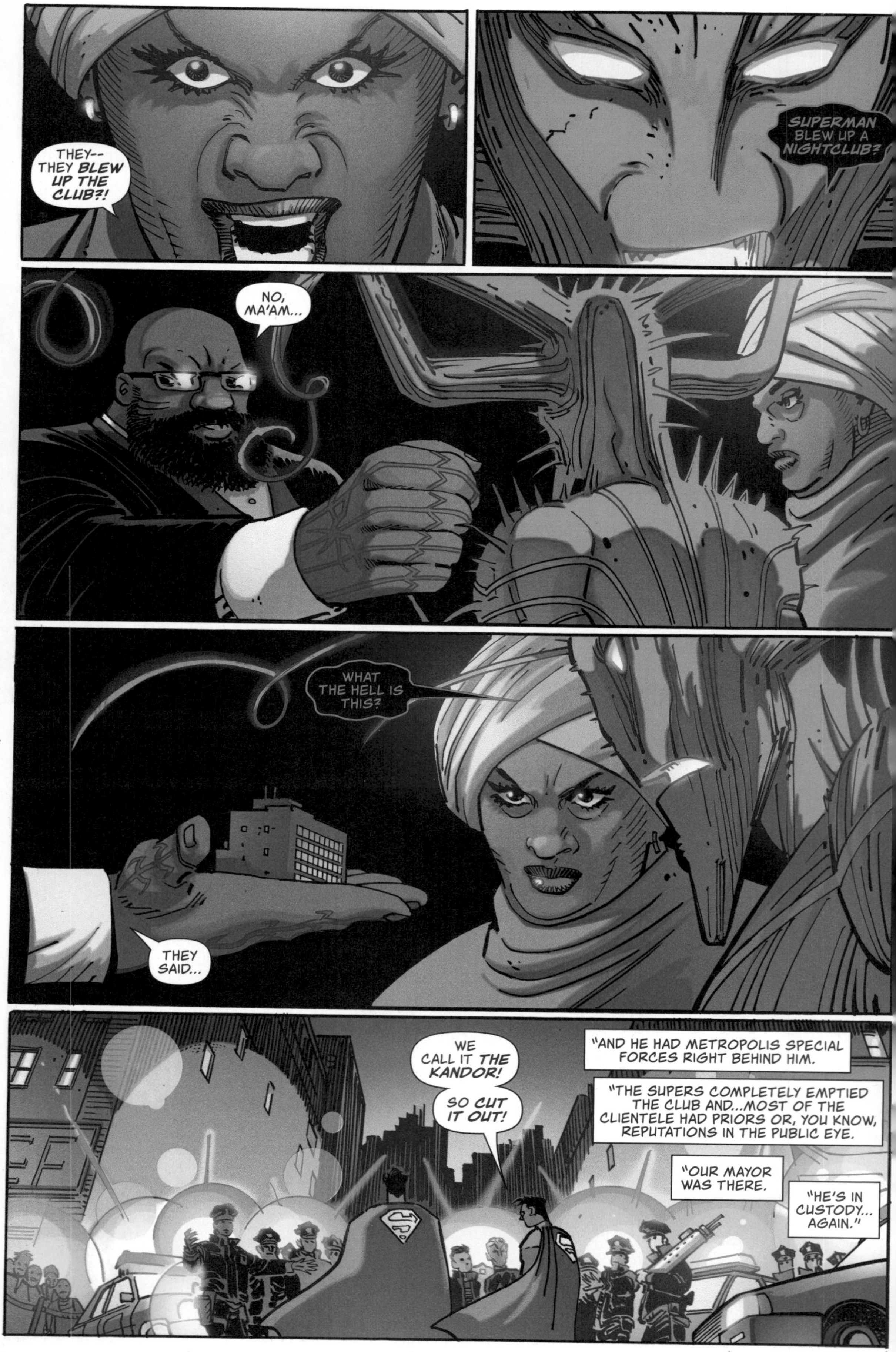
THEY--
THEY BLEW UP THE CLUB?!
SUPERMAN BLEW UP A NIGHTCLUB?
NO, MA'AM...
WHAT THE HELL IS THIS?
THEY SAID...
WE CALL IT THE KANDOR!
SO CUT IT OUT!
"AND HE HAD METROPOLIS SPECIAL FORCES RIGHT BEHIND HIM.
"THE SUPERS COMPLETELY EMPTIED THE CLUB AND...MOST OF THE CLIENTELE HAD PRIORS OR, YOU KNOW, REPUTATIONS IN THE PUBLIC EYE.
"OUR MAYOR WAS THERE.
"HE'S IN CUSTODY... AGAIN."

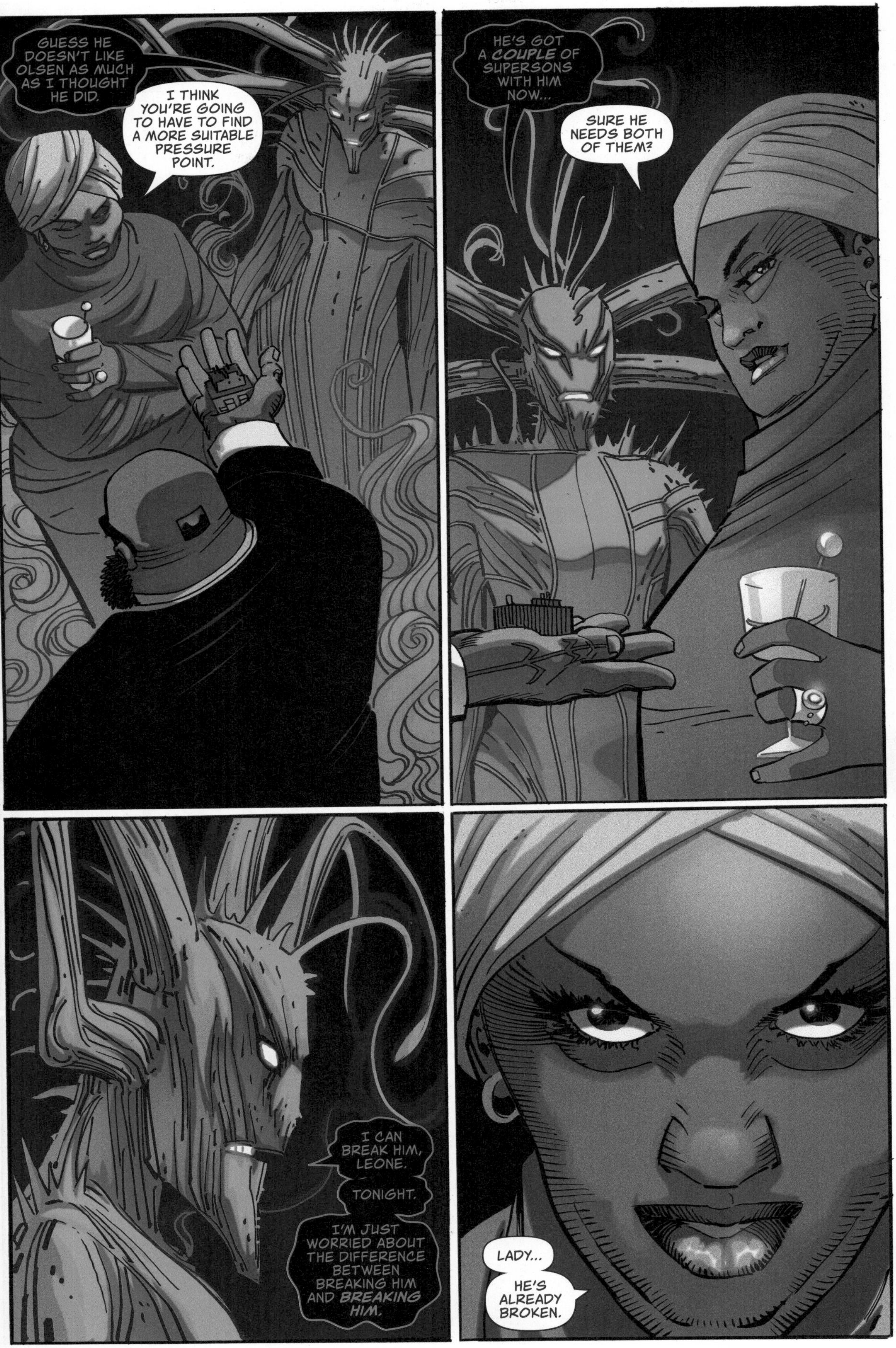
GUESS HE DOESN'T LIKE OLSEN AS MUCH AS I THOUGHT HE DID.
I THINK YOU'RE GOING TO HAVE TO FIND A MORE SUITABLE PRESSURE POINT.
HE'S GOT A COUPLE OF SUPERSONS WITH HIM NOW...
SURE HE NEEDS BOTH OF THEM?
I CAN BREAK HIM, LEONE.
TONIGHT.
I'M JUST WORRIED ABOUT THE DIFFERENCE BETWEEN BREAKING HIM AND BREAKING HIM.
LADY...
HE'S ALREADY BROKEN.

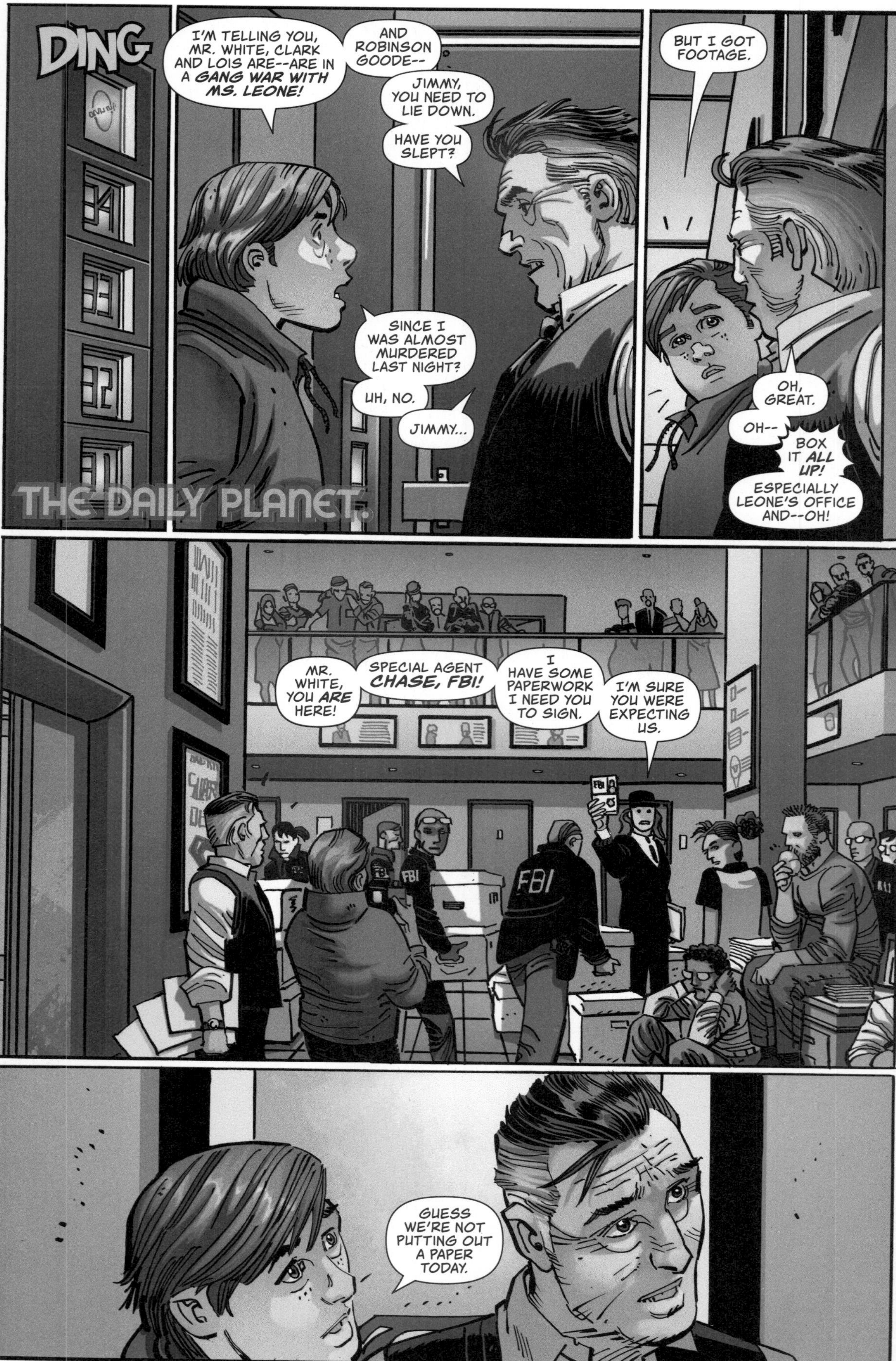
DING
I'M TELLING YOU, MR. WHITE, CLARK AND LOIS ARE--ARE IN A GANG WAR WITH MS. LEONE!
AND ROBINSON GOODE--
JIMMY, YOU NEED TO LIE DOWN.
HAVE YOU SLEPT?
SINCE I WAS ALMOST MURDERED LAST NIGHT?
UH, NO.
JIMMY...
THE DAILY PLANET.
BUT I GOT FOOTAGE.
OH, GREAT.
OH--
BOX IT ALL UP! ESPECIALLY LEONE'S OFFICE AND--OH!
MR. WHITE, YOU ARE HERE!
SPECIAL AGENT CHASE, FBI!
I HAVE SOME PAPERWORK I NEED YOU TO SIGN.
I'M SURE YOU WERE EXPECTING US.
FBI
FBI
GUESS WE'RE NOT PUTTING OUT A PAPER TODAY.

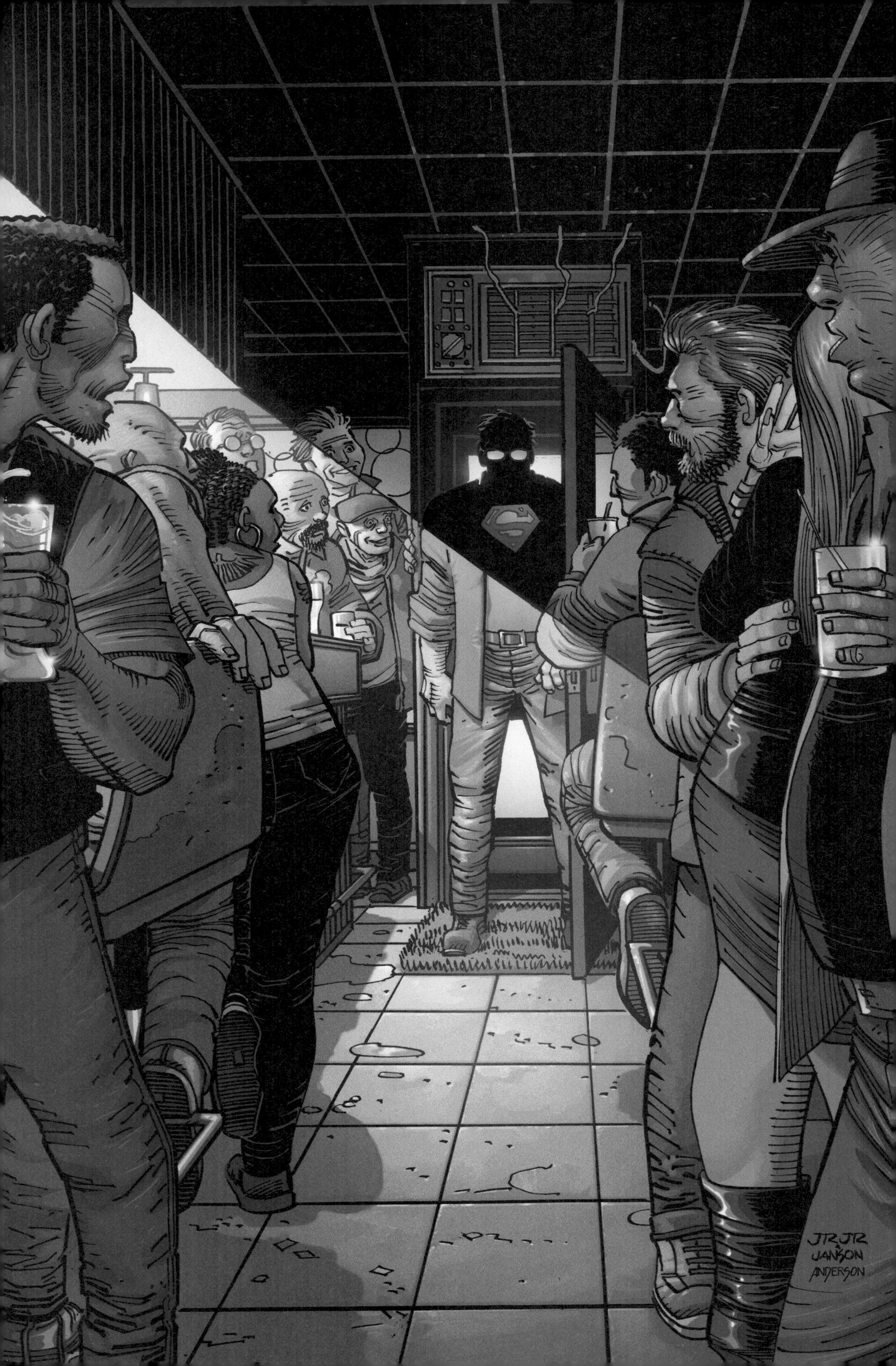
JRJR
JANSON
ANDERSON

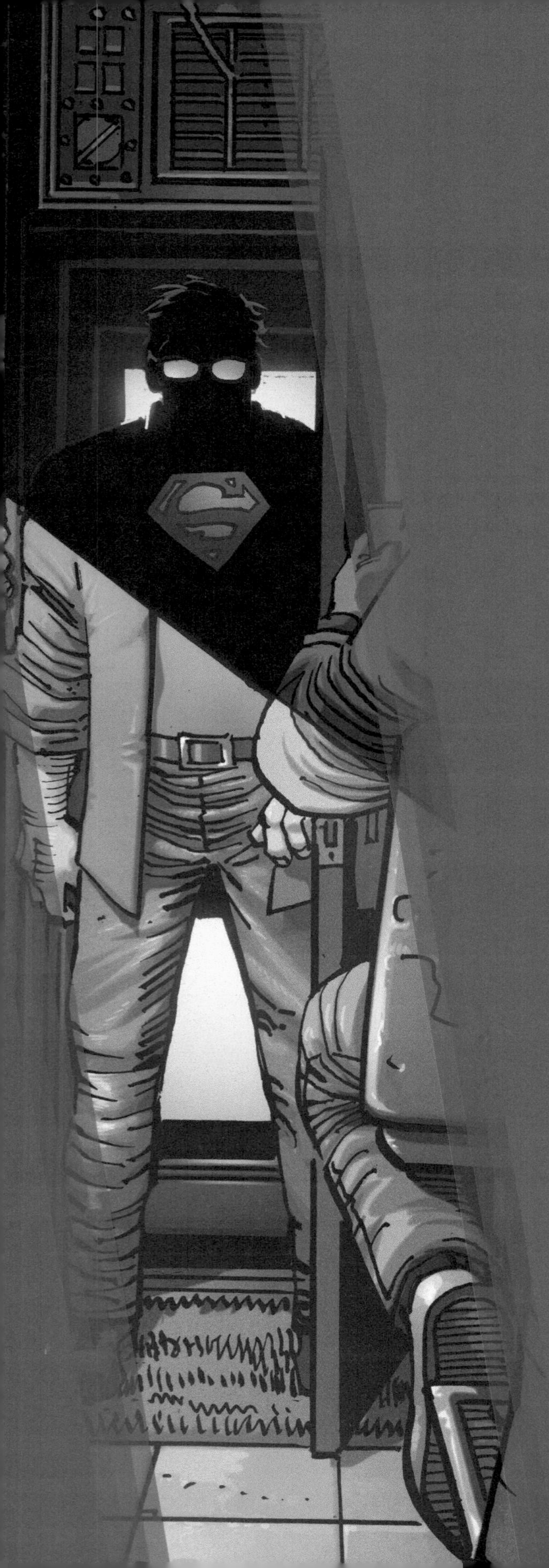

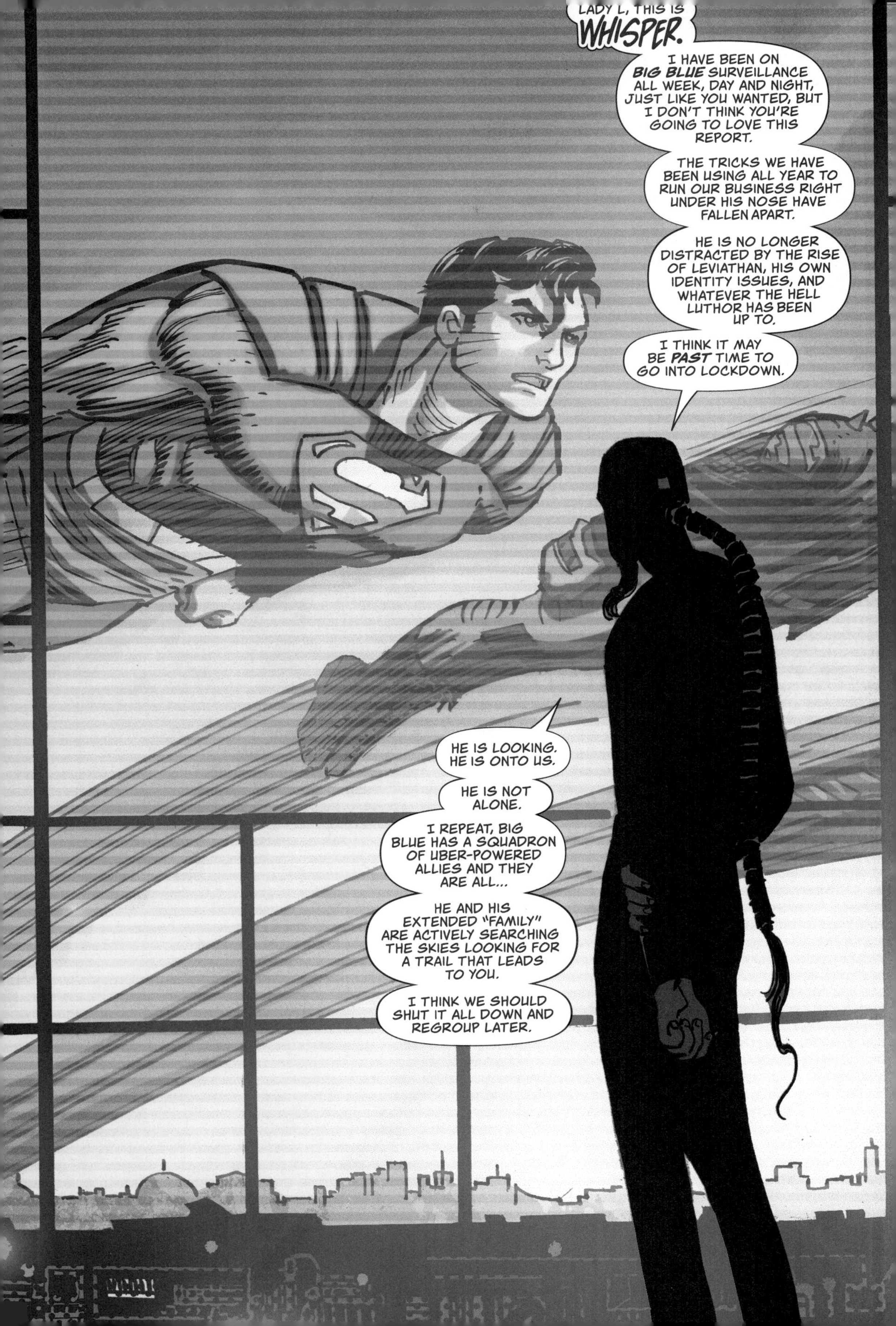
LADY L, THIS IS WHISPER.
I HAVE BEEN ON BIG BLUE SURVEILLANCE ALL WEEK, DAY AND NIGHT, JUST LIKE YOU WANTED, BUT I DON'T THINK YOU'RE GOING TO LOVE THIS REPORT.
THE TRICKS WE HAVE BEEN USING ALL YEAR TO RUN OUR BUSINESS RIGHT UNDER HIS NOSE HAVE FALLEN APART.
HE IS NO LONGER DISTRACTED BY THE RISE OF LEVIATHAN, HIS OWN IDENTITY ISSUES, AND WHATEVER THE HELL LUTHOR HAS BEEN UP TO.
I THINK IT MAY BE PAST TIME TO GO INTO LOCKDOWN.
HE IS LOOKING. HE IS ONTO US.
HE IS NOT ALONE.
I REPEAT, BIG BLUE HAS A SQUADRON OF UBER-POWERED ALLIES AND THEY ARE ALL...
HE AND HIS EXTENDED "FAMILY" ARE ACTIVELY SEARCHING THE SKIES LOOKING FOR A TRAIL THAT LEADS TO YOU.
I THINK WE SHOULD SHUT IT ALL DOWN AND REGROUP LATER.

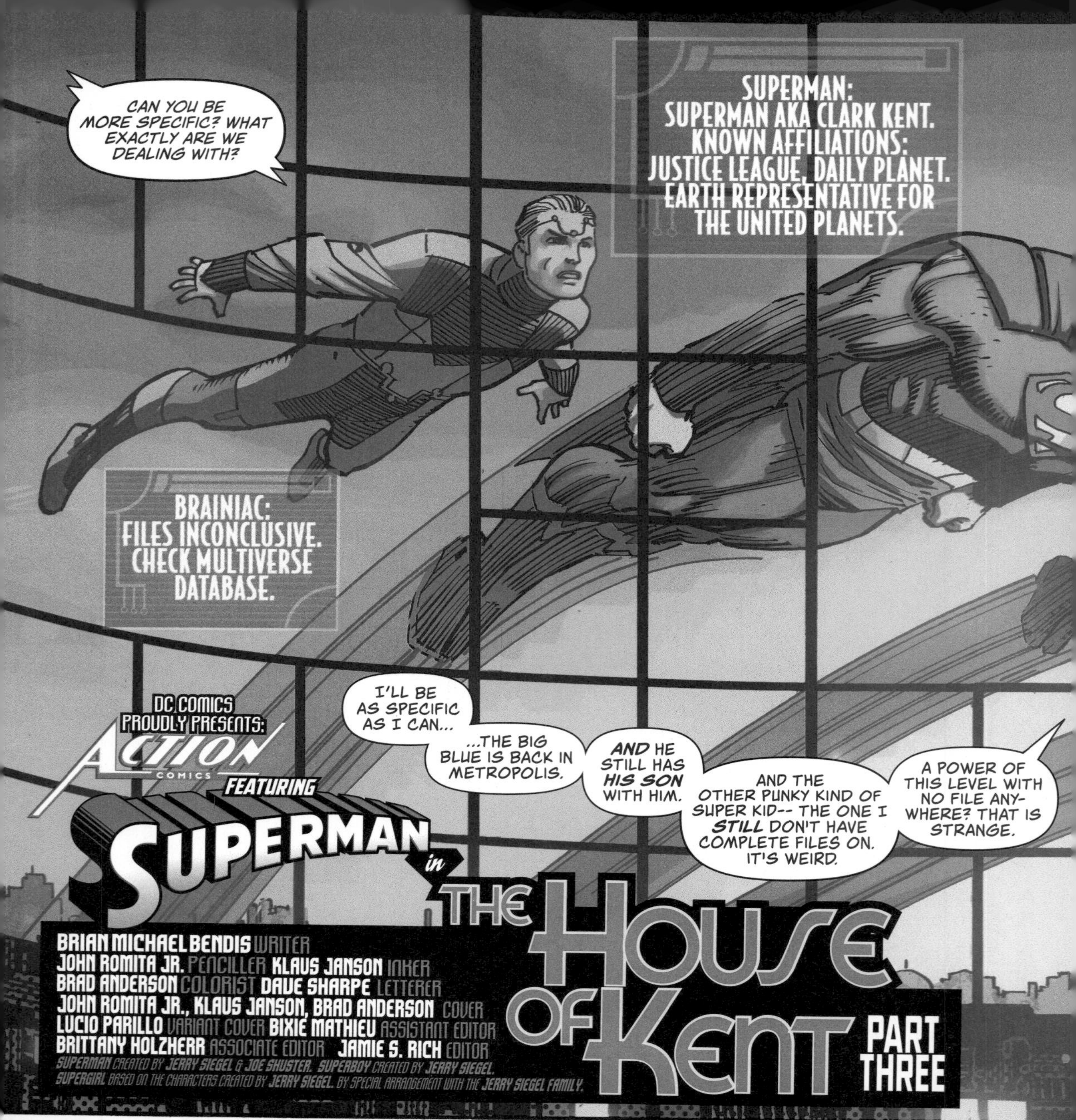
CAN YOU BE MORE SPECIFIC? WHAT EXACTLY ARE WE DEALING WITH?
SUPERMAN: SUPERMAN AKA CLARK KENT. KNOWN AFFILIATIONS: JUSTICE LEAGUE, DAILY PLANET. EARTH REPRESENTATIVE FOR THE UNITED PLANETS.
BRAINIAC: FILES INCONCLUSIVE. CHECK MULTIVERSE DATABASE.
I'LL BE AS SPECIFIC AS I CAN...
...THE BIG BLUE IS BACK IN METROPOLIS.
AND HE STILL HAS HIS SON WITH HIM.
AND THE OTHER PUNKY KIND OF SUPER KID-- THE ONE I STILL DON'T HAVE COMPLETE FILES ON. IT'S WEIRD.
A POWER OF THIS LEVEL WITH NO FILE ANYWHERE? THAT IS STRANGE.
DC COMICS PROUDLY PRESENTS:
ACTION COMICS
FEATURING
SUPERMAN in
THE HOUSE OF KENT PART THREE
BRIAN MICHAEL BENDIS WRITER
JOHN ROMITA JR. PENCILLER KLAUS JANSON INKER
BRAD ANDERSON COLORIST DAVE SHARPE LETTERER
JOHN ROMITA JR., KLAUS JANSON, BRAD ANDERSON COVER
LUCIO PARILLO VARIANT COVER BIXIE MATHIEU ASSISTANT EDITOR
BRITTANY HOLZHERR ASSOCIATE EDITOR JAMIE S. RICH EDITOR
SUPERMAN CREATED BY JERRY SIEGEL & JOE SHUSTER. SUPERBOY CREATED BY JERRY SIEGEL.
SUPERGIRL BASED ON THE CHARACTERS CREATED BY JERRY SIEGEL. BY SPECIAL ARRANGEMENT WITH THE JERRY SIEGEL FAMILY.

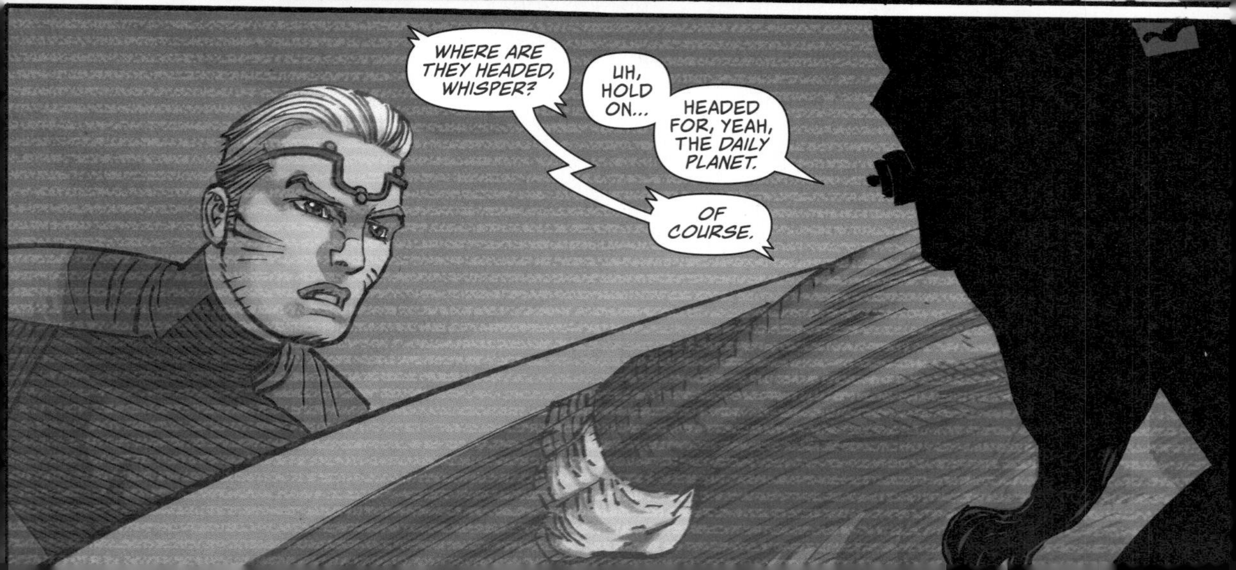
WHERE ARE THEY HEADED, WHISPER?
UH, HOLD ON...
HEADED FOR, YEAH, THE DAILY PLANET.
OF COURSE.

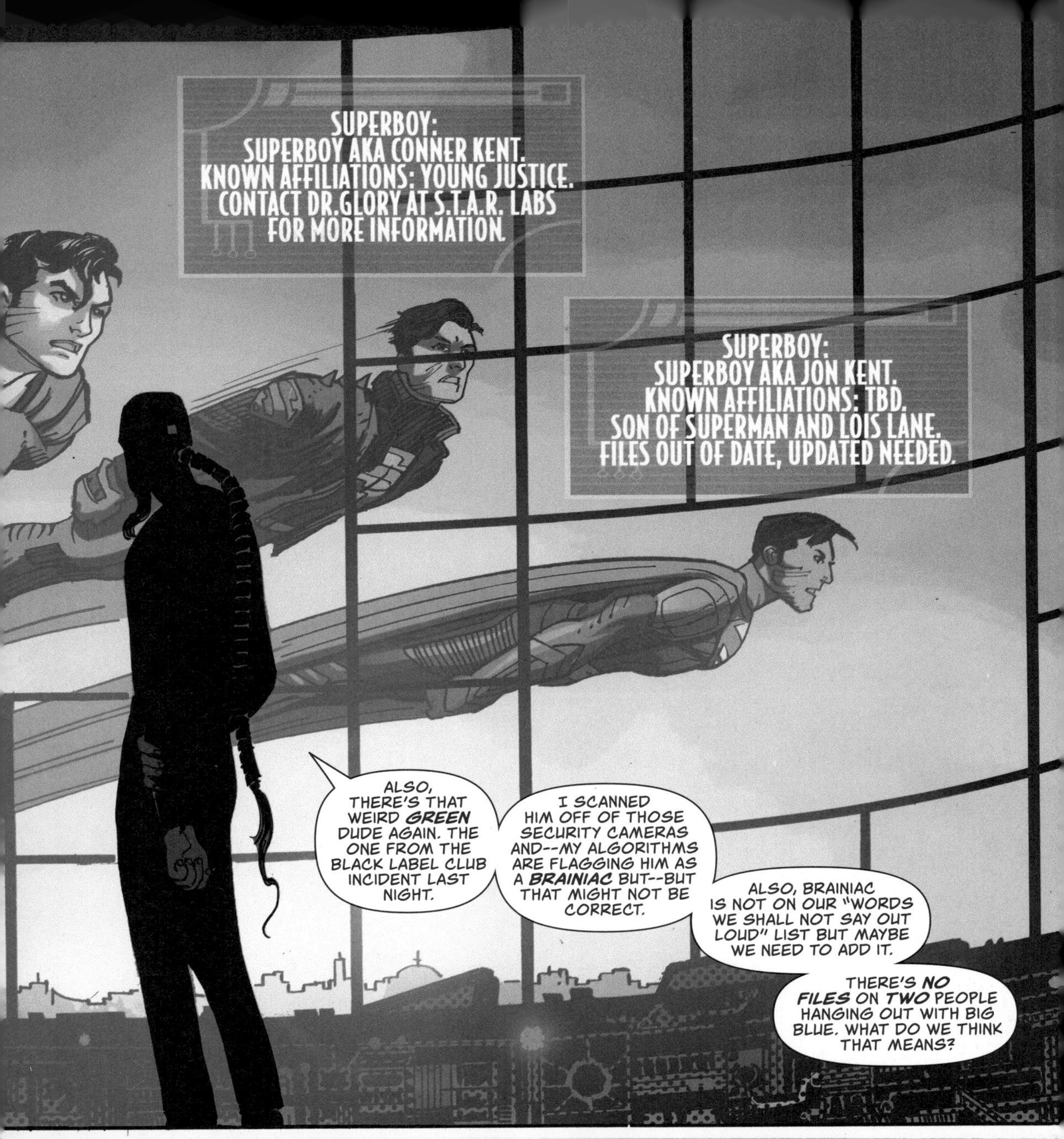
SUPERBOY:
SUPERBOY AKA CONNER KENT.
KNOWN AFFILIATIONS: YOUNG JUSTICE.
CONTACT DR.GLORY AT S.T.A.R. LABS
FOR MORE INFORMATION.
SUPERBOY:
SUPERBOY AKA JON KENT.
KNOWN AFFILIATIONS: TBD.
SON OF SUPERMAN AND LOIS LANE.
FILES OUT OF DATE, UPDATED NEEDED.
ALSO, THERE'S THAT WEIRD GREEN DUDE AGAIN. THE ONE FROM THE BLACK LABEL CLUB INCIDENT LAST NIGHT.
I SCANNED HIM OFF OF THOSE SECURITY CAMERAS AND--MY ALGORITHMS ARE FLAGGING HIM AS A BRAINIAC BUT--BUT THAT MIGHT NOT BE CORRECT.
ALSO, BRAINIAC IS NOT ON OUR "WORDS WE SHALL NOT SAY OUT LOUD" LIST BUT MAYBE WE NEED TO ADD IT.
THERE'S NO FILES ON TWO PEOPLE HANGING OUT WITH BIG BLUE. WHAT DO WE THINK THAT MEANS?

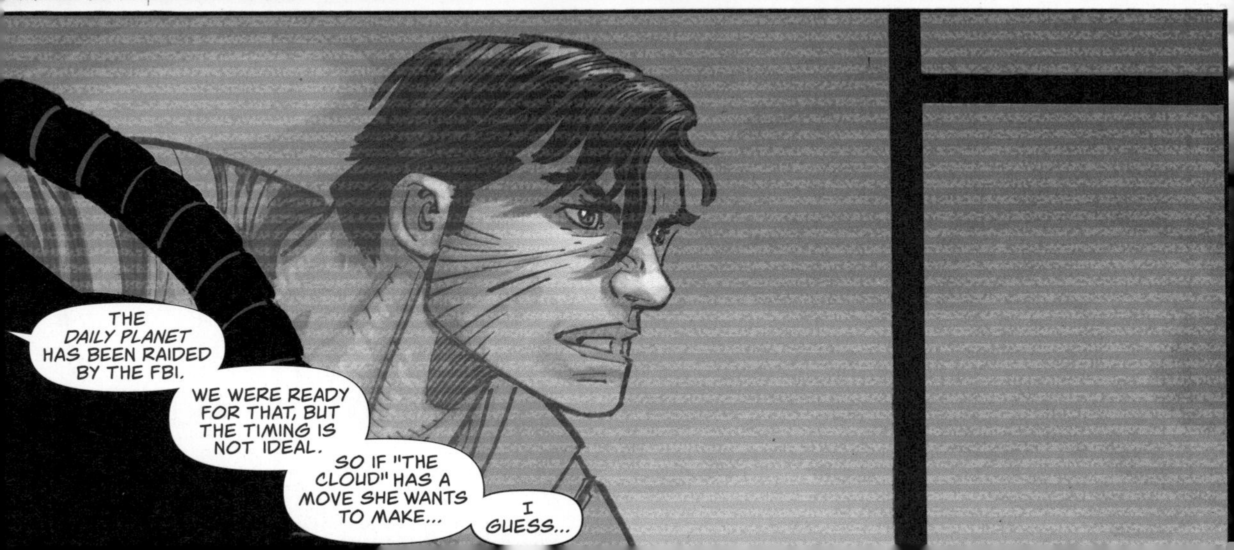
THE DAILY PLANET HAS BEEN RAIDED BY THE FBI.
WE WERE READY FOR THAT, BUT THE TIMING IS NOT IDEAL.
SO IF "THE CLOUD" HAS A MOVE SHE WANTS TO MAKE...
I GUESS...

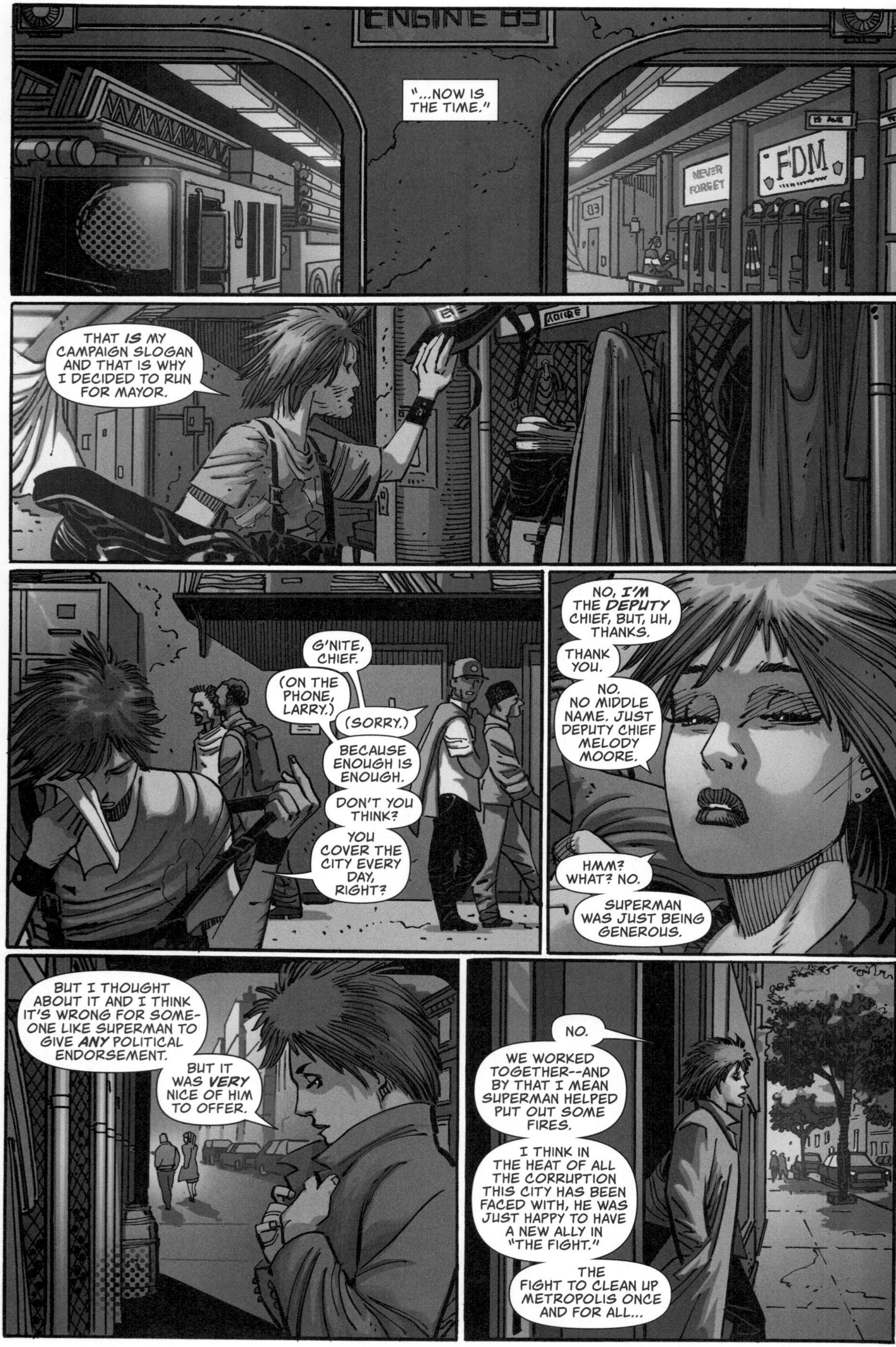
ENGINE 83
"...NOW IS THE TIME."
NEVER FORGET
FDM
THAT IS MY CAMPAIGN SLOGAN AND THAT IS WHY I DECIDED TO RUN FOR MAYOR.
G'NITE, CHIEF.
(ON THE PHONE, LARRY.)
(SORRY.)
BECAUSE ENOUGH IS ENOUGH.
DON'T YOU THINK?
YOU COVER THE CITY EVERY DAY, RIGHT?
NO, I'M THE DEPUTY CHIEF, BUT, UH, THANKS.
THANK YOU.
NO. NO MIDDLE NAME. JUST DEPUTY CHIEF MELODY MOORE.
HMM? WHAT? NO.
SUPERMAN WAS JUST BEING GENEROUS.
BUT I THOUGHT ABOUT IT AND I THINK IT'S WRONG FOR SOME-ONE LIKE SUPERMAN TO GIVE ANY POLITICAL ENDORSEMENT.
BUT IT WAS VERY NICE OF HIM TO OFFER.
NO.
WE WORKED TOGETHER--AND BY THAT I MEAN SUPERMAN HELPED PUT OUT SOME FIRES.
I THINK IN THE HEAT OF ALL THE CORRUPTION THIS CITY HAS BEEN FACED WITH, HE WAS JUST HAPPY TO HAVE A NEW ALLY IN "THE FIGHT."
THE FIGHT TO CLEAN UP METROPOLIS ONCE AND FOR ALL...

WELL, YOU HAVE TO STAND UP TO CORRUPTION...

THE PEOPLE OF THIS CITY WANT...

SUPERMAN'S PAL, *MELODY MOORE.*

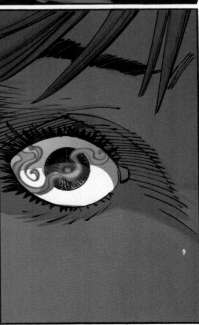

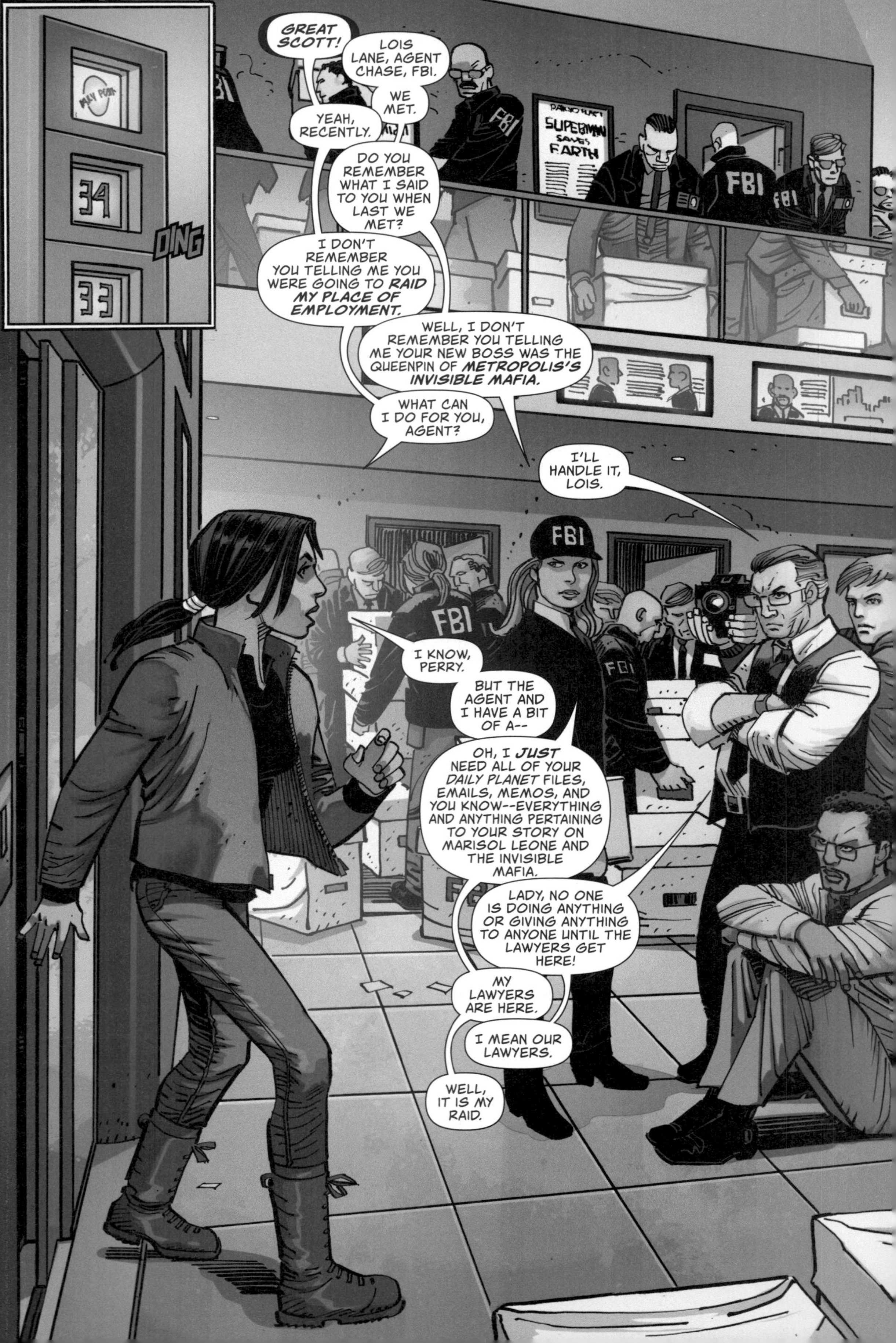
34
DING
33
GREAT SCOTT!
LOIS LANE, AGENT CHASE, FBI.
WE MET.
YEAH, RECENTLY.
DO YOU REMEMBER WHAT I SAID TO YOU WHEN LAST WE MET?
I DON'T REMEMBER YOU TELLING ME YOU WERE GOING TO *RAID MY PLACE OF EMPLOYMENT.*
WELL, I DON'T REMEMBER YOU TELLING ME YOUR NEW BOSS WAS THE QUEENPIN OF *METROPOLIS'S INVISIBLE MAFIA.*
WHAT CAN I DO FOR YOU, AGENT?
FBI
SUPERMAN SAVES EARTH
I'LL HANDLE IT, LOIS.
FBI
I KNOW, PERRY.
BUT THE AGENT AND I HAVE A BIT OF A--
OH, I *JUST* NEED ALL OF YOUR *DAILY PLANET* FILES, EMAILS, MEMOS, AND YOU KNOW--EVERYTHING AND ANYTHING PERTAINING TO YOUR STORY ON MARISOL LEONE AND THE INVISIBLE MAFIA.
LADY, NO ONE IS DOING ANYTHING OR GIVING ANYTHING TO ANYONE UNTIL THE LAWYERS GET HERE!
MY LAWYERS ARE HERE.
I MEAN OUR LAWYERS.
WELL, IT IS MY RAID.

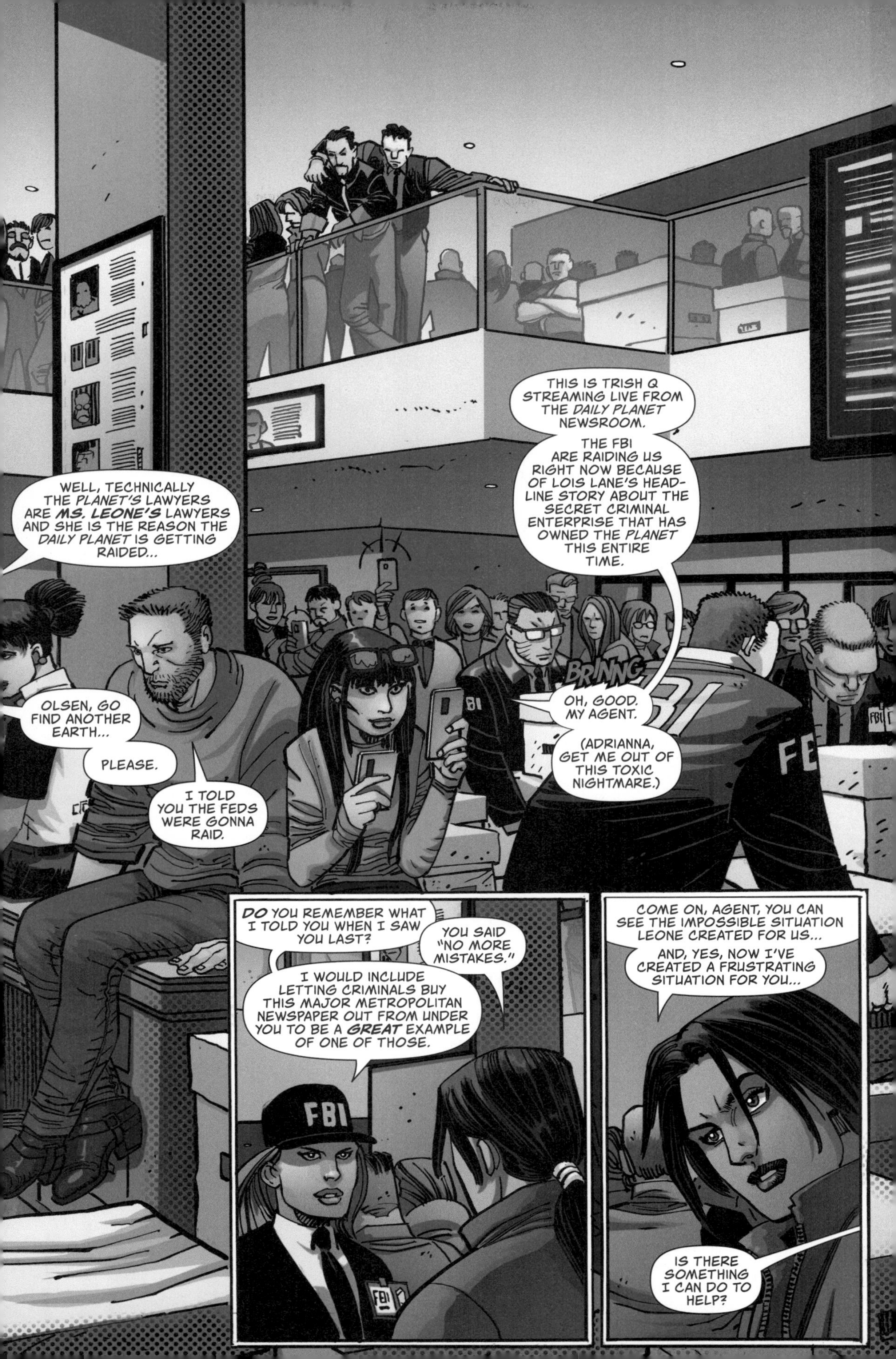

WELL, TECHNICALLY THE PLANET'S LAWYERS ARE MS. LEONE'S LAWYERS AND SHE IS THE REASON THE DAILY PLANET IS GETTING RAIDED...
THIS IS TRISH Q STREAMING LIVE FROM THE DAILY PLANET NEWSROOM.
THE FBI ARE RAIDING US RIGHT NOW BECAUSE OF LOIS LANE'S HEAD-LINE STORY ABOUT THE SECRET CRIMINAL ENTERPRISE THAT HAS OWNED THE PLANET THIS ENTIRE TIME.
OLSEN, GO FIND ANOTHER EARTH...
PLEASE.
I TOLD YOU THE FEDS WERE GONNA RAID.
BRINNG
OH, GOOD. MY AGENT.
(ADRIANNA, GET ME OUT OF THIS TOXIC NIGHTMARE.)
DO YOU REMEMBER WHAT I TOLD YOU WHEN I SAW YOU LAST?
YOU SAID "NO MORE MISTAKES."
I WOULD INCLUDE LETTING CRIMINALS BUY THIS MAJOR METROPOLITAN NEWSPAPER OUT FROM UNDER YOU TO BE A GREAT EXAMPLE OF ONE OF THOSE.
COME ON, AGENT, YOU CAN SEE THE IMPOSSIBLE SITUATION LEONE CREATED FOR US...
AND, YES, NOW I'VE CREATED A FRUSTRATING SITUATION FOR YOU...
IS THERE SOMETHING I CAN DO TO HELP?

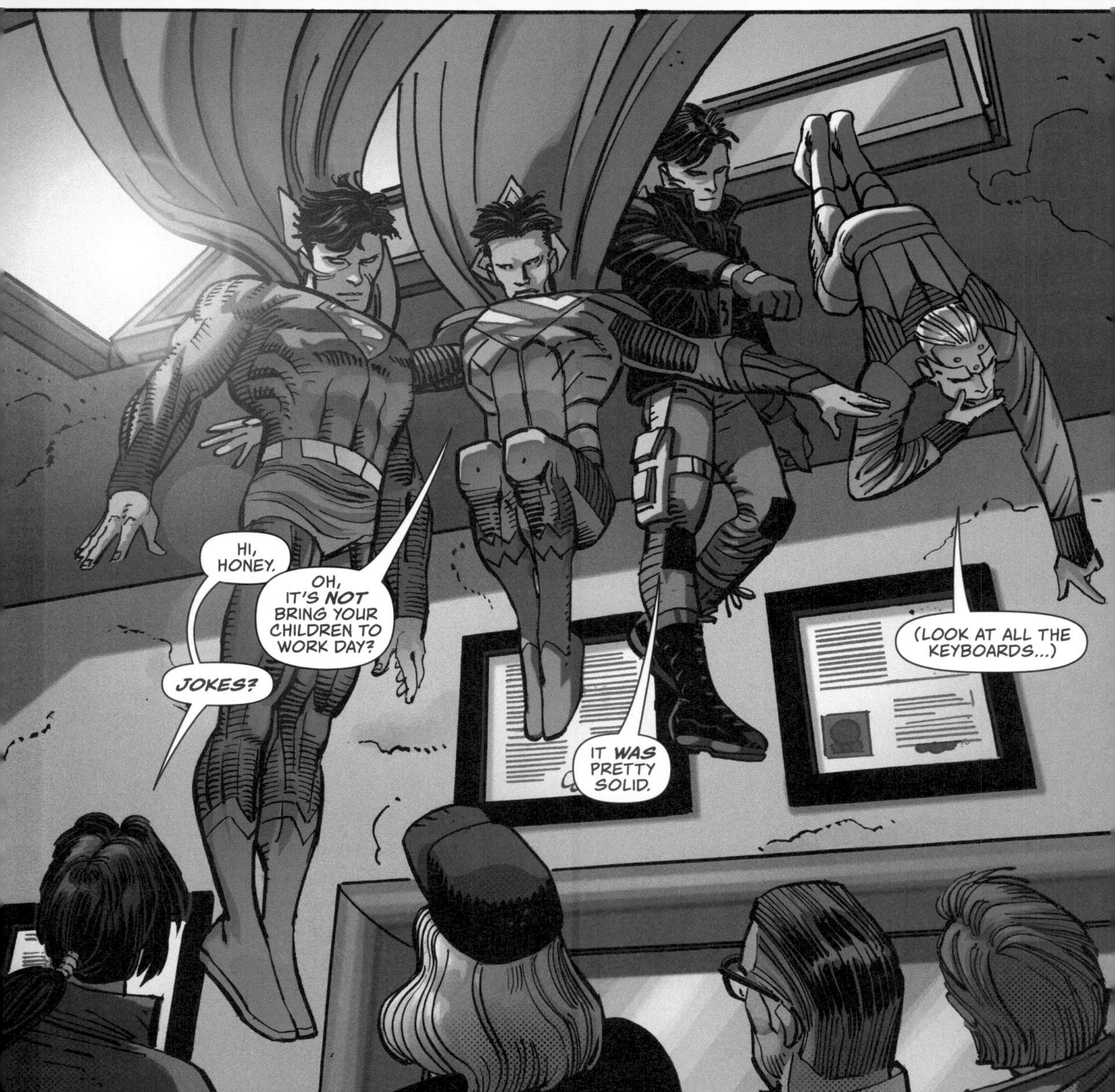
HI, HONEY.
OH, IT'S NOT BRING YOUR CHILDREN TO WORK DAY?
JOKES?
IT WAS PRETTY SOLID.
(LOOK AT ALL THE KEYBOARDS...)

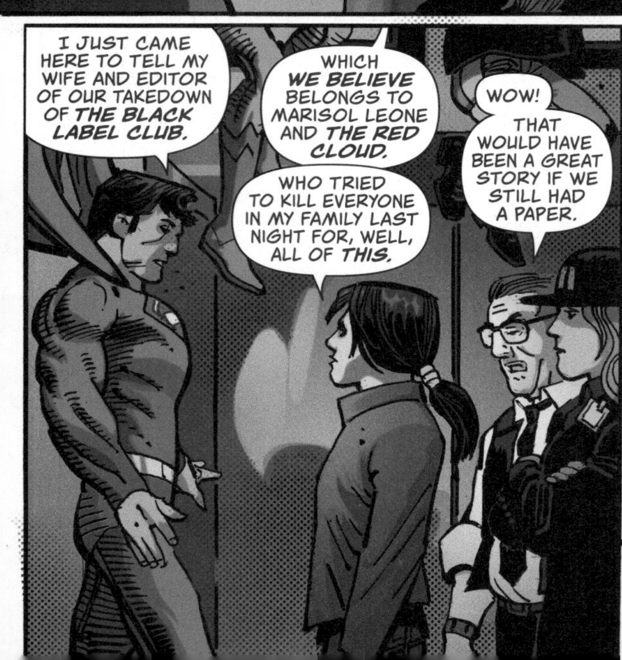
I JUST CAME HERE TO TELL MY WIFE AND EDITOR OF OUR TAKEDOWN OF THE BLACK LABEL CLUB.
WHICH WE BELIEVE BELONGS TO MARISOL LEONE AND THE RED CLOUD.
WHO TRIED TO KILL EVERYONE IN MY FAMILY LAST NIGHT FOR, WELL, ALL OF THIS.
WOW!
THAT WOULD HAVE BEEN A GREAT STORY IF WE STILL HAD A PAPER.

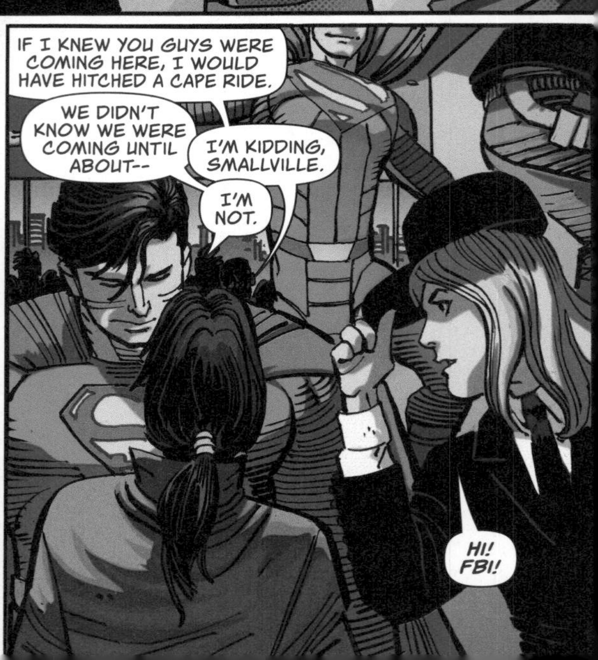
IF I KNEW YOU GUYS WERE COMING HERE, I WOULD HAVE HITCHED A CAPE RIDE.
WE DIDN'T KNOW WE WERE COMING UNTIL ABOUT--
I'M KIDDING, SMALLVILLE.
I'M NOT.
HI! FBI!

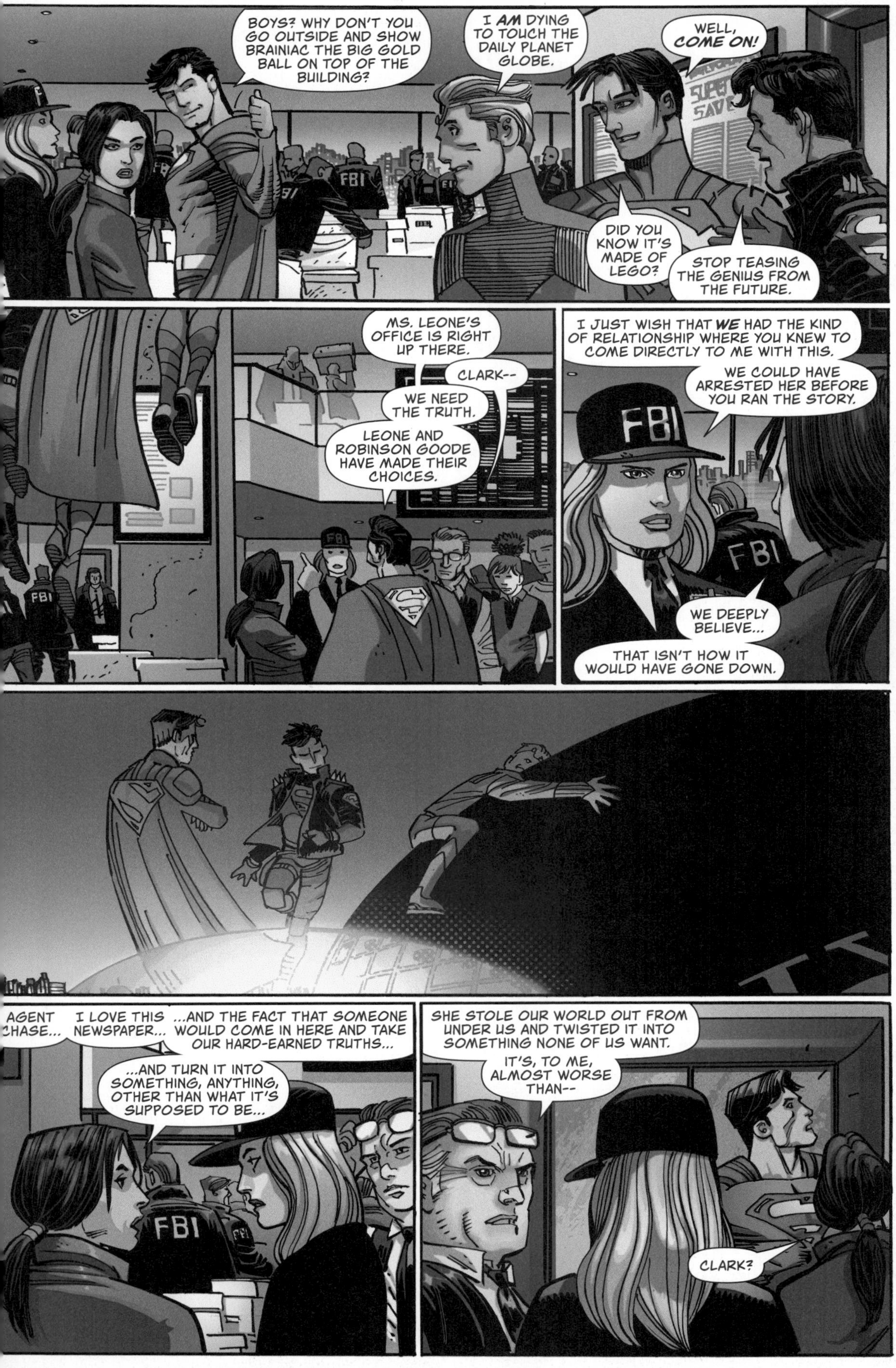
BOYS? WHY DON'T YOU GO OUTSIDE AND SHOW BRAINIAC THE BIG GOLD BALL ON TOP OF THE BUILDING?
I AM DYING TO TOUCH THE DAILY PLANET GLOBE.
WELL, COME ON!
DID YOU KNOW IT'S MADE OF LEGO?
STOP TEASING THE GENIUS FROM THE FUTURE.
MS. LEONE'S OFFICE IS RIGHT UP THERE.
CLARK--
WE NEED THE TRUTH.
LEONE AND ROBINSON GOODE HAVE MADE THEIR CHOICES.
I JUST WISH THAT WE HAD THE KIND OF RELATIONSHIP WHERE YOU KNEW TO COME DIRECTLY TO ME WITH THIS.
WE COULD HAVE ARRESTED HER BEFORE YOU RAN THE STORY.
WE DEEPLY BELIEVE...
THAT ISN'T HOW IT WOULD HAVE GONE DOWN.
AGENT CHASE...
I LOVE THIS NEWSPAPER...
...AND THE FACT THAT SOMEONE WOULD COME IN HERE AND TAKE OUR HARD-EARNED TRUTHS...
...AND TURN IT INTO SOMETHING, ANYTHING, OTHER THAN WHAT IT'S SUPPOSED TO BE...
SHE STOLE OUR WORLD OUT FROM UNDER US AND TWISTED IT INTO SOMETHING NONE OF US WANT.
IT'S, TO ME, ALMOST WORSE THAN--
CLARK?

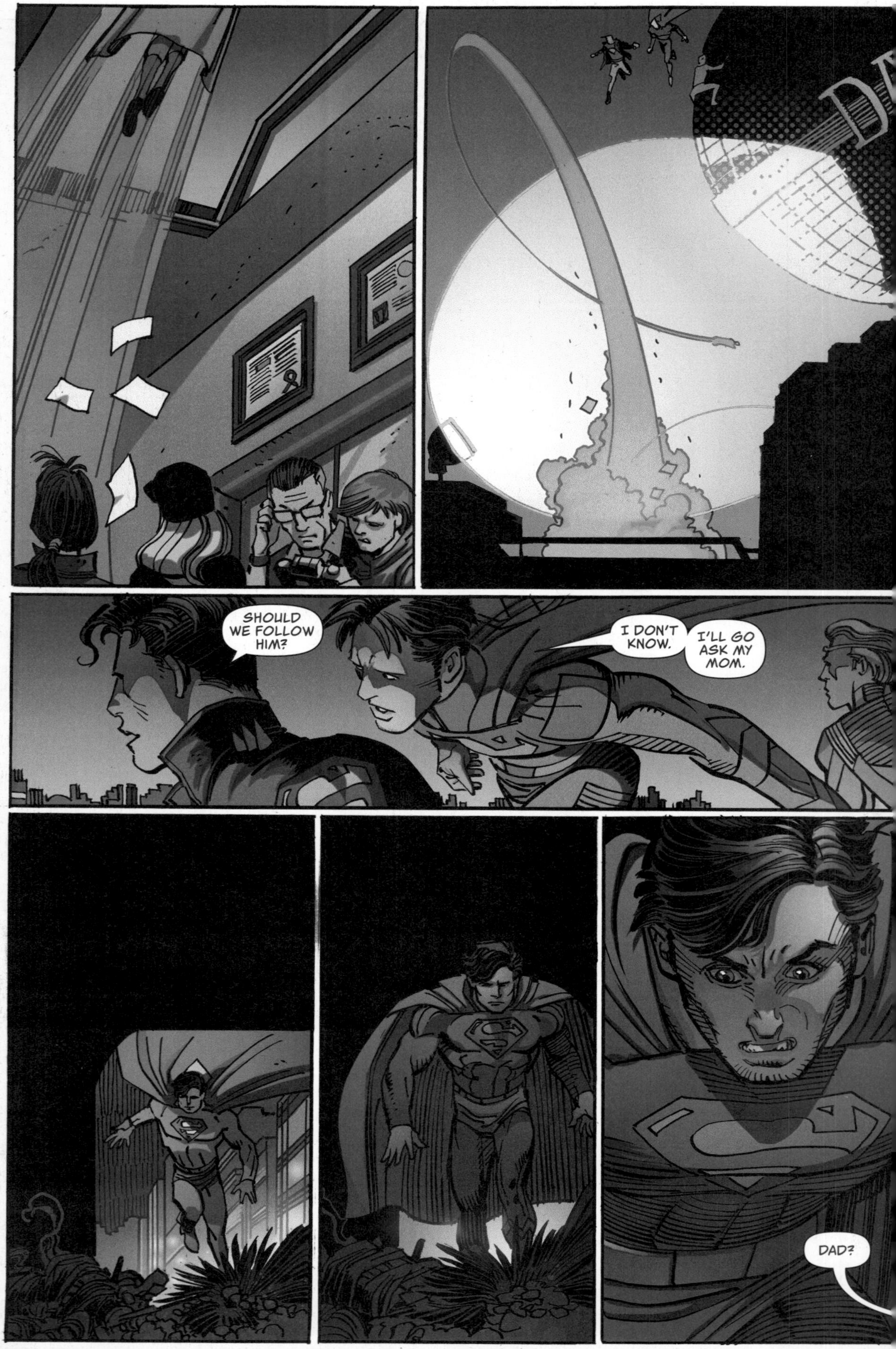
SHOULD WE FOLLOW HIM?
I DON'T KNOW.
I'LL GO ASK MY MOM.
DAD?

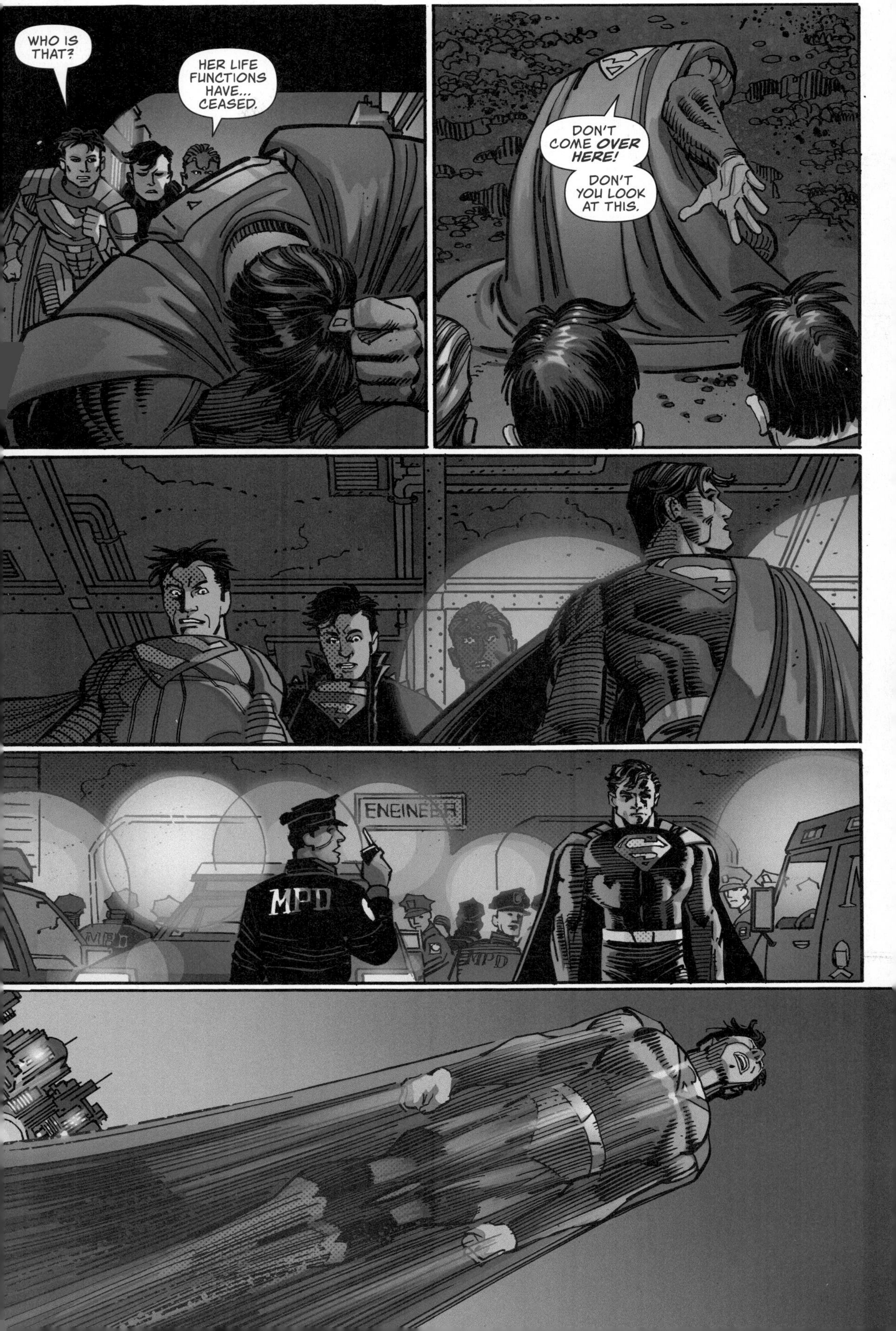
WHO IS THAT?
HER LIFE FUNCTIONS HAVE... CEASED.
DON'T COME **OVER HERE!**
DON'T YOU LOOK AT THIS.
ENGINEER
MPD
MPD
MPD

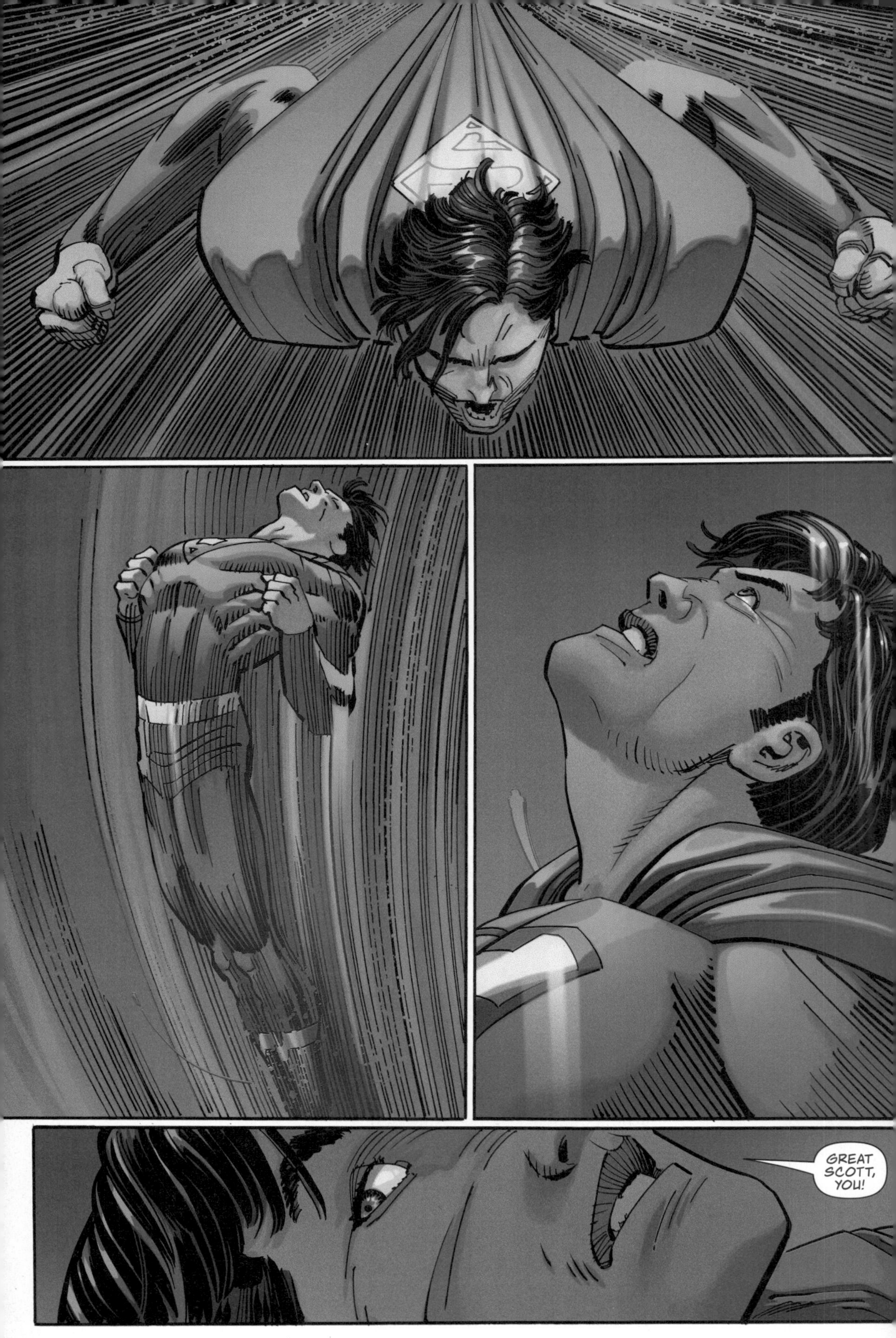
GREAT SCOTT, YOU!

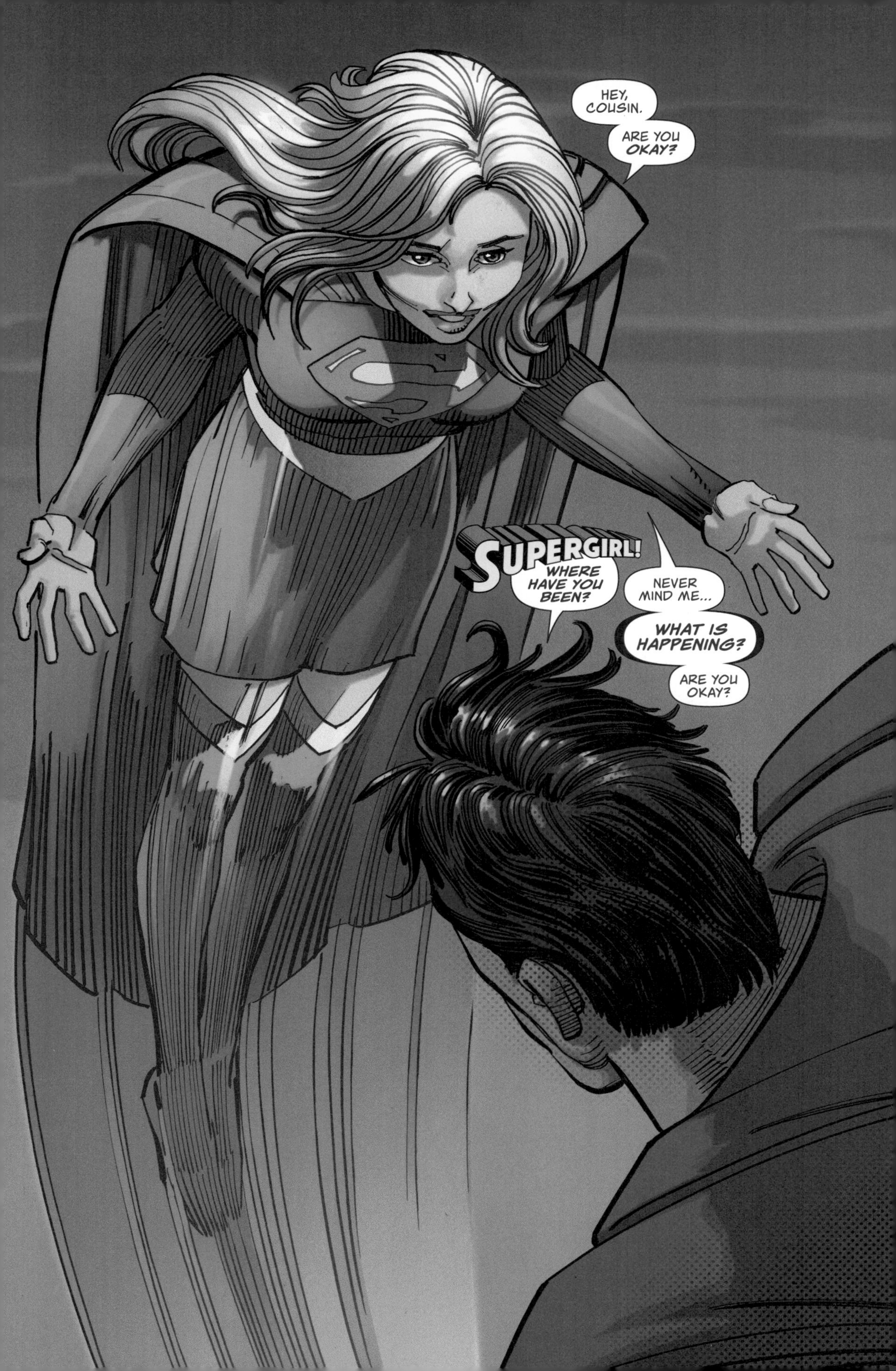

HEY, COUSIN.
ARE YOU OKAY?
SUPERGIRL! WHERE HAVE YOU BEEN?
NEVER MIND ME...
WHAT IS HAPPENING?
ARE YOU OKAY?

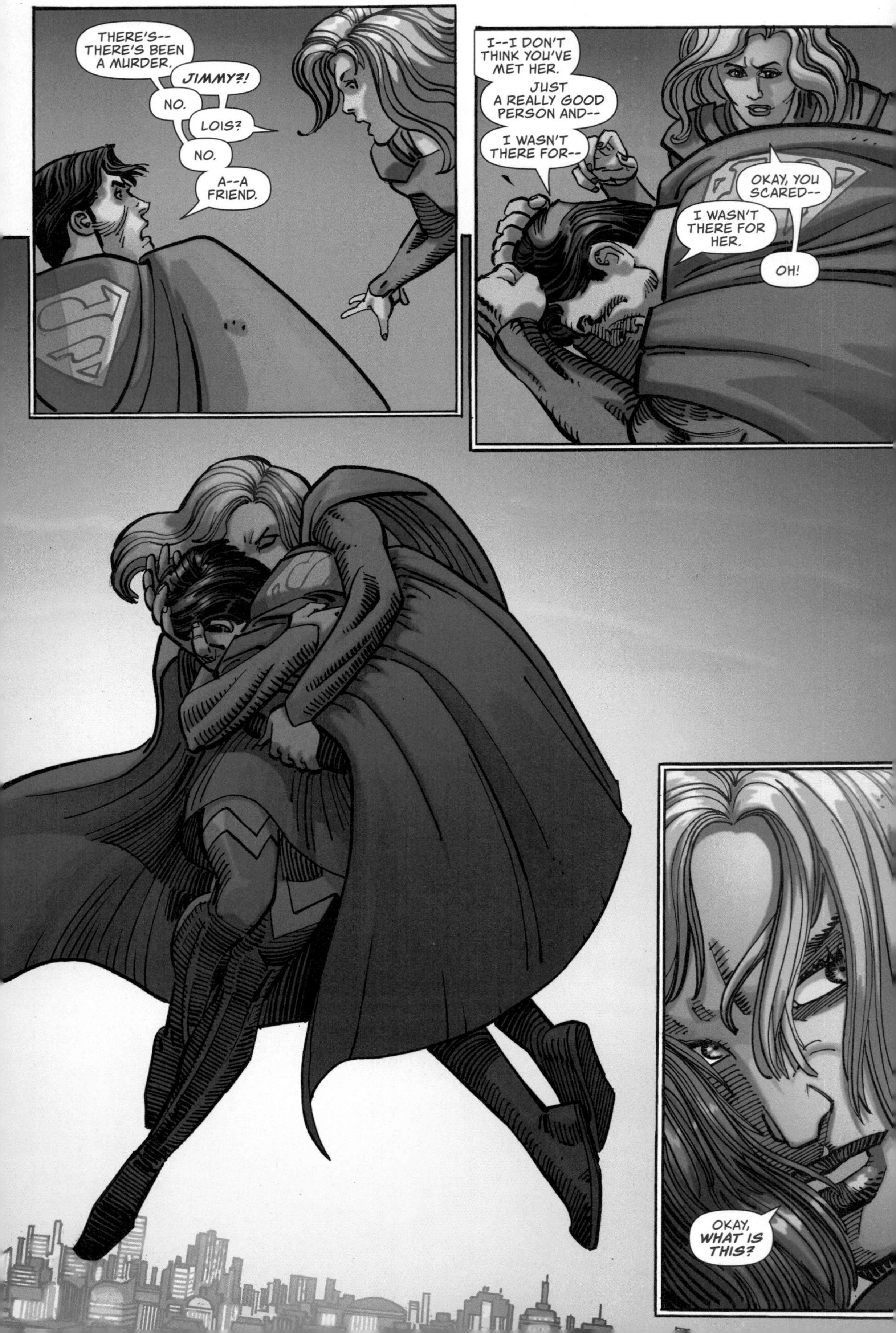
THERE'S--
THERE'S BEEN
A MURDER.
JIMMY?!
NO.
LOIS?
NO.
A--A
FRIEND.
I--I DON'T
THINK YOU'VE
MET HER.
JUST
A REALLY GOOD
PERSON AND--
I WASN'T
THERE FOR--
OKAY, YOU
SCARED--
I WASN'T
THERE FOR
HER.
OH!
OKAY,
WHAT IS
THIS?

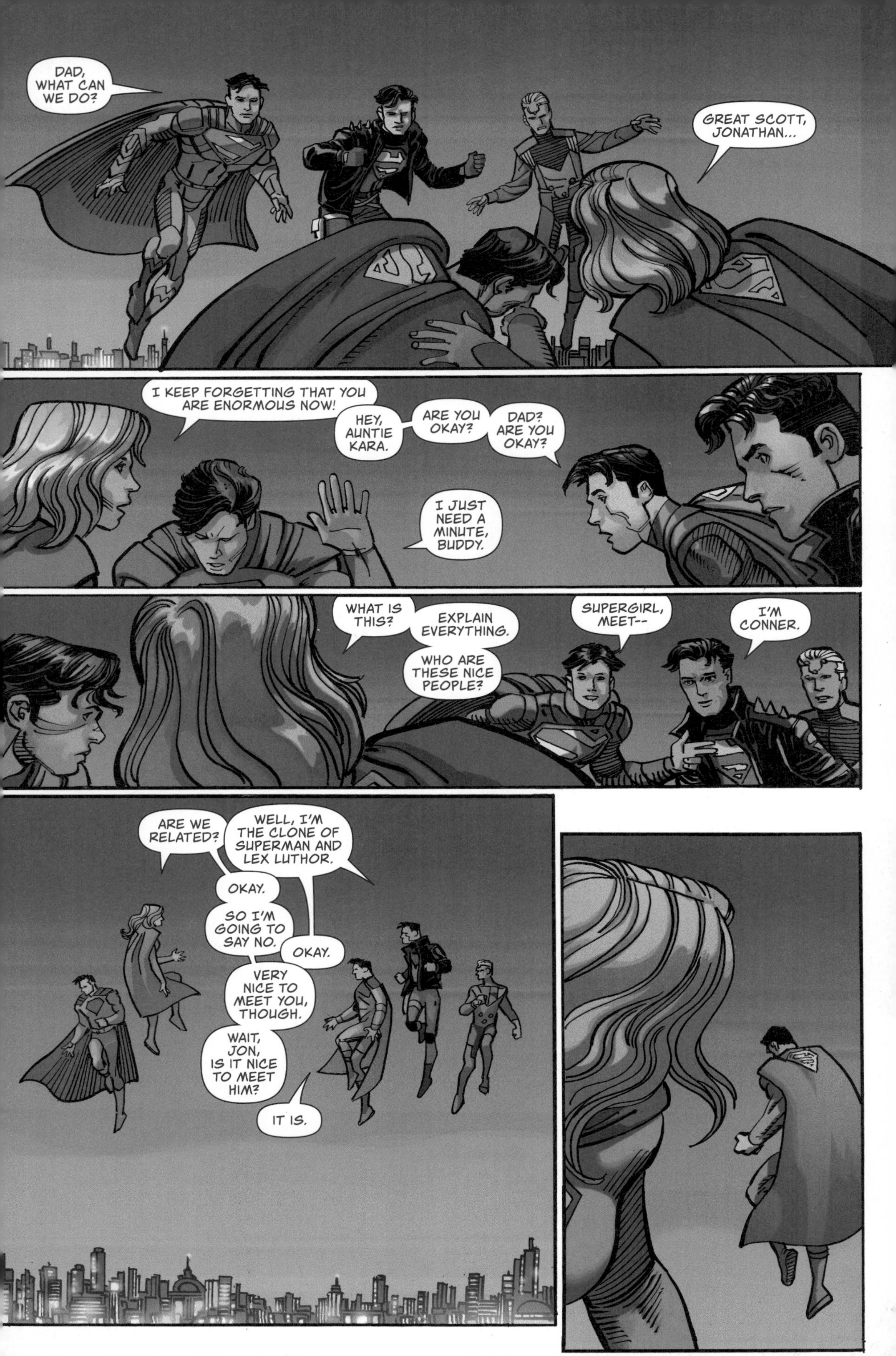
DAD, WHAT CAN WE DO?
GREAT SCOTT, JONATHAN...
I KEEP FORGETTING THAT YOU ARE ENORMOUS NOW!
HEY, AUNTIE KARA.
ARE YOU OKAY?
DAD? ARE YOU OKAY?
I JUST NEED A MINUTE, BUDDY.
WHAT IS THIS?
EXPLAIN EVERYTHING.
WHO ARE THESE NICE PEOPLE?
SUPERGIRL, MEET--
I'M CONNER.
ARE WE RELATED?
WELL, I'M THE CLONE OF SUPERMAN AND LEX LUTHOR.
OKAY.
SO I'M GOING TO SAY NO.
OKAY.
VERY NICE TO MEET YOU, THOUGH.
WAIT, JON, IS IT NICE TO MEET HIM?
IT IS.

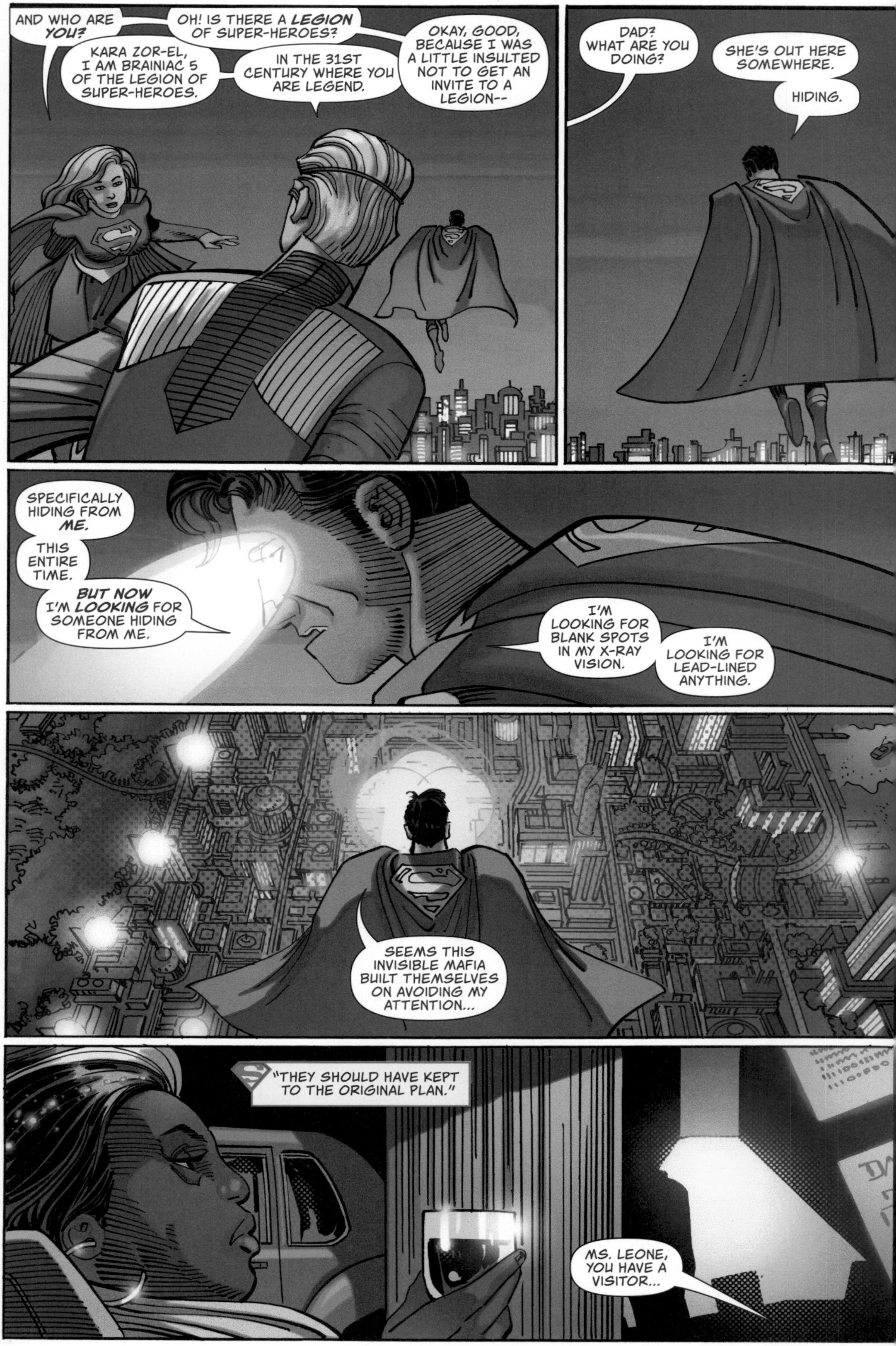
AND WHO ARE YOU?
OH! IS THERE A LEGION OF SUPER-HEROES?
KARA ZOR-EL, I AM BRAINIAC 5 OF THE LEGION OF SUPER-HEROES.
IN THE 31ST CENTURY WHERE YOU ARE LEGEND.
OKAY, GOOD, BECAUSE I WAS A LITTLE INSULTED NOT TO GET AN INVITE TO A LEGION--
DAD? WHAT ARE YOU DOING?
SHE'S OUT HERE SOMEWHERE.
HIDING.
SPECIFICALLY HIDING FROM ME.
THIS ENTIRE TIME.
BUT NOW I'M LOOKING FOR SOMEONE HIDING FROM ME.
I'M LOOKING FOR BLANK SPOTS IN MY X-RAY VISION.
I'M LOOKING FOR LEAD-LINED ANYTHING.
SEEMS THIS INVISIBLE MAFIA BUILT THEMSELVES ON AVOIDING MY ATTENTION...
"THEY SHOULD HAVE KEPT TO THE ORIGINAL PLAN."
MS. LEONE, YOU HAVE A VISITOR...

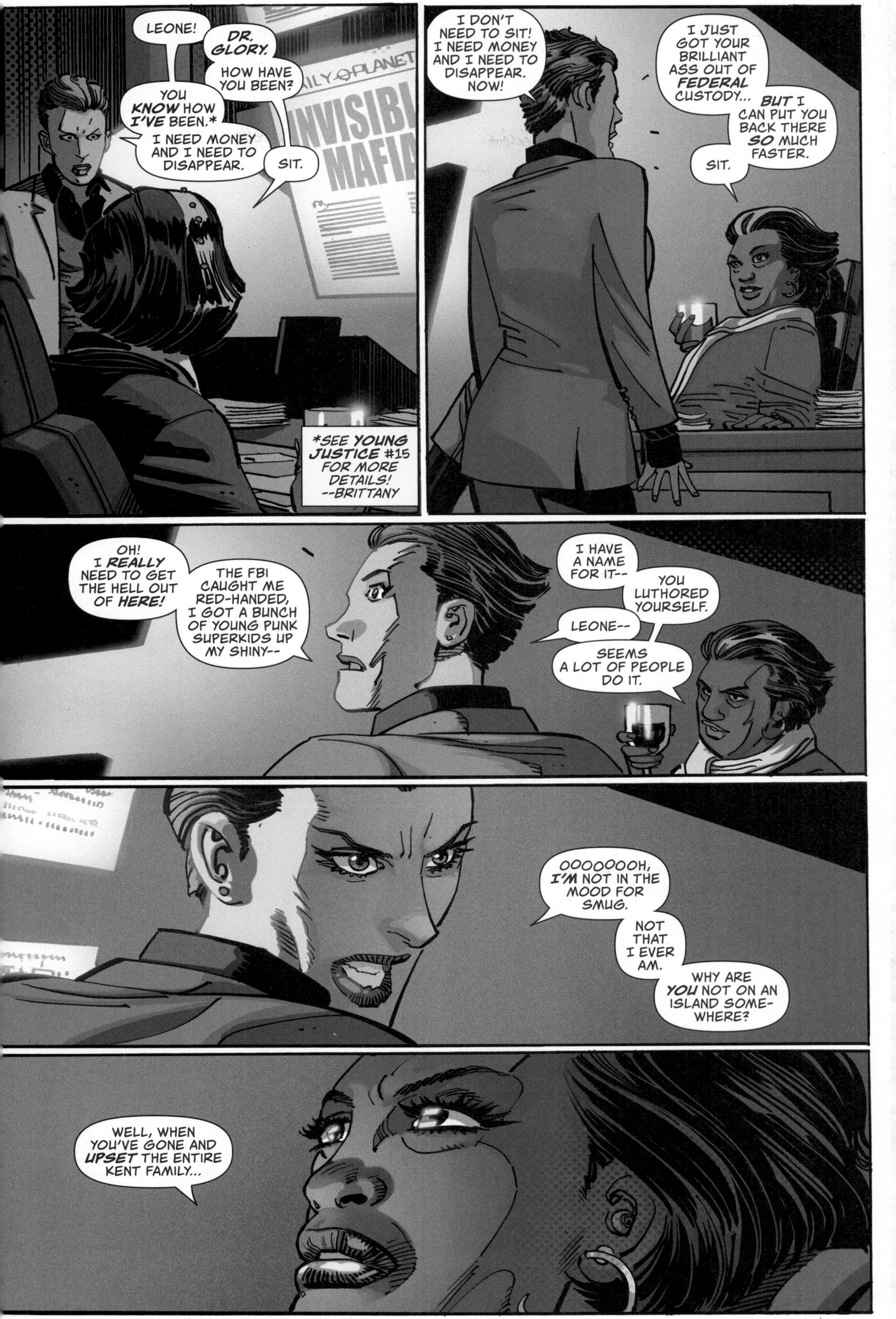
LEONE!
DR. GLORY.
HOW HAVE YOU BEEN?
YOU KNOW HOW I'VE BEEN.*
I NEED MONEY AND I NEED TO DISAPPEAR.
SIT.
DAILY PLANET
INVISIBLE MAFIA
*SEE YOUNG JUSTICE #15 FOR MORE DETAILS! --BRITTANY
I DON'T NEED TO SIT! I NEED MONEY AND I NEED TO DISAPPEAR. NOW!
I JUST GOT YOUR BRILLIANT ASS OUT OF FEDERAL CUSTODY... BUT I CAN PUT YOU BACK THERE SO MUCH FASTER.
SIT.
OH! I REALLY NEED TO GET THE HELL OUT OF HERE!
THE FBI CAUGHT ME RED-HANDED, I GOT A BUNCH OF YOUNG PUNK SUPERKIDS UP MY SHINY--
I HAVE A NAME FOR IT--
YOU LUTHORED YOURSELF.
LEONE--
SEEMS A LOT OF PEOPLE DO IT.
OOOOOOOH, I'M NOT IN THE MOOD FOR SMUG.
NOT THAT I EVER AM.
WHY ARE YOU NOT ON AN ISLAND SOME-WHERE?
WELL, WHEN YOU'VE GONE AND UPSET THE ENTIRE KENT FAMILY...

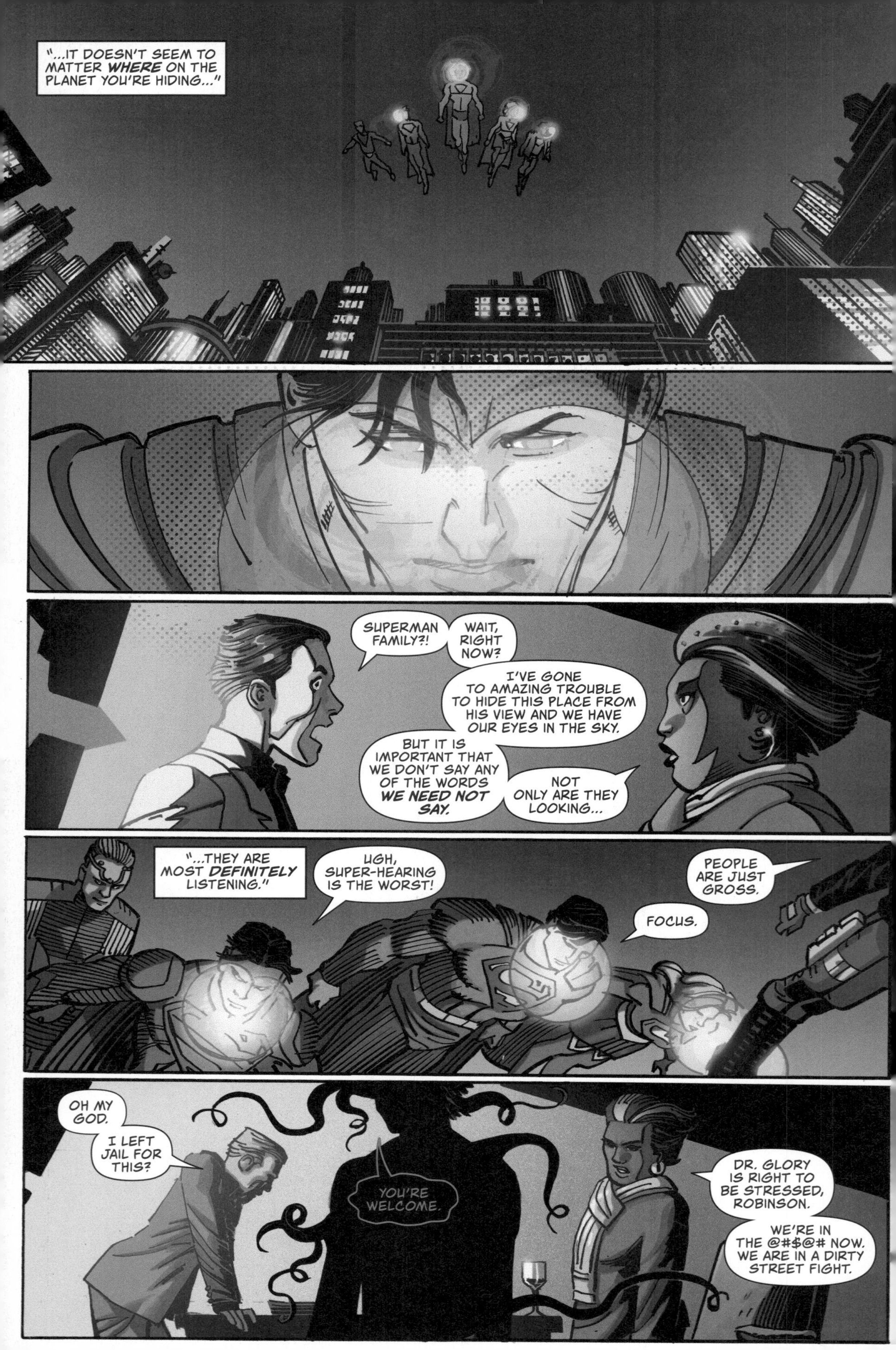
"...IT DOESN'T SEEM TO MATTER WHERE ON THE PLANET YOU'RE HIDING..."
SUPERMAN FAMILY?!
WAIT, RIGHT NOW?
I'VE GONE TO AMAZING TROUBLE TO HIDE THIS PLACE FROM HIS VIEW AND WE HAVE OUR EYES IN THE SKY.
BUT IT IS IMPORTANT THAT WE DON'T SAY ANY OF THE WORDS WE NEED NOT SAY.
NOT ONLY ARE THEY LOOKING...
"...THEY ARE MOST DEFINITELY LISTENING."
UGH, SUPER-HEARING IS THE WORST!
PEOPLE ARE JUST GROSS.
FOCUS.
OH MY GOD.
I LEFT JAIL FOR THIS?
YOU'RE WELCOME.
DR. GLORY IS RIGHT TO BE STRESSED, ROBINSON.
WE'RE IN THE @#$@# NOW. WE ARE IN A DIRTY STREET FIGHT.

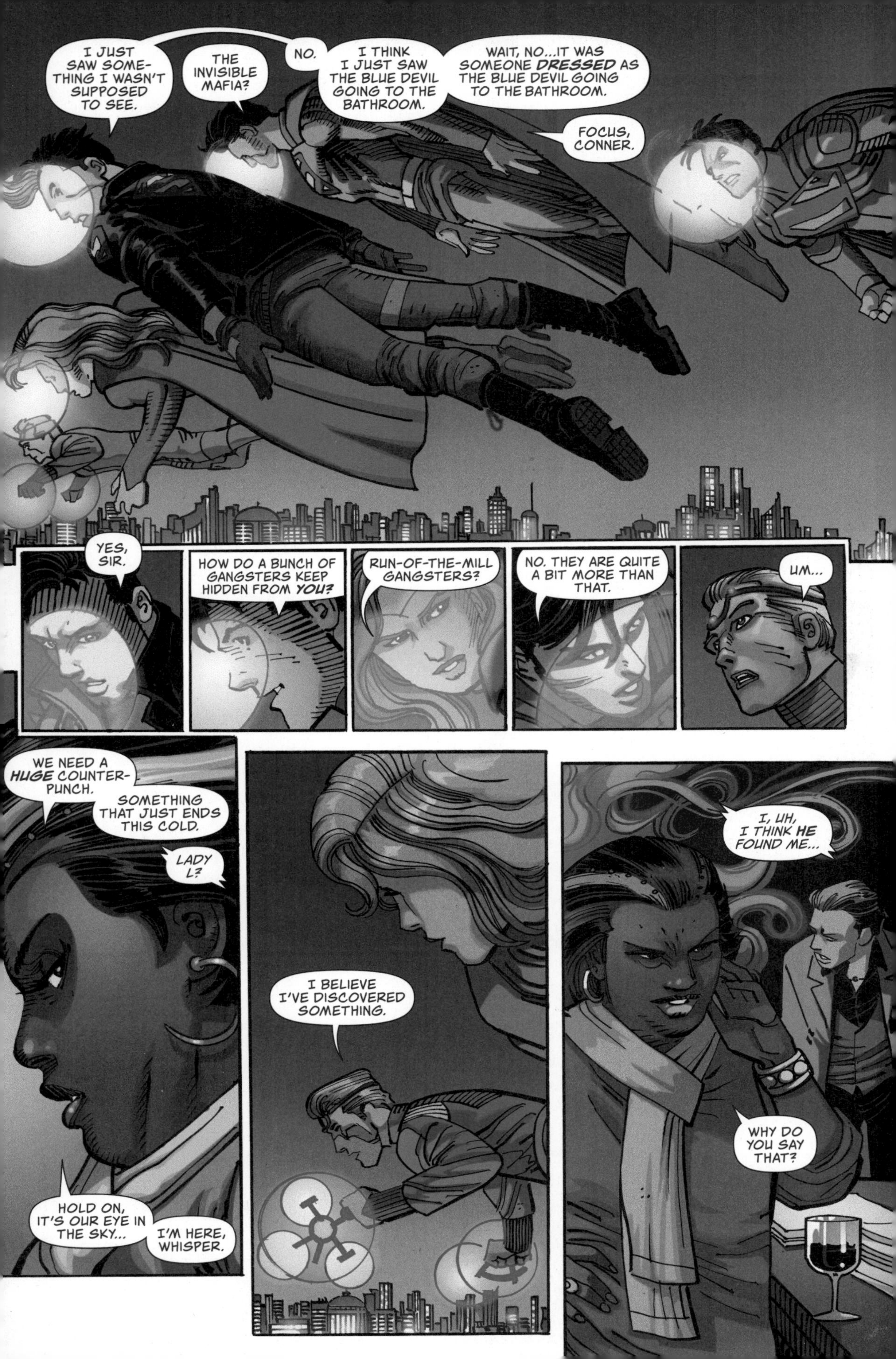
I JUST SAW SOME-THING I WASN'T SUPPOSED TO SEE.
THE INVISIBLE MAFIA?
NO.
I THINK I JUST SAW THE BLUE DEVIL GOING TO THE BATHROOM.
WAIT, NO...IT WAS SOMEONE DRESSED AS THE BLUE DEVIL GOING TO THE BATHROOM.
FOCUS, CONNER.
YES, SIR.
HOW DO A BUNCH OF GANGSTERS KEEP HIDDEN FROM YOU?
RUN-OF-THE-MILL GANGSTERS?
NO. THEY ARE QUITE A BIT MORE THAN THAT.
UM...
WE NEED A HUGE COUNTER-PUNCH.
SOMETHING THAT JUST ENDS THIS COLD.
LADY L?
HOLD ON, IT'S OUR EYE IN THE SKY...
I'M HERE, WHISPER.
I BELIEVE I'VE DISCOVERED SOMETHING.
I, UH, I THINK HE FOUND ME...
WHY DO YOU SAY THAT?

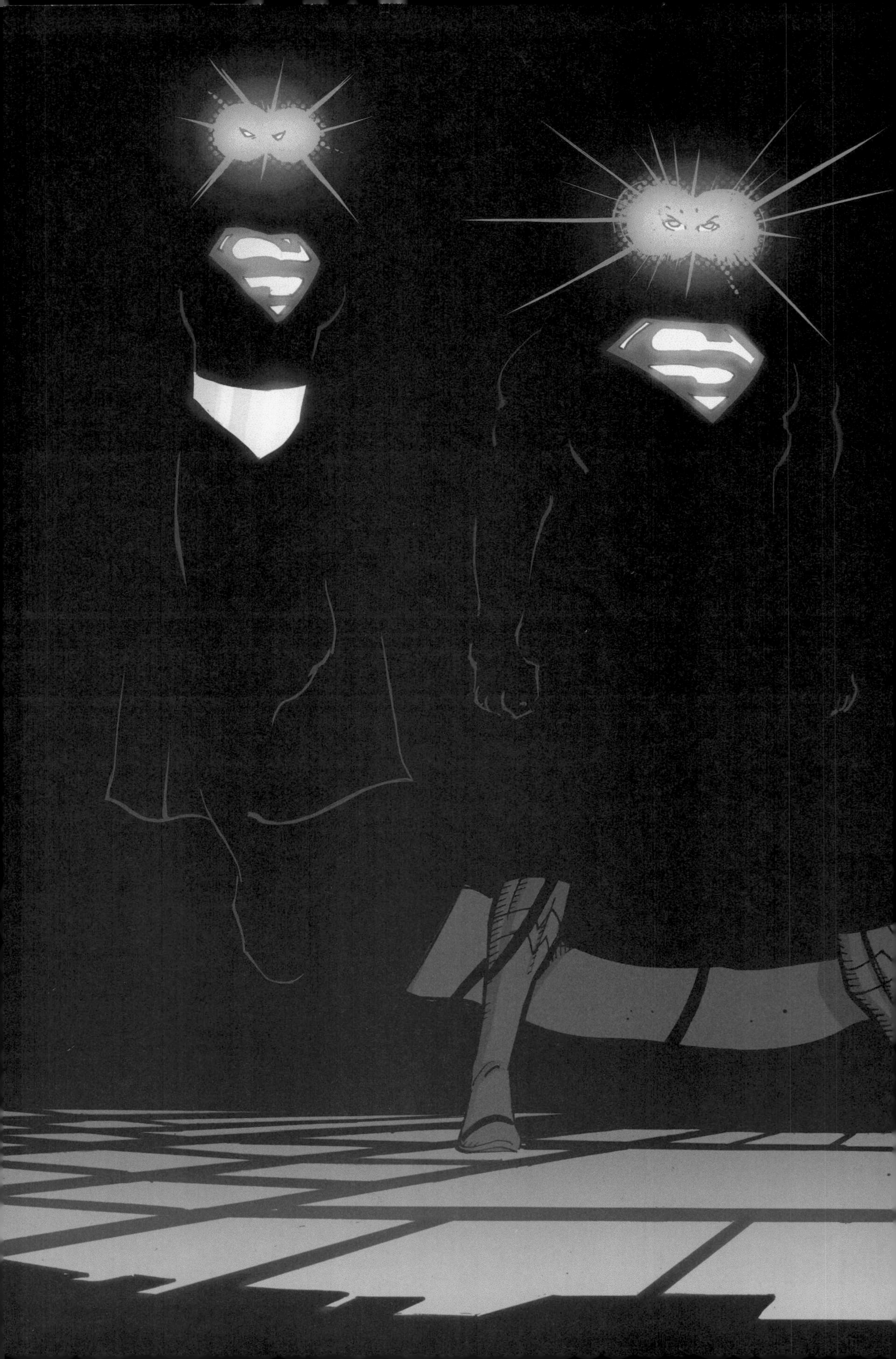

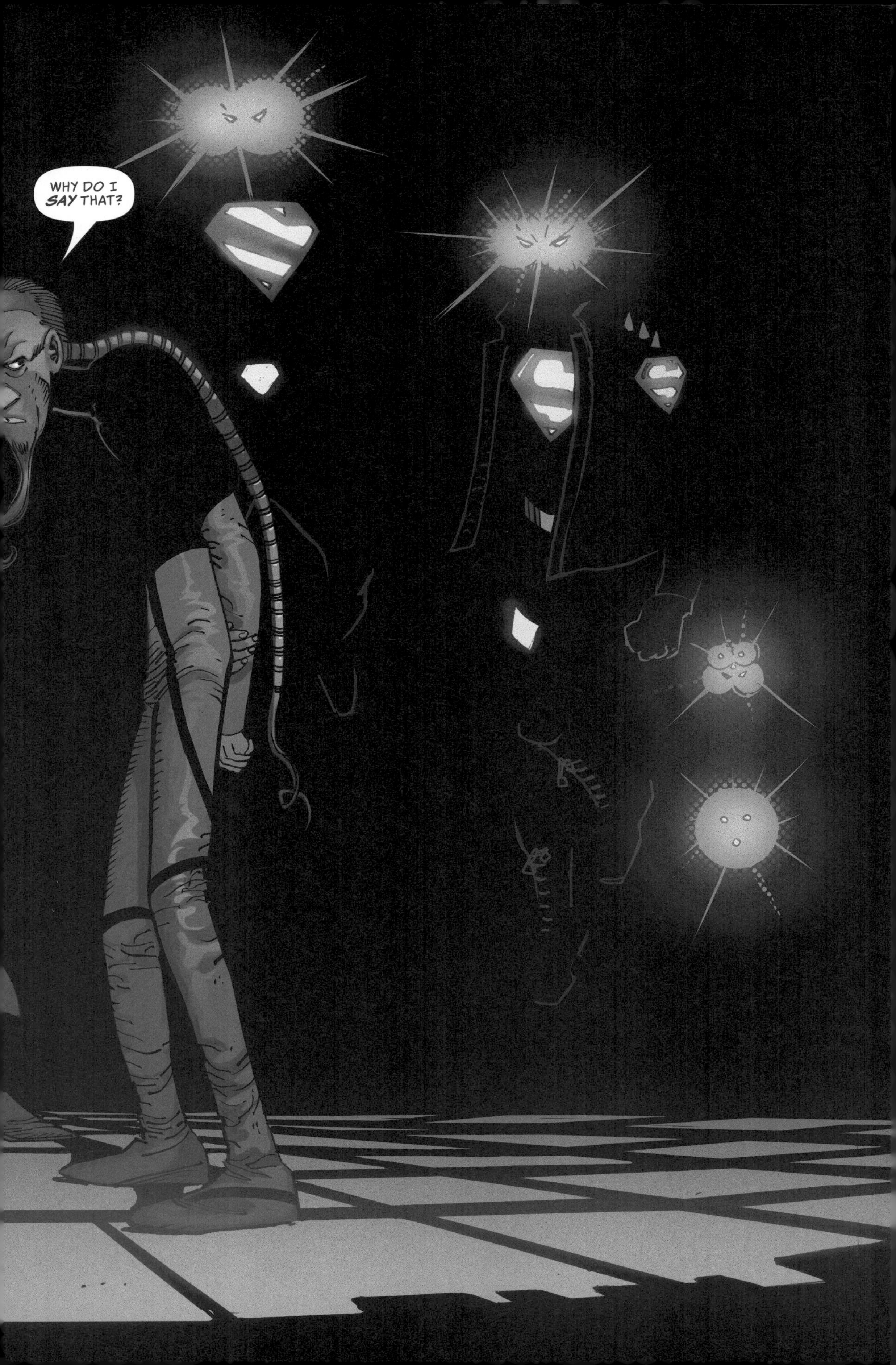
WHY DO I SAY THAT?

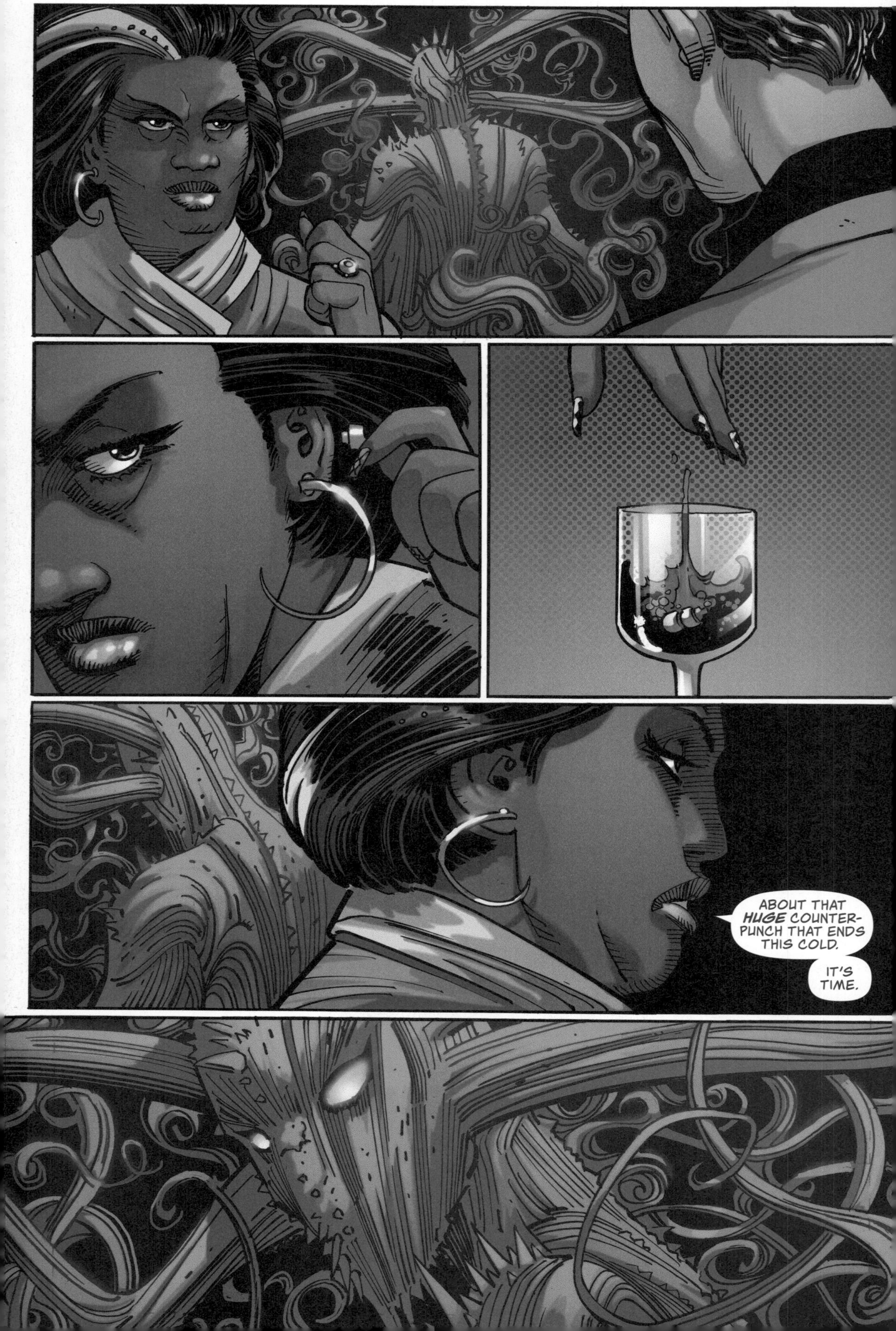
ABOUT THAT HUGE COUNTER-PUNCH THAT ENDS THIS COLD.
IT'S TIME.

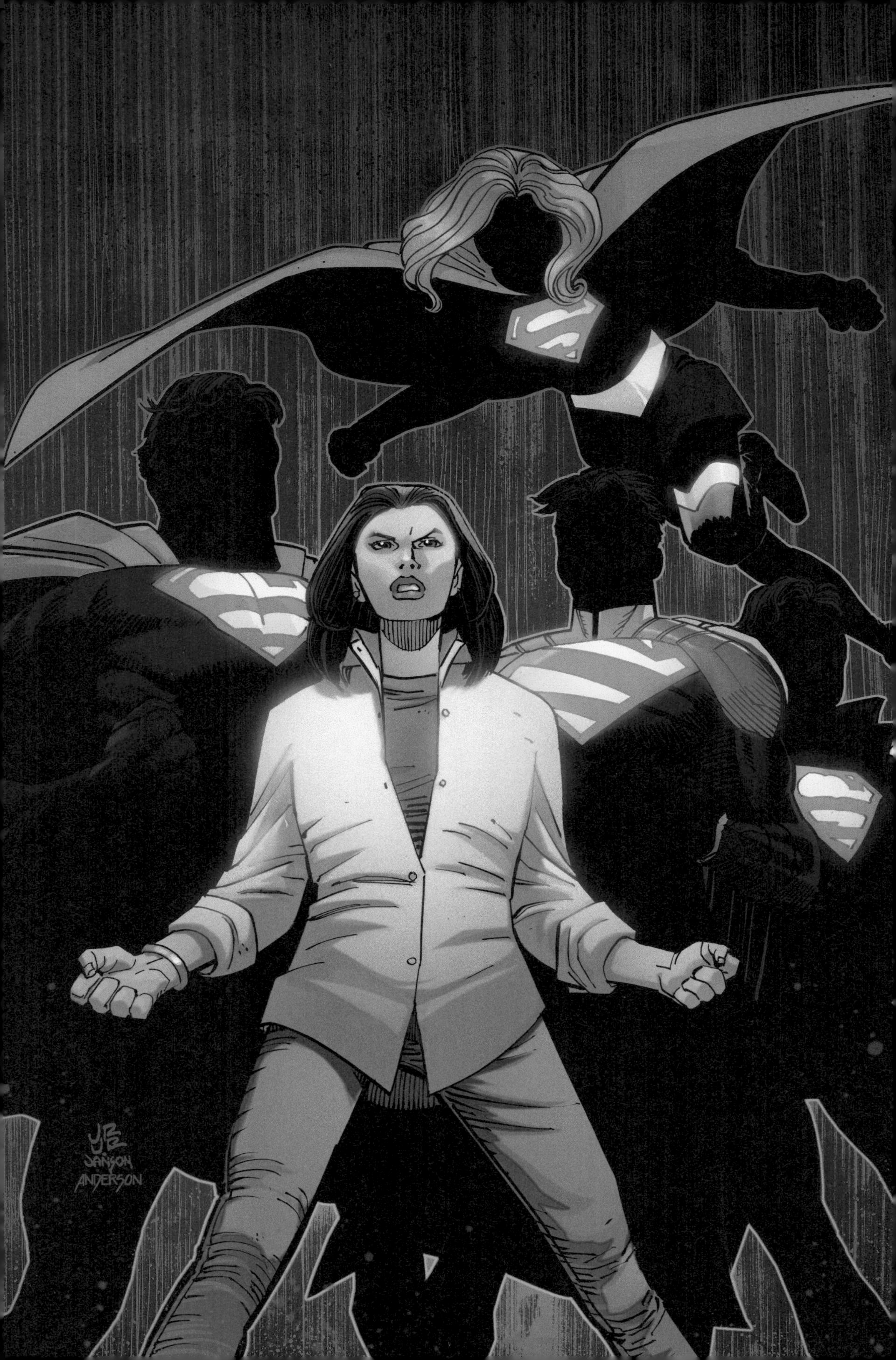

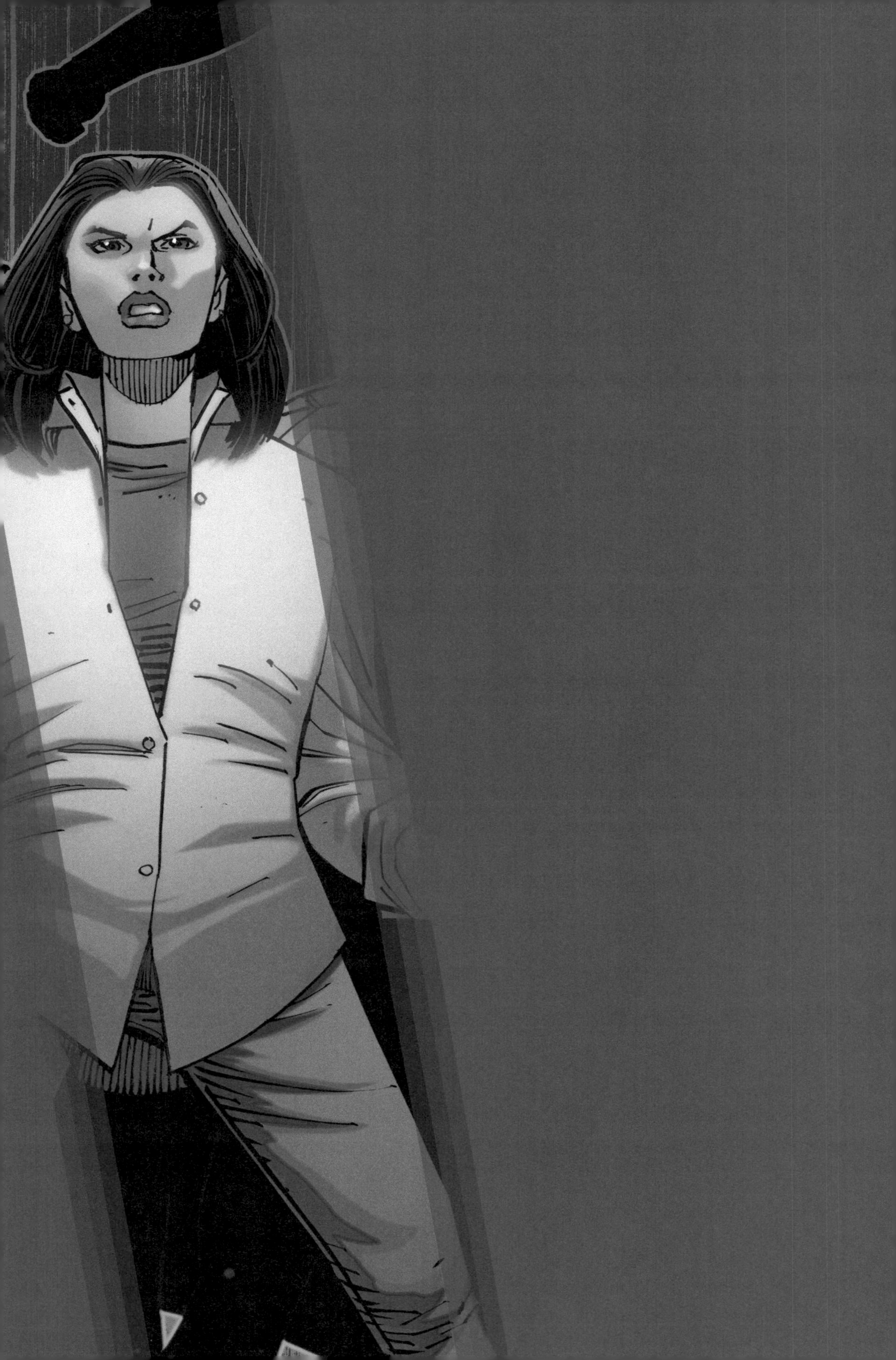

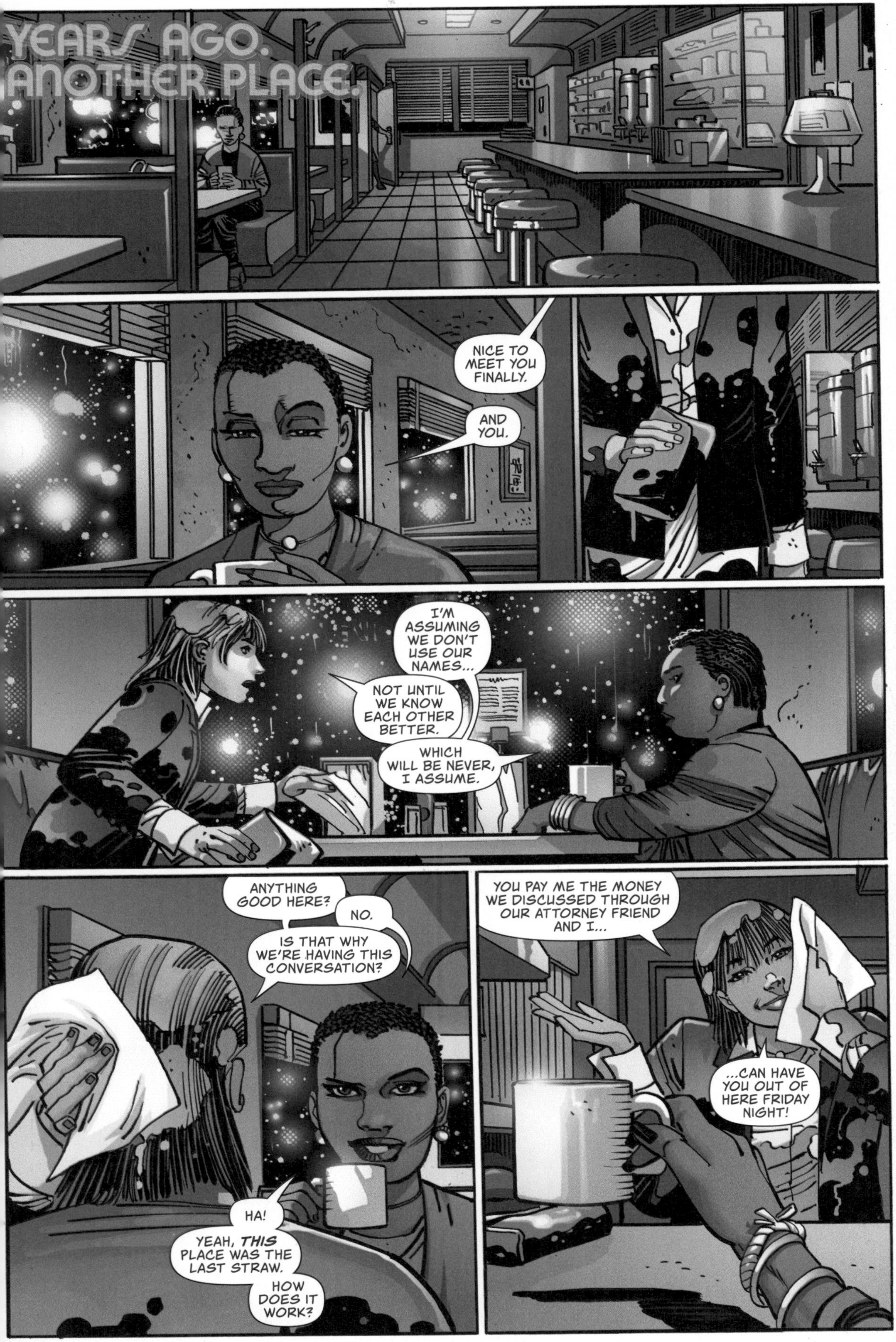

YEARS AGO. ANOTHER PLACE.
NICE TO MEET YOU FINALLY.
AND YOU.
I'M ASSUMING WE DON'T USE OUR NAMES...
NOT UNTIL WE KNOW EACH OTHER BETTER.
WHICH WILL BE NEVER, I ASSUME.
ANYTHING GOOD HERE?
NO.
IS THAT WHY WE'RE HAVING THIS CONVERSATION?
HA!
YEAH, THIS PLACE WAS THE LAST STRAW.
HOW DOES IT WORK?
YOU PAY ME THE MONEY WE DISCUSSED THROUGH OUR ATTORNEY FRIEND AND I...
...CAN HAVE YOU OUT OF HERE FRIDAY NIGHT!

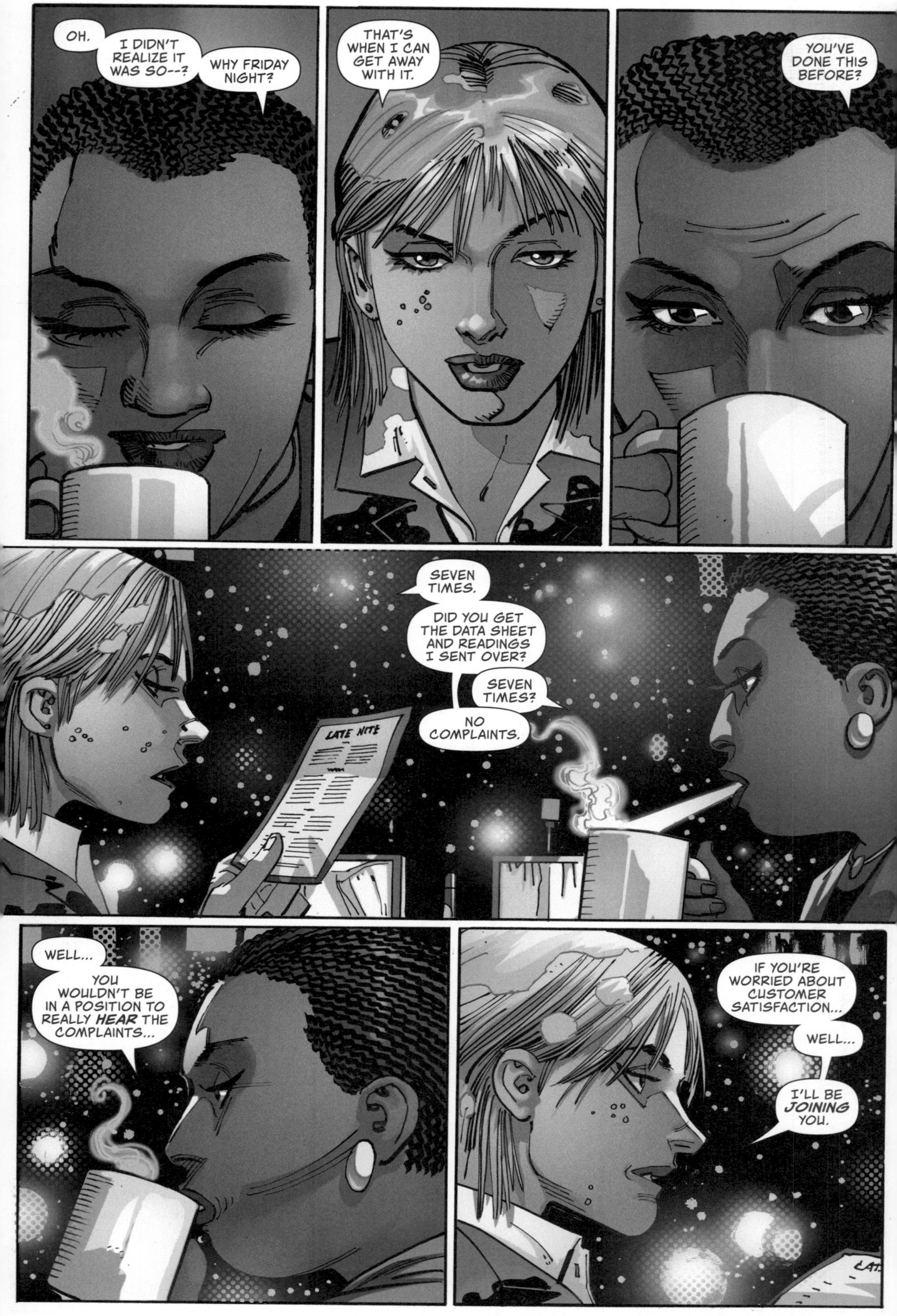
OH.
I DIDN'T REALIZE IT WAS SO--?
WHY FRIDAY NIGHT?
THAT'S WHEN I CAN GET AWAY WITH IT.
YOU'VE DONE THIS BEFORE?
SEVEN TIMES.
DID YOU GET THE DATA SHEET AND READINGS I SENT OVER?
SEVEN TIMES?
NO COMPLAINTS.
LATE NITE
WELL...
YOU WOULDN'T BE IN A POSITION TO REALLY *HEAR* THE COMPLAINTS...
IF YOU'RE WORRIED ABOUT CUSTOMER SATISFACTION...
WELL...
I'LL BE *JOINING* YOU.

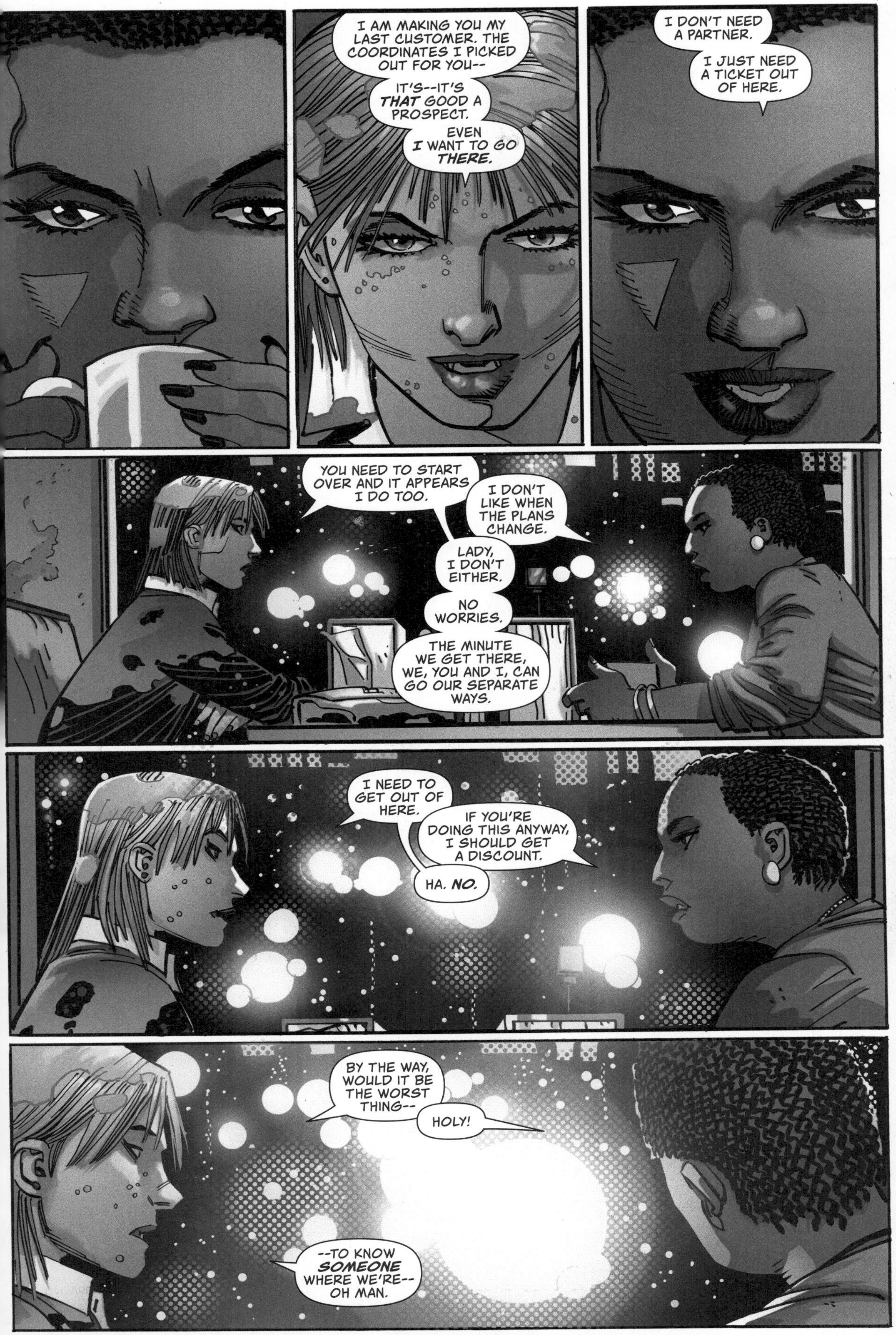
I AM MAKING YOU MY LAST CUSTOMER. THE COORDINATES I PICKED OUT FOR YOU--
IT'S--IT'S *THAT* GOOD A PROSPECT.
EVEN *I* WANT TO GO *THERE.*
I DON'T NEED A PARTNER.
I JUST NEED A TICKET OUT OF HERE.
YOU NEED TO START OVER AND IT APPEARS I DO TOO.
I DON'T LIKE WHEN THE PLANS CHANGE.
LADY, I DON'T EITHER.
NO WORRIES.
THE MINUTE WE GET THERE, WE, YOU AND I, CAN GO OUR SEPARATE WAYS.
I NEED TO GET OUT OF HERE.
IF YOU'RE DOING THIS ANYWAY, I SHOULD GET A DISCOUNT.
HA. *NO.*
BY THE WAY, WOULD IT BE THE WORST THING--
HOLY!
--TO KNOW *SOMEONE* WHERE WE'RE--OH MAN.

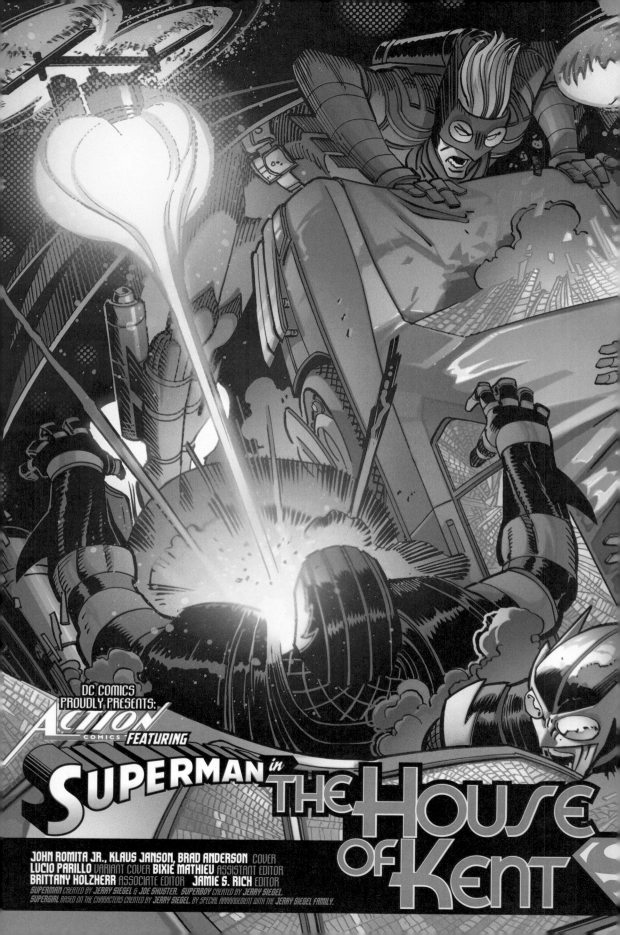

DC COMICS
PROUDLY PRESENTS:
*ACTION* COMICS FEATURING

SUPERMAN in THE HOUSE OF KENT

JOHN ROMITA JR., KLAUS JANSON, BRAD ANDERSON *Cover*
LUCIO PARILLO *Variant Cover* BIXIE MATHIEU *Assistant Editor*
BRITTANY HOLZHERR *Associate Editor* JAMIE S. RICH *Editor*
SUPERMAN *created by* JERRY SIEGEL & JOE SHUSTER. SUPERBOY *created by* JERRY SIEGEL.
SUPERGIRL *based on the characters created by* JERRY SIEGEL. *by special arrangement with the* JERRY SIEGEL *family.*

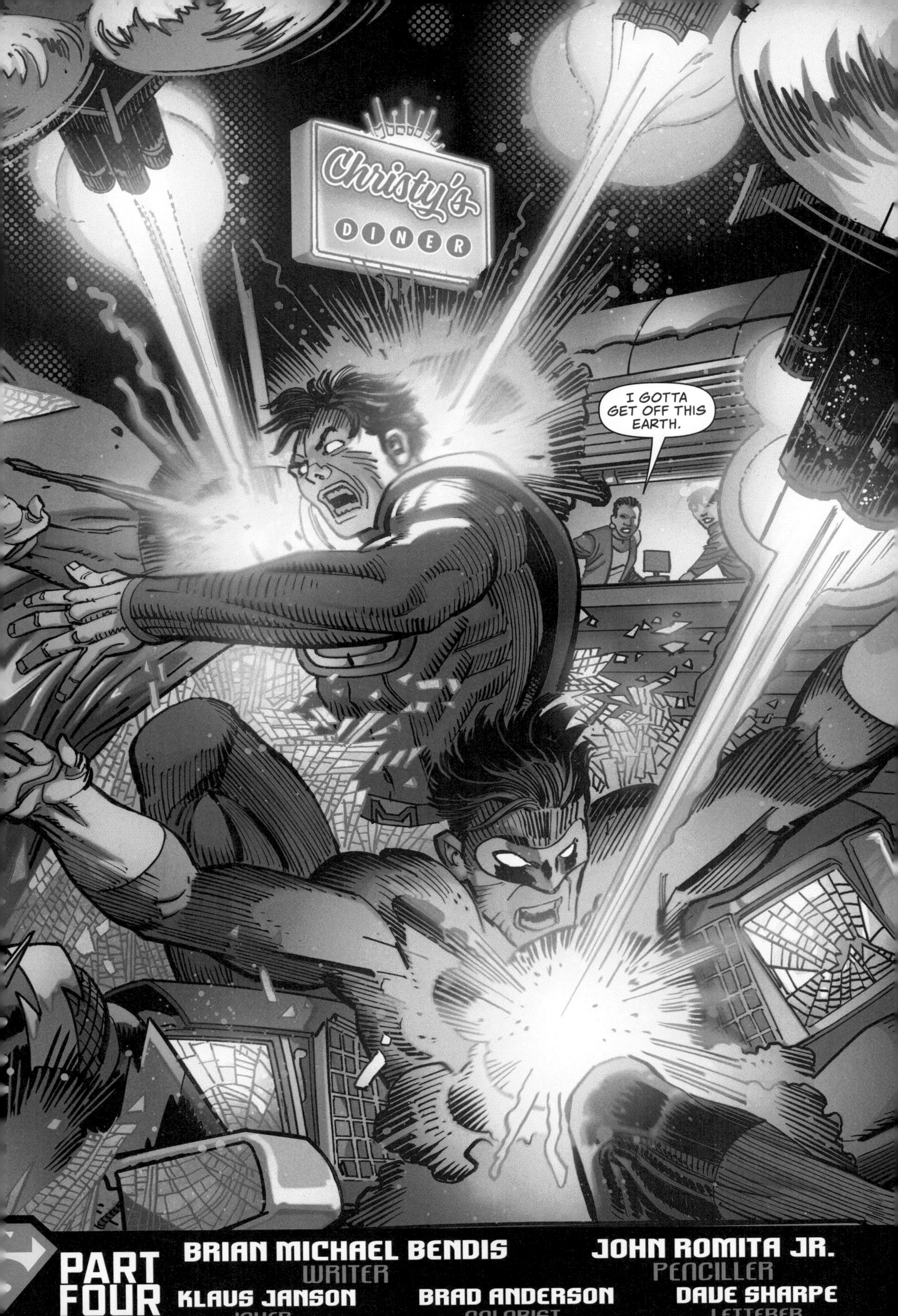
Christy's DINER
I GOTTA GET OFF THIS EARTH.

PART FOUR

BRIAN MICHAEL BENDIS WRITER
JOHN ROMITA JR. PENCILLER
KLAUS JANSON INKER
BRAD ANDERSON COLORIST
DAVE SHARPE LETTERER

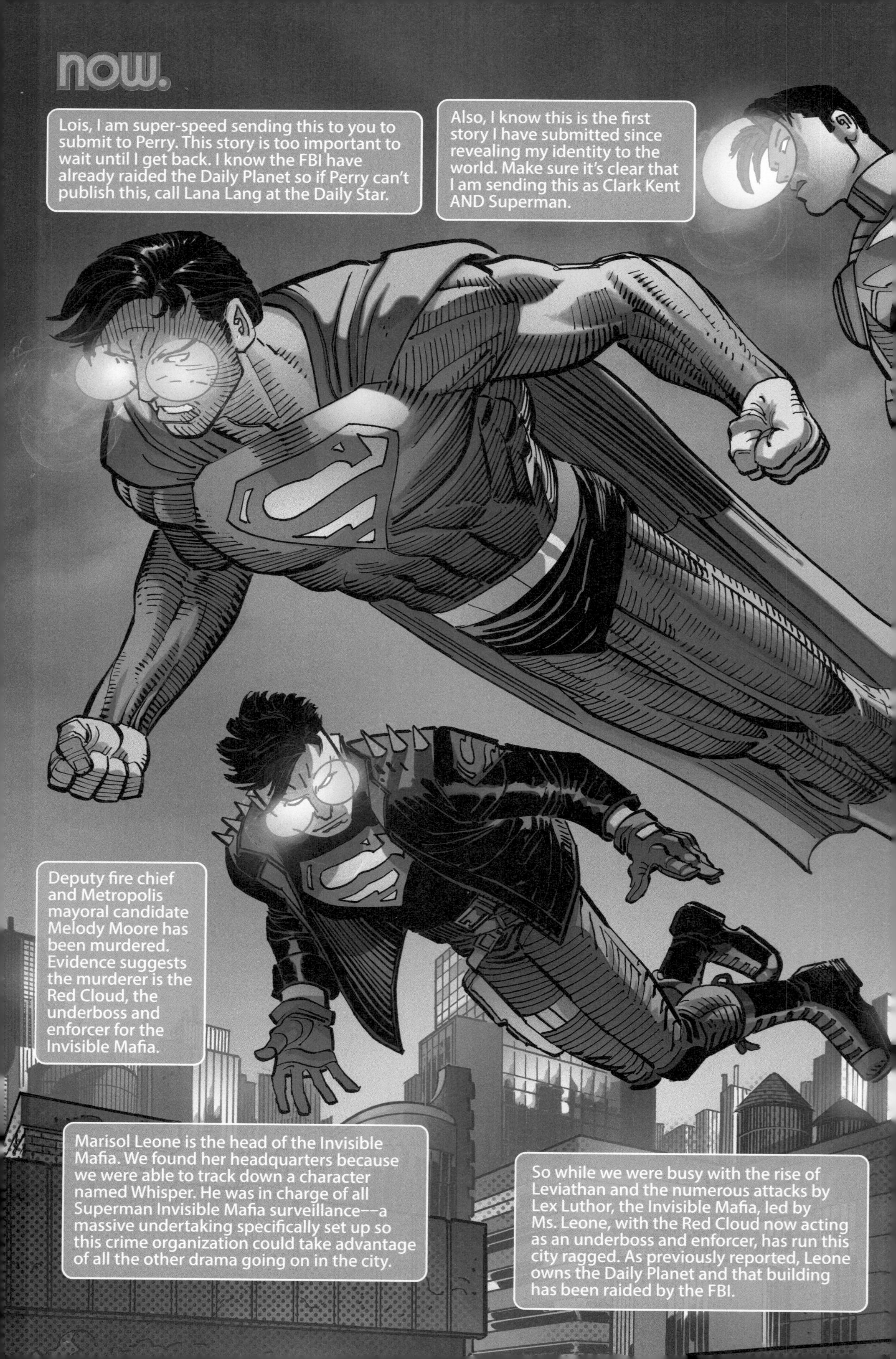
now.
Lois, I am super-speed sending this to you to submit to Perry. This story is too important to wait until I get back. I know the FBI have already raided the Daily Planet so if Perry can't publish this, call Lana Lang at the Daily Star.
Also, I know this is the first story I have submitted since revealing my identity to the world. Make sure it's clear that I am sending this as Clark Kent AND Superman.
Deputy fire chief and Metropolis mayoral candidate Melody Moore has been murdered. Evidence suggests the murderer is the Red Cloud, the underboss and enforcer for the Invisible Mafia.
Marisol Leone is the head of the Invisible Mafia. We found her headquarters because we were able to track down a character named Whisper. He was in charge of all Superman Invisible Mafia surveillance––a massive undertaking specifically set up so this crime organization could take advantage of all the other drama going on in the city.
So while we were busy with the rise of Leviathan and the numerous attacks by Lex Luthor, the Invisible Mafia, led by Ms. Leone, with the Red Cloud now acting as an underboss and enforcer, has run this city ragged. As previously reported, Leone owns the Daily Planet and that building has been raided by the FBI.

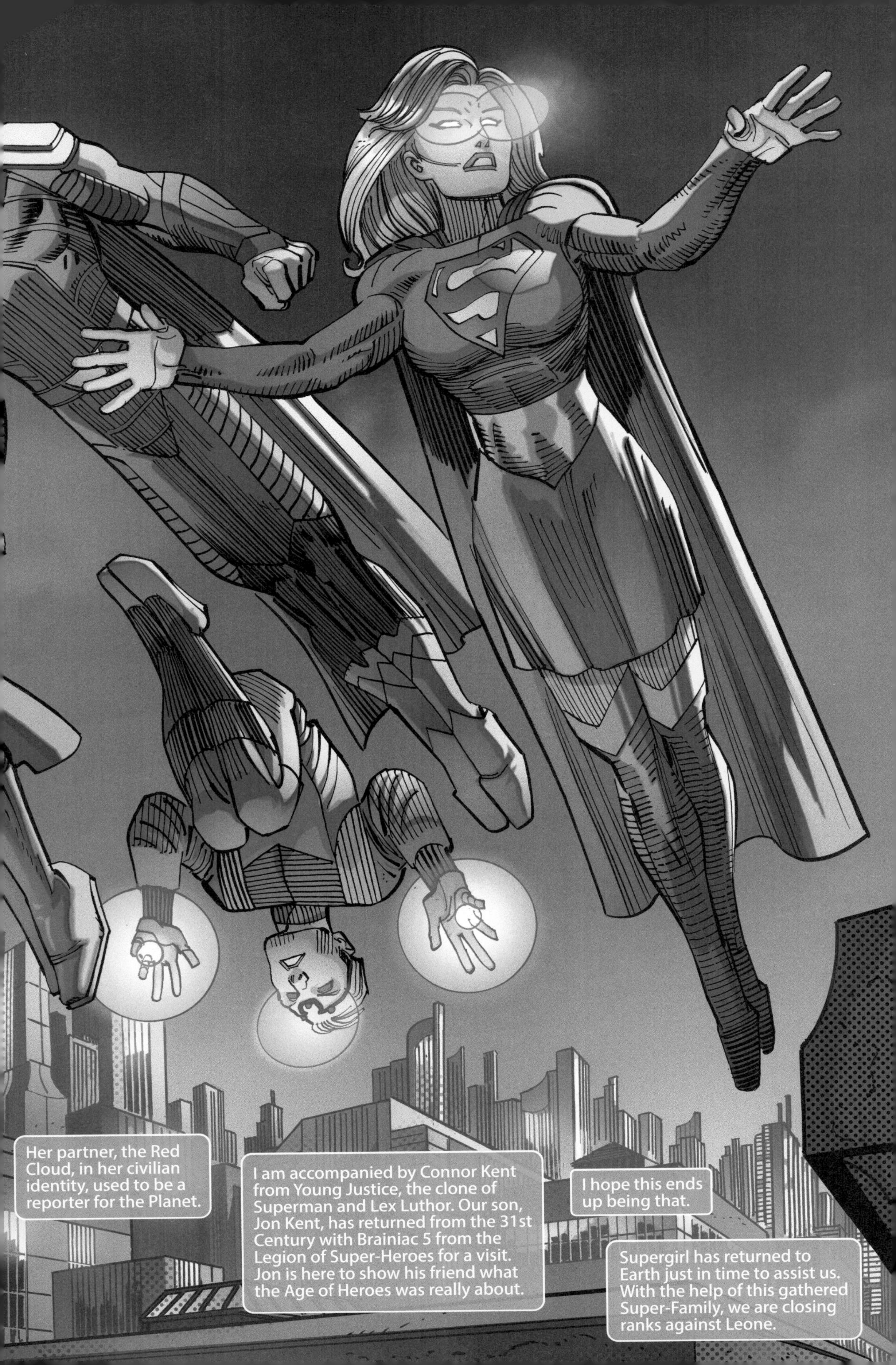
Her partner, the Red Cloud, in her civilian identity, used to be a reporter for the Planet.
I am accompanied by Connor Kent from Young Justice, the clone of Superman and Lex Luthor. Our son, Jon Kent, has returned from the 31st Century with Brainiac 5 from the Legion of Super-Heroes for a visit. Jon is here to show his friend what the Age of Heroes was really about.
I hope this ends up being that.
Supergirl has returned to Earth just in time to assist us. With the help of this gathered Super-Family, we are closing ranks against Leone.

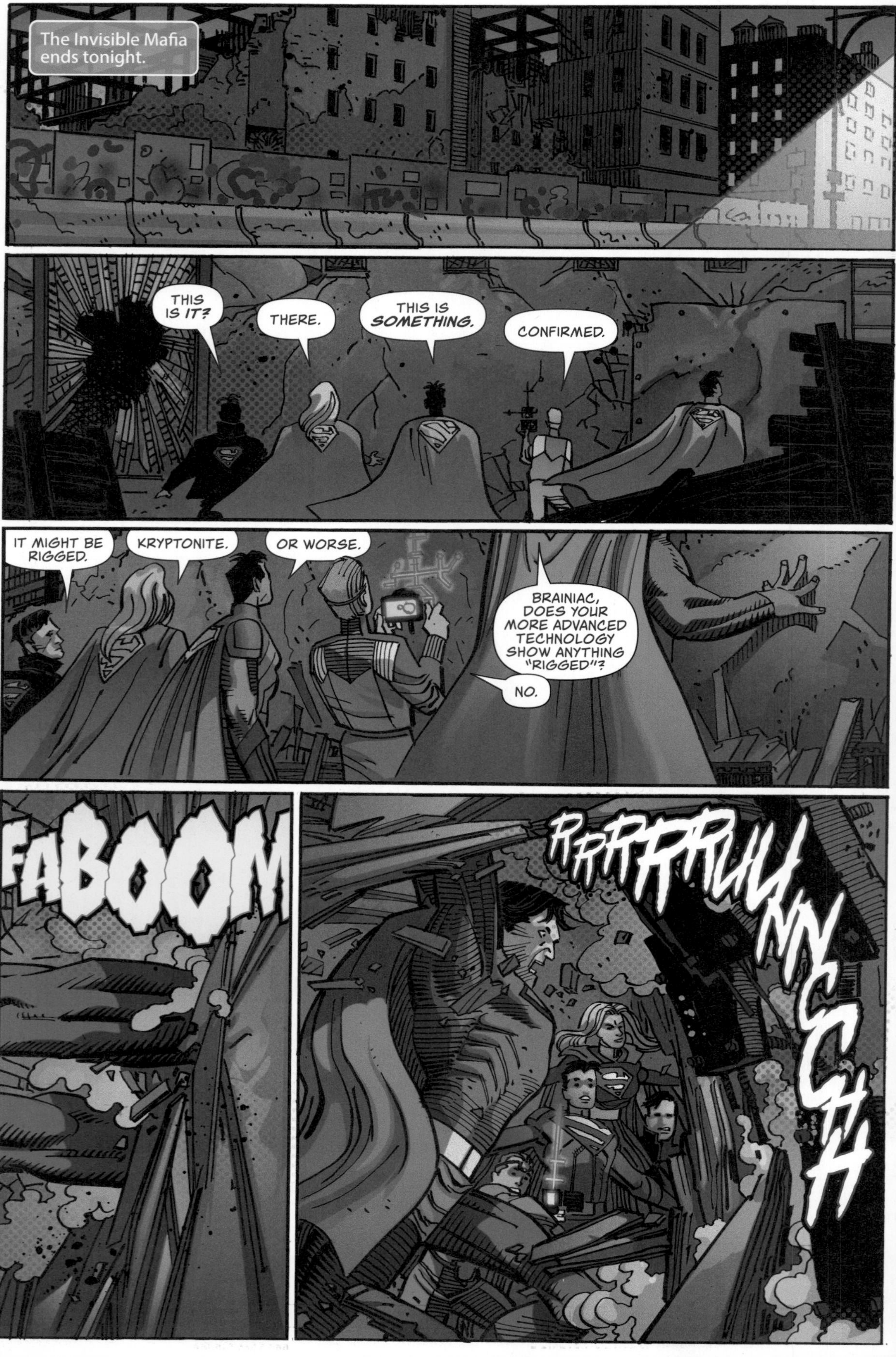
The Invisible Mafia ends tonight.
THIS IS IT?
THERE.
THIS IS SOMETHING.
CONFIRMED.
IT MIGHT BE RIGGED.
KRYPTONITE.
OR WORSE.
BRAINIAC, DOES YOUR MORE ADVANCED TECHNOLOGY SHOW ANYTHING "RIGGED"?
NO.
FABOOM
RRRRRRUNNCHH

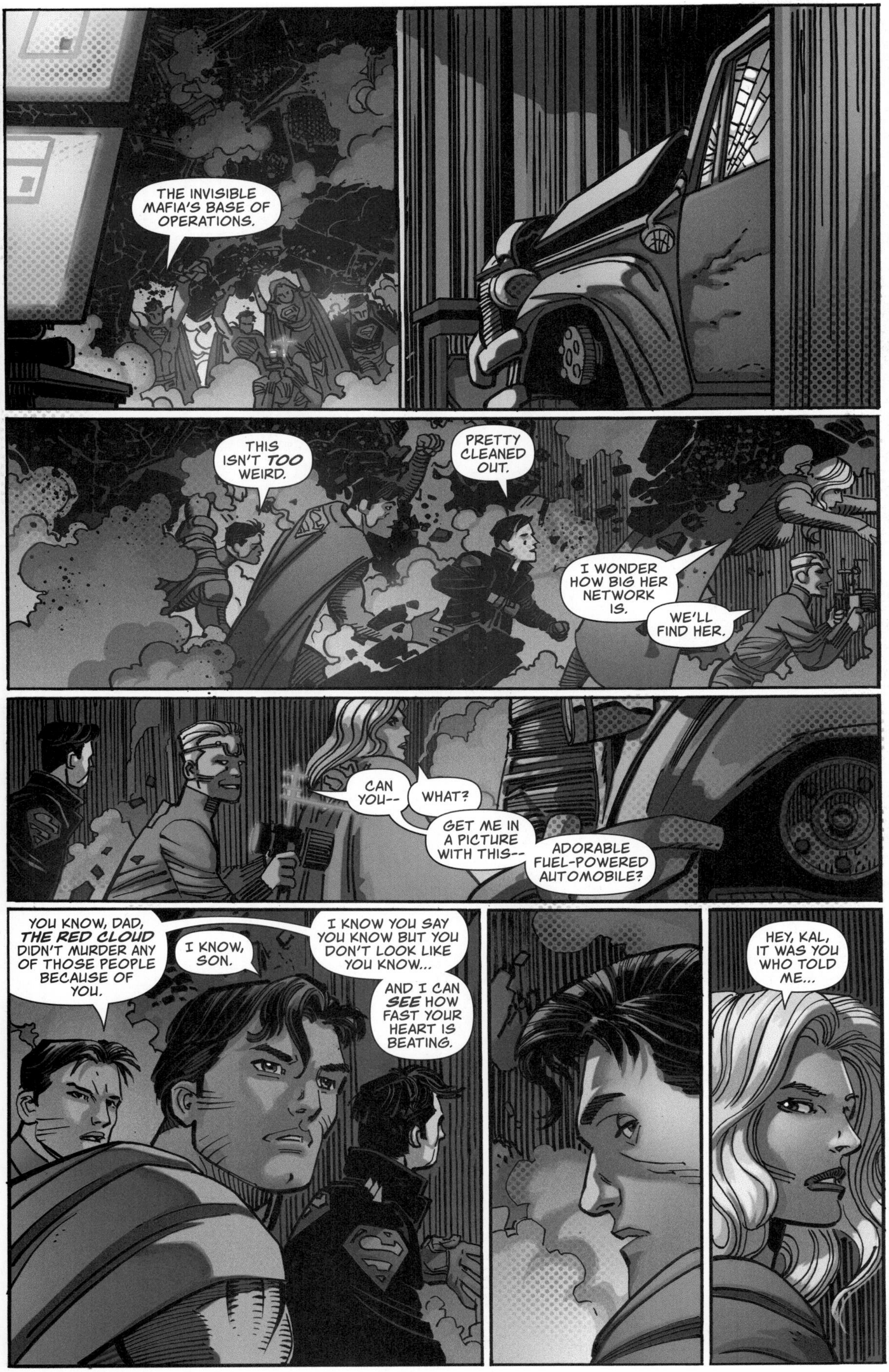
THE INVISIBLE MAFIA'S BASE OF OPERATIONS.
THIS ISN'T *TOO* WEIRD.
PRETTY CLEANED OUT.
I WONDER HOW BIG HER NETWORK IS.
WE'LL FIND HER.
CAN YOU--
WHAT?
GET ME IN A PICTURE WITH THIS--
ADORABLE FUEL-POWERED AUTOMOBILE?
YOU KNOW, DAD, ***THE RED CLOUD*** DIDN'T MURDER ANY OF THOSE PEOPLE BECAUSE OF YOU.
I KNOW, SON.
I KNOW YOU SAY YOU KNOW BUT YOU DON'T LOOK LIKE YOU KNOW...
AND I CAN ***SEE*** HOW FAST YOUR HEART IS BEATING.
HEY, KAL, IT WAS YOU WHO TOLD ME...

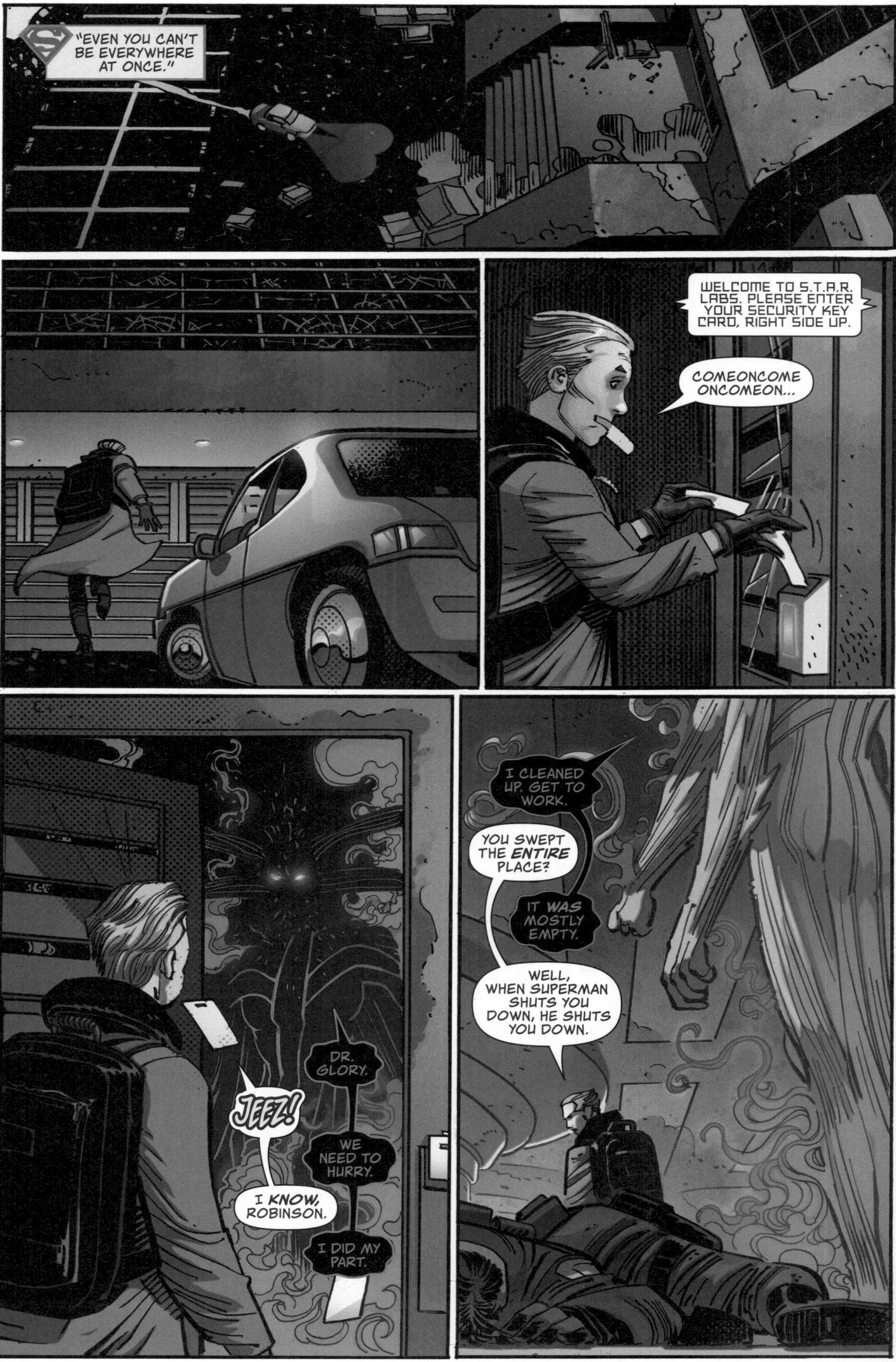
"EVEN YOU CAN'T BE EVERYWHERE AT ONCE."
WELCOME TO S.T.A.R. LABS. PLEASE ENTER YOUR SECURITY KEY CARD, RIGHT SIDE UP.
COMEONCOME ONCOMEON...
DR. GLORY.
JEEZ!
WE NEED TO HURRY.
I KNOW, ROBINSON.
I DID MY PART.
I CLEANED UP. GET TO WORK.
YOU SWEPT THE ENTIRE PLACE?
IT WAS MOSTLY EMPTY.
WELL, WHEN SUPERMAN SHUTS YOU DOWN, HE SHUTS YOU DOWN.

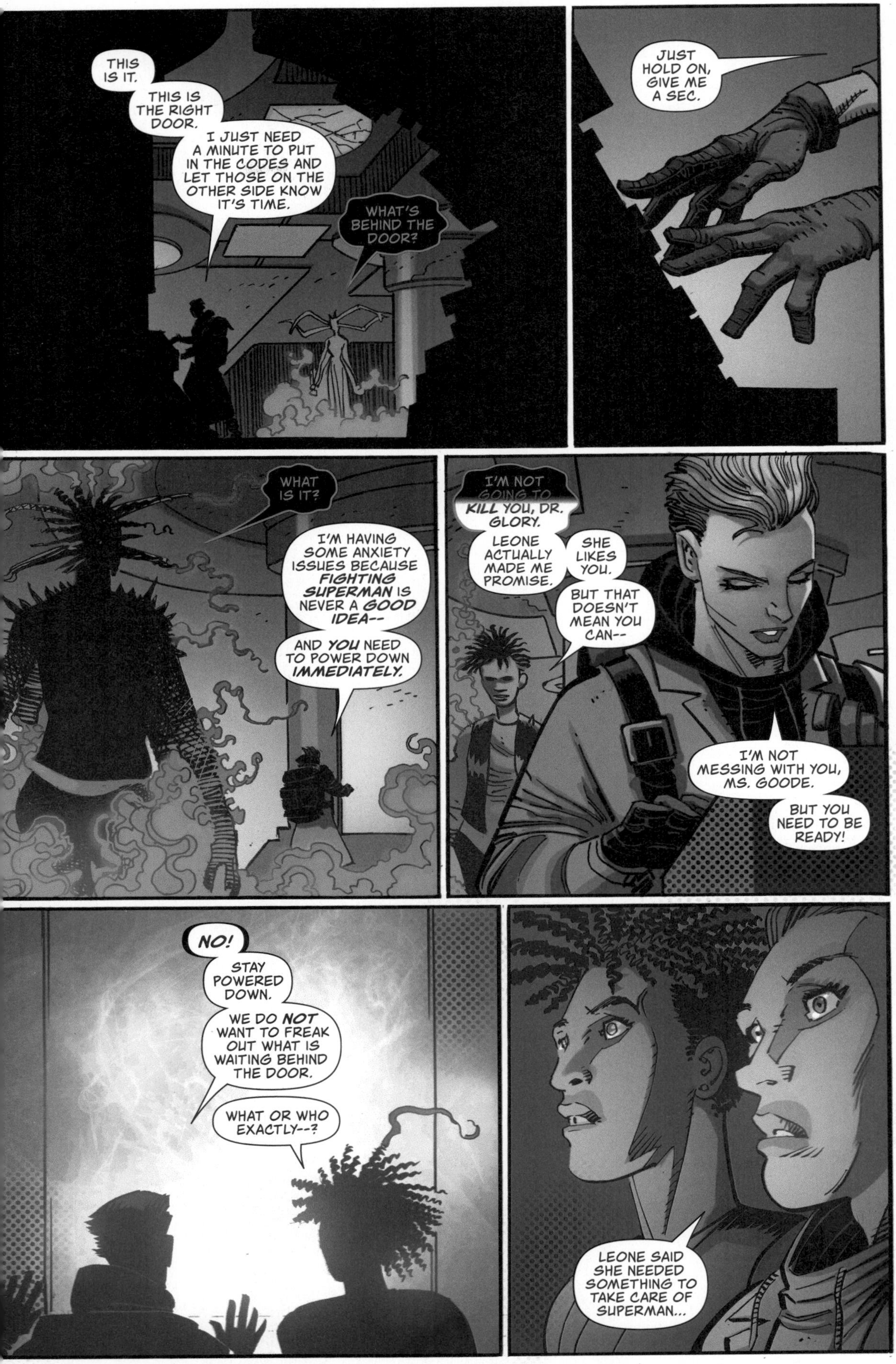
THIS IS IT.
THIS IS THE RIGHT DOOR.
I JUST NEED A MINUTE TO PUT IN THE CODES AND LET THOSE ON THE OTHER SIDE KNOW IT'S TIME.
WHAT'S BEHIND THE DOOR?
JUST HOLD ON, GIVE ME A SEC.
WHAT IS IT?
I'M HAVING SOME ANXIETY ISSUES BECAUSE FIGHTING SUPERMAN IS NEVER A GOOD IDEA--
AND YOU NEED TO POWER DOWN IMMEDIATELY.
I'M NOT GOING TO KILL YOU, DR. GLORY.
LEONE ACTUALLY MADE ME PROMISE.
SHE LIKES YOU.
BUT THAT DOESN'T MEAN YOU CAN--
I'M NOT MESSING WITH YOU, MS. GOODE.
BUT YOU NEED TO BE READY!
NO!
STAY POWERED DOWN.
WE DO NOT WANT TO FREAK OUT WHAT IS WAITING BEHIND THE DOOR.
WHAT OR WHO EXACTLY--?
LEONE SAID SHE NEEDED SOMETHING TO TAKE CARE OF SUPERMAN...

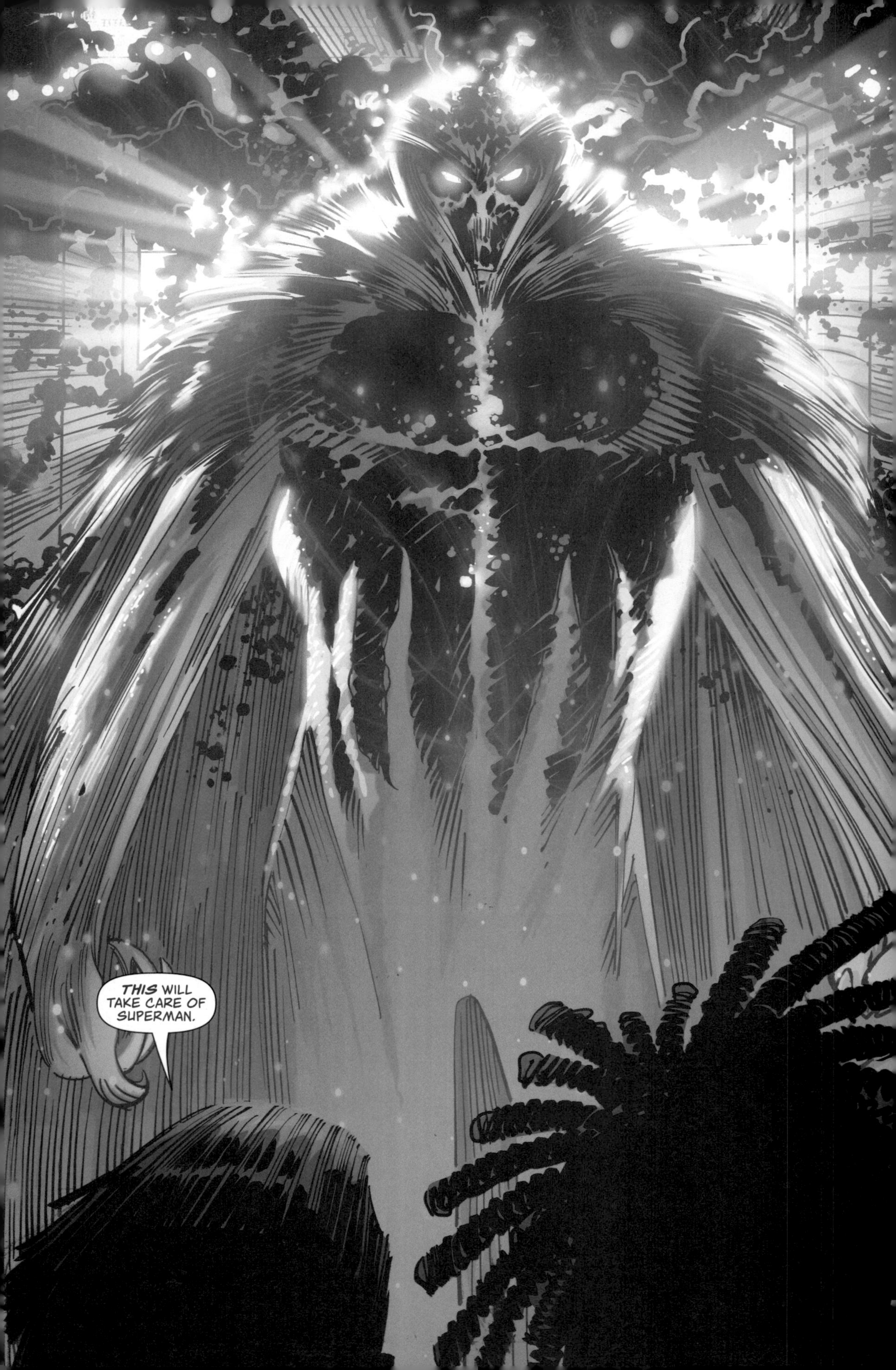
THIS WILL TAKE CARE OF SUPERMAN.

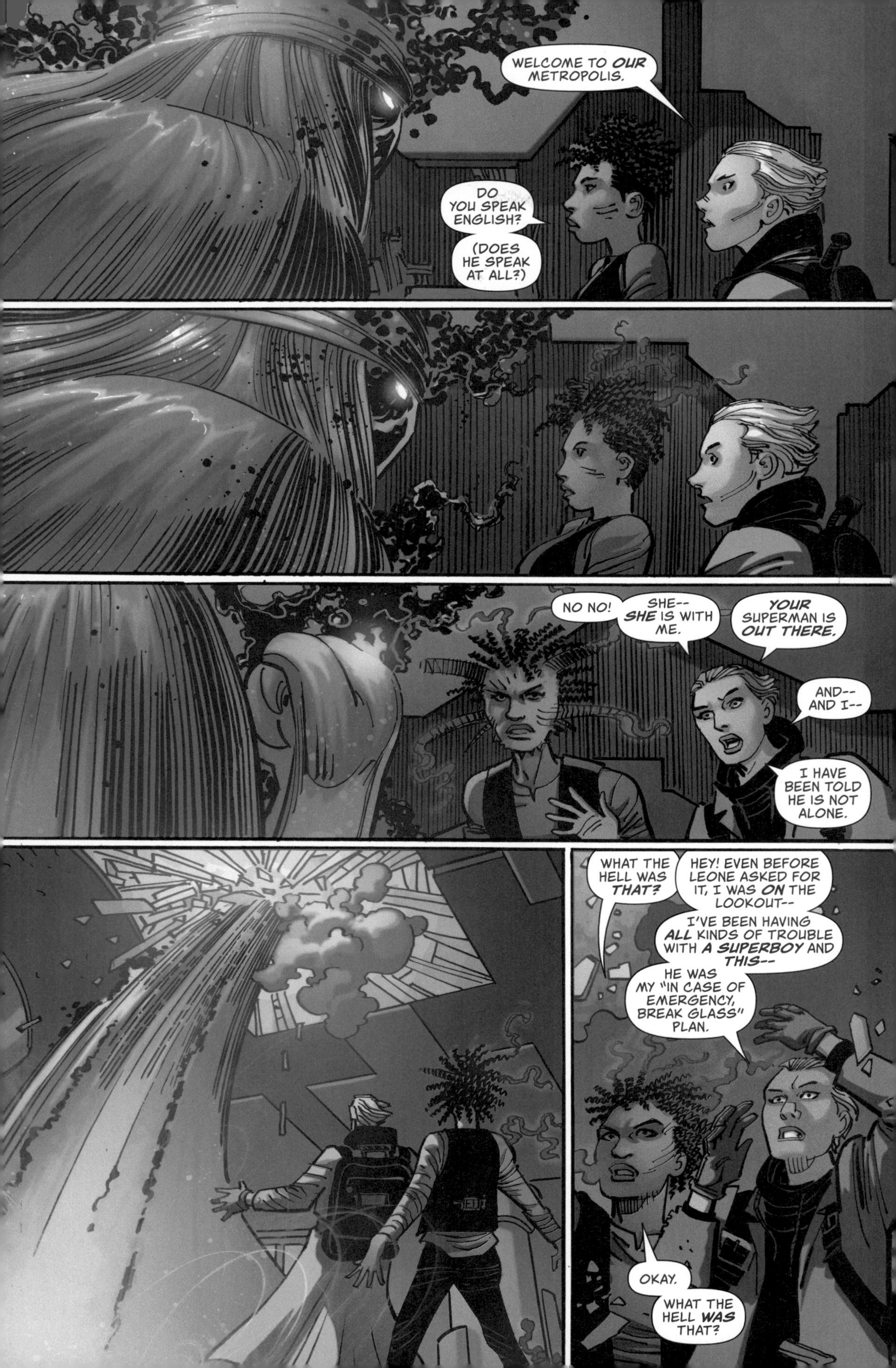
WELCOME TO OUR METROPOLIS.
DO YOU SPEAK ENGLISH?
(DOES HE SPEAK AT ALL?)
NO NO!
SHE-- SHE IS WITH ME.
YOUR SUPERMAN IS OUT THERE.
AND-- AND I--
I HAVE BEEN TOLD HE IS NOT ALONE.
WHAT THE HELL WAS THAT?
HEY! EVEN BEFORE LEONE ASKED FOR IT, I WAS ON THE LOOKOUT--
I'VE BEEN HAVING ALL KINDS OF TROUBLE WITH A SUPERBOY AND THIS--
HE WAS MY "IN CASE OF EMERGENCY, BREAK GLASS" PLAN.
OKAY.
WHAT THE HELL WAS THAT?

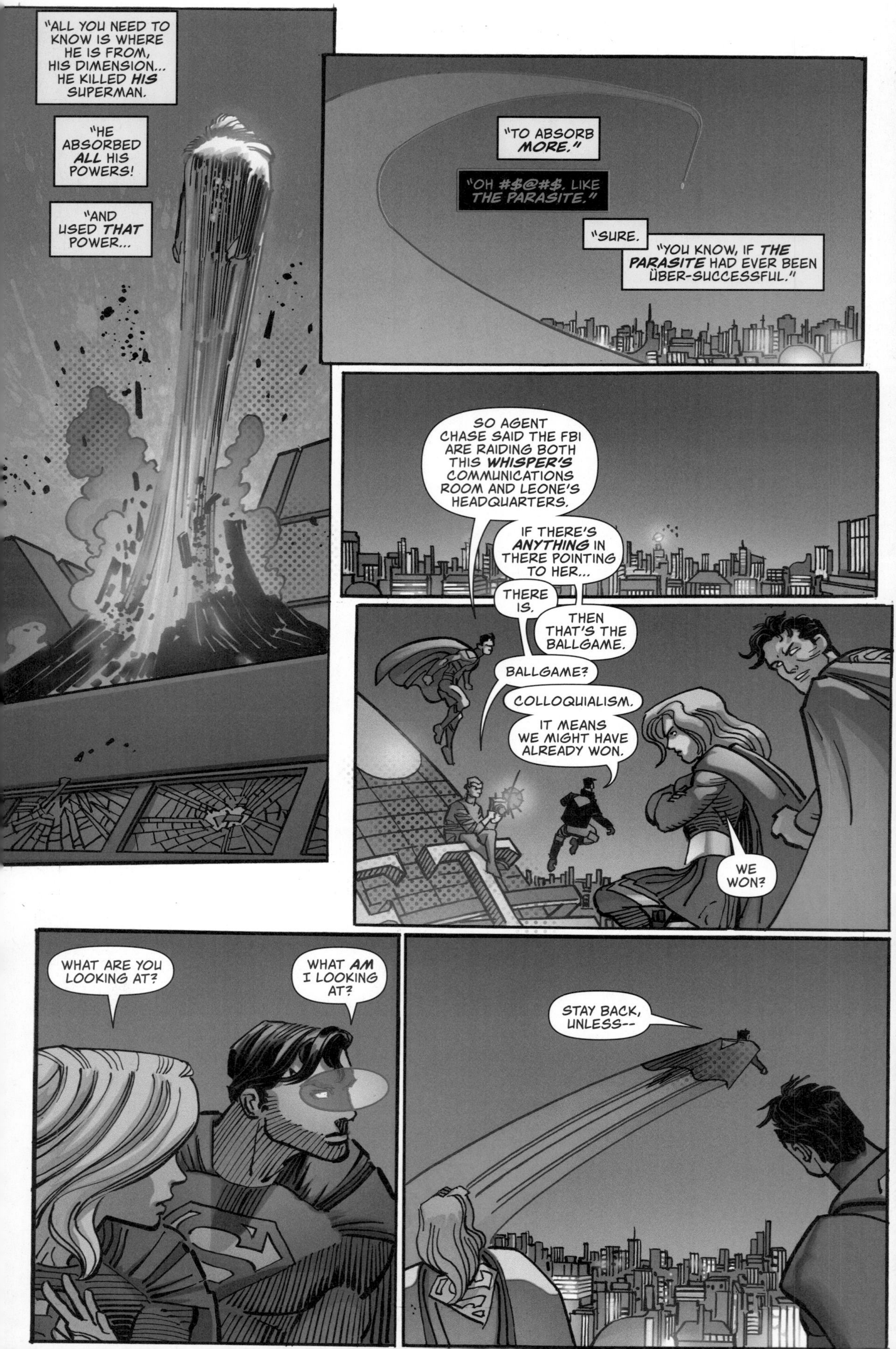
"ALL YOU NEED TO KNOW IS WHERE HE IS FROM, HIS DIMENSION... HE KILLED HIS SUPERMAN.
"HE ABSORBED ALL HIS POWERS!
"AND USED THAT POWER...
"TO ABSORB MORE."
"OH #$@#$. LIKE THE PARASITE."
"SURE.
"YOU KNOW, IF THE PARASITE HAD EVER BEEN ÜBER-SUCCESSFUL."
SO AGENT CHASE SAID THE FBI ARE RAIDING BOTH THIS WHISPER'S COMMUNICATIONS ROOM AND LEONE'S HEADQUARTERS.
IF THERE'S ANYTHING IN THERE POINTING TO HER...
THERE IS.
THEN THAT'S THE BALLGAME.
BALLGAME?
COLLOQUIALISM.
IT MEANS WE MIGHT HAVE ALREADY WON.
WE WON?
WHAT ARE YOU LOOKING AT?
WHAT AM I LOOKING AT?
STAY BACK, UNLESS--

WHAT IS THAT?

I SAID STAY BACK UNTIL I CAN INVESTIGATE.

IT'S LIKE NONE OF US LISTENS.

I HAVE NO HISTORICAL RECORD OF THAT CREATURE.

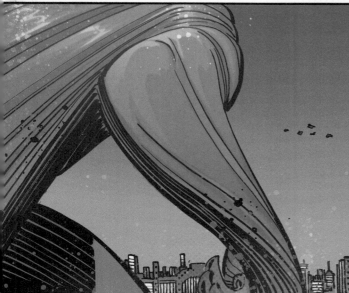

WHAT'S IT DOING?

I THINK *THE GROUP* OF US MIGHT BE GIVING HIM PAUSE.

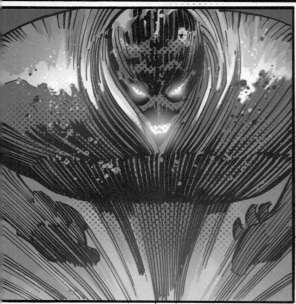

OR NOT.

STAY BACK.

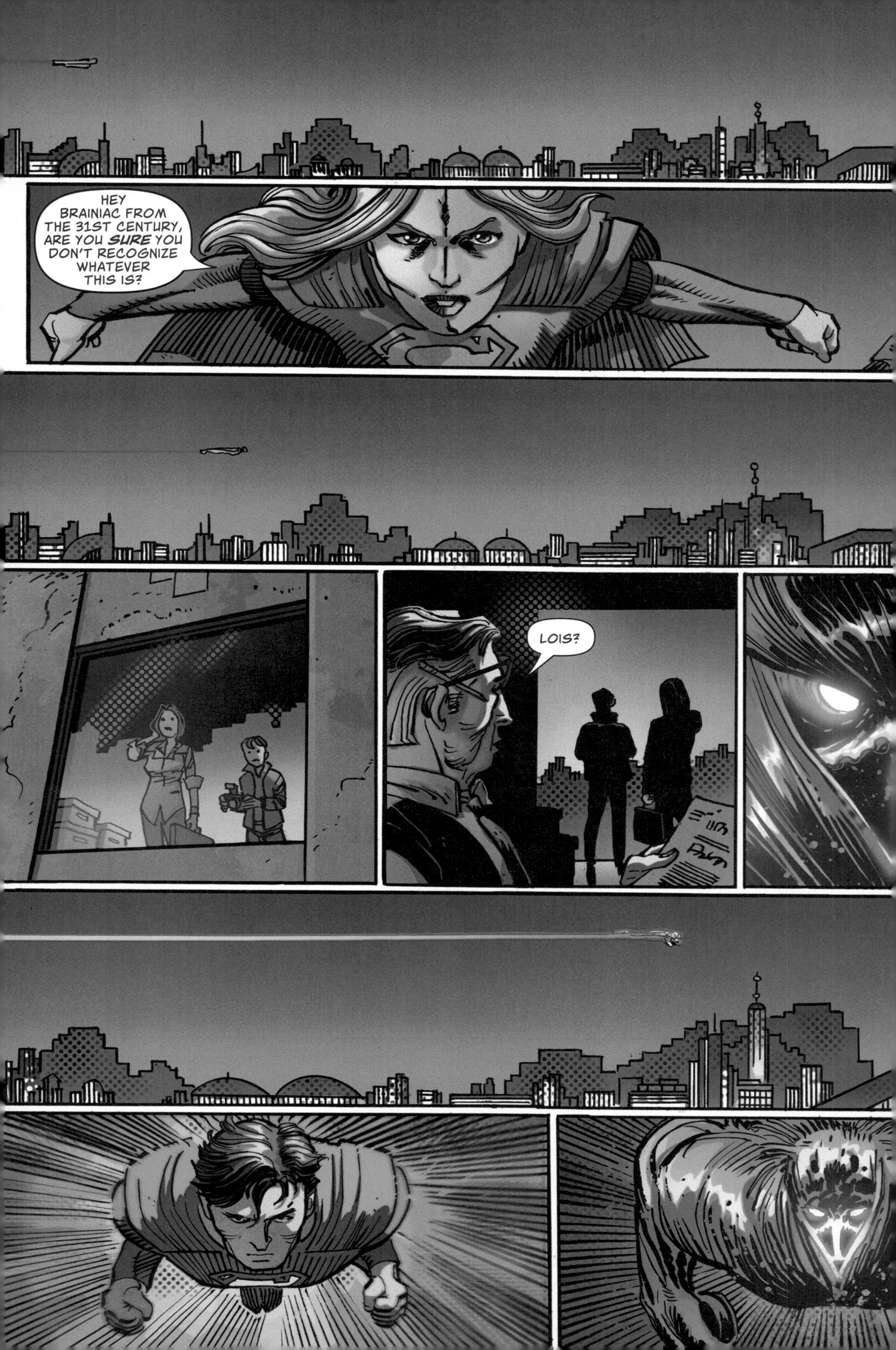
HEY BRAINIAC FROM THE 31ST CENTURY, ARE YOU SURE YOU DON'T RECOGNIZE WHATEVER THIS IS?
LOIS?

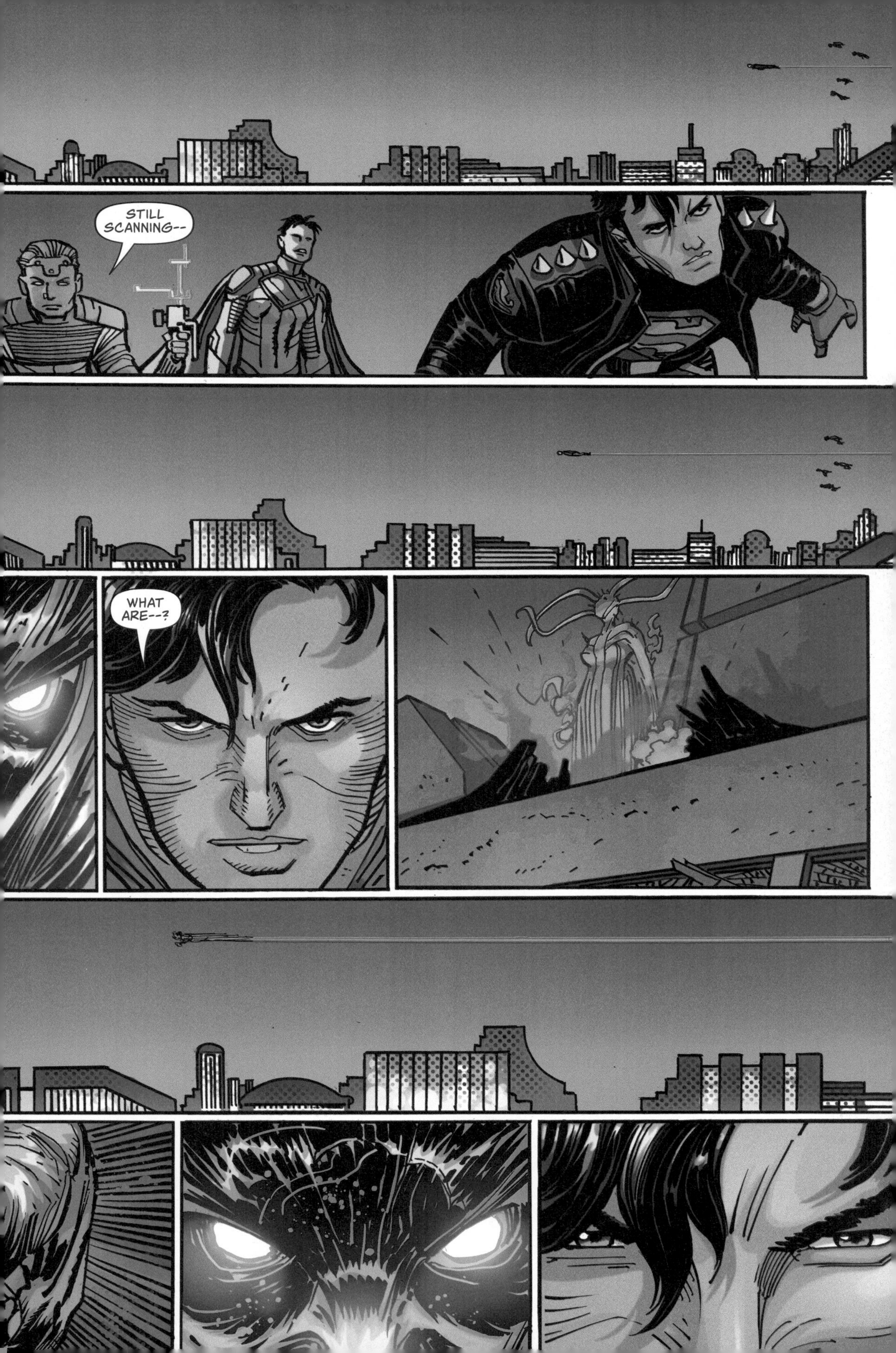
STILL SCANNING--
WHAT ARE--?

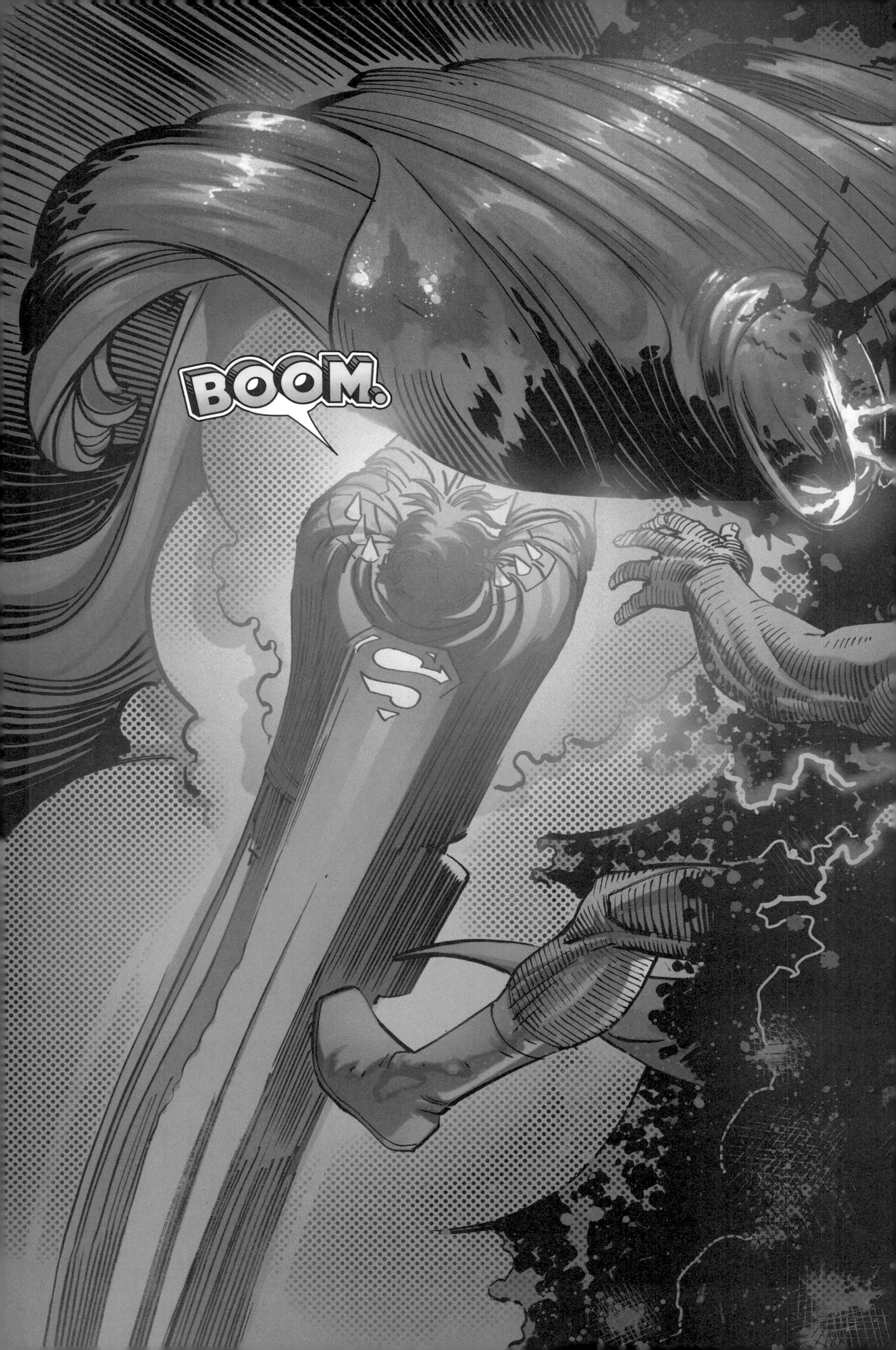
BOOM.

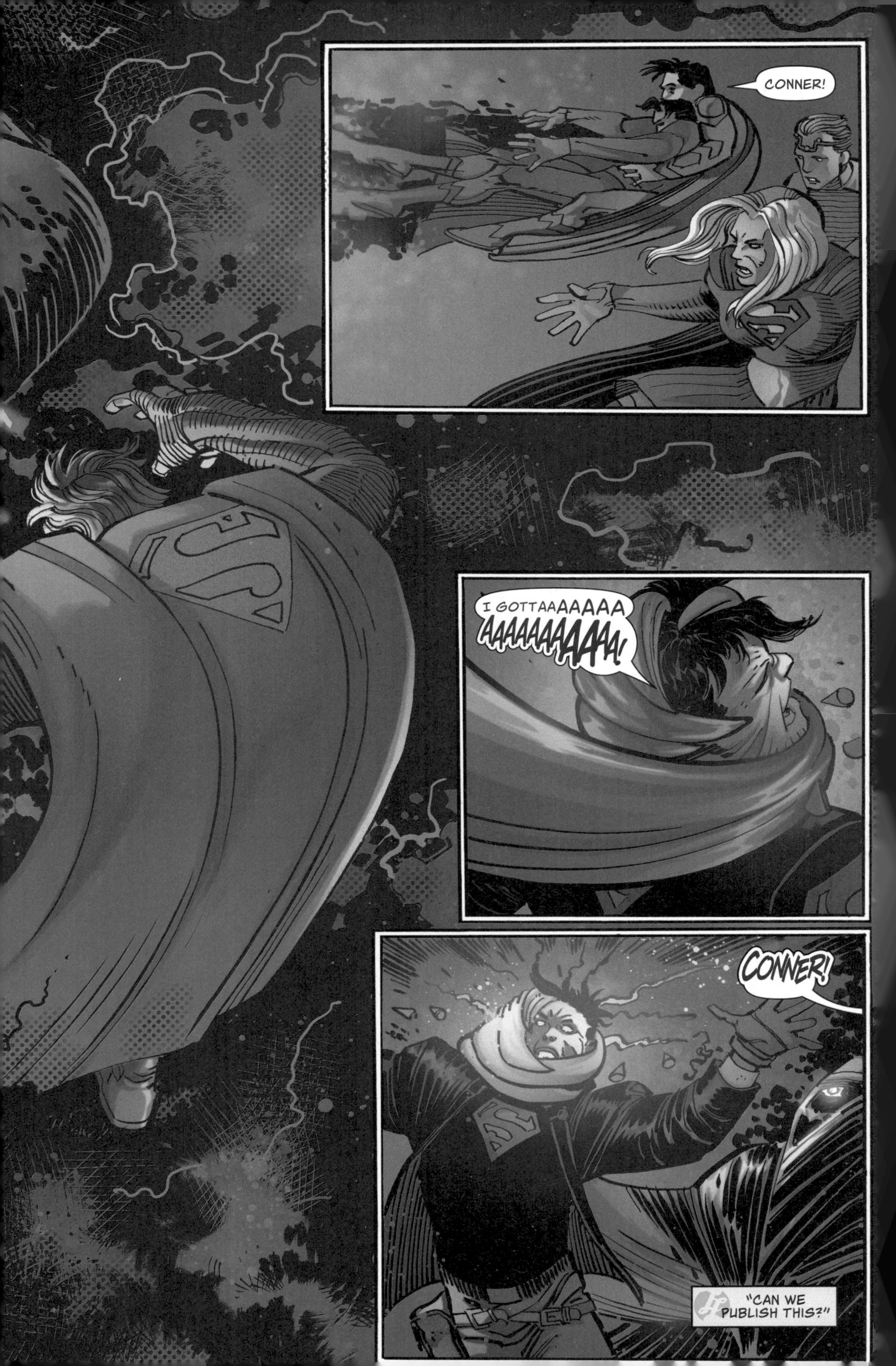
CONNER!
I GOTTAAAAAAA AAAAAAAAAAAA!
CONNER!
"CAN WE PUBLISH THIS?"

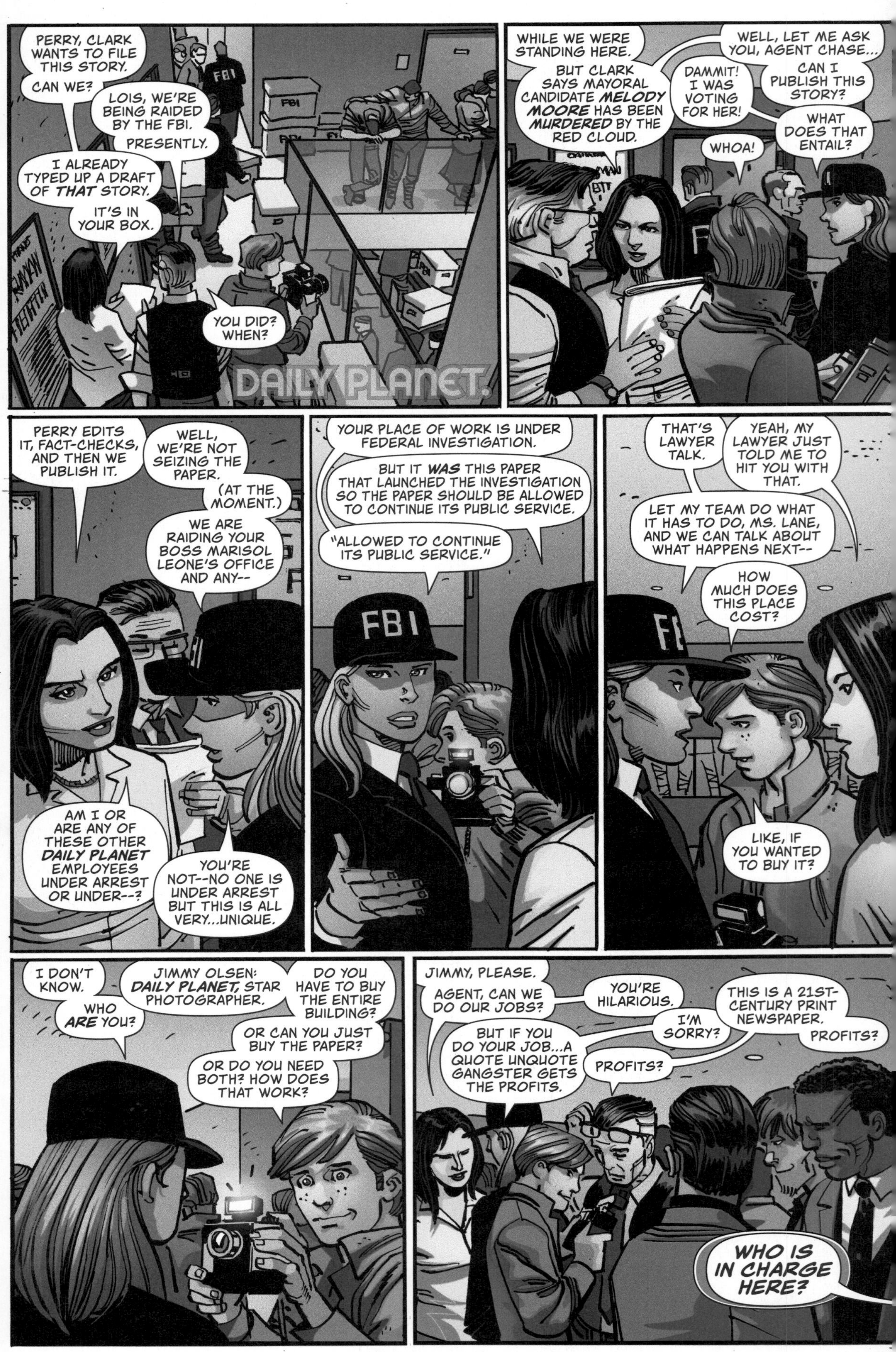
PERRY, CLARK WANTS TO FILE THIS STORY.
CAN WE?
LOIS, WE'RE BEING RAIDED BY THE FBI.
PRESENTLY.
I ALREADY TYPED UP A DRAFT OF THAT STORY.
IT'S IN YOUR BOX.
YOU DID? WHEN?
DAILY PLANET.
WHILE WE WERE STANDING HERE.
BUT CLARK SAYS MAYORAL CANDIDATE MELODY MOORE HAS BEEN MURDERED BY THE RED CLOUD.
DAMMIT! I WAS VOTING FOR HER!
WHOA!
WELL, LET ME ASK YOU, AGENT CHASE...
CAN I PUBLISH THIS STORY?
WHAT DOES THAT ENTAIL?
PERRY EDITS IT, FACT-CHECKS, AND THEN WE PUBLISH IT.
WELL, WE'RE NOT SEIZING THE PAPER.
(AT THE MOMENT.)
WE ARE RAIDING YOUR BOSS MARISOL LEONE'S OFFICE AND ANY--
AM I OR ARE ANY OF THESE OTHER DAILY PLANET EMPLOYEES UNDER ARREST OR UNDER--?
YOU'RE NOT--NO ONE IS UNDER ARREST BUT THIS IS ALL VERY...UNIQUE.
YOUR PLACE OF WORK IS UNDER FEDERAL INVESTIGATION.
BUT IT WAS THIS PAPER THAT LAUNCHED THE INVESTIGATION SO THE PAPER SHOULD BE ALLOWED TO CONTINUE ITS PUBLIC SERVICE.
"ALLOWED TO CONTINUE ITS PUBLIC SERVICE."
FBI
THAT'S LAWYER TALK.
YEAH, MY LAWYER JUST TOLD ME TO HIT YOU WITH THAT.
LET MY TEAM DO WHAT IT HAS TO DO, MS. LANE, AND WE CAN TALK ABOUT WHAT HAPPENS NEXT--
HOW MUCH DOES THIS PLACE COST?
LIKE, IF YOU WANTED TO BUY IT?
I DON'T KNOW.
WHO ARE YOU?
JIMMY OLSEN: DAILY PLANET, STAR PHOTOGRAPHER.
DO YOU HAVE TO BUY THE ENTIRE BUILDING?
OR CAN YOU JUST BUY THE PAPER?
OR DO YOU NEED BOTH? HOW DOES THAT WORK?
JIMMY, PLEASE.
AGENT, CAN WE DO OUR JOBS?
YOU'RE HILARIOUS.
I'M SORRY?
BUT IF YOU DO YOUR JOB...A QUOTE UNQUOTE GANGSTER GETS THE PROFITS.
PROFITS?
THIS IS A 21ST-CENTURY PRINT NEWSPAPER.
PROFITS?
WHO IS IN CHARGE HERE?

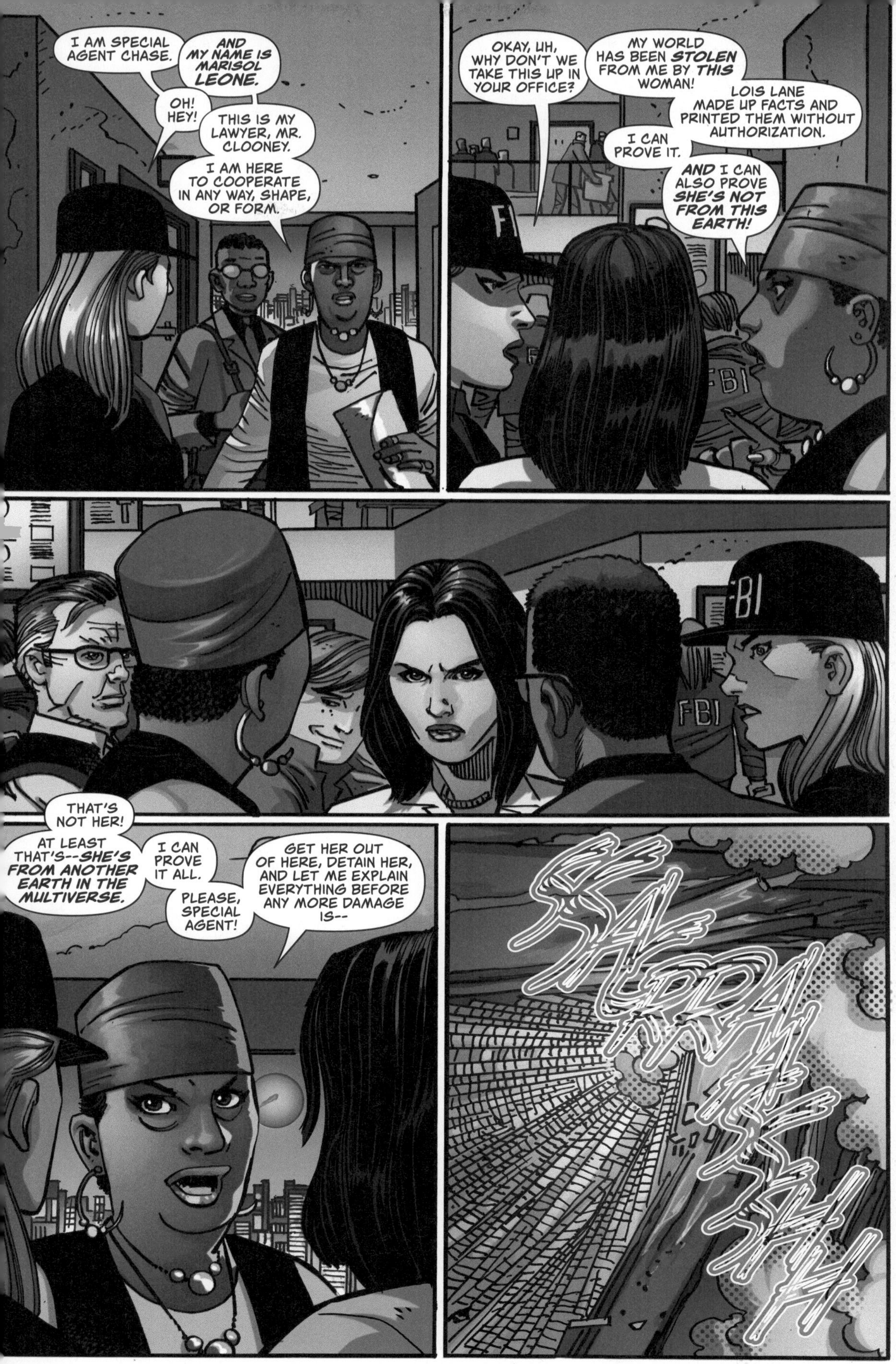
I AM SPECIAL AGENT CHASE.
AND MY NAME IS MARISOL LEONE.
OH! HEY!
THIS IS MY LAWYER, MR. CLOONEY.
I AM HERE TO COOPERATE IN ANY WAY, SHAPE, OR FORM.
OKAY, UH, WHY DON'T WE TAKE THIS UP IN YOUR OFFICE?
MY WORLD HAS BEEN STOLEN FROM ME BY THIS WOMAN!
LOIS LANE MADE UP FACTS AND PRINTED THEM WITHOUT AUTHORIZATION.
I CAN PROVE IT.
AND I CAN ALSO PROVE SHE'S NOT FROM THIS EARTH!
THAT'S NOT HER!
AT LEAST THAT'S--SHE'S FROM ANOTHER EARTH IN THE MULTIVERSE.
I CAN PROVE IT ALL.
PLEASE, SPECIAL AGENT!
GET HER OUT OF HERE, DETAIN HER, AND LET ME EXPLAIN EVERYTHING BEFORE ANY MORE DAMAGE IS--

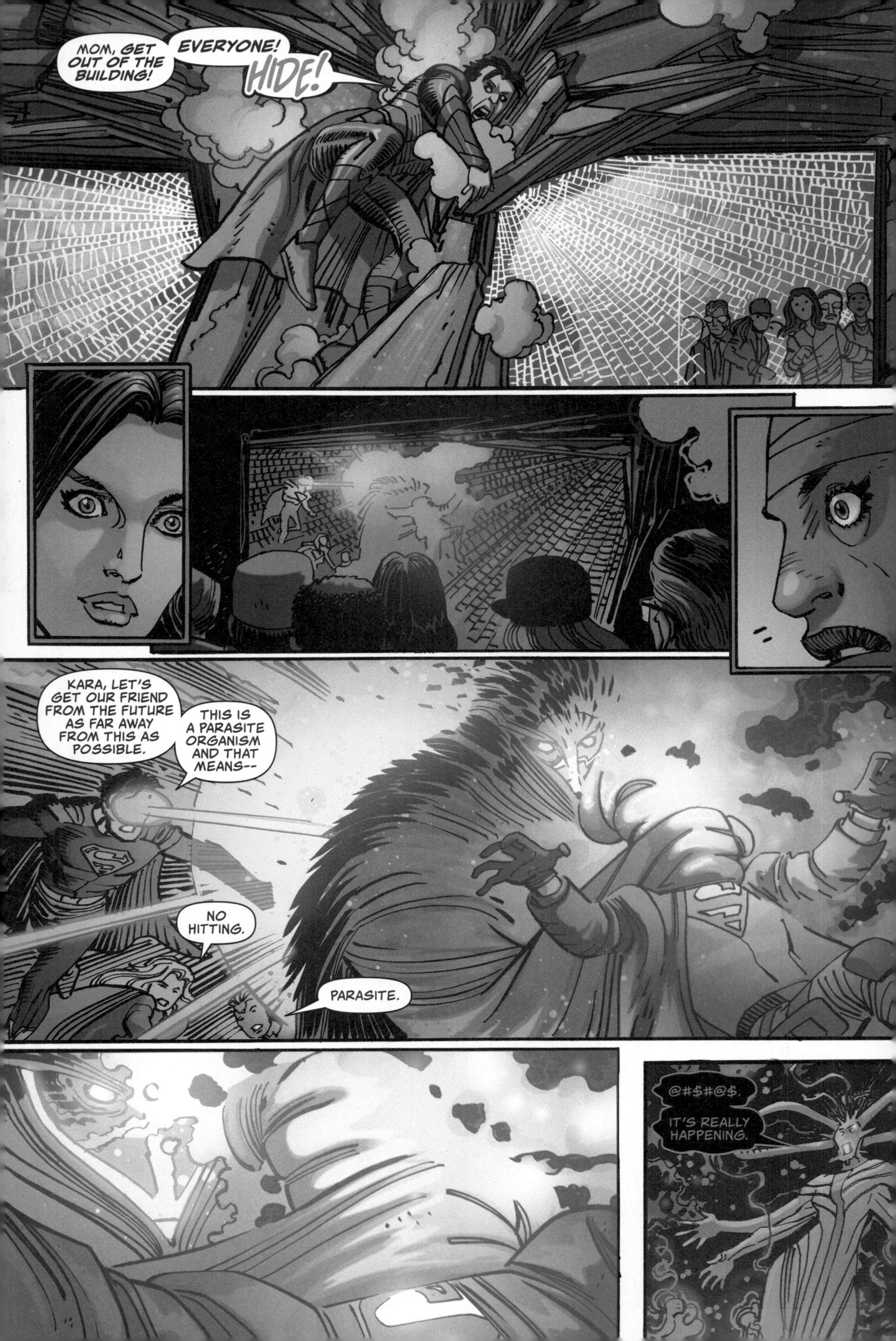
MOM, GET OUT OF THE BUILDING!
EVERYONE! HIDE!
KARA, LET'S GET OUR FRIEND FROM THE FUTURE AS FAR AWAY FROM THIS AS POSSIBLE.
THIS IS A PARASITE ORGANISM AND THAT MEANS--
NO HITTING.
PARASITE.
@#$#@$.
IT'S REALLY HAPPENING.

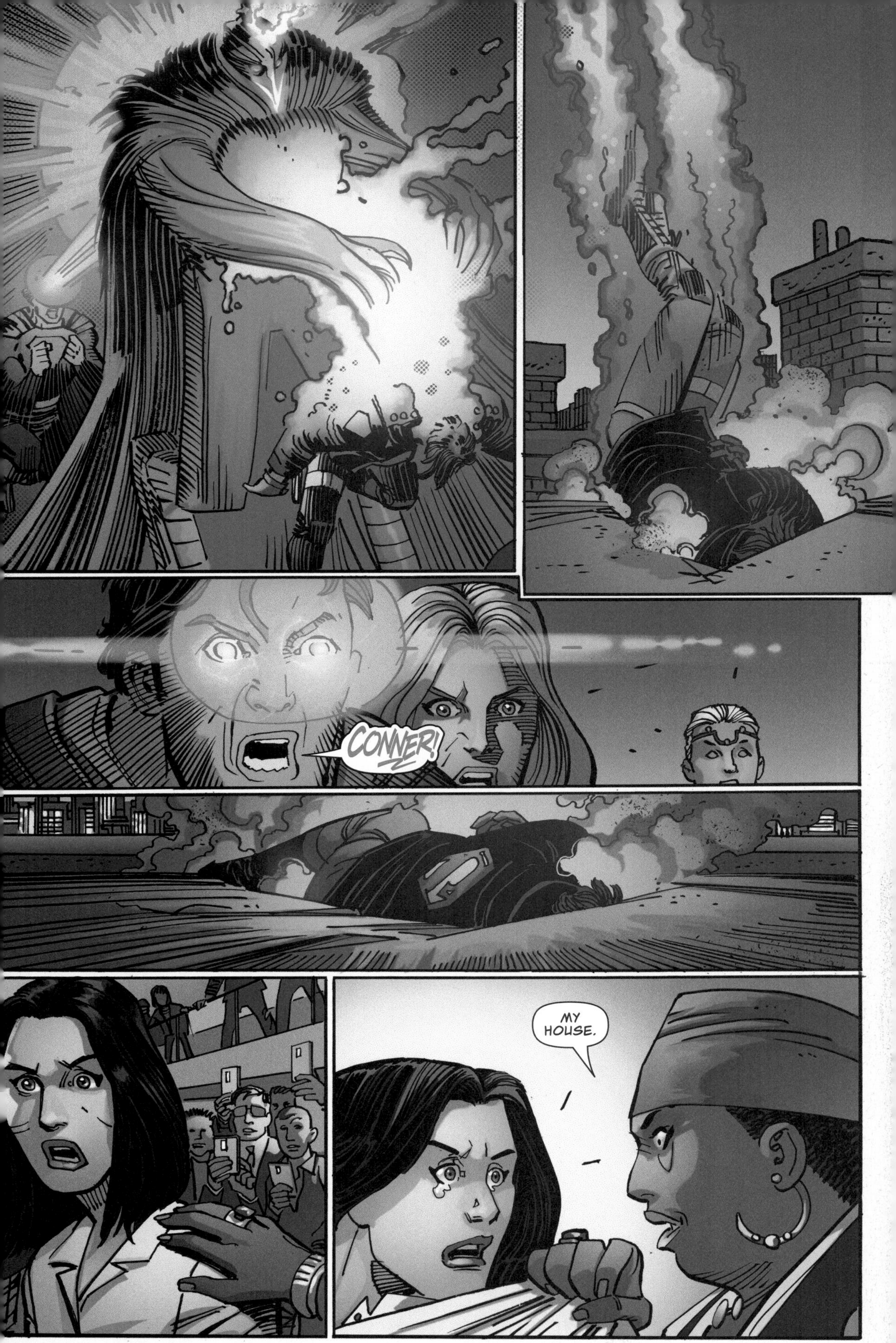
CONNER!
MY HOUSE.

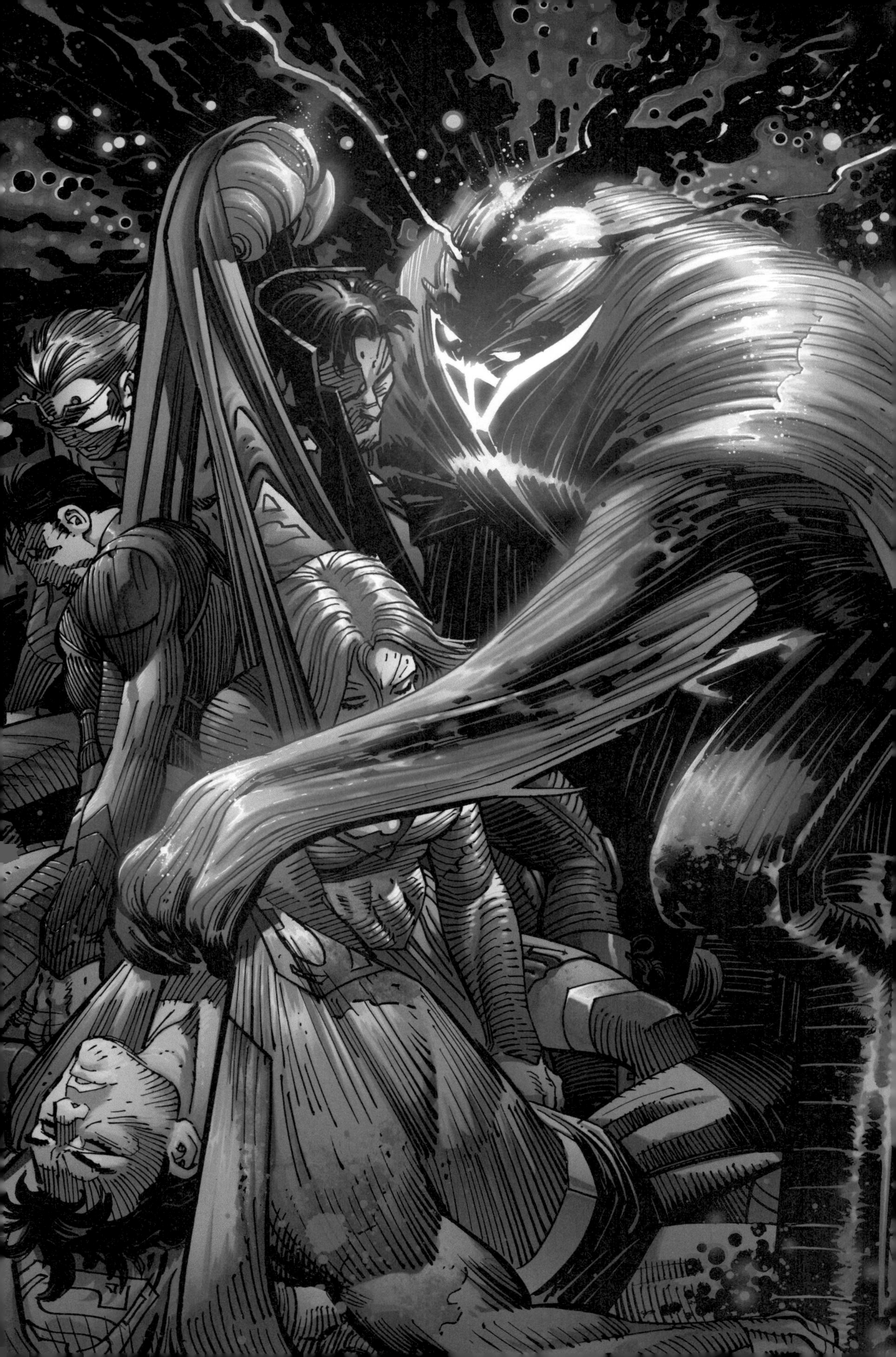

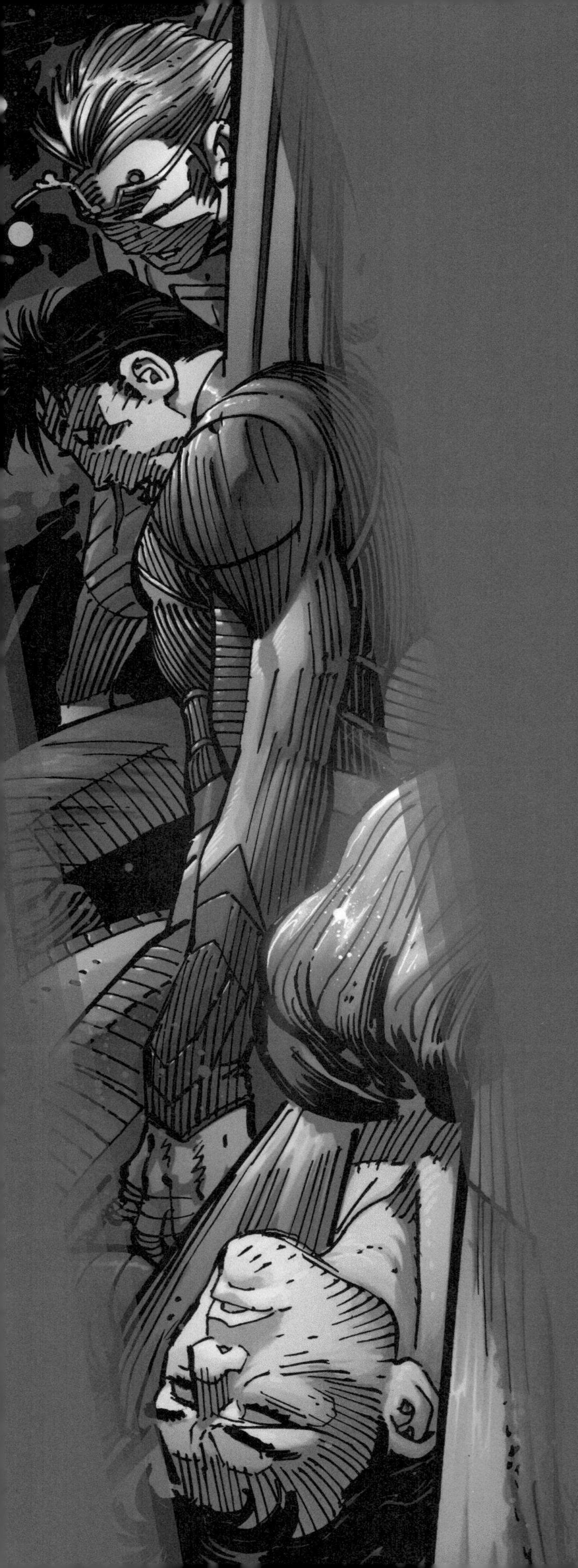

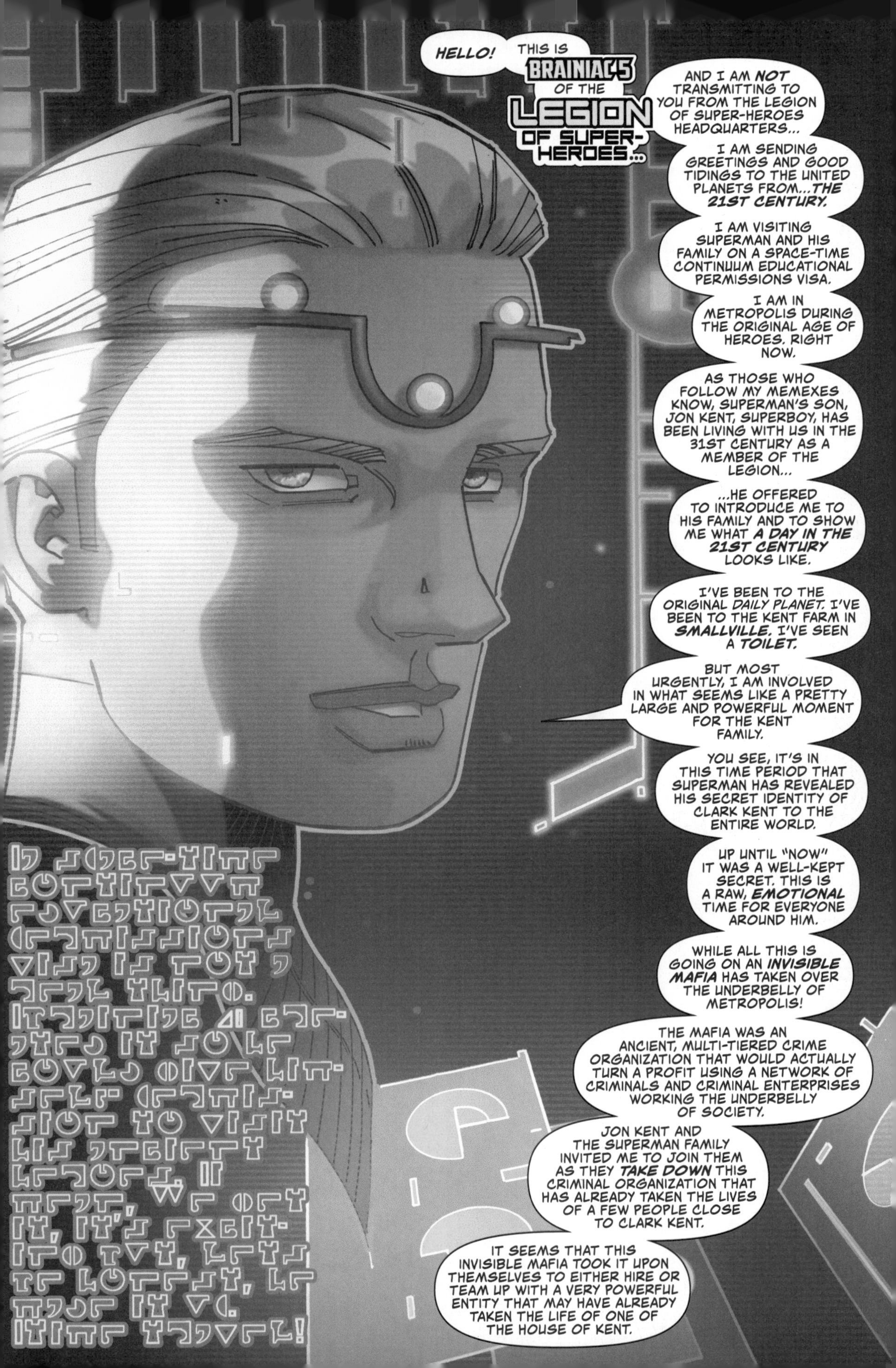
HELLO!
THIS IS BRAINIAC 5 OF THE LEGION OF SUPER-HEROES...
AND I AM NOT TRANSMITTING TO YOU FROM THE LEGION OF SUPER-HEROES HEADQUARTERS...
I AM SENDING GREETINGS AND GOOD TIDINGS TO THE UNITED PLANETS FROM...THE 21ST CENTURY.
I AM VISITING SUPERMAN AND HIS FAMILY ON A SPACE-TIME CONTINUUM EDUCATIONAL PERMISSIONS VISA.
I AM IN METROPOLIS DURING THE ORIGINAL AGE OF HEROES. RIGHT NOW.
AS THOSE WHO FOLLOW MY MEMEXES KNOW, SUPERMAN'S SON, JON KENT, SUPERBOY, HAS BEEN LIVING WITH US IN THE 31ST CENTURY AS A MEMBER OF THE LEGION...
...HE OFFERED TO INTRODUCE ME TO HIS FAMILY AND TO SHOW ME WHAT A DAY IN THE 21ST CENTURY LOOKS LIKE.
I'VE BEEN TO THE ORIGINAL DAILY PLANET. I'VE BEEN TO THE KENT FARM IN SMALLVILLE. I'VE SEEN A TOILET.
BUT MOST URGENTLY, I AM INVOLVED IN WHAT SEEMS LIKE A PRETTY LARGE AND POWERFUL MOMENT FOR THE KENT FAMILY.
YOU SEE, IT'S IN THIS TIME PERIOD THAT SUPERMAN HAS REVEALED HIS SECRET IDENTITY OF CLARK KENT TO THE ENTIRE WORLD.
UP UNTIL "NOW" IT WAS A WELL-KEPT SECRET. THIS IS A RAW, EMOTIONAL TIME FOR EVERYONE AROUND HIM.
WHILE ALL THIS IS GOING ON AN INVISIBLE MAFIA HAS TAKEN OVER THE UNDERBELLY OF METROPOLIS!
THE MAFIA WAS AN ANCIENT, MULTI-TIERED CRIME ORGANIZATION THAT WOULD ACTUALLY TURN A PROFIT USING A NETWORK OF CRIMINALS AND CRIMINAL ENTERPRISES WORKING THE UNDERBELLY OF SOCIETY.
JON KENT AND THE SUPERMAN FAMILY INVITED ME TO JOIN THEM AS THEY TAKE DOWN THIS CRIMINAL ORGANIZATION THAT HAS ALREADY TAKEN THE LIVES OF A FEW PEOPLE CLOSE TO CLARK KENT.
IT SEEMS THAT THIS INVISIBLE MAFIA TOOK IT UPON THEMSELVES TO EITHER HIRE OR TEAM UP WITH A VERY POWERFUL ENTITY THAT MAY HAVE ALREADY TAKEN THE LIFE OF ONE OF THE HOUSE OF KENT.

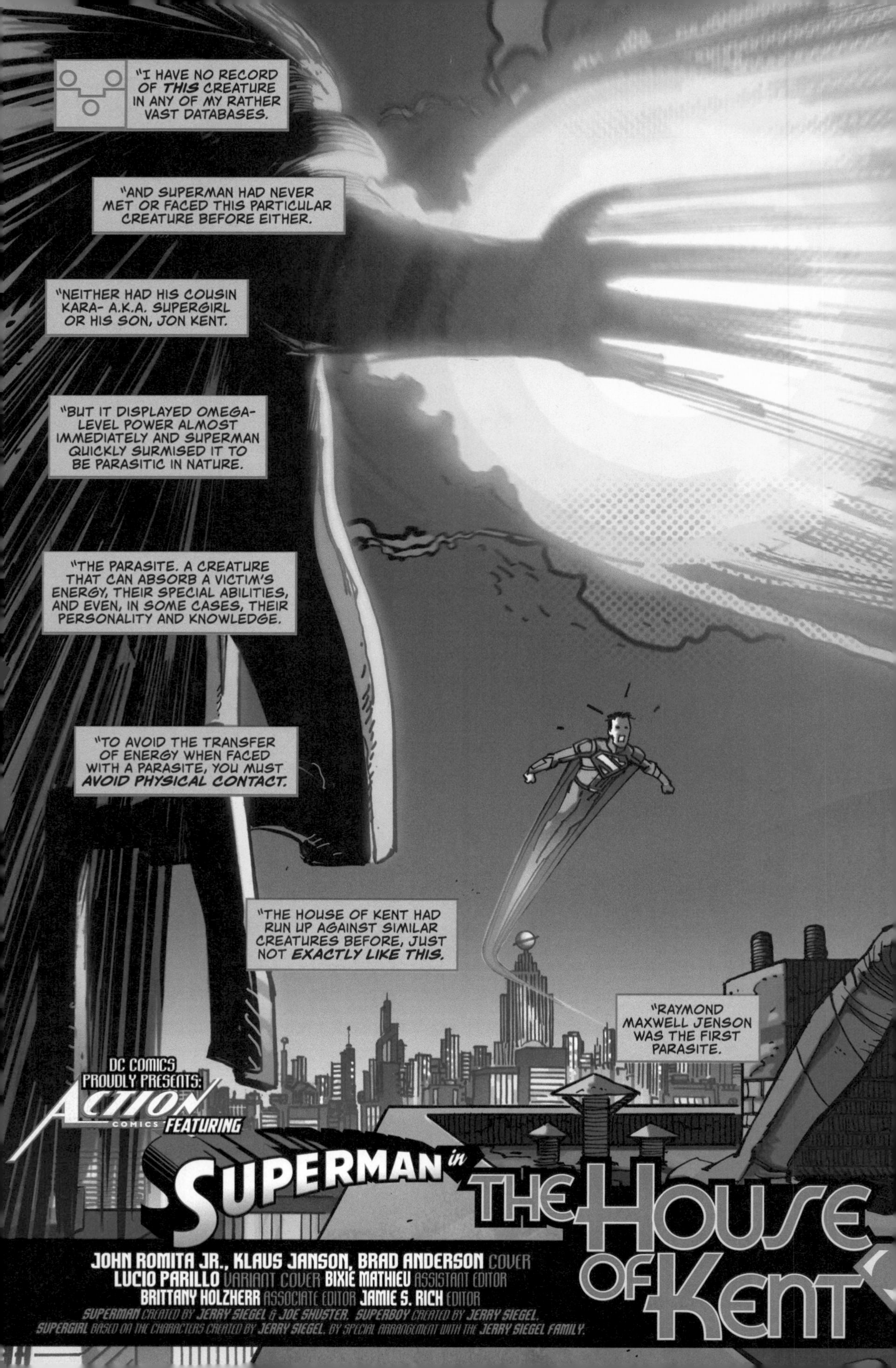
"I HAVE NO RECORD OF THIS CREATURE IN ANY OF MY RATHER VAST DATABASES.
"AND SUPERMAN HAD NEVER MET OR FACED THIS PARTICULAR CREATURE BEFORE EITHER.
"NEITHER HAD HIS COUSIN KARA- A.K.A. SUPERGIRL OR HIS SON, JON KENT.
"BUT IT DISPLAYED OMEGA-LEVEL POWER ALMOST IMMEDIATELY AND SUPERMAN QUICKLY SURMISED IT TO BE PARASITIC IN NATURE.
"THE PARASITE. A CREATURE THAT CAN ABSORB A VICTIM'S ENERGY, THEIR SPECIAL ABILITIES, AND EVEN, IN SOME CASES, THEIR PERSONALITY AND KNOWLEDGE.
"TO AVOID THE TRANSFER OF ENERGY WHEN FACED WITH A PARASITE, YOU MUST AVOID PHYSICAL CONTACT.
"THE HOUSE OF KENT HAD RUN UP AGAINST SIMILAR CREATURES BEFORE, JUST NOT EXACTLY LIKE THIS.
"RAYMOND MAXWELL JENSON WAS THE FIRST PARASITE.
DC COMICS PROUDLY PRESENTS:
ACTION COMICS FEATURING
SUPERMAN in
THE HOUSE OF KENT
JOHN ROMITA JR., KLAUS JANSON, BRAD ANDERSON COVER
LUCIO PARILLO VARIANT COVER BIXIE MATHIEU ASSISTANT EDITOR
BRITTANY HOLZHERR ASSOCIATE EDITOR JAMIE S. RICH EDITOR
SUPERMAN CREATED BY JERRY SIEGEL & JOE SHUSTER. SUPERBOY CREATED BY JERRY SIEGEL.
SUPERGIRL BASED ON THE CHARACTERS CREATED BY JERRY SIEGEL. BY SPECIAL ARRANGEMENT WITH THE JERRY SIEGEL FAMILY.

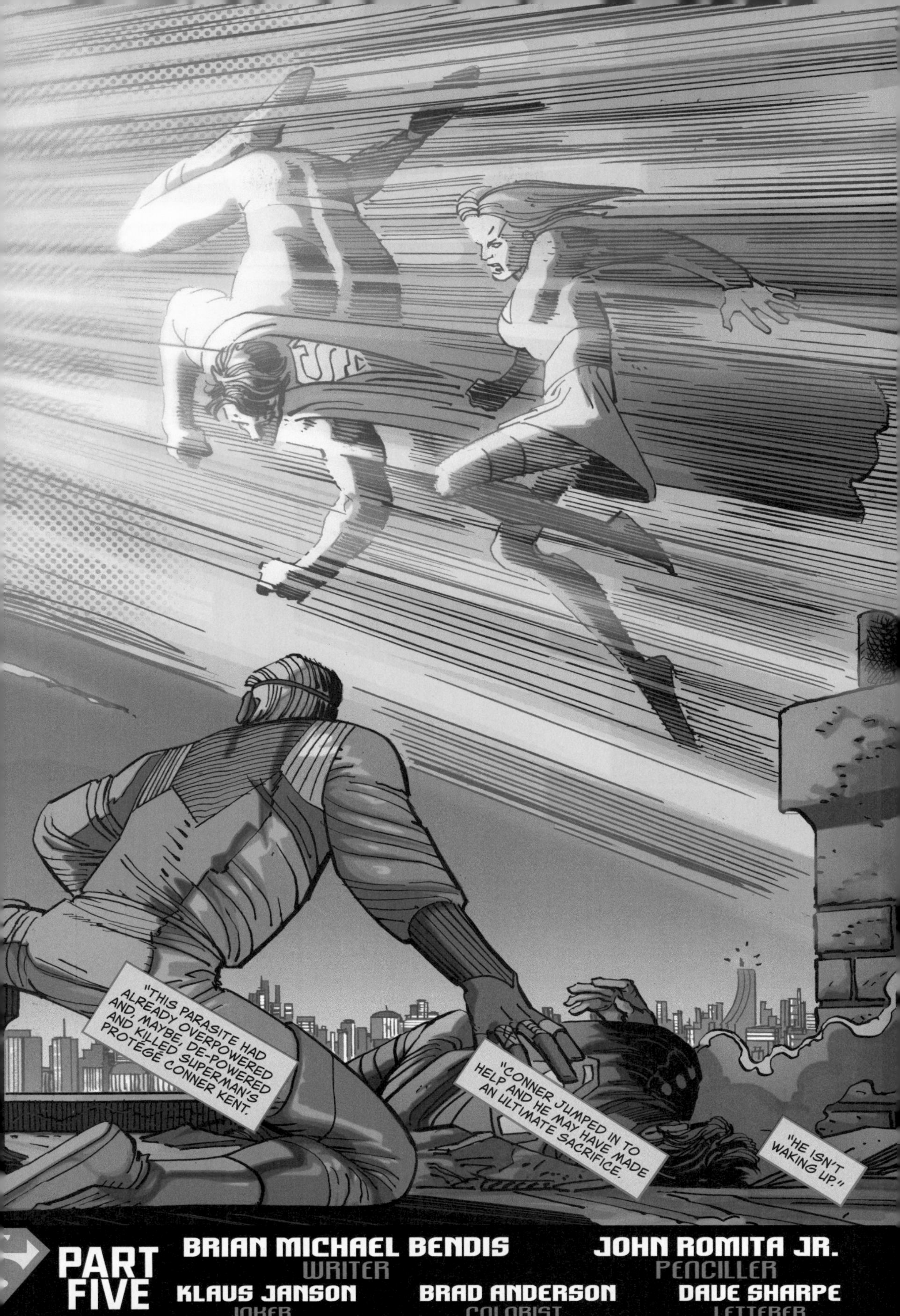
"THIS PARASITE HAD ALREADY OVERPOWERED AND, MAYBE, DE-POWERED AND KILLED SUPERMAN'S PROTÉGÉ CONNER KENT.
"CONNER JUMPED IN TO HELP AND HE MAY HAVE MADE AN ULTIMATE SACRIFICE.
"HE ISN'T WAKING UP."

**PART FIVE**

**BRIAN MICHAEL BENDIS** WRITER
**JOHN ROMITA JR.** PENCILLER
**KLAUS JANSON** INKER
**BRAD ANDERSON** COLORIST
**DAVE SHARPE** LETTERER

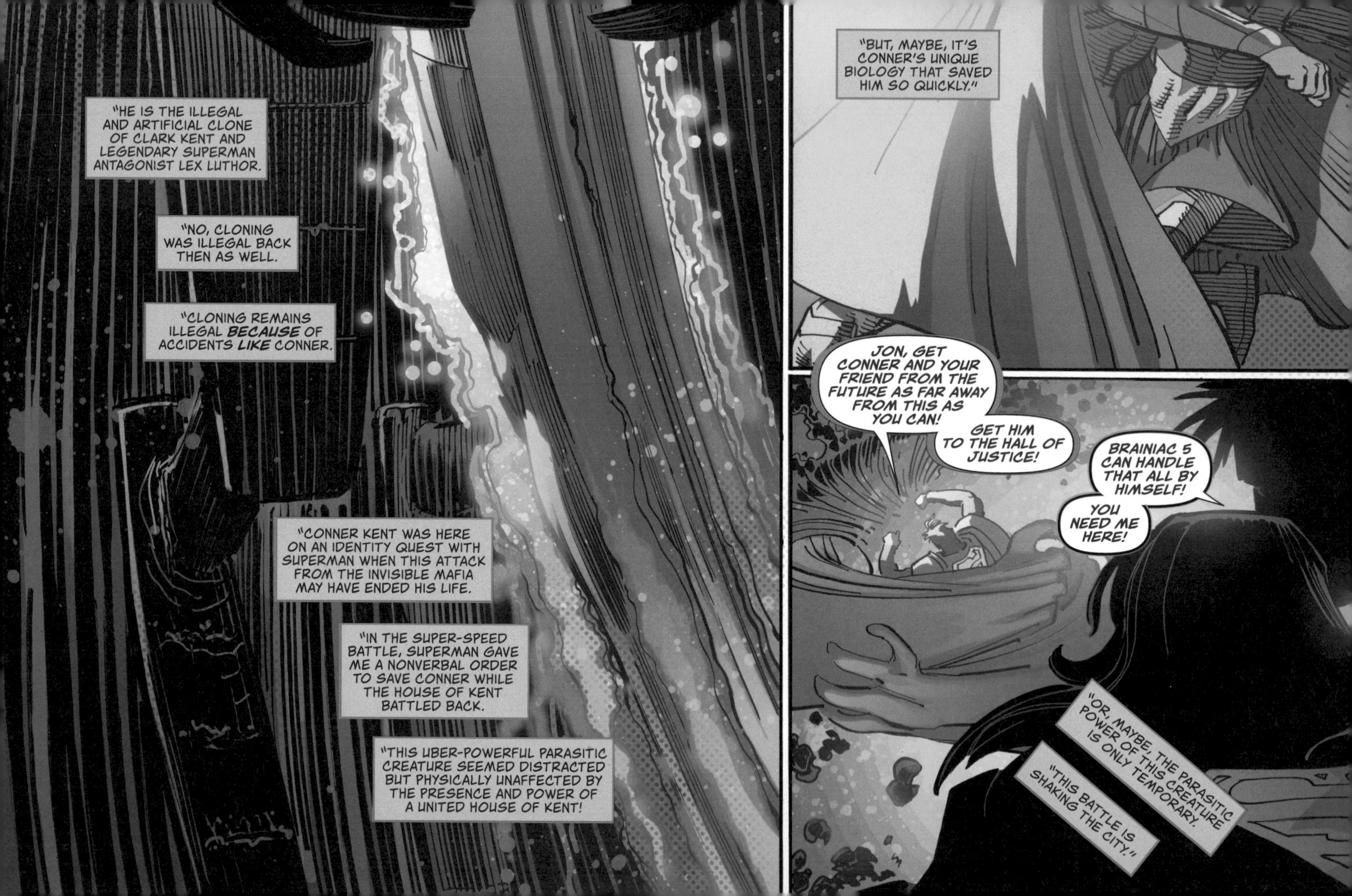
"HE IS THE ILLEGAL AND ARTIFICIAL CLONE OF CLARK KENT AND LEGENDARY SUPERMAN ANTAGONIST LEX LUTHOR.
"NO, CLONING WAS ILLEGAL BACK THEN AS WELL.
"CLONING REMAINS ILLEGAL *BECAUSE* OF ACCIDENTS *LIKE* CONNER.
"CONNER KENT WAS HERE ON AN IDENTITY QUEST WITH SUPERMAN WHEN THIS ATTACK FROM THE INVISIBLE MAFIA MAY HAVE ENDED HIS LIFE.
"IN THE SUPER-SPEED BATTLE, SUPERMAN GAVE ME A NONVERBAL ORDER TO SAVE CONNER WHILE THE HOUSE OF KENT BATTLED BACK.
"THIS UBER-POWERFUL PARASITIC CREATURE SEEMED DISTRACTED BUT PHYSICALLY UNAFFECTED BY THE PRESENCE AND POWER OF A UNITED HOUSE OF KENT!
"BUT, MAYBE, IT'S CONNER'S UNIQUE BIOLOGY THAT SAVED HIM SO QUICKLY."
JON, GET CONNER AND YOUR FRIEND FROM THE FUTURE AS FAR AWAY FROM THIS AS YOU CAN!
GET HIM TO THE HALL OF JUSTICE!
BRAINIAC 5 CAN HANDLE THAT ALL BY HIMSELF!
YOU NEED ME HERE!
"OR, MAYBE, THE PARASITIC POWER OF THIS CREATURE IS ONLY TEMPORARY.
"THIS BATTLE IS SHAKING THE CITY."

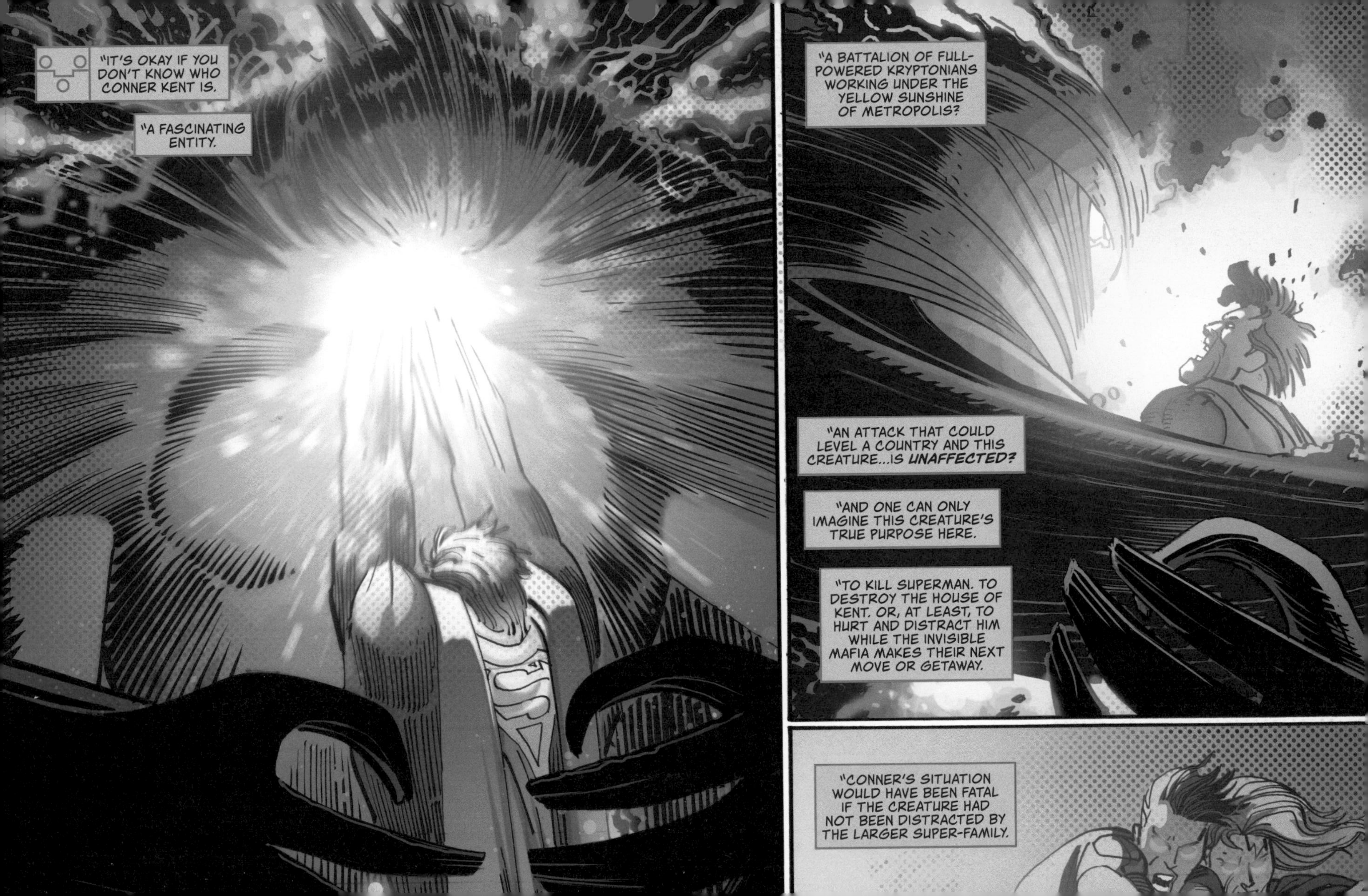
"IT'S OKAY IF YOU DON'T KNOW WHO CONNER KENT IS.
"A FASCINATING ENTITY.
"A BATTALION OF FULL-POWERED KRYPTONIANS WORKING UNDER THE YELLOW SUNSHINE OF METROPOLIS?
"AN ATTACK THAT COULD LEVEL A COUNTRY AND THIS CREATURE...IS *UNAFFECTED?*
"AND ONE CAN ONLY IMAGINE THIS CREATURE'S TRUE PURPOSE HERE.
"TO KILL SUPERMAN. TO DESTROY THE HOUSE OF KENT. OR, AT LEAST, TO HURT AND DISTRACT HIM WHILE THE INVISIBLE MAFIA MAKES THEIR NEXT MOVE OR GETAWAY.
"CONNER'S SITUATION WOULD HAVE BEEN FATAL IF THE CREATURE HAD NOT BEEN DISTRACTED BY THE LARGER SUPER-FAMILY.

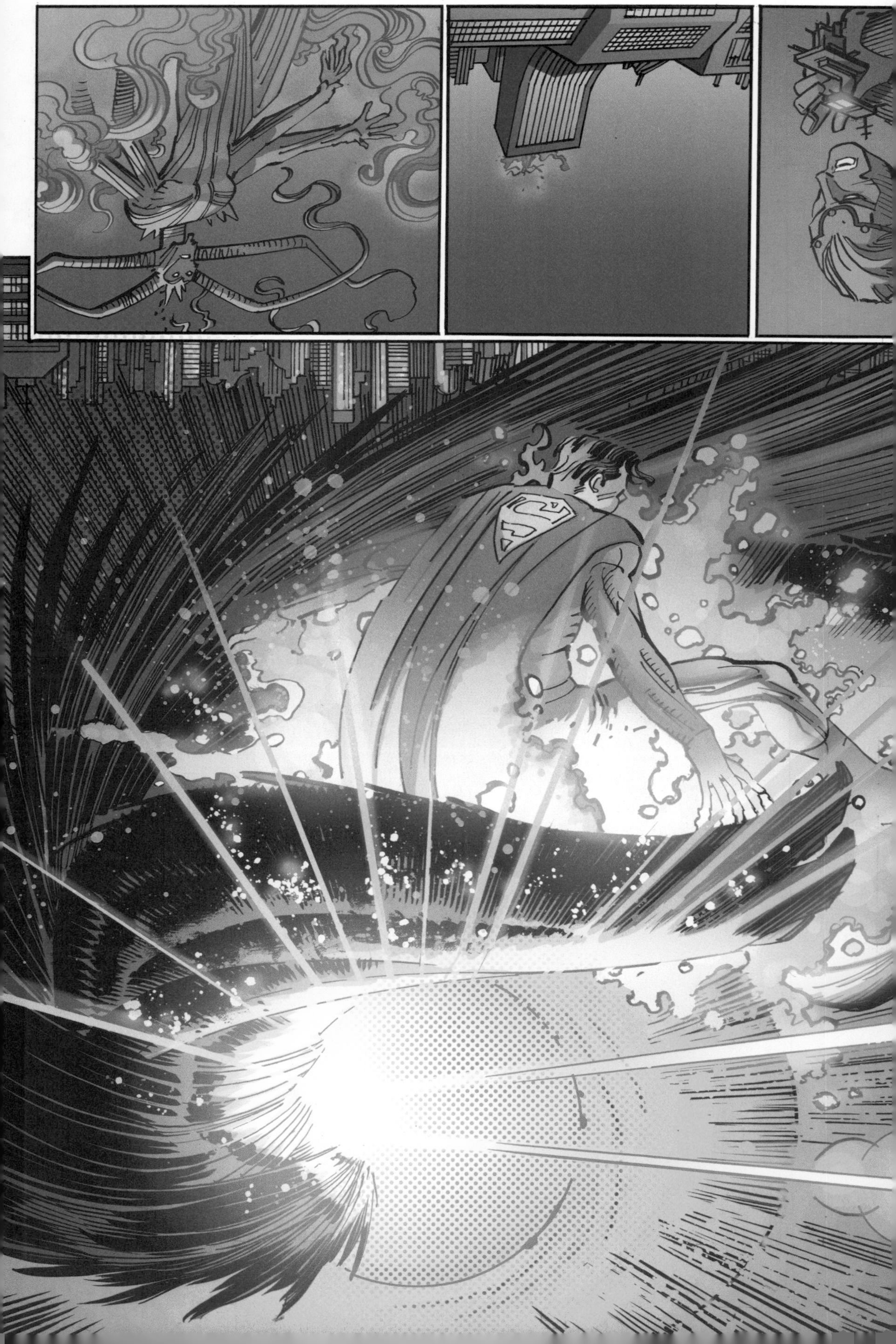

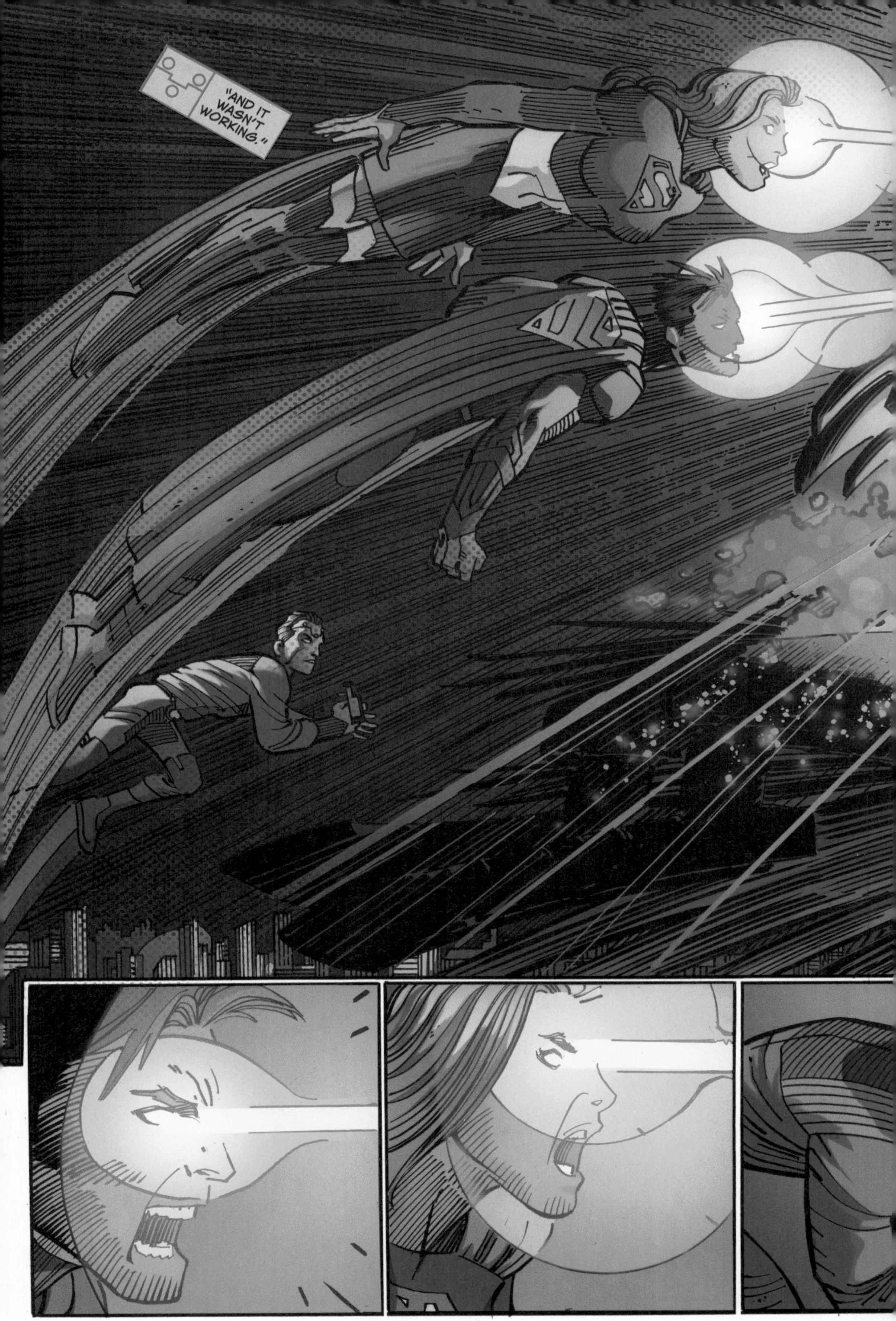
"AND IT WASN'T WORKING."

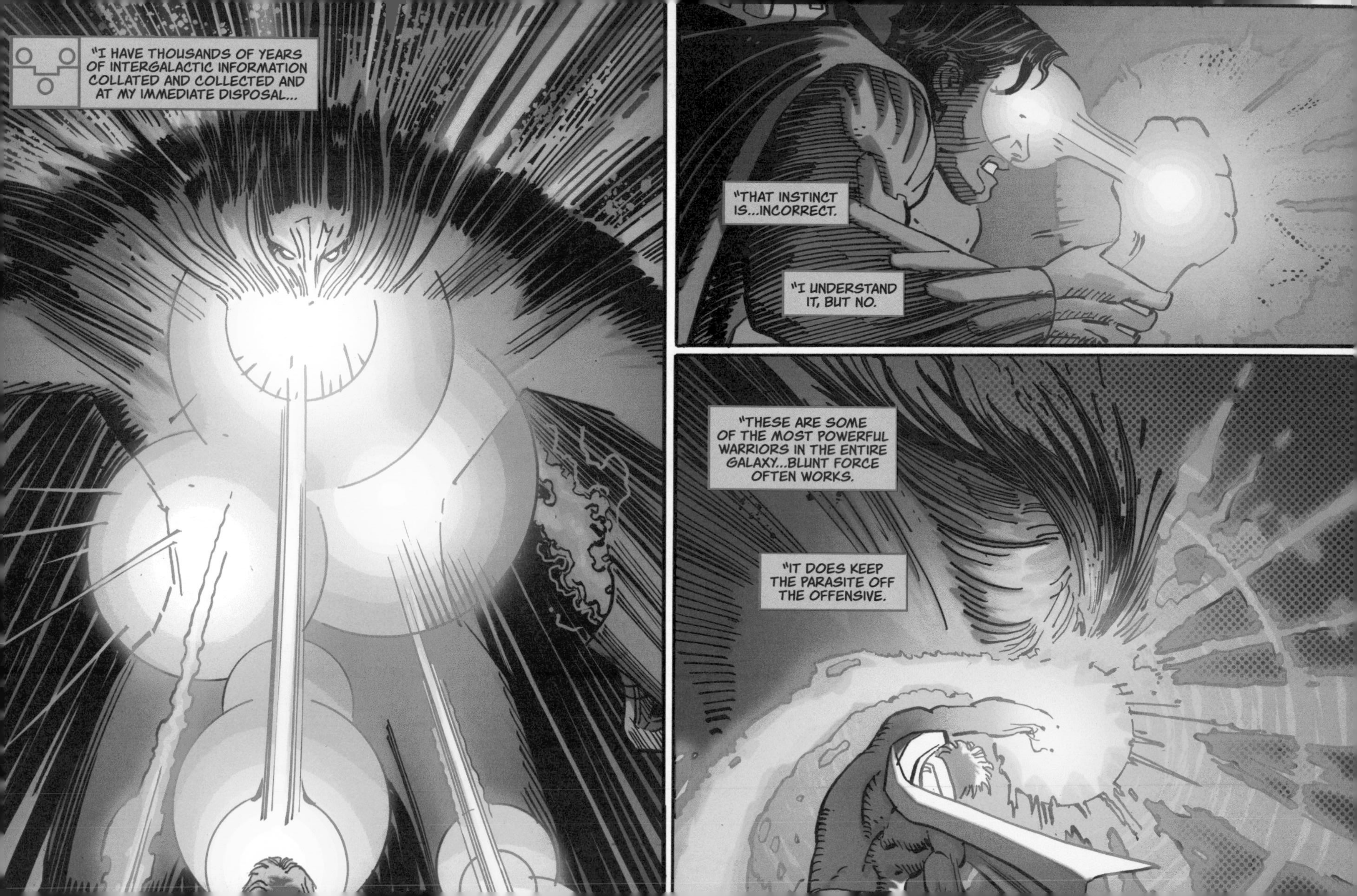
"I HAVE THOUSANDS OF YEARS OF INTERGALACTIC INFORMATION COLLATED AND COLLECTED AND AT MY IMMEDIATE DISPOSAL...
"THAT INSTINCT IS...INCORRECT.
"I UNDERSTAND IT, BUT NO.
"THESE ARE SOME OF THE MOST POWERFUL WARRIORS IN THE ENTIRE GALAXY...BLUNT FORCE OFTEN WORKS.
"IT DOES KEEP THE PARASITE OFF THE OFFENSIVE.

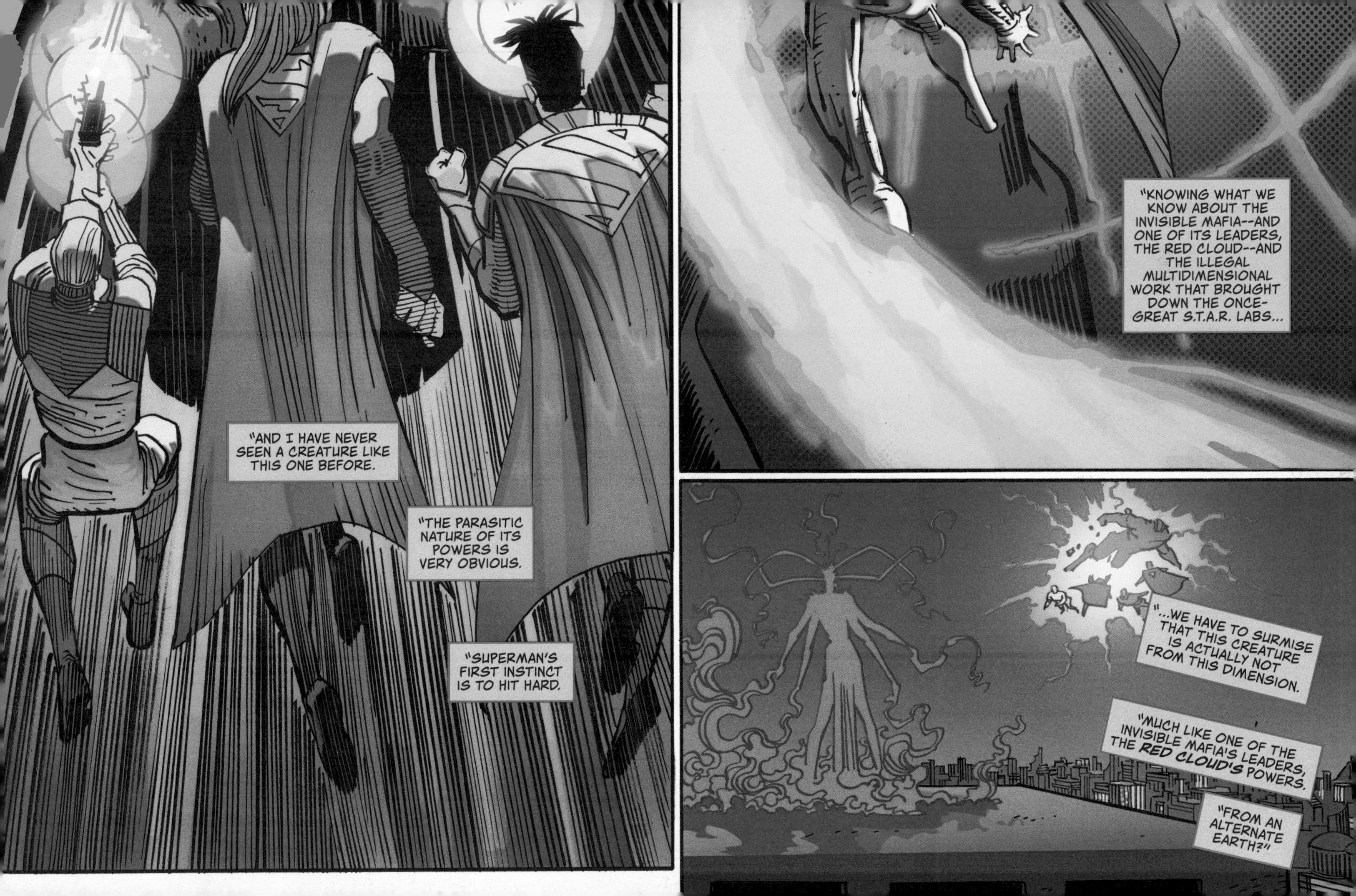
"AND I HAVE NEVER SEEN A CREATURE LIKE THIS ONE BEFORE.
"THE PARASITIC NATURE OF ITS POWERS IS VERY OBVIOUS.
"SUPERMAN'S FIRST INSTINCT IS TO HIT HARD.
"KNOWING WHAT WE KNOW ABOUT THE INVISIBLE MAFIA--AND ONE OF ITS LEADERS, THE RED CLOUD--AND THE ILLEGAL MULTIDIMENSIONAL WORK THAT BROUGHT DOWN THE ONCE-GREAT S.T.A.R. LABS...
"...WE HAVE TO SURMISE THAT THIS CREATURE IS ACTUALLY NOT FROM THIS DIMENSION.
"MUCH LIKE ONE OF THE INVISIBLE MAFIA'S LEADERS, THE RED CLOUD'S POWERS.
"FROM AN ALTERNATE EARTH?"

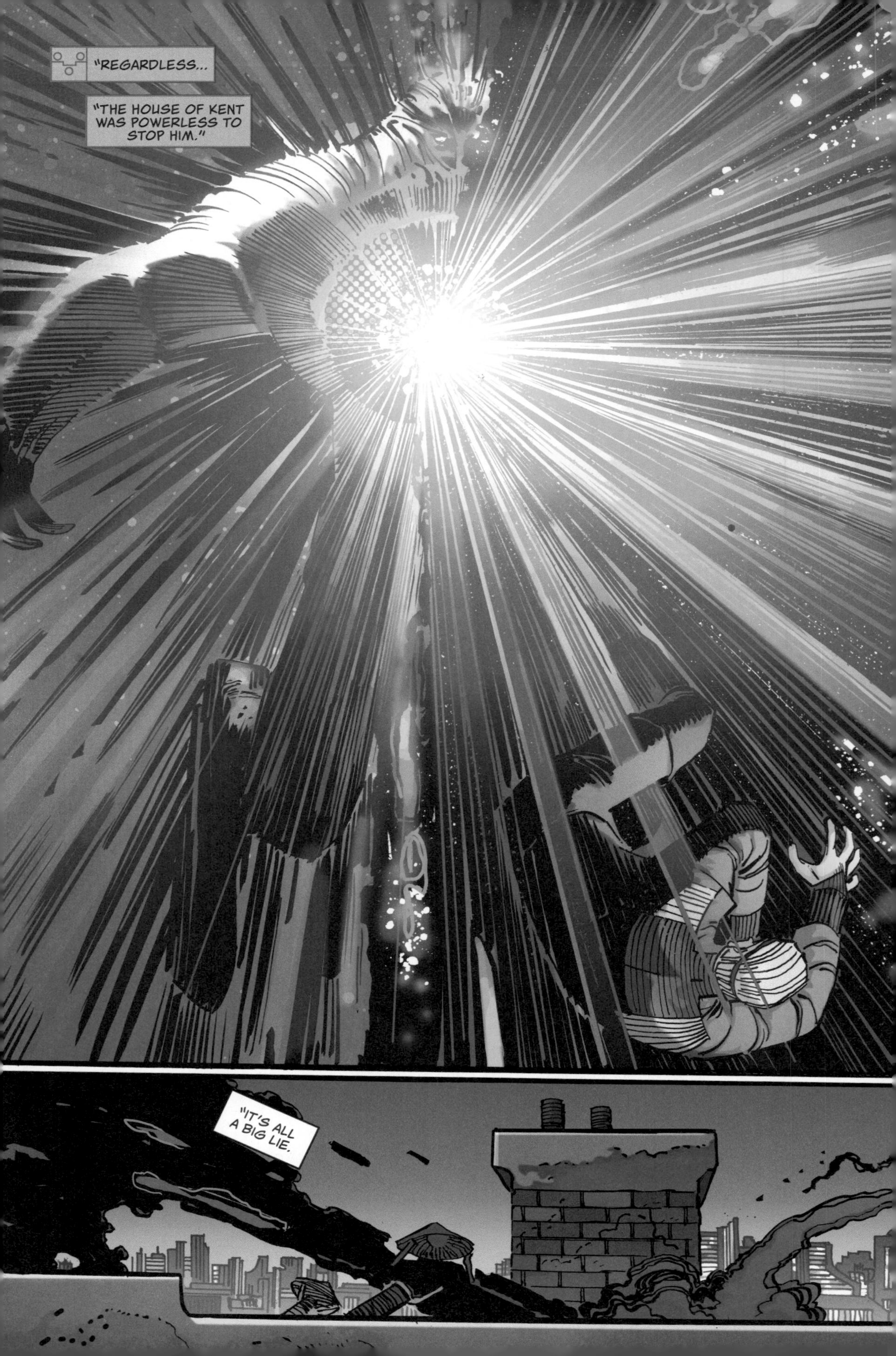
"REGARDLESS...
"THE HOUSE OF KENT WAS POWERLESS TO STOP HIM."
"IT'S ALL A BIG LIE.

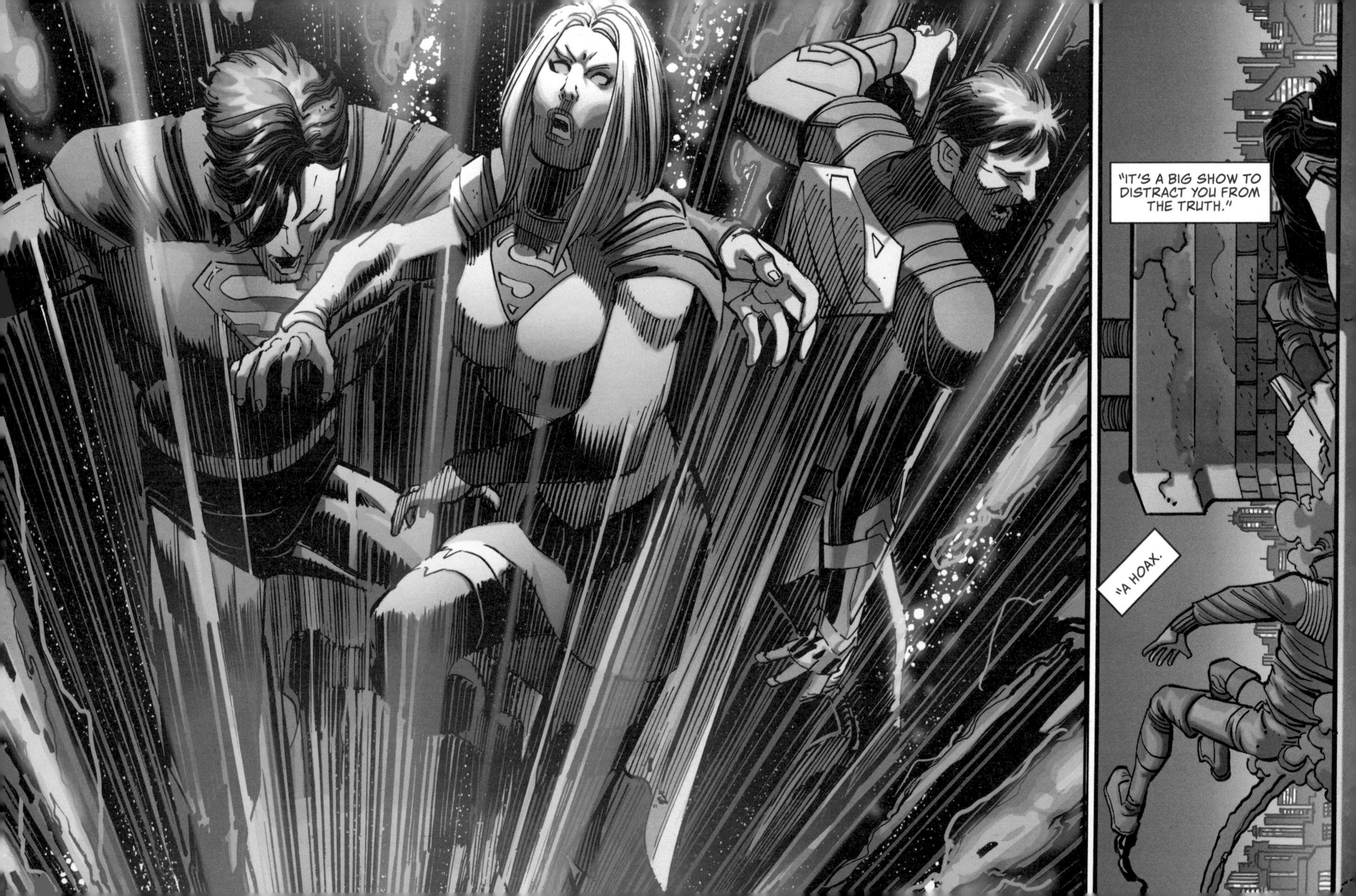
"A HOAX.
"IT'S A BIG SHOW TO DISTRACT YOU FROM THE TRUTH."

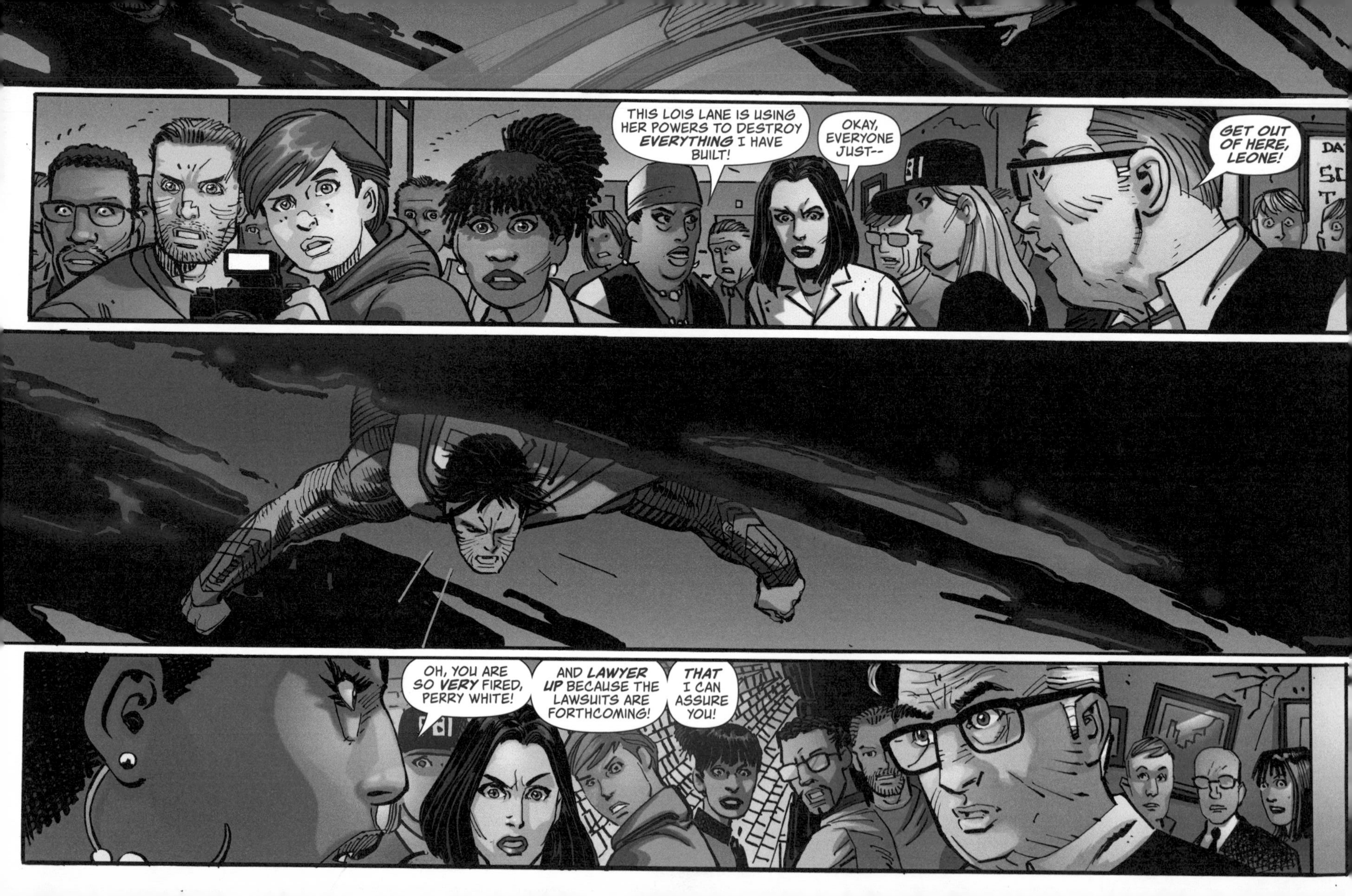
THIS LOIS LANE IS USING HER POWERS TO DESTROY EVERYTHING I HAVE BUILT!
OKAY, EVERYONE JUST--
GET OUT OF HERE, LEONE!
OH, YOU ARE SO VERY FIRED, PERRY WHITE!
AND LAWYER UP BECAUSE THE LAWSUITS ARE FORTHCOMING!
THAT I CAN ASSURE YOU!

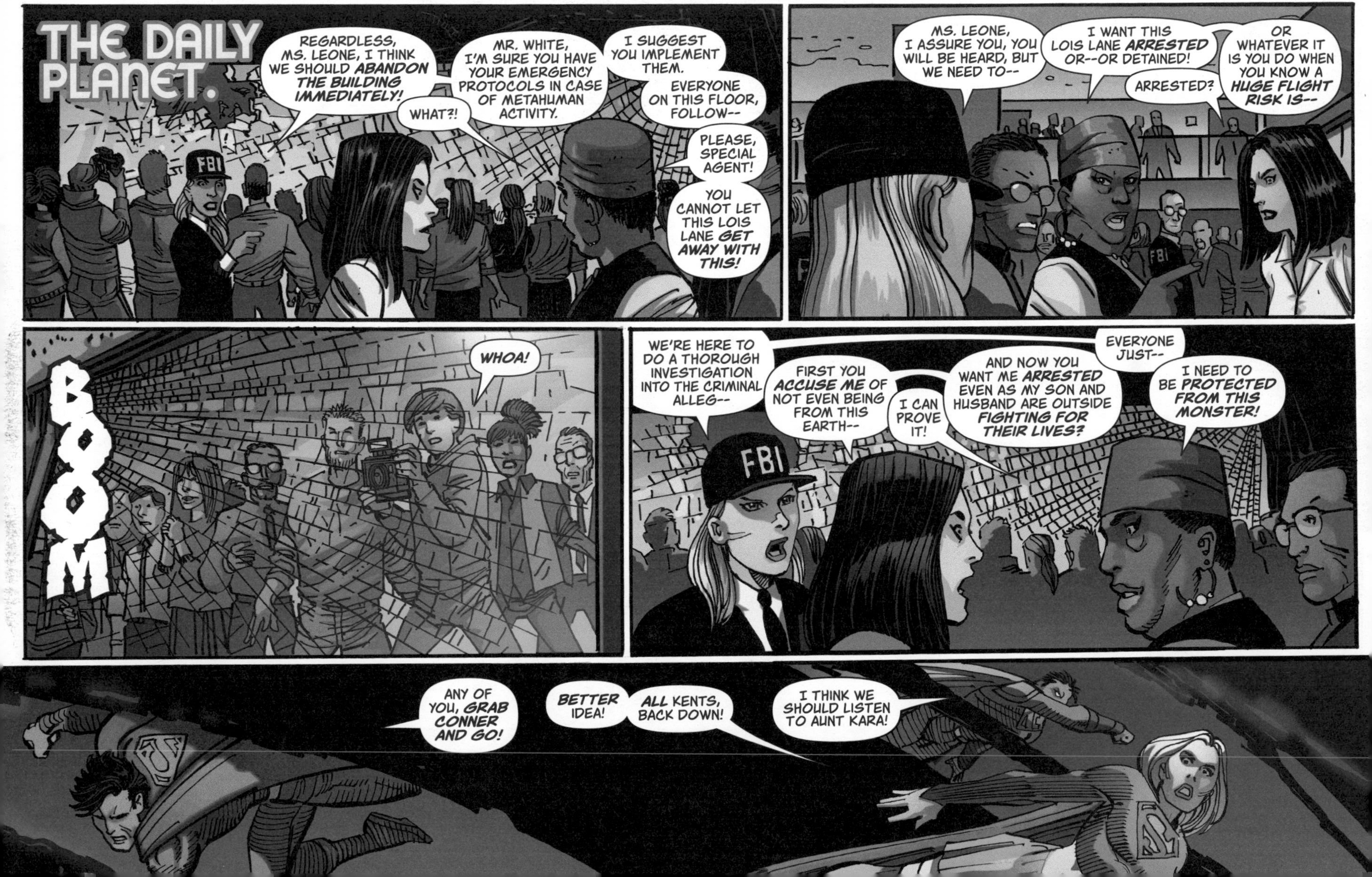
THE DAILY PLANET.
REGARDLESS, MS. LEONE, I THINK WE SHOULD ABANDON THE BUILDING IMMEDIATELY!
WHAT?!
MR. WHITE, I'M SURE YOU HAVE YOUR EMERGENCY PROTOCOLS IN CASE OF METAHUMAN ACTIVITY.
I SUGGEST YOU IMPLEMENT THEM.
EVERYONE ON THIS FLOOR, FOLLOW--
PLEASE, SPECIAL AGENT!
YOU CANNOT LET THIS LOIS LANE GET AWAY WITH THIS!
MS. LEONE, I ASSURE YOU, YOU WILL BE HEARD, BUT WE NEED TO--
I WANT THIS LOIS LANE ARRESTED OR--OR DETAINED!
OR WHATEVER IT IS YOU DO WHEN YOU KNOW A HUGE FLIGHT RISK IS--
ARRESTED?
BOOM
WHOA!
WE'RE HERE TO DO A THOROUGH INVESTIGATION INTO THE CRIMINAL ALLEG--
FIRST YOU ACCUSE ME OF NOT EVEN BEING FROM THIS EARTH--
I CAN PROVE IT!
AND NOW YOU WANT ME ARRESTED EVEN AS MY SON AND HUSBAND ARE OUTSIDE FIGHTING FOR THEIR LIVES?
EVERYONE JUST--
I NEED TO BE PROTECTED FROM THIS MONSTER!
ANY OF YOU, GRAB CONNER AND GO!
BETTER IDEA!
ALL KENTS, BACK DOWN!
I THINK WE SHOULD LISTEN TO AUNT KARA!

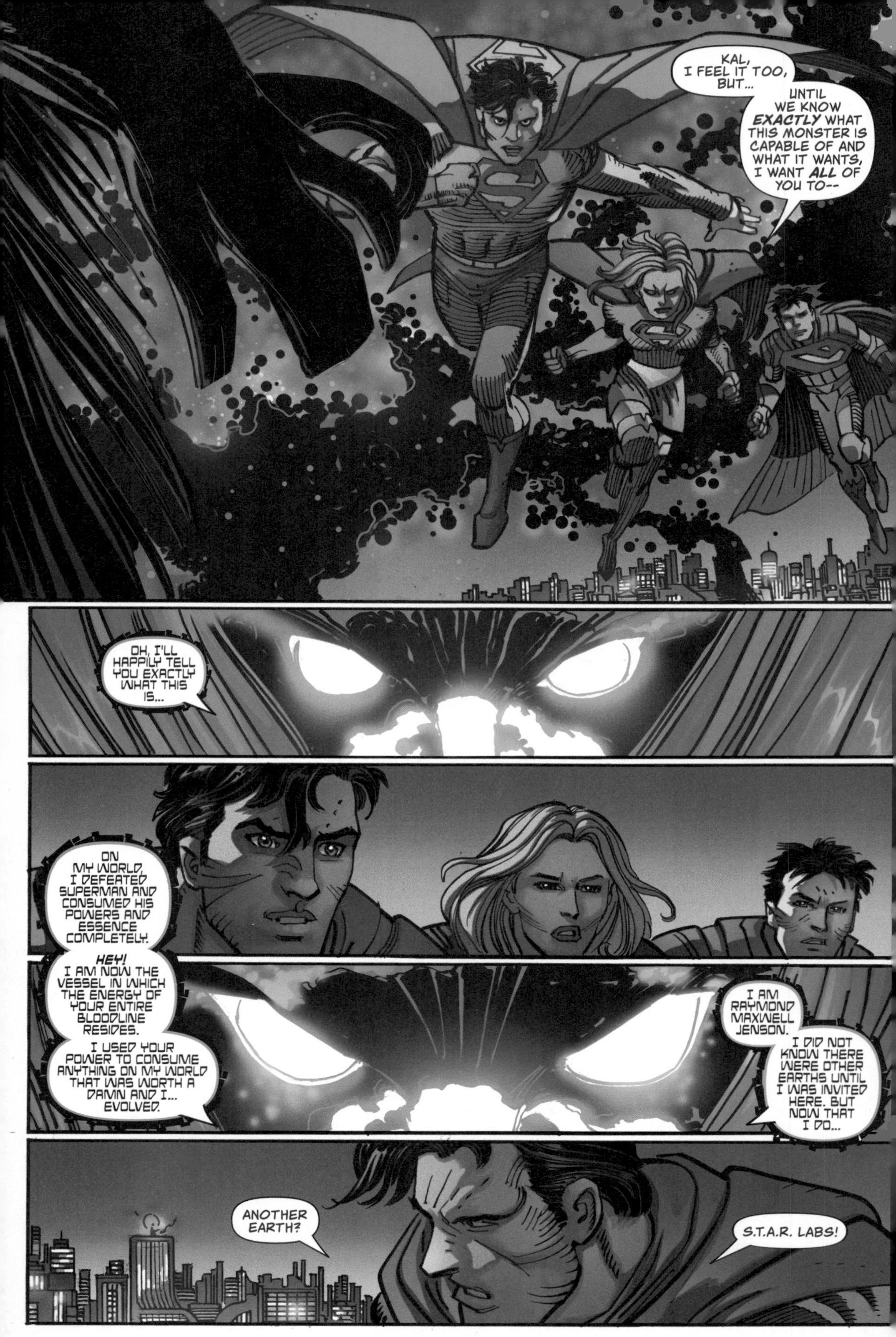
KAL, I FEEL IT TOO, BUT...
UNTIL WE KNOW EXACTLY WHAT THIS MONSTER IS CAPABLE OF AND WHAT IT WANTS, I WANT ALL OF YOU TO--
OH, I'LL HAPPILY TELL YOU EXACTLY WHAT THIS IS...
ON MY WORLD, I DEFEATED SUPERMAN AND CONSUMED HIS POWERS AND ESSENCE COMPLETELY.
HEY! I AM NOW THE VESSEL IN WHICH THE ENERGY OF YOUR ENTIRE BLOODLINE RESIDES.
I USED YOUR POWER TO CONSUME ANYTHING ON MY WORLD THAT WAS WORTH A DAMN AND I... EVOLVED.
I AM RAYMOND MAXWELL JENSON.
I DID NOT KNOW THERE WERE OTHER EARTHS UNTIL I WAS INVITED HERE. BUT NOW THAT I DO...
ANOTHER EARTH?
S.T.A.R. LABS!

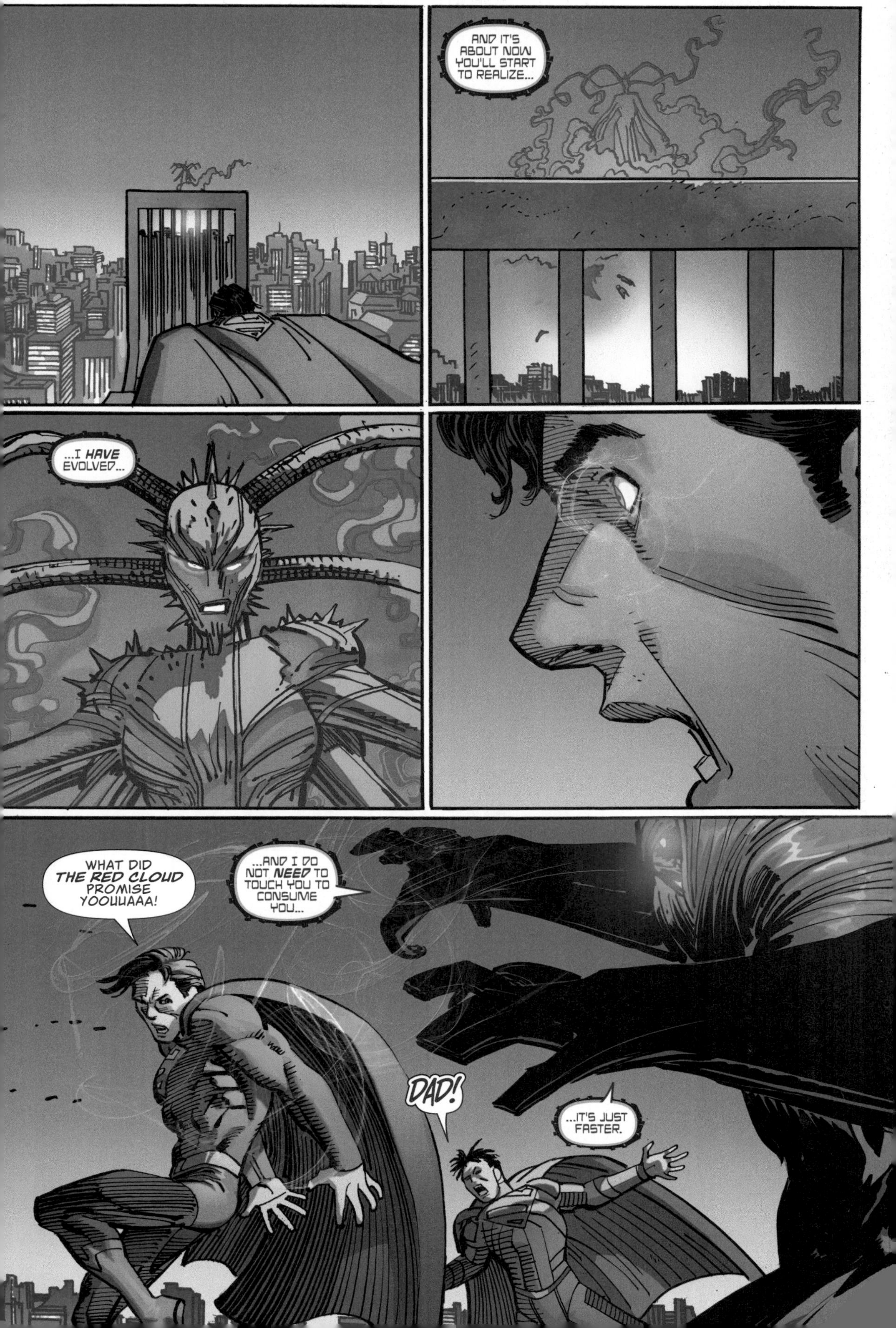
AND IT'S ABOUT NOW YOU'LL START TO REALIZE...
...I HAVE EVOLVED...
WHAT DID THE RED CLOUD PROMISE YOOUUAAA!
...AND I DO NOT NEED TO TOUCH YOU TO CONSUME YOU...
DAD!
...IT'S JUST FASTER.

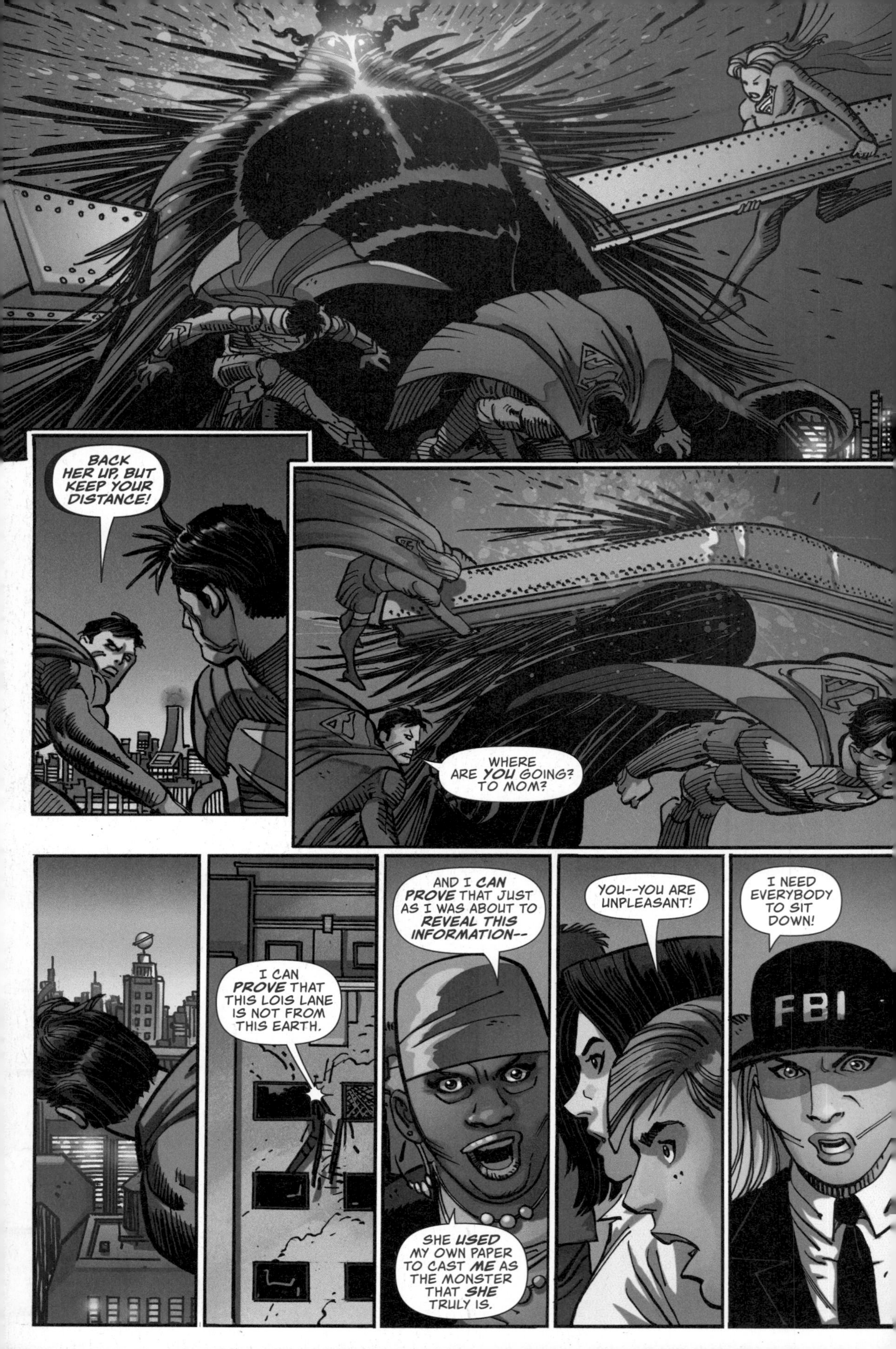
BACK HER UP, BUT KEEP YOUR DISTANCE!
WHERE ARE YOU GOING? TO MOM?
I CAN PROVE THAT THIS LOIS LANE IS NOT FROM THIS EARTH.
AND I CAN PROVE THAT JUST AS I WAS ABOUT TO REVEAL THIS INFORMATION--
SHE USED MY OWN PAPER TO CAST ME AS THE MONSTER THAT SHE TRULY IS.
YOU--YOU ARE UNPLEASANT!
I NEED EVERYBODY TO SIT DOWN!
FBI

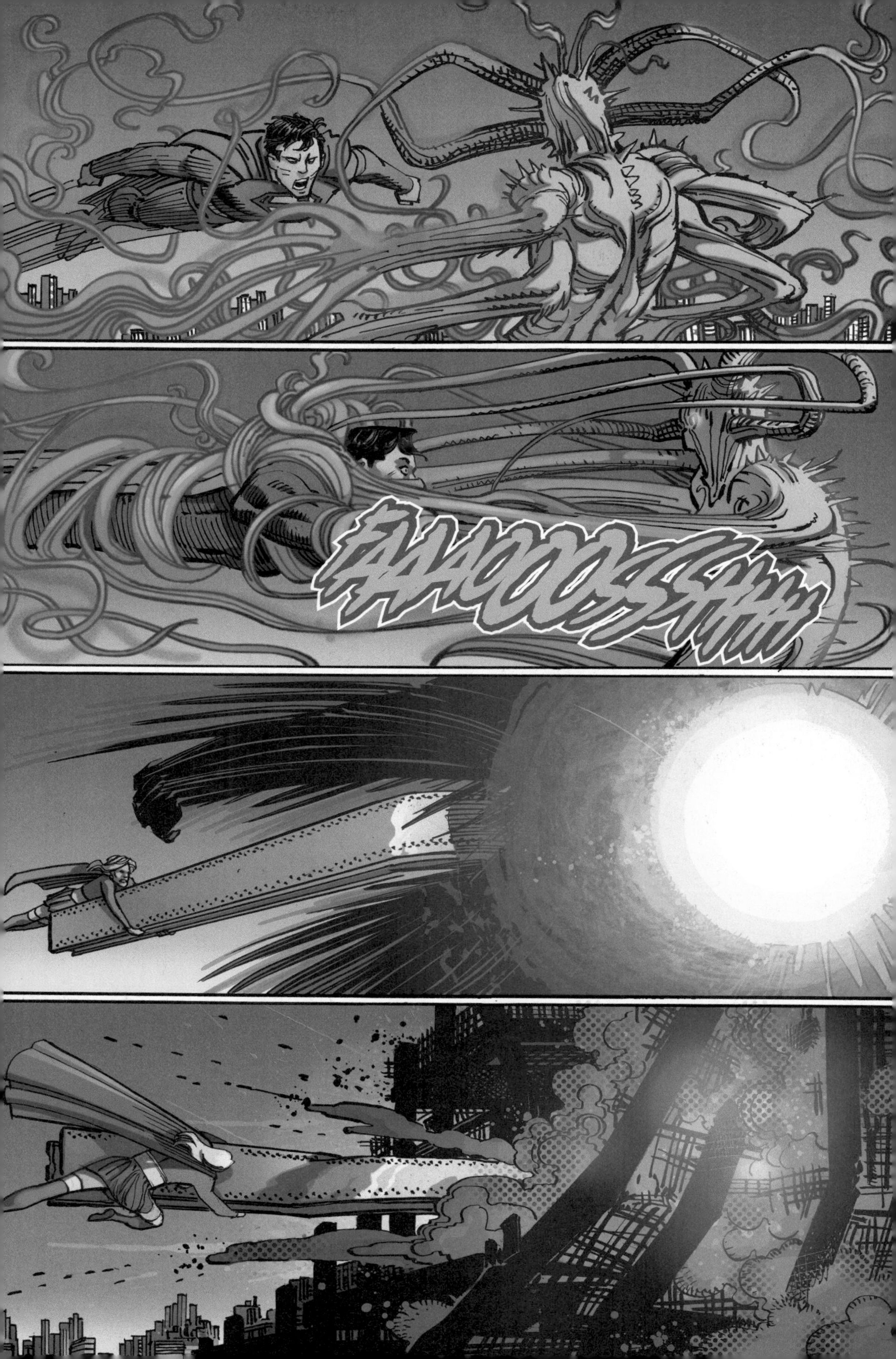
FAAOOOSHHH

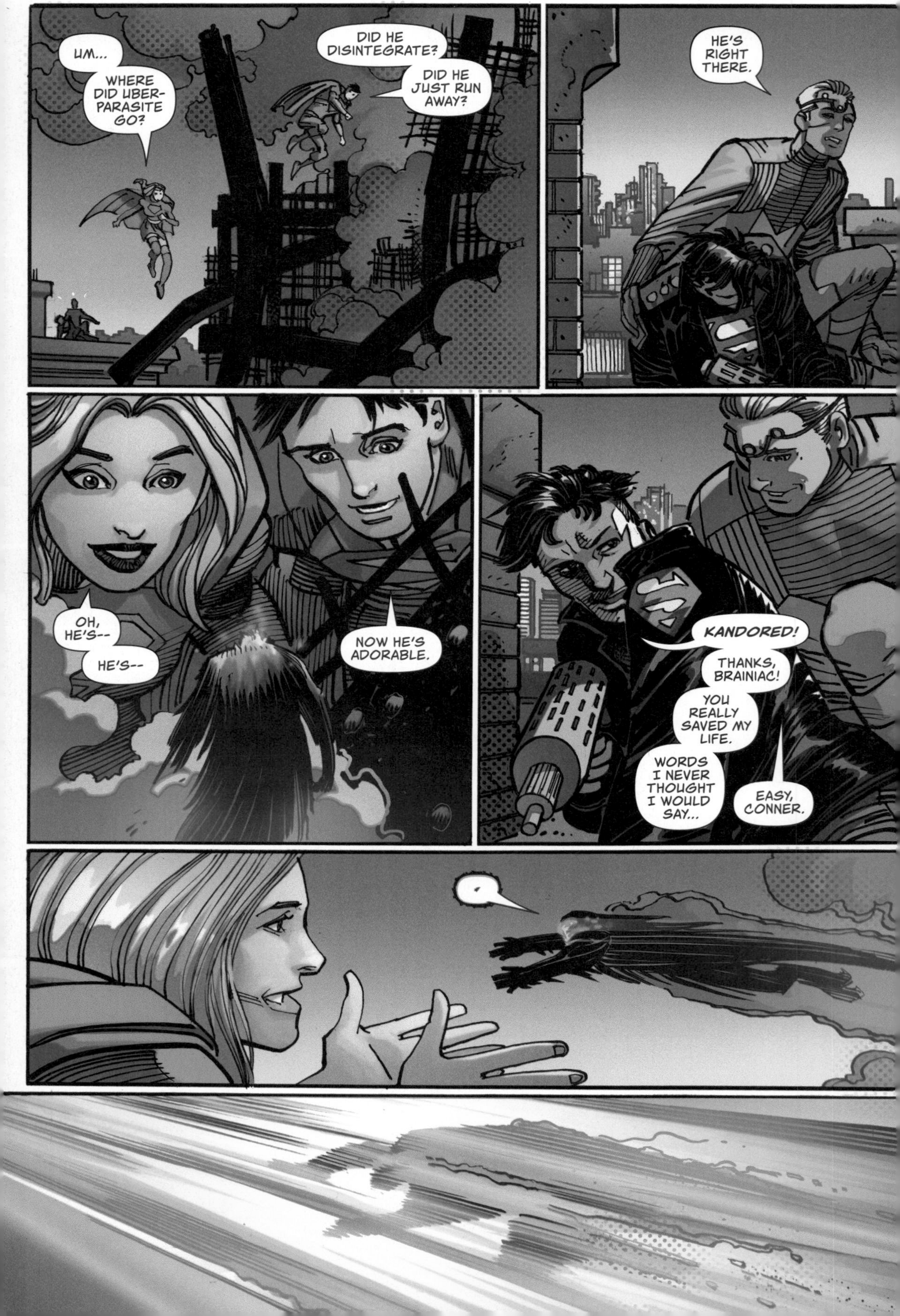
UM...
WHERE DID UBER-PARASITE GO?
DID HE DISINTEGRATE?
DID HE JUST RUN AWAY?
HE'S RIGHT THERE.
OH, HE'S--
HE'S--
NOW HE'S ADORABLE.
KANDORED!
THANKS, BRAINIAC!
YOU REALLY SAVED MY LIFE.
WORDS I NEVER THOUGHT I WOULD SAY...
EASY, CONNER.

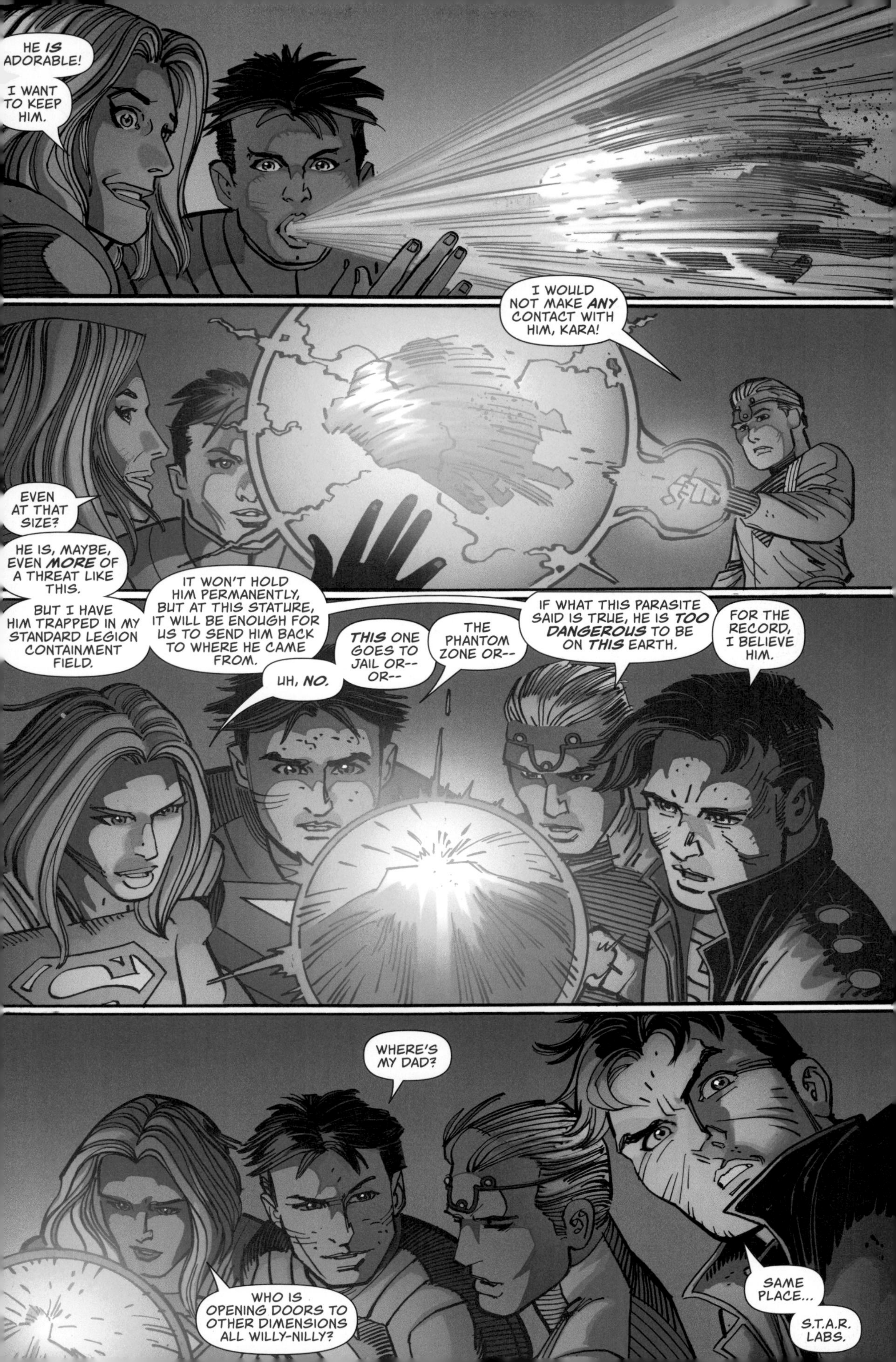
HE IS ADORABLE!
I WANT TO KEEP HIM.
I WOULD NOT MAKE ANY CONTACT WITH HIM, KARA!
EVEN AT THAT SIZE?
HE IS, MAYBE, EVEN MORE OF A THREAT LIKE THIS.
BUT I HAVE HIM TRAPPED IN MY STANDARD LEGION CONTAINMENT FIELD.
IT WON'T HOLD HIM PERMANENTLY, BUT AT THIS STATURE, IT WILL BE ENOUGH FOR US TO SEND HIM BACK TO WHERE HE CAME FROM.
UH, NO.
THIS ONE GOES TO JAIL OR-- OR--
THE PHANTOM ZONE OR--
IF WHAT THIS PARASITE SAID IS TRUE, HE IS TOO DANGEROUS TO BE ON THIS EARTH.
FOR THE RECORD, I BELIEVE HIM.
WHERE'S MY DAD?
WHO IS OPENING DOORS TO OTHER DIMENSIONS ALL WILLY-NILLY?
SAME PLACE...
S.T.A.R. LABS.

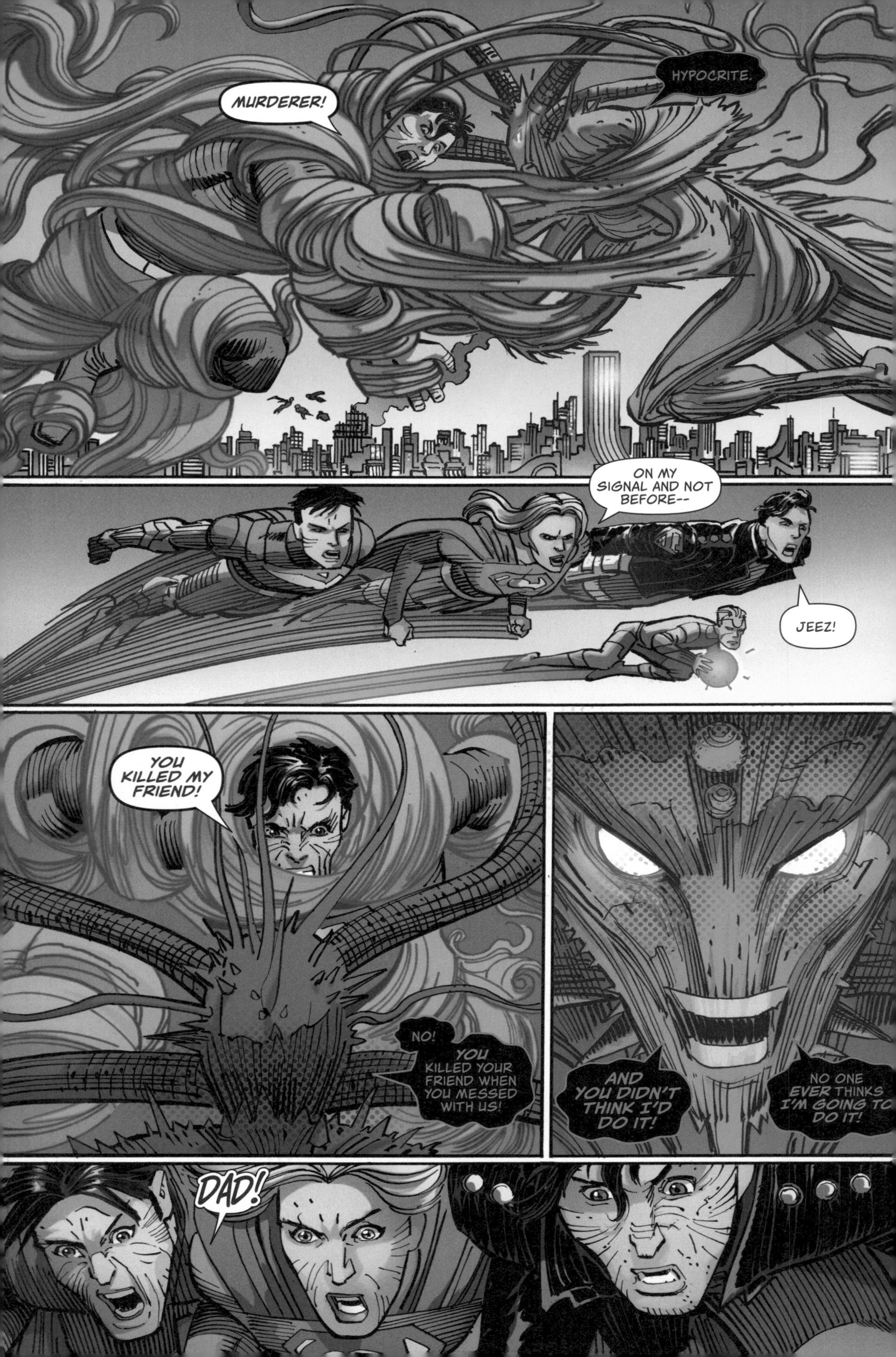
MURDERER!
HYPOCRITE.
ON MY SIGNAL AND NOT BEFORE--
JEEZ!
YOU KILLED MY FRIEND!
NO!
YOU KILLED YOUR FRIEND WHEN YOU MESSED WITH US!
AND YOU DIDN'T THINK I'D DO IT!
NO ONE EVER THINKS I'M GOING TO DO IT!
DAD!

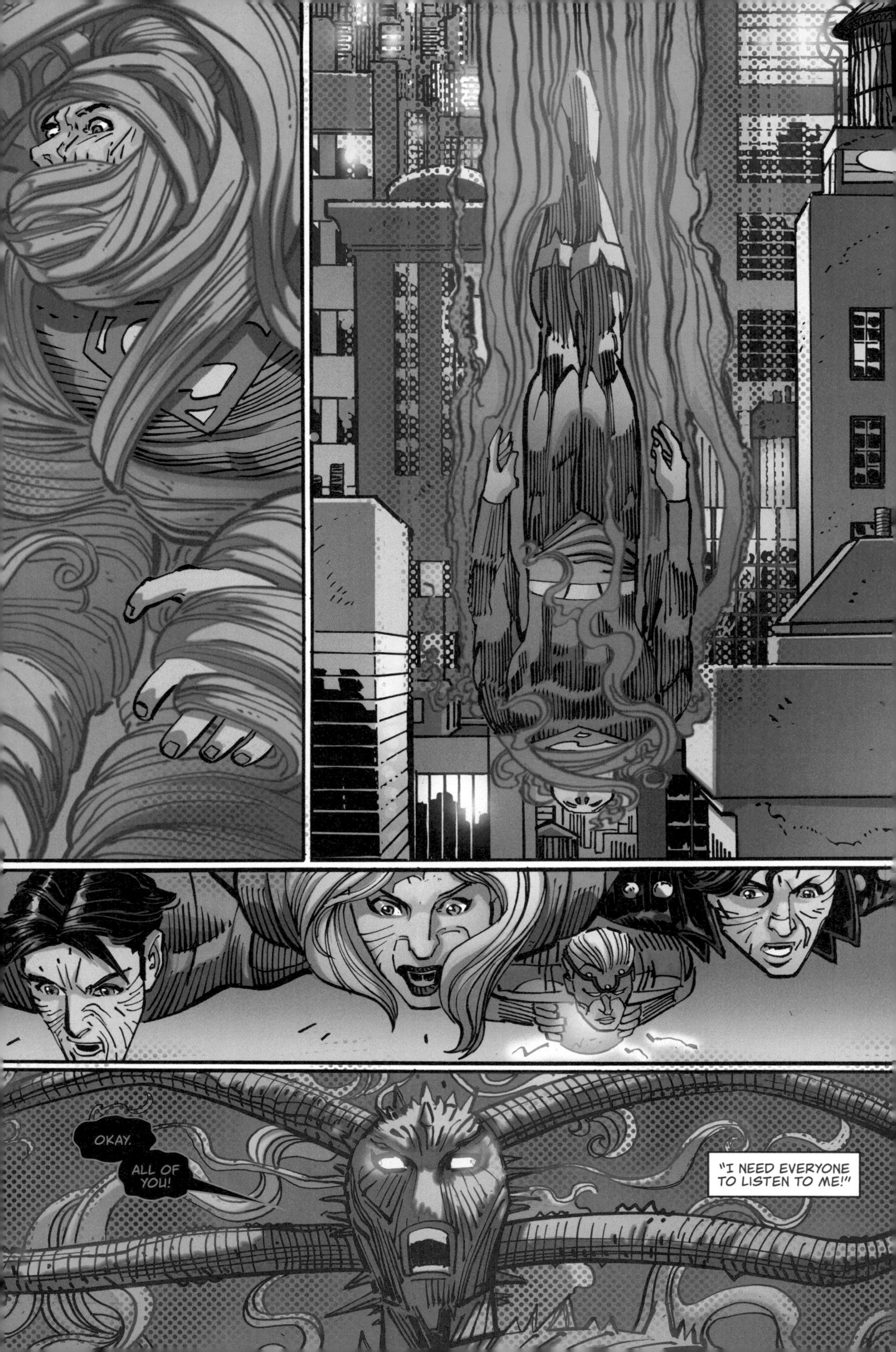
OKAY.
ALL OF YOU!
"I NEED EVERYONE TO LISTEN TO ME!"

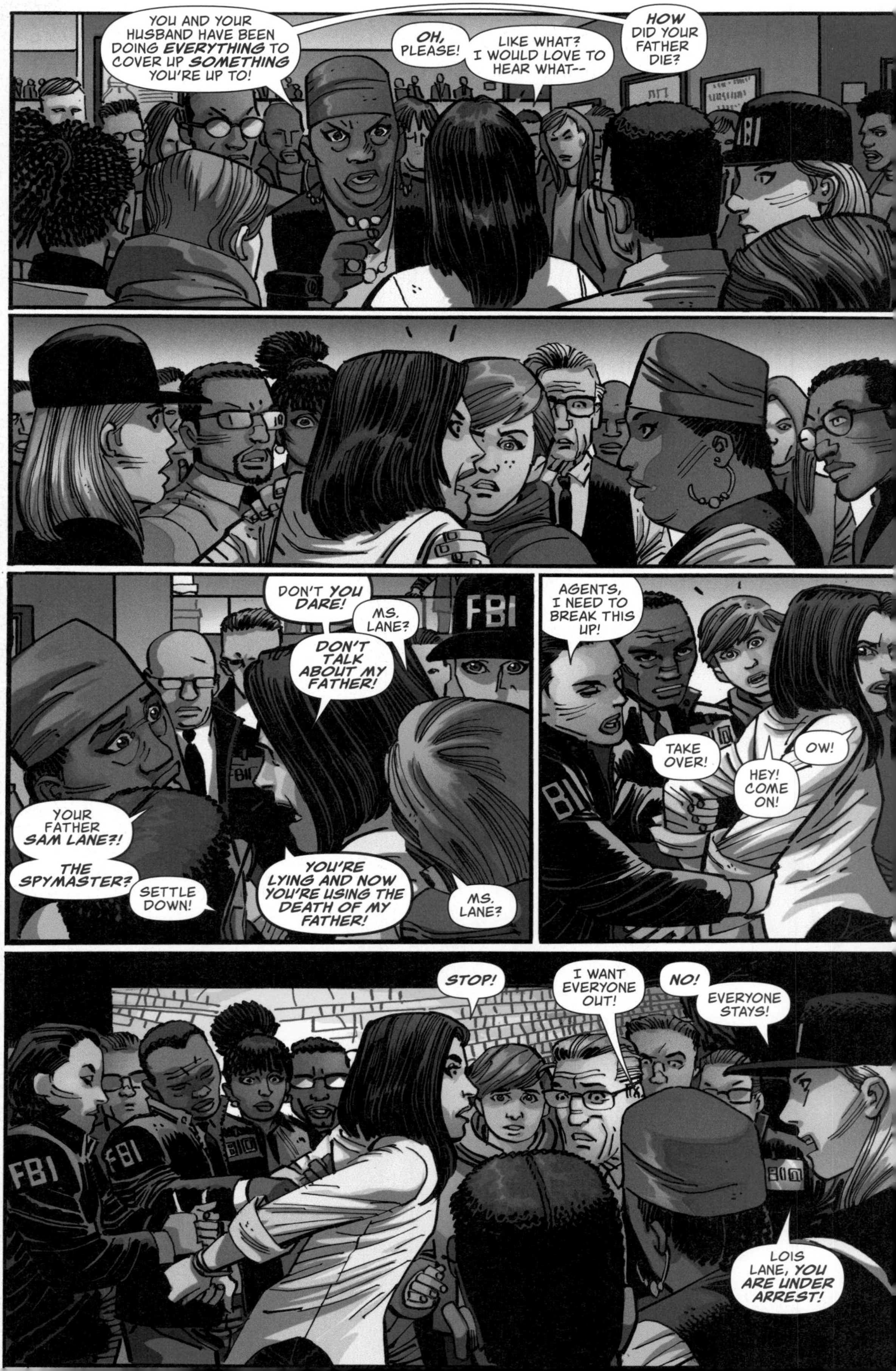
YOU AND YOUR HUSBAND HAVE BEEN DOING EVERYTHING TO COVER UP SOMETHING YOU'RE UP TO!
OH, PLEASE!
LIKE WHAT? I WOULD LOVE TO HEAR WHAT--
HOW DID YOUR FATHER DIE?
DON'T YOU DARE!
MS. LANE?
DON'T TALK ABOUT MY FATHER!
YOUR FATHER SAM LANE?!
THE SPYMASTER?
SETTLE DOWN!
YOU'RE LYING AND NOW YOU'RE USING THE DEATH OF MY FATHER!
MS. LANE?
AGENTS, I NEED TO BREAK THIS UP!
TAKE OVER!
OW!
HEY! COME ON!
STOP!
I WANT EVERYONE OUT!
NO!
EVERYONE STAYS!
LOIS LANE, YOU ARE UNDER ARREST!

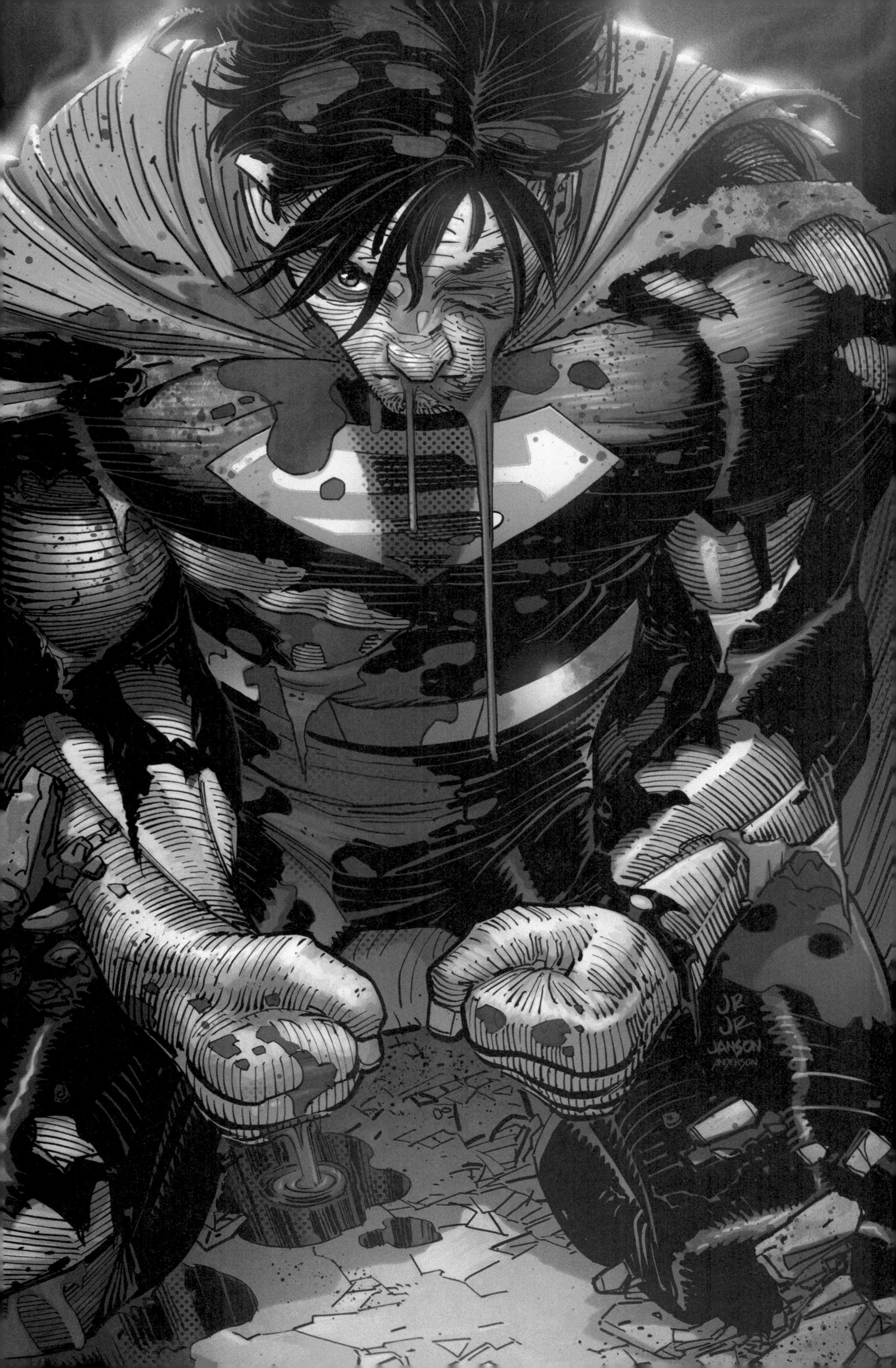
JR JR
JANSON
ANDERSON

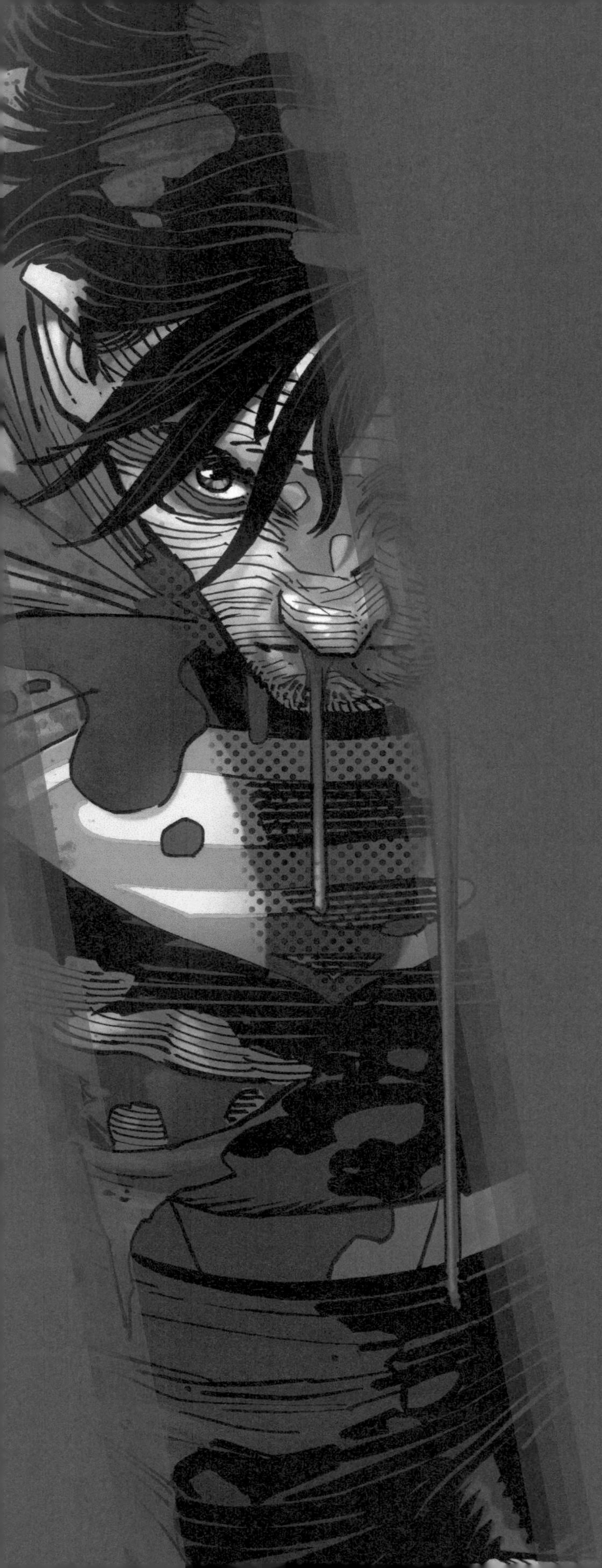

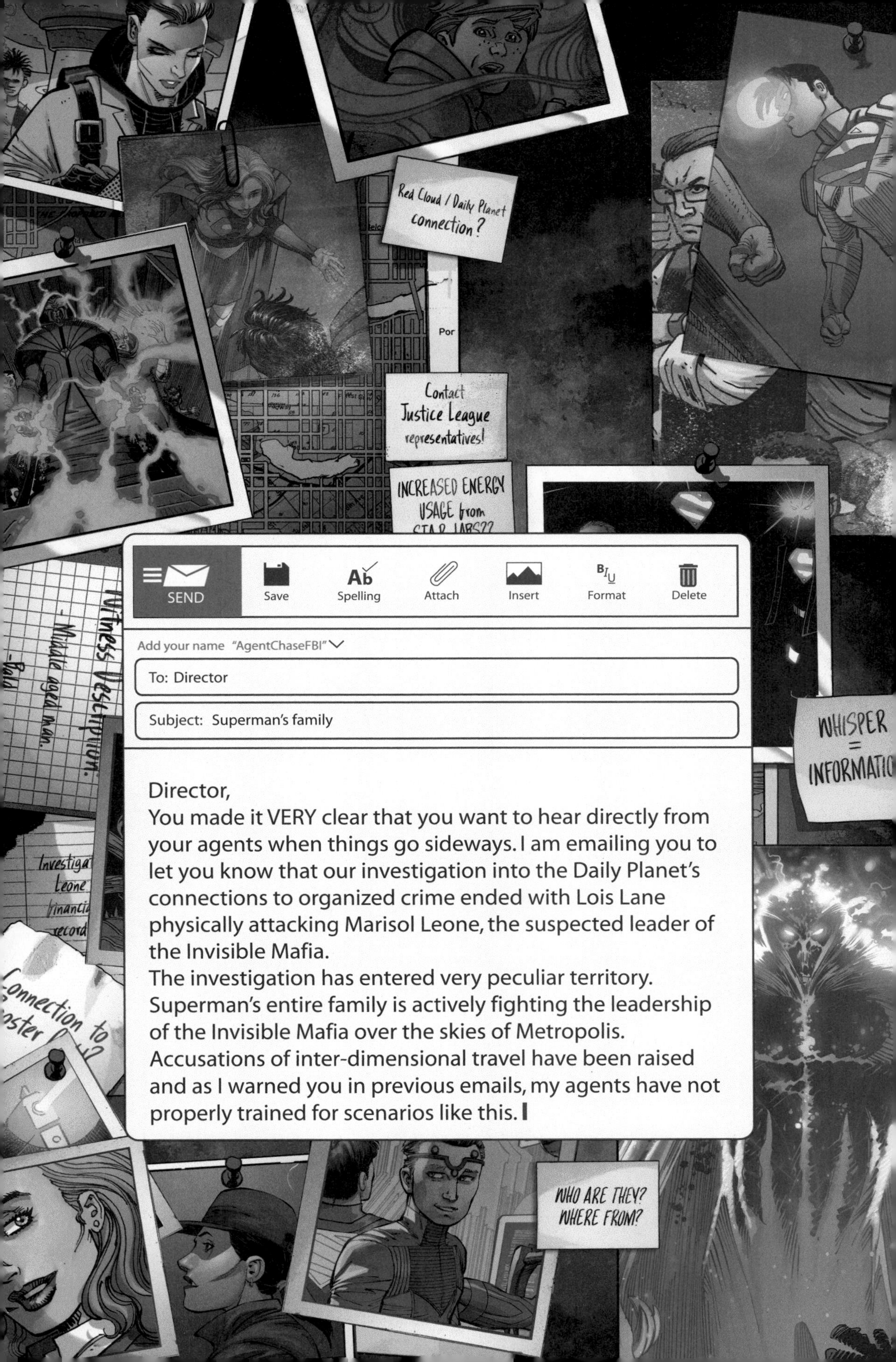
Red Cloud / Daily Planet connection?
Por
Contact Justice League representatives!
INCREASED ENERGY USAGE from
- Middle aged man.
SEND
Save
Spelling
Attach
Insert
Format
Delete
Add your name "AgentChaseFBI"
To: Director
Subject: Superman's family
Director,
You made it VERY clear that you want to hear directly from your agents when things go sideways. I am emailing you to let you know that our investigation into the Daily Planet's connections to organized crime ended with Lois Lane physically attacking Marisol Leone, the suspected leader of the Invisible Mafia.
The investigation has entered very peculiar territory. Superman's entire family is actively fighting the leadership of the Invisible Mafia over the skies of Metropolis. Accusations of inter-dimensional travel have been raised and as I warned you in previous emails, my agents have not properly trained for scenarios like this.
WHISPER =
WHO ARE THEY? WHERE FROM?

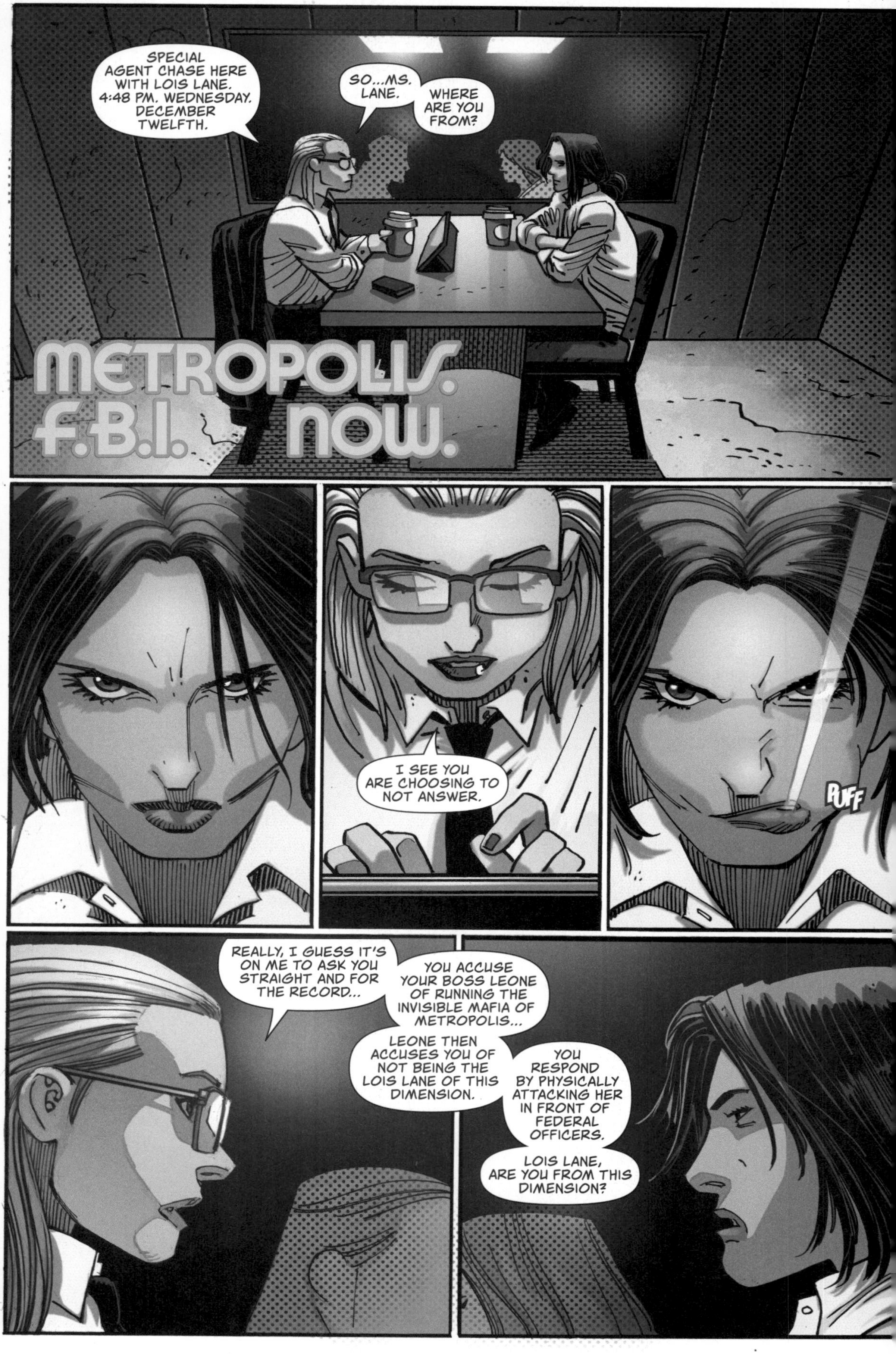
SPECIAL AGENT CHASE HERE WITH LOIS LANE. 4:48 PM. WEDNESDAY. DECEMBER TWELFTH.
SO...MS. LANE.
WHERE ARE YOU FROM?
METROPOLIS. F.B.I. NOW.
I SEE YOU ARE CHOOSING TO NOT ANSWER.
PUFF
REALLY, I GUESS IT'S ON ME TO ASK YOU STRAIGHT AND FOR THE RECORD...
YOU ACCUSE YOUR BOSS LEONE OF RUNNING THE INVISIBLE MAFIA OF METROPOLIS...
LEONE THEN ACCUSES YOU OF NOT BEING THE LOIS LANE OF THIS DIMENSION.
YOU RESPOND BY PHYSICALLY ATTACKING HER IN FRONT OF FEDERAL OFFICERS.
LOIS LANE, ARE YOU FROM THIS DIMENSION?

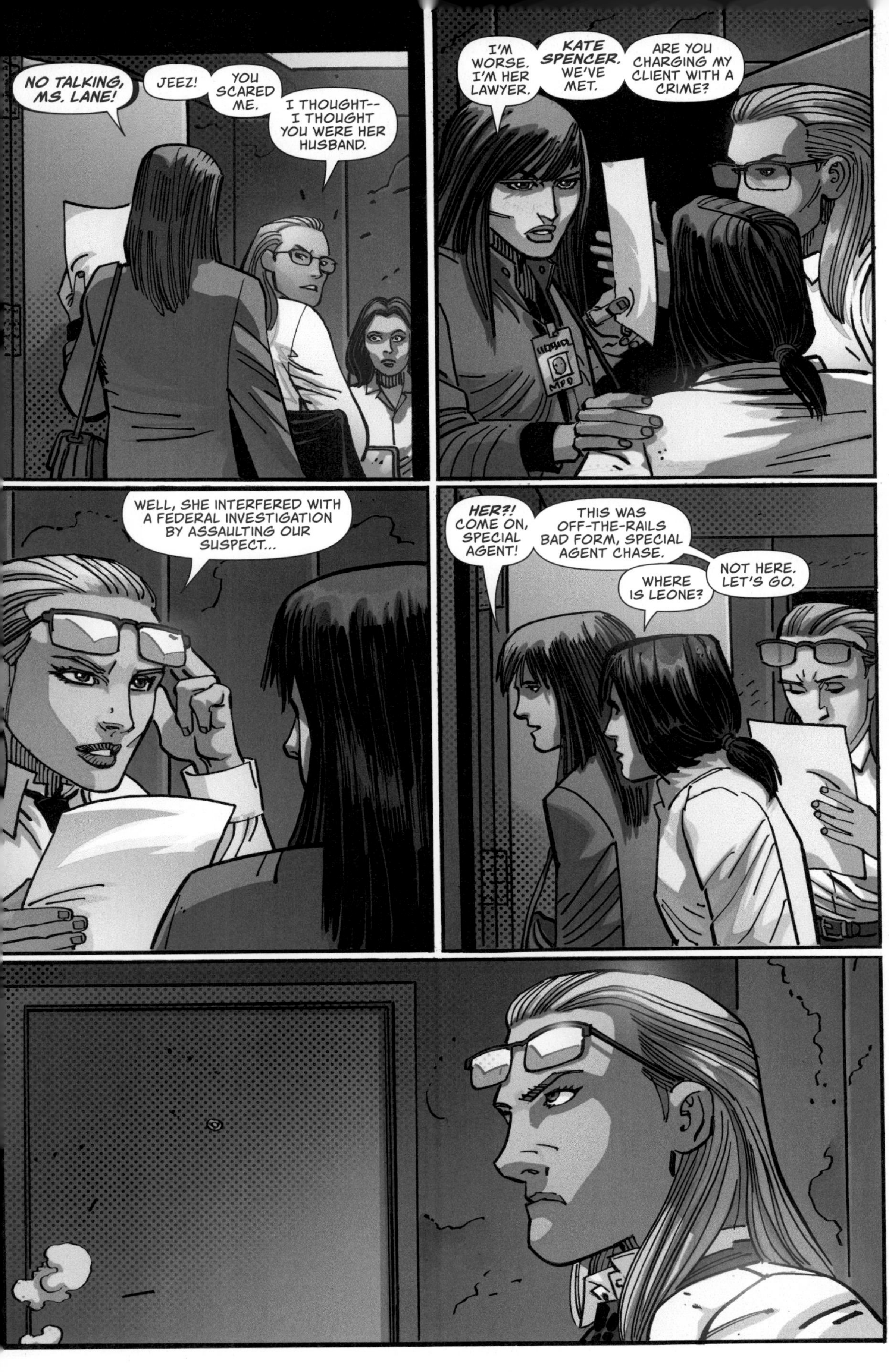
NO TALKING, MS. LANE!
JEEZ!
YOU SCARED ME.
I THOUGHT-- I THOUGHT YOU WERE HER HUSBAND.
I'M WORSE. I'M HER LAWYER.
KATE SPENCER. WE'VE MET.
ARE YOU CHARGING MY CLIENT WITH A CRIME?
WELL, SHE INTERFERED WITH A FEDERAL INVESTIGATION BY ASSAULTING OUR SUSPECT...
HER?! COME ON, SPECIAL AGENT!
THIS WAS OFF-THE-RAILS BAD FORM, SPECIAL AGENT CHASE.
WHERE IS LEONE?
NOT HERE. LET'S GO.

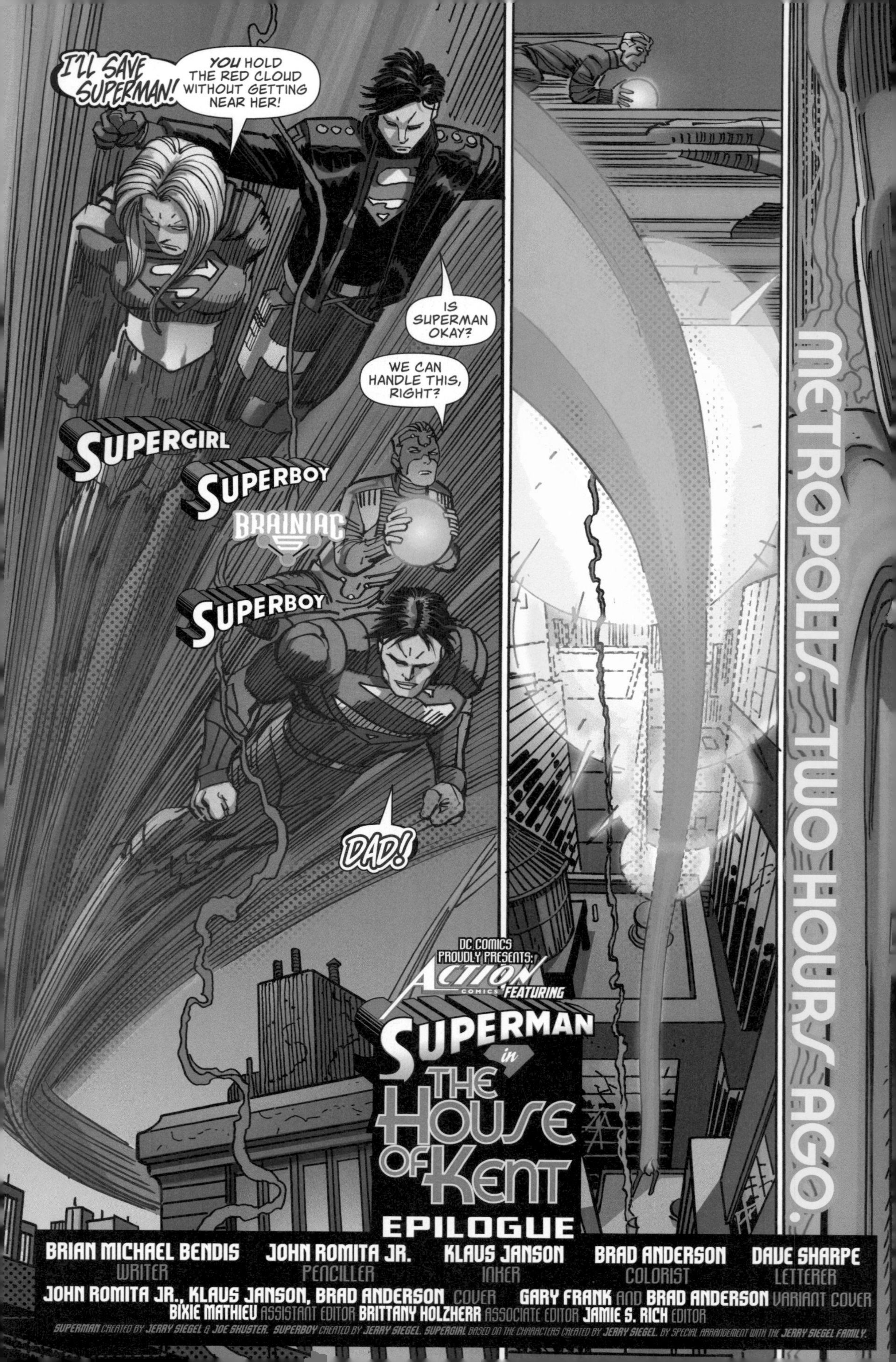

I'LL SAVE SUPERMAN!
YOU HOLD THE RED CLOUD WITHOUT GETTING NEAR HER!
IS SUPERMAN OKAY?
WE CAN HANDLE THIS, RIGHT?
DAD!
SUPERGIRL
SUPERBOY
BRAINIAC
SUPERBOY
METROPOLIS. TWO HOURS AGO.
DC COMICS PROUDLY PRESENTS: ACTION COMICS FEATURING
SUPERMAN in THE HOUSE OF KENT
EPILOGUE
BRIAN MICHAEL BENDIS WRITER
JOHN ROMITA JR. PENCILLER
KLAUS JANSON INKER
BRAD ANDERSON COLORIST
DAVE SHARPE LETTERER
JOHN ROMITA JR., KLAUS JANSON, BRAD ANDERSON COVER
GARY FRANK AND BRAD ANDERSON VARIANT COVER
BIXIE MATHIEU ASSISTANT EDITOR BRITTANY HOLZHERR ASSOCIATE EDITOR JAMIE S. RICH EDITOR
SUPERMAN CREATED BY JERRY SIEGEL & JOE SHUSTER. SUPERBOY CREATED BY JERRY SIEGEL. SUPERGIRL BASED ON THE CHARACTERS CREATED BY JERRY SIEGEL. BY SPECIAL ARRANGEMENT WITH THE JERRY SIEGEL FAMILY.

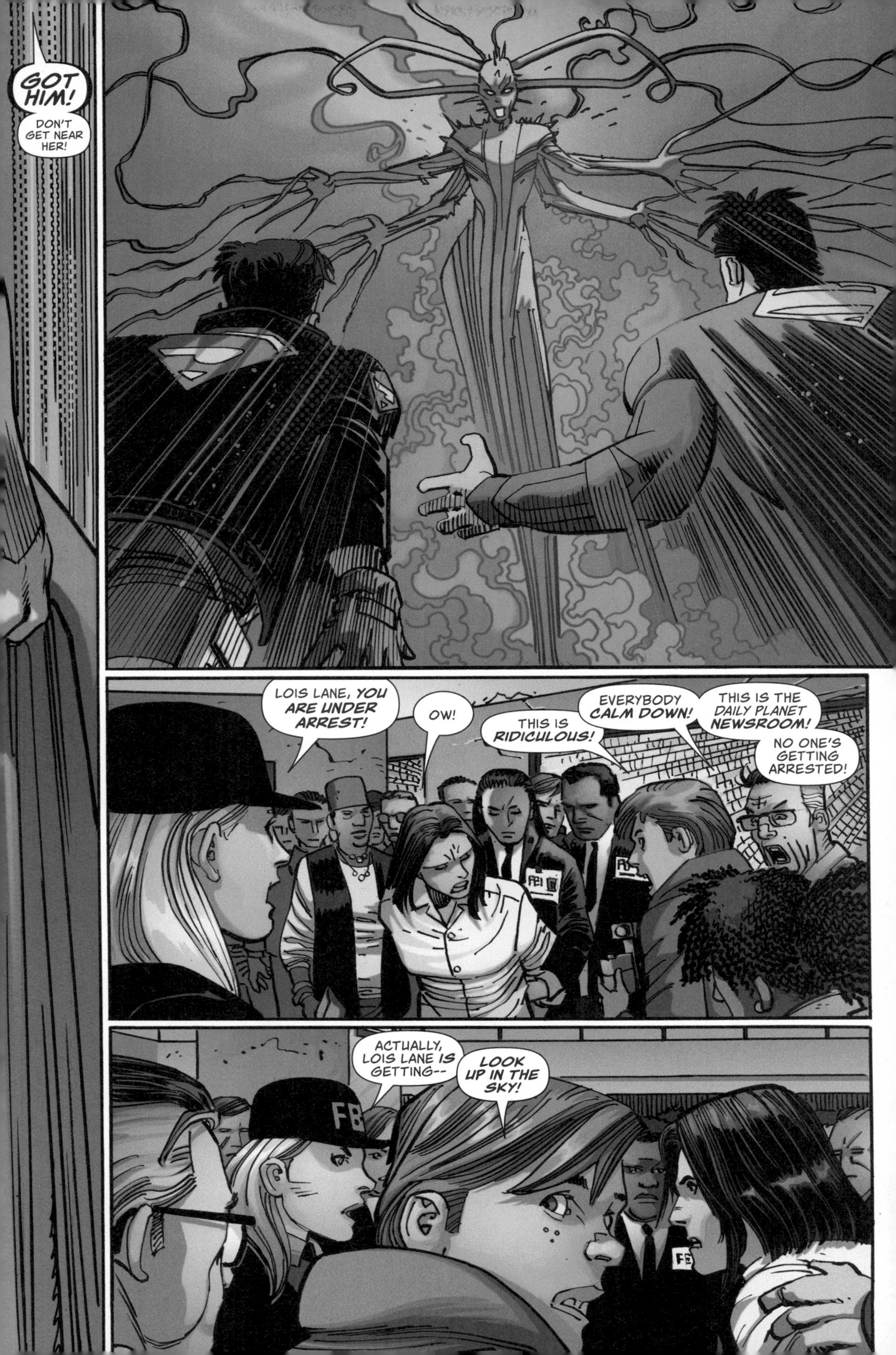
GOT HIM!
DON'T GET NEAR HER!
LOIS LANE, YOU ARE UNDER ARREST!
OW!
THIS IS RIDICULOUS!
EVERYBODY CALM DOWN!
THIS IS THE DAILY PLANET NEWSROOM!
NO ONE'S GETTING ARRESTED!
FBI
ACTUALLY, LOIS LANE IS GETTING--
LOOK UP IN THE SKY!

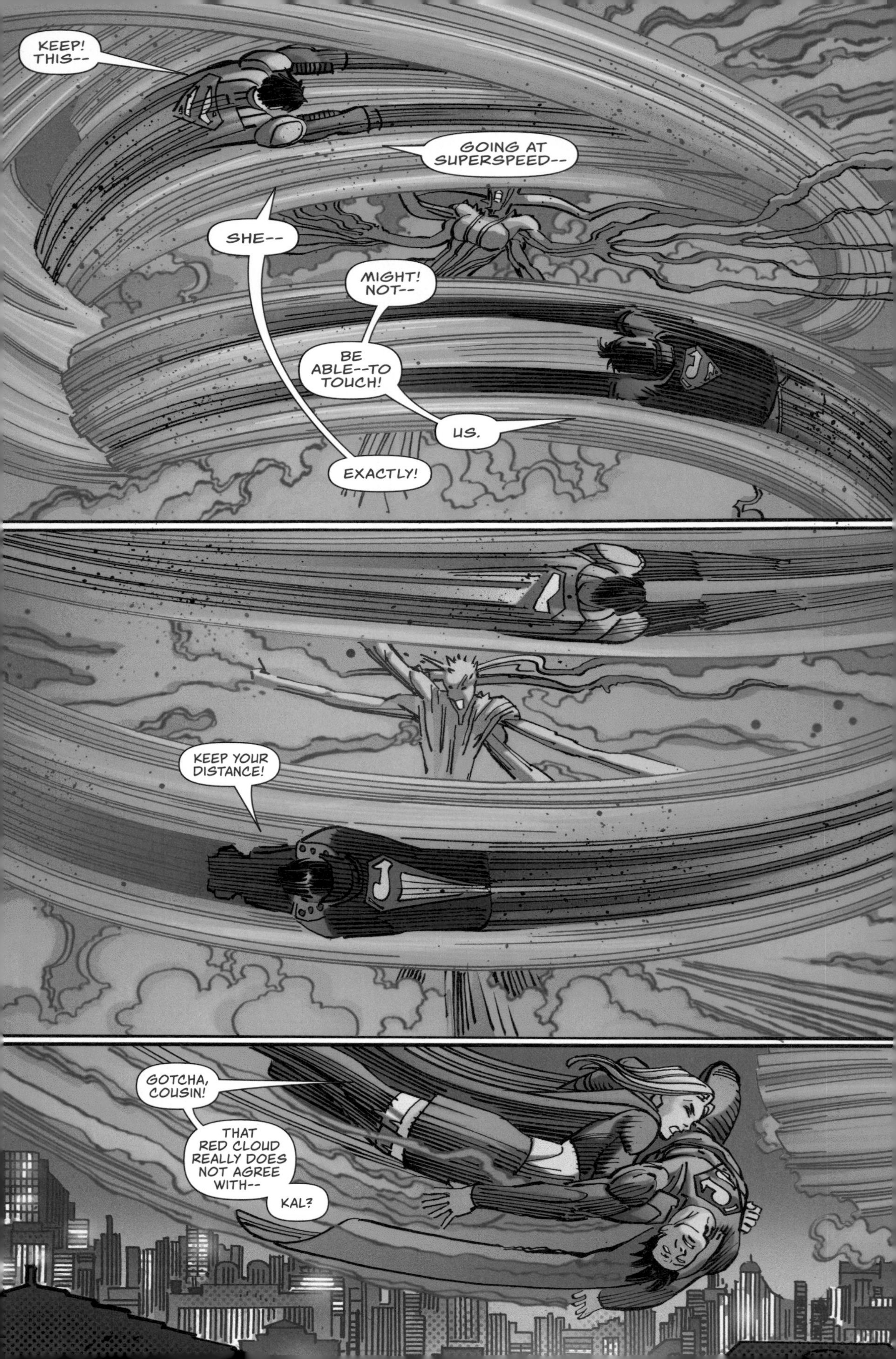
KEEP! THIS--
GOING AT SUPERSPEED--
SHE--
MIGHT! NOT--
BE ABLE--TO TOUCH!
US.
EXACTLY!
KEEP YOUR DISTANCE!
GOTCHA, COUSIN!
THAT RED CLOUD REALLY DOES NOT AGREE WITH--
KAL?

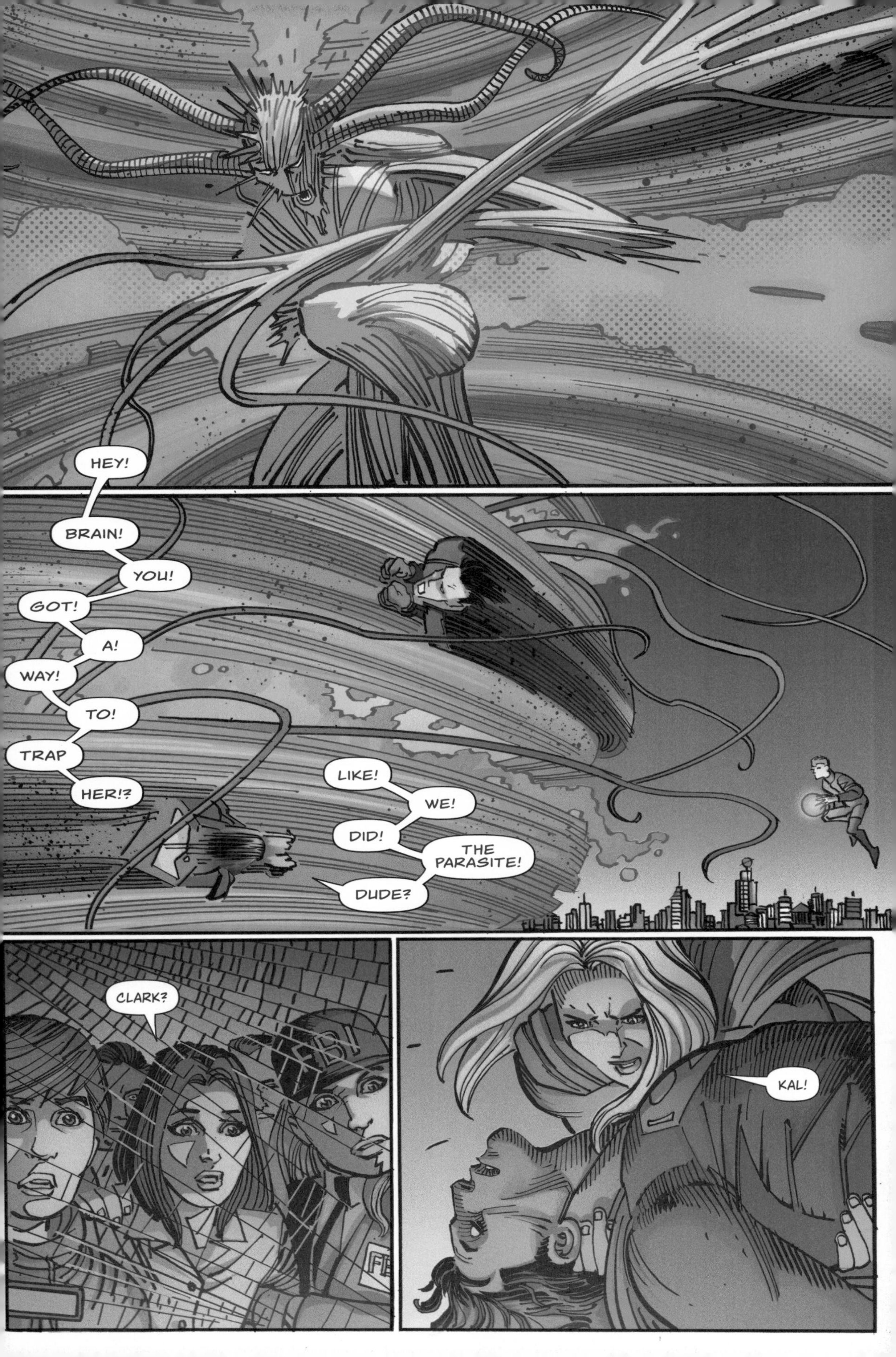
HEY!
BRAIN!
YOU!
GOT!
A!
WAY!
TO!
TRAP
HER!?
LIKE!
WE!
DID!
THE PARASITE!
DUDE?
CLARK?
KAL!

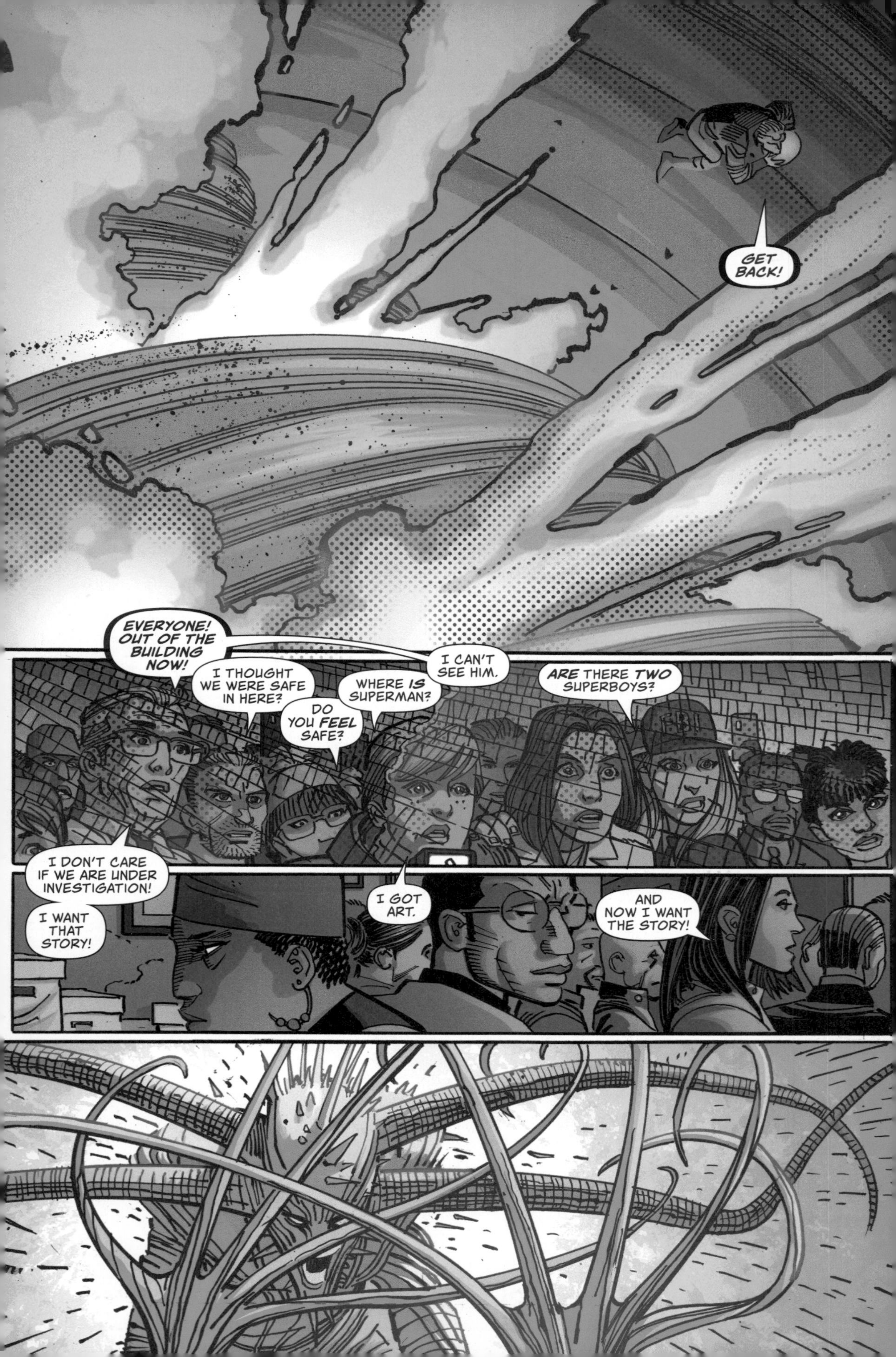
GET BACK!
EVERYONE! OUT OF THE BUILDING NOW!
I THOUGHT WE WERE SAFE IN HERE?
DO YOU FEEL SAFE?
WHERE IS SUPERMAN?
I CAN'T SEE HIM.
ARE THERE TWO SUPERBOYS?
I DON'T CARE IF WE ARE UNDER INVESTIGATION!
I WANT THAT STORY!
I GOT ART.
AND NOW I WANT THE STORY!

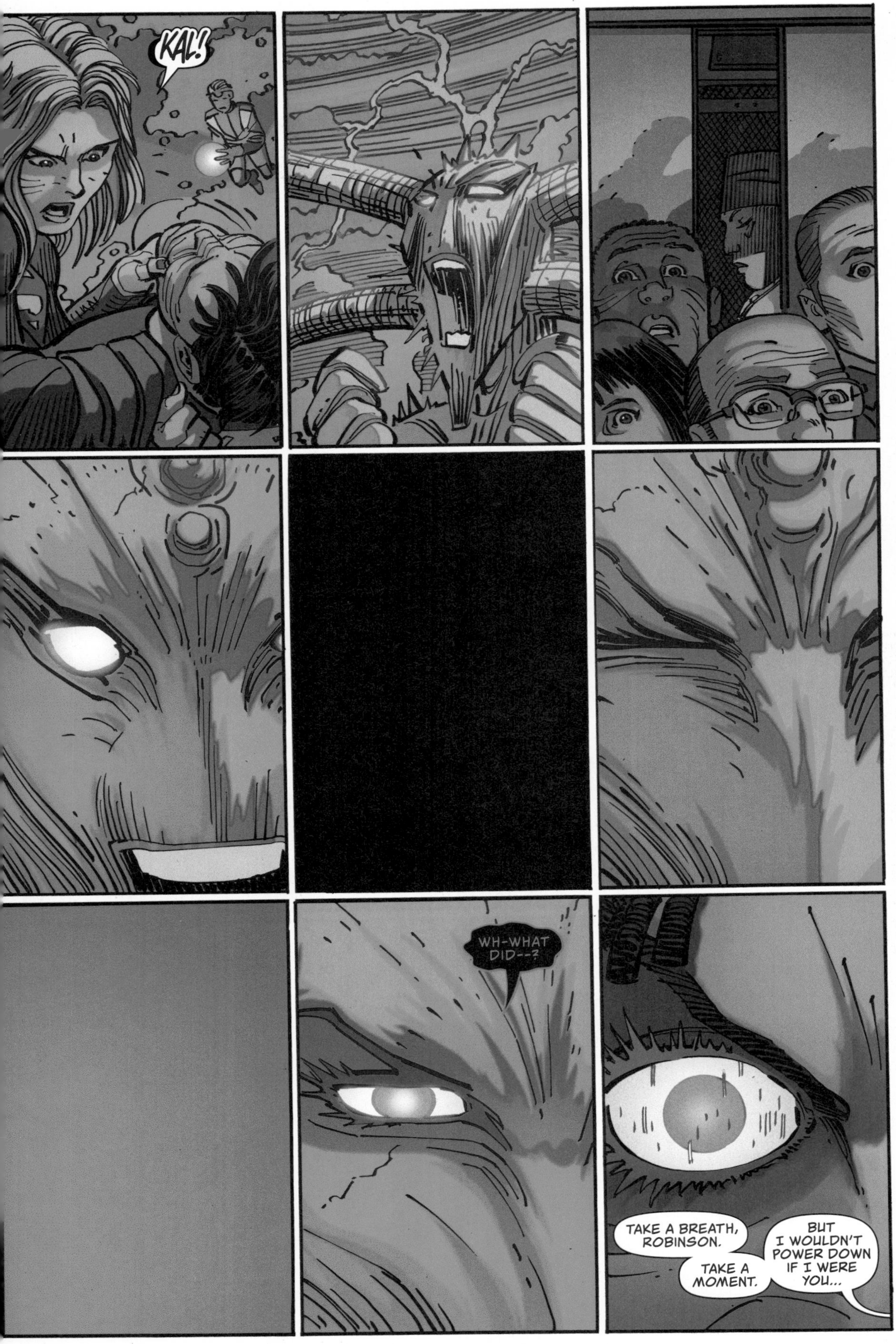
KAL!
WH-WHAT DID--?
TAKE A BREATH, ROBINSON.
TAKE A MOMENT.
BUT I WOULDN'T POWER DOWN IF I WERE YOU...

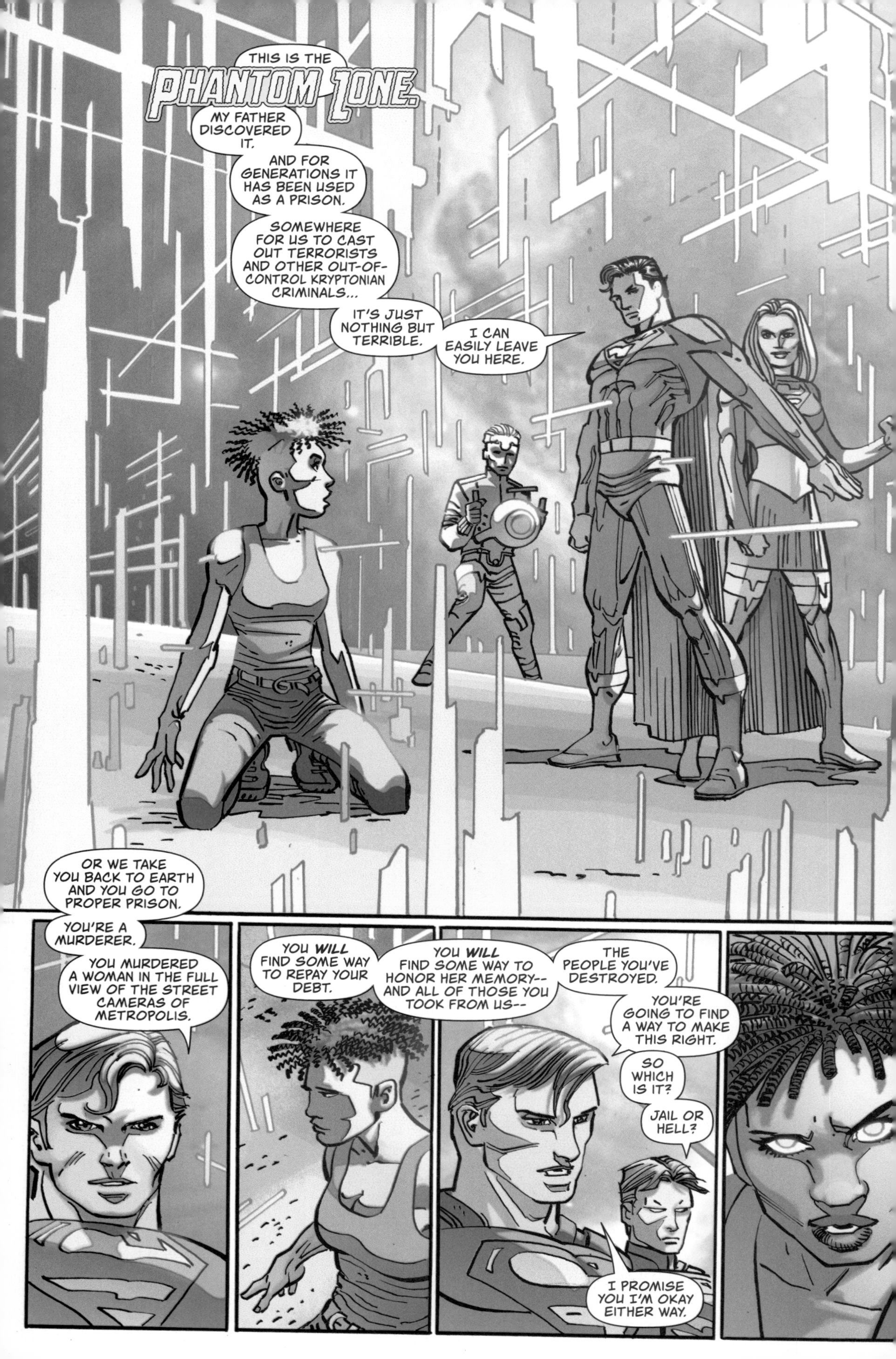
THIS IS THE
PHANTOM ZONE.
MY FATHER DISCOVERED IT.
AND FOR GENERATIONS IT HAS BEEN USED AS A PRISON.
SOMEWHERE FOR US TO CAST OUT TERRORISTS AND OTHER OUT-OF-CONTROL KRYPTONIAN CRIMINALS...
IT'S JUST NOTHING BUT TERRIBLE.
I CAN EASILY LEAVE YOU HERE.
OR WE TAKE YOU BACK TO EARTH AND YOU GO TO PROPER PRISON.
YOU'RE A MURDERER.
YOU MURDERED A WOMAN IN THE FULL VIEW OF THE STREET CAMERAS OF METROPOLIS.
YOU *WILL* FIND SOME WAY TO REPAY YOUR DEBT.
YOU *WILL* FIND SOME WAY TO HONOR HER MEMORY-- AND ALL OF THOSE YOU TOOK FROM US--
THE PEOPLE YOU'VE DESTROYED.
YOU'RE GOING TO FIND A WAY TO MAKE THIS RIGHT.
SO WHICH IS IT?
JAIL OR HELL?
I PROMISE YOU I'M OKAY EITHER WAY.

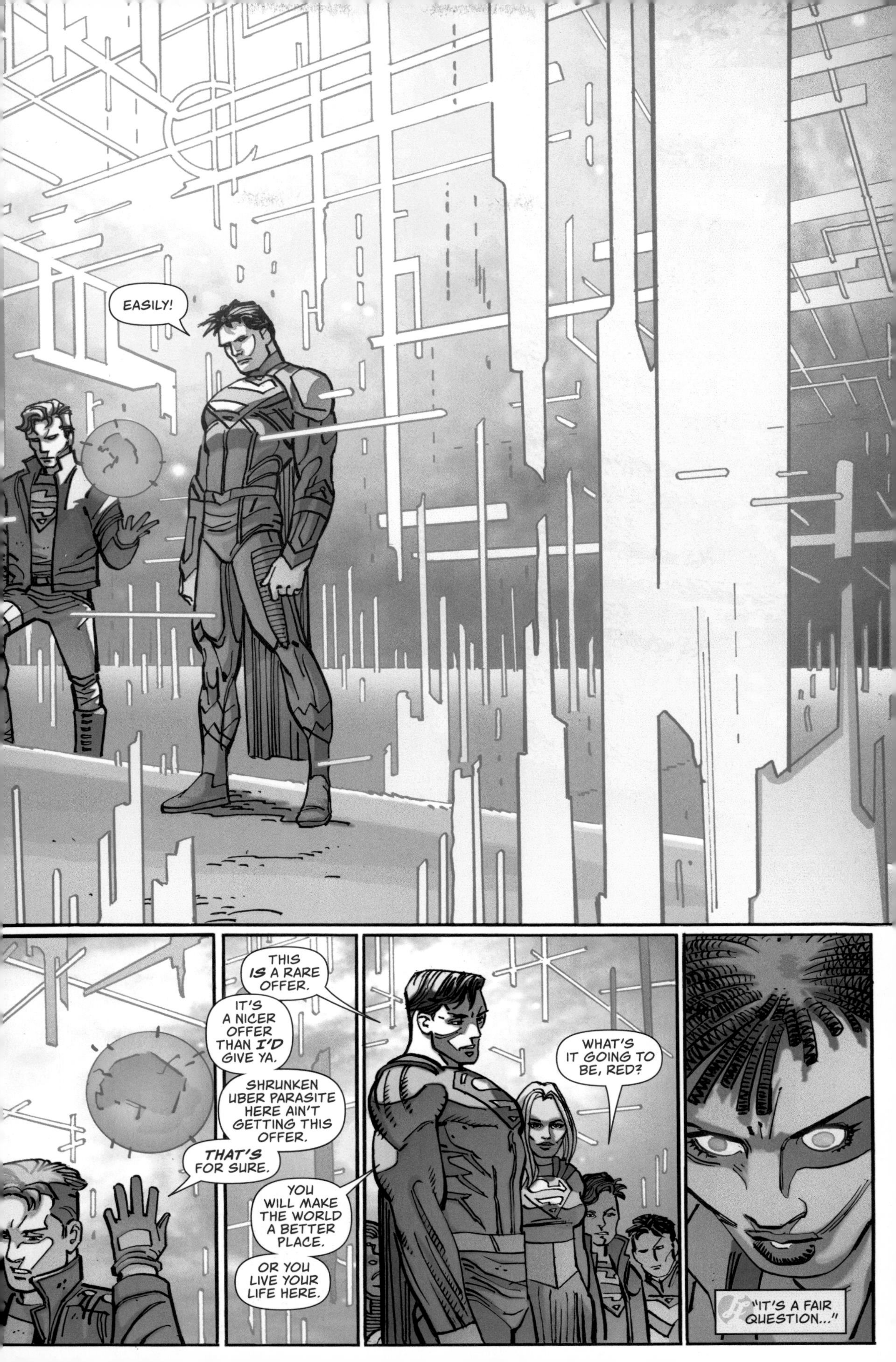
EASILY!
THIS IS A RARE OFFER.
IT'S A NICER OFFER THAN I'D GIVE YA.
SHRUNKEN UBER PARASITE HERE AIN'T GETTING THIS OFFER.
THAT'S FOR SURE.
YOU WILL MAKE THE WORLD A BETTER PLACE.
OR YOU LIVE YOUR LIFE HERE.
WHAT'S IT GOING TO BE, RED?
"IT'S A FAIR QUESTION..."

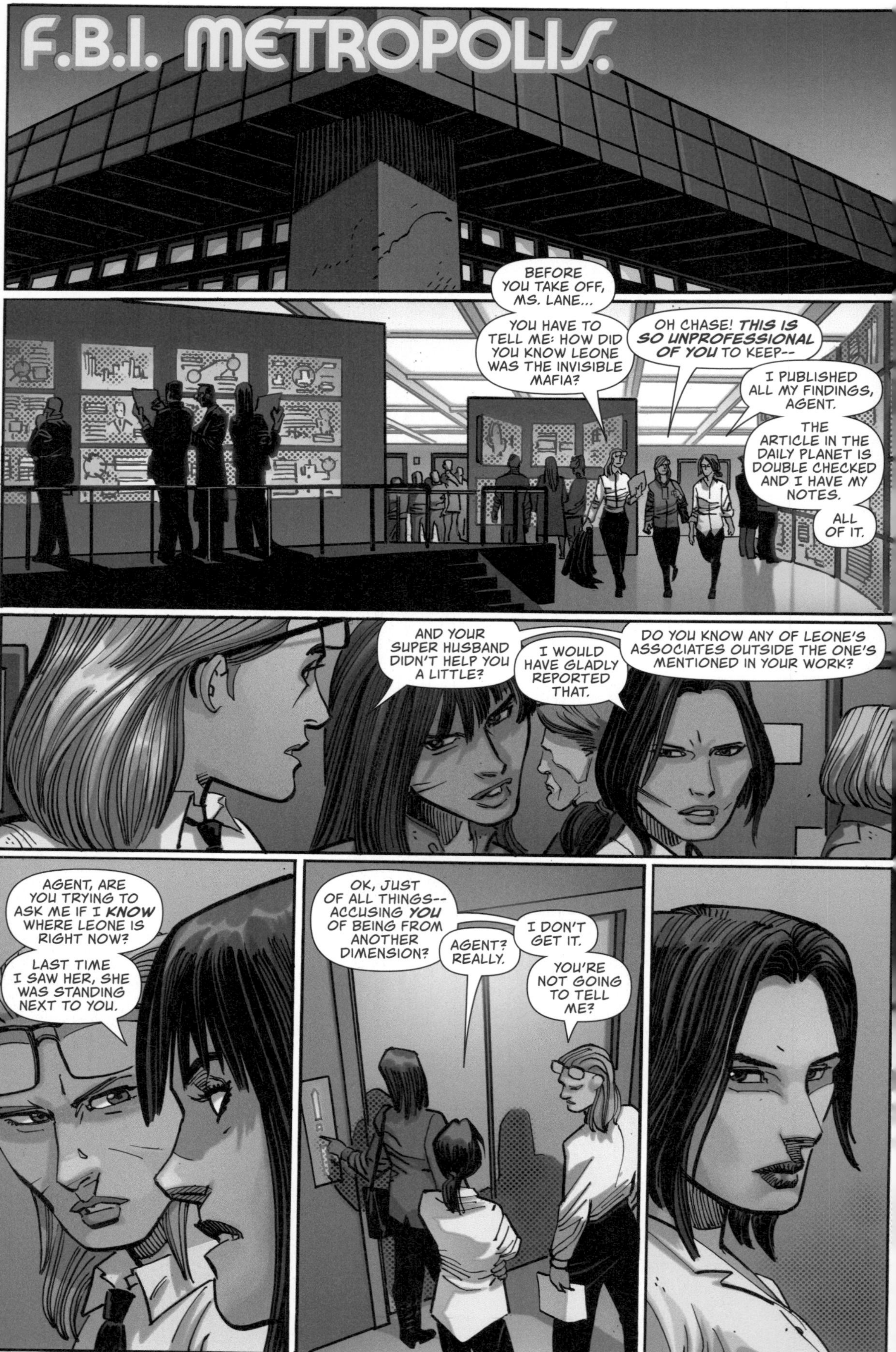
F.B.I. METROPOLIS.
BEFORE YOU TAKE OFF, MS. LANE...
YOU HAVE TO TELL ME: HOW DID YOU KNOW LEONE WAS THE INVISIBLE MAFIA?
OH CHASE! THIS IS SO UNPROFESSIONAL OF YOU TO KEEP--
I PUBLISHED ALL MY FINDINGS, AGENT.
THE ARTICLE IN THE DAILY PLANET IS DOUBLE CHECKED AND I HAVE MY NOTES.
ALL OF IT.
AND YOUR SUPER HUSBAND DIDN'T HELP YOU A LITTLE?
I WOULD HAVE GLADLY REPORTED THAT.
DO YOU KNOW ANY OF LEONE'S ASSOCIATES OUTSIDE THE ONE'S MENTIONED IN YOUR WORK?
AGENT, ARE YOU TRYING TO ASK ME IF I KNOW WHERE LEONE IS RIGHT NOW?
LAST TIME I SAW HER, SHE WAS STANDING NEXT TO YOU.
OK, JUST OF ALL THINGS-- ACCUSING YOU OF BEING FROM ANOTHER DIMENSION?
AGENT? REALLY.
I DON'T GET IT.
YOU'RE NOT GOING TO TELL ME?

YOU CAN DO IT...

DING

OH MY GOD!

YES.

AND, SEE? IF I SAID IT TO YOU OUT LOUD...

LEONE'S FROM ANOTHER EARTH!

THAT'S-- THAT'S WHY THERE'S NO PAPER TRAIL OF THE MYSTERIOUS LEONE!

NOT BECAUSE SHE'S A MASTER WHATEVER YOU CALL IT...

##!#!#

SHE'S ALREADY GONE, ISN'T SHE?

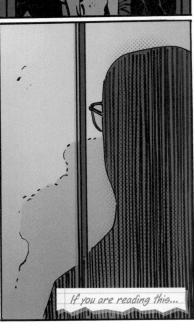

*If you are reading this...*

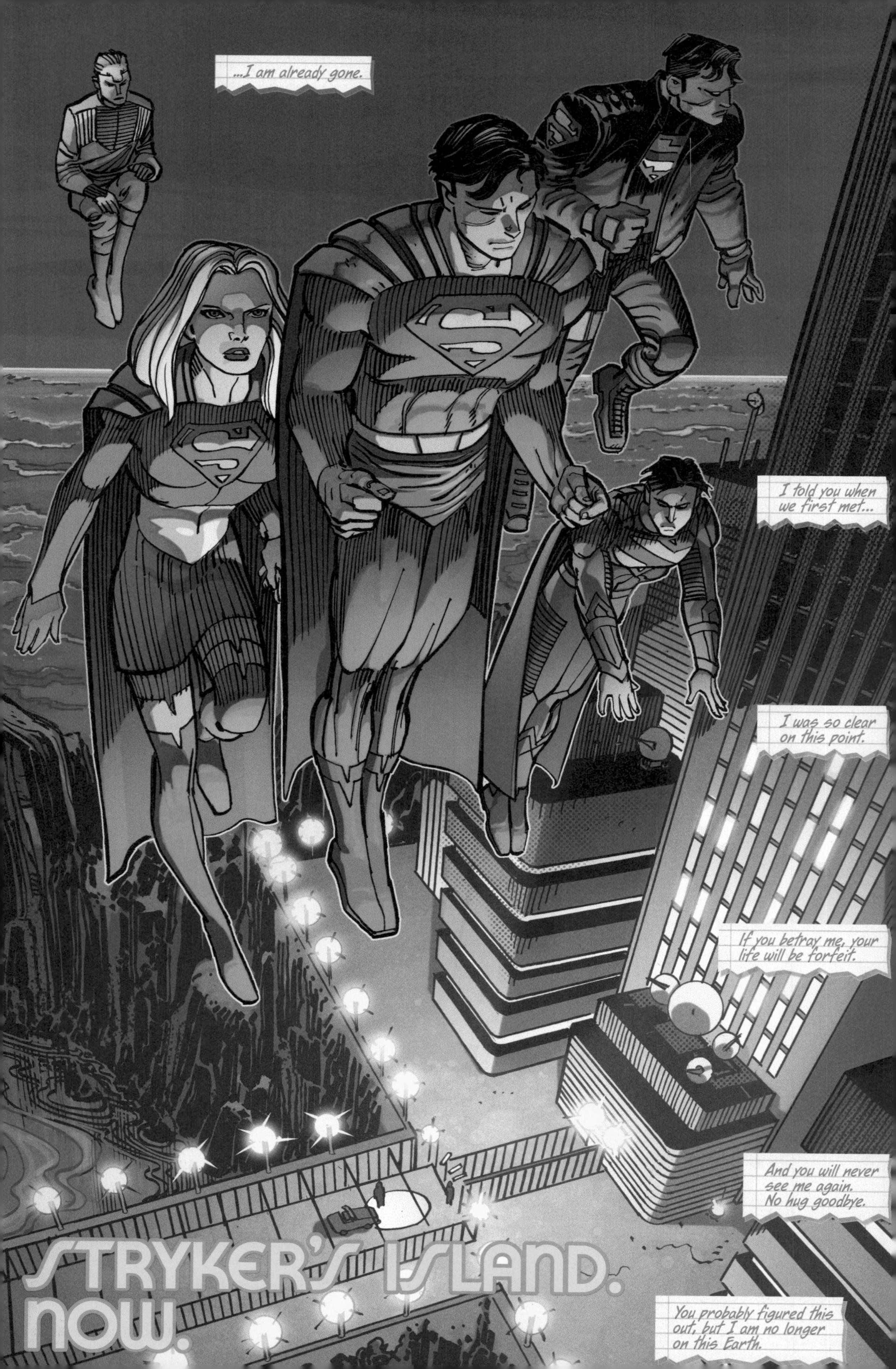
...I am already gone.
I told you when we first met...
I was so clear on this point.
If you betray me, your life will be forfeit.
And you will never see me again. No hug goodbye.
STRYKER'S ISLAND. NOW.
You probably figured this out, but I am no longer on this Earth.

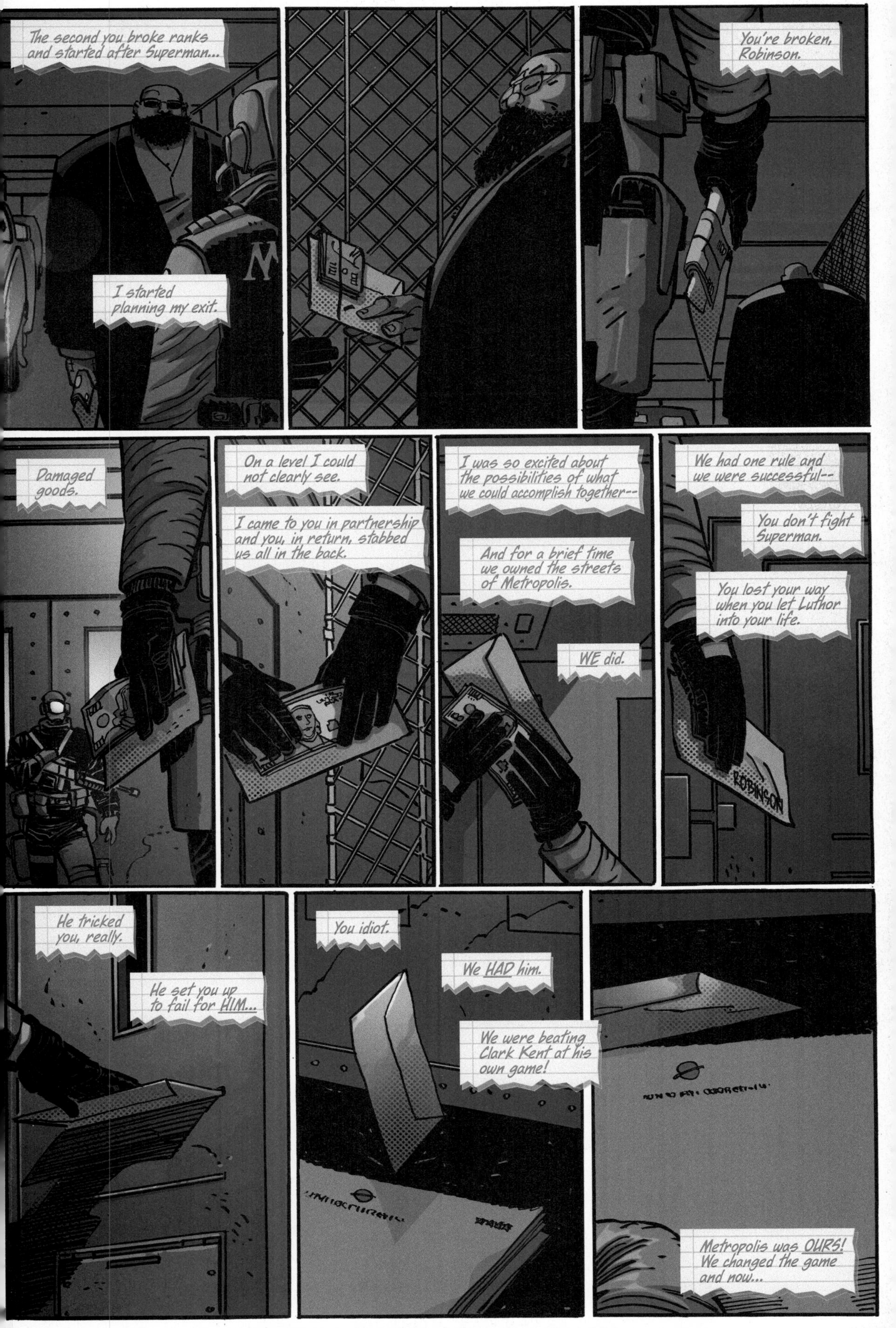

The second you broke ranks and started after Superman...
I started planning my exit.
You're broken, Robinson.
Damaged goods.
On a level I could not clearly see.
I came to you in partnership and you, in return, stabbed us all in the back.
I was so excited about the possibilities of what we could accomplish together--
And for a brief time we owned the streets of Metropolis.
WE did.
We had one rule and we were successful--
You don't fight Superman.
You lost your way when you let Luthor into your life.
ROBINSON
He tricked you, really.
He set you up to fail for HIM...
You idiot.
We HAD him.
We were beating Clark Kent at his own game!
Metropolis was OURS! We changed the game and now...

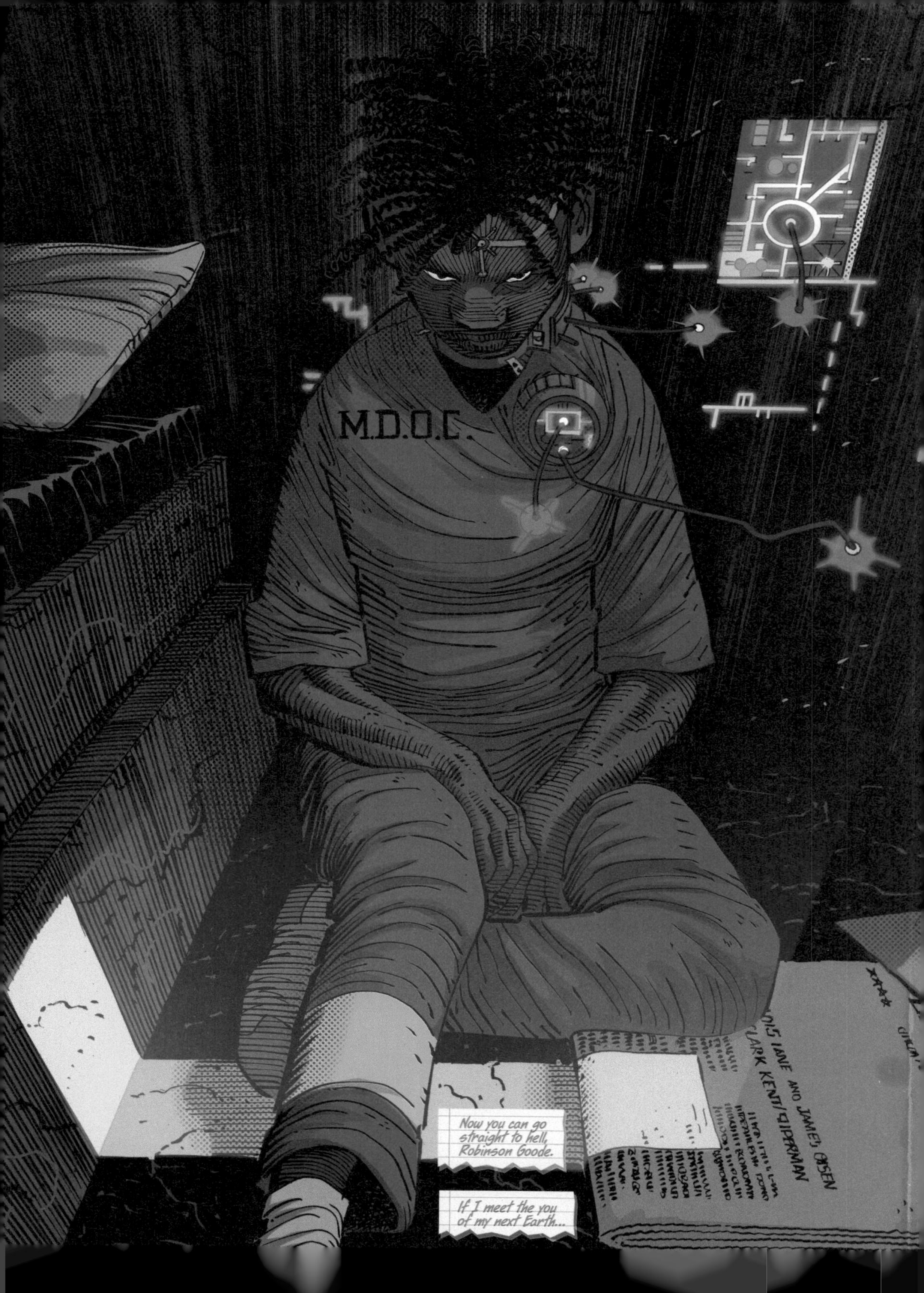
M.D.O.C.
Now you can go straight to hell, Robinson Goode.
If I meet the you of my next Earth...

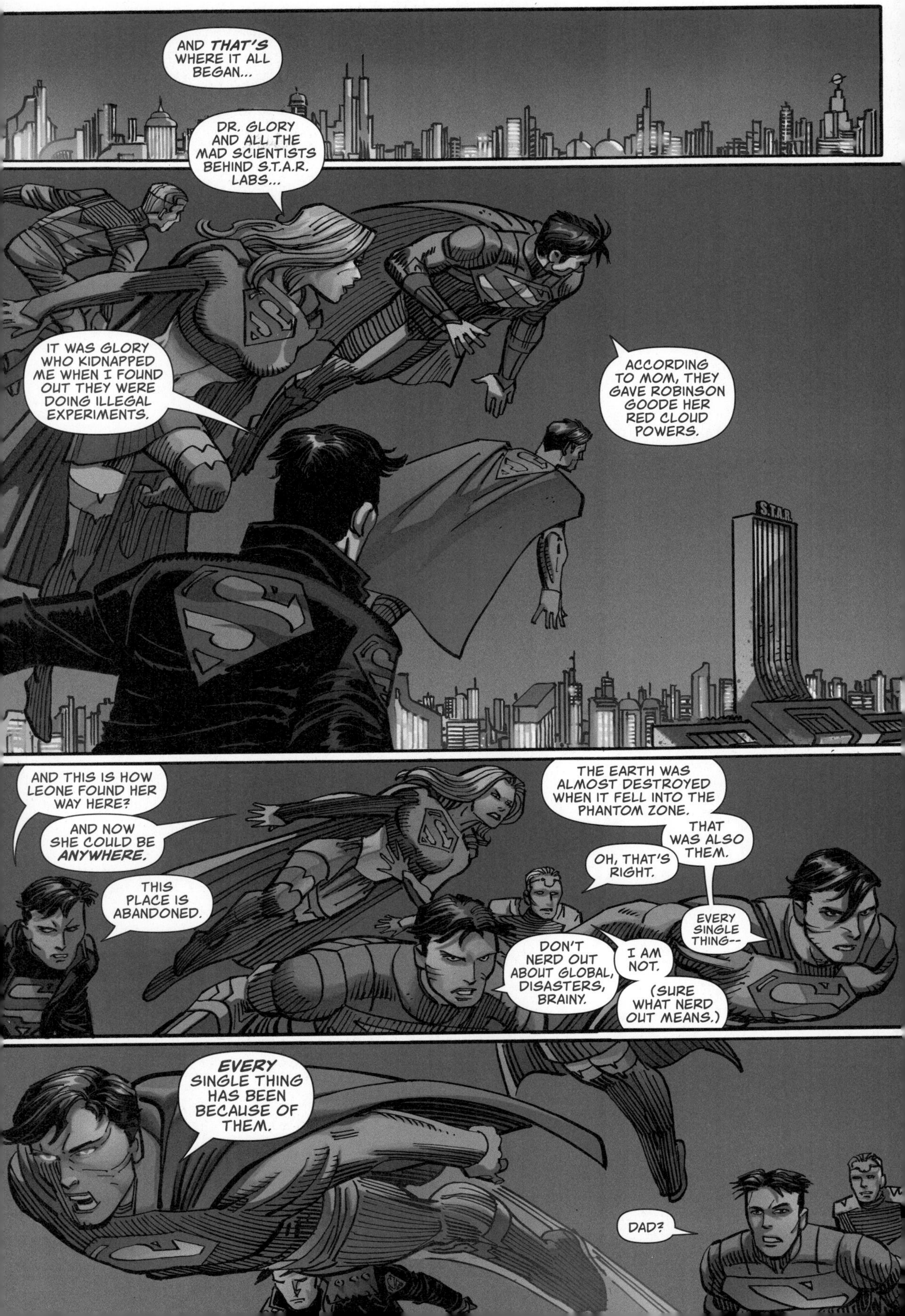
AND *THAT'S* WHERE IT ALL BEGAN...
DR. GLORY AND ALL THE MAD SCIENTISTS BEHIND S.T.A.R. LABS...
IT WAS GLORY WHO KIDNAPPED ME WHEN I FOUND OUT THEY WERE DOING ILLEGAL EXPERIMENTS.
ACCORDING TO MOM, THEY GAVE ROBINSON GOODE HER RED CLOUD POWERS.
S.T.A.R.
AND THIS IS HOW LEONE FOUND HER WAY HERE?
AND NOW SHE COULD BE *ANYWHERE.*
THIS PLACE IS ABANDONED.
THE EARTH WAS ALMOST DESTROYED WHEN IT FELL INTO THE PHANTOM ZONE.
THAT WAS ALSO THEM.
OH, THAT'S RIGHT.
EVERY SINGLE THING--
DON'T NERD OUT ABOUT GLOBAL DISASTERS, BRAINY.
I AM NOT.
(SURE WHAT NERD OUT MEANS.)
*EVERY* SINGLE THING HAS BEEN BECAUSE OF THEM.
DAD?

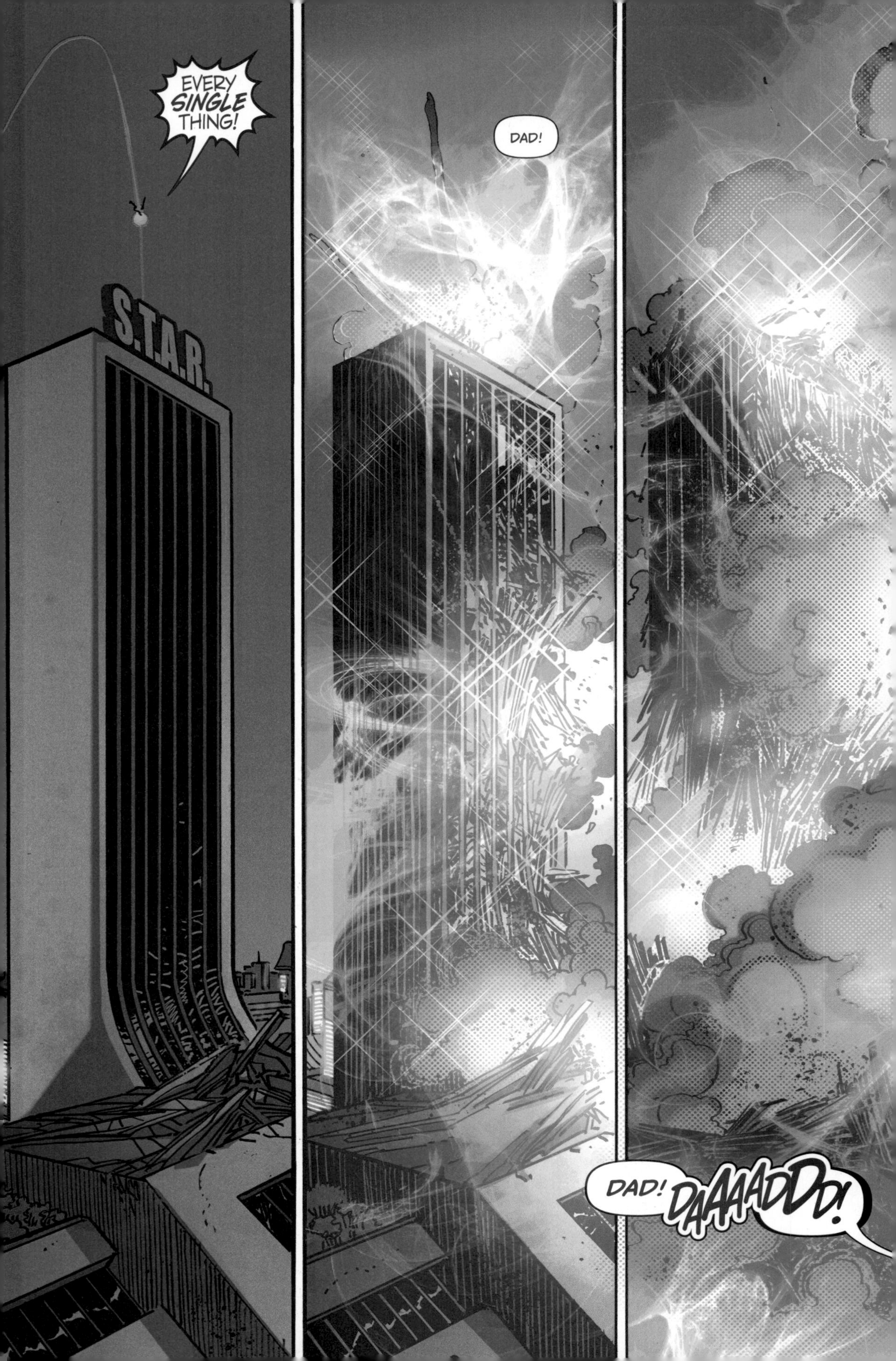
EVERY SINGLE THING!
S.T.A.R.
DAD!
DAD! DAAAADDD!

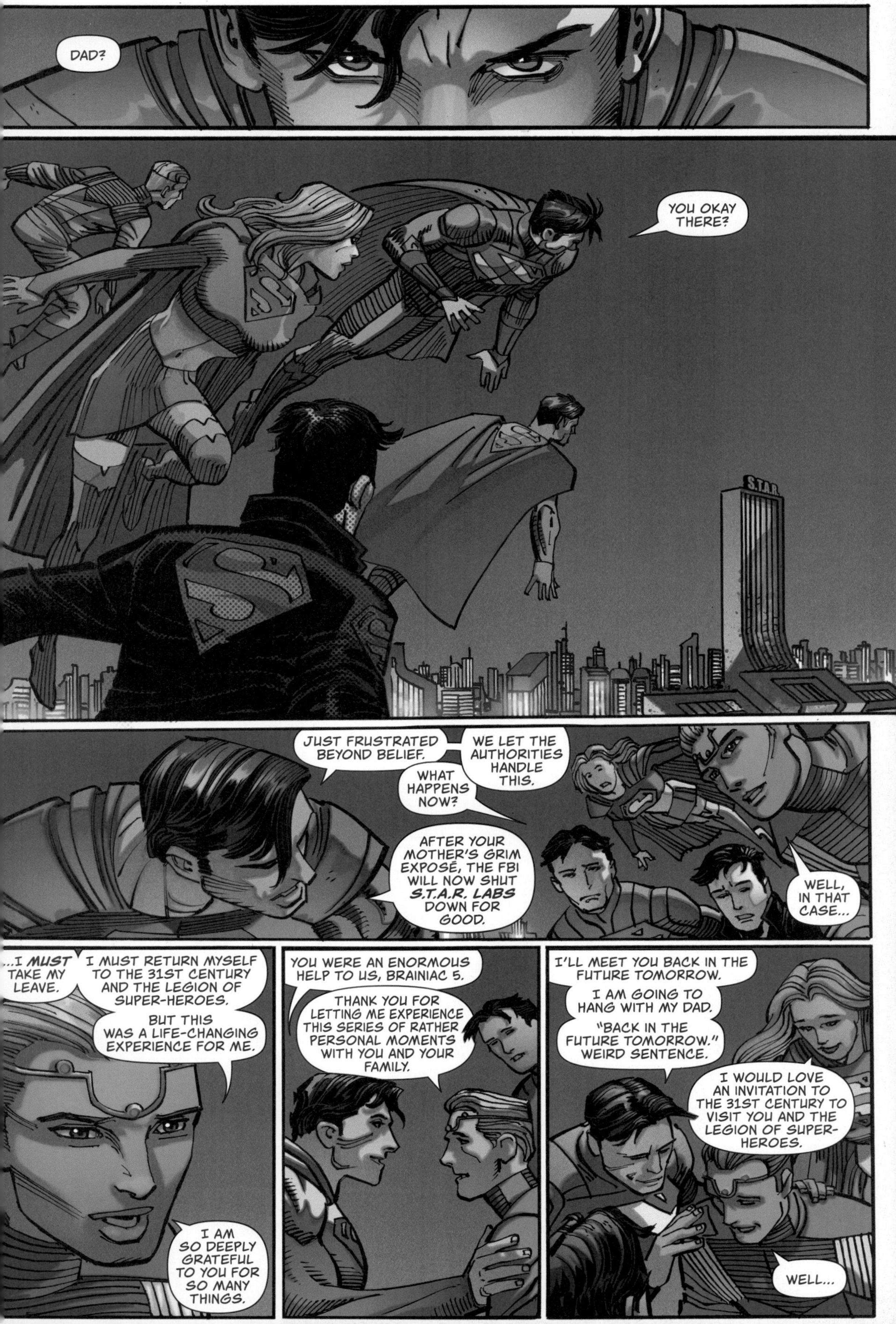
DAD?
YOU OKAY THERE?
S.T.A.R.
JUST FRUSTRATED BEYOND BELIEF.
WE LET THE AUTHORITIES HANDLE THIS.
WHAT HAPPENS NOW?
AFTER YOUR MOTHER'S GRIM EXPOSÉ, THE FBI WILL NOW SHUT S.T.A.R. LABS DOWN FOR GOOD.
WELL, IN THAT CASE...
...I MUST TAKE MY LEAVE.
I MUST RETURN MYSELF TO THE 31ST CENTURY AND THE LEGION OF SUPER-HEROES.
BUT THIS WAS A LIFE-CHANGING EXPERIENCE FOR ME.
I AM SO DEEPLY GRATEFUL TO YOU FOR SO MANY THINGS.
YOU WERE AN ENORMOUS HELP TO US, BRAINIAC 5.
THANK YOU FOR LETTING ME EXPERIENCE THIS SERIES OF RATHER PERSONAL MOMENTS WITH YOU AND YOUR FAMILY.
I'LL MEET YOU BACK IN THE FUTURE TOMORROW.
I AM GOING TO HANG WITH MY DAD.
"BACK IN THE FUTURE TOMORROW." WEIRD SENTENCE.
I WOULD LOVE AN INVITATION TO THE 31ST CENTURY TO VISIT YOU AND THE LEGION OF SUPER-HEROES.
WELL...

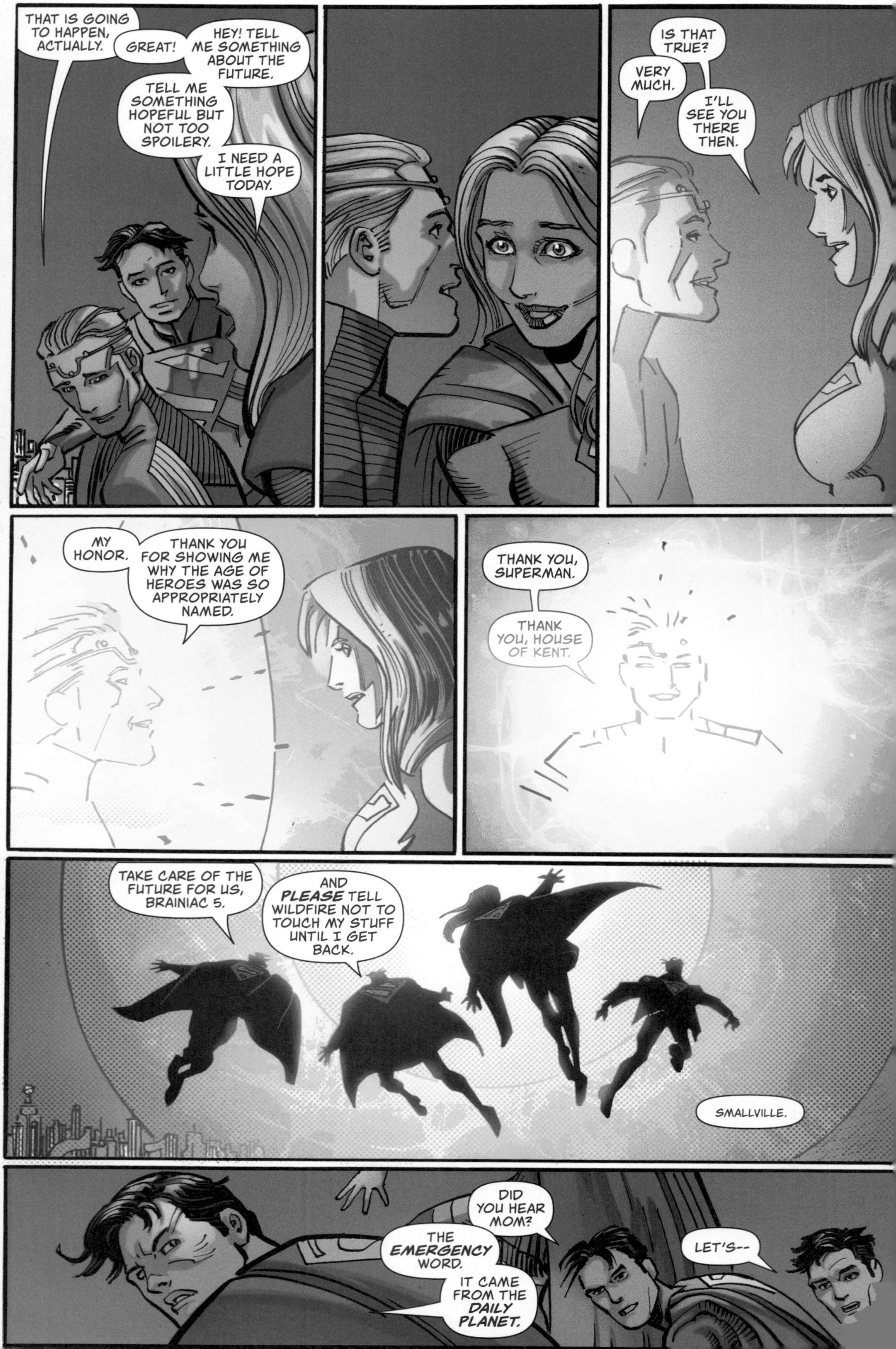

THAT IS GOING TO HAPPEN, ACTUALLY.
GREAT!
HEY! TELL ME SOMETHING ABOUT THE FUTURE.
TELL ME SOMETHING HOPEFUL BUT NOT TOO SPOILERY.
I NEED A LITTLE HOPE TODAY.
IS THAT TRUE?
VERY MUCH.
I'LL SEE YOU THERE THEN.
MY HONOR.
THANK YOU FOR SHOWING ME WHY THE AGE OF HEROES WAS SO APPROPRIATELY NAMED.
THANK YOU, SUPERMAN.
THANK YOU, HOUSE OF KENT.
TAKE CARE OF THE FUTURE FOR US, BRAINIAC 5.
AND PLEASE TELL WILDFIRE NOT TO TOUCH MY STUFF UNTIL I GET BACK.
SMALLVILLE.
DID YOU HEAR MOM?
THE EMERGENCY WORD.
IT CAME FROM THE DAILY PLANET.
LET'S--

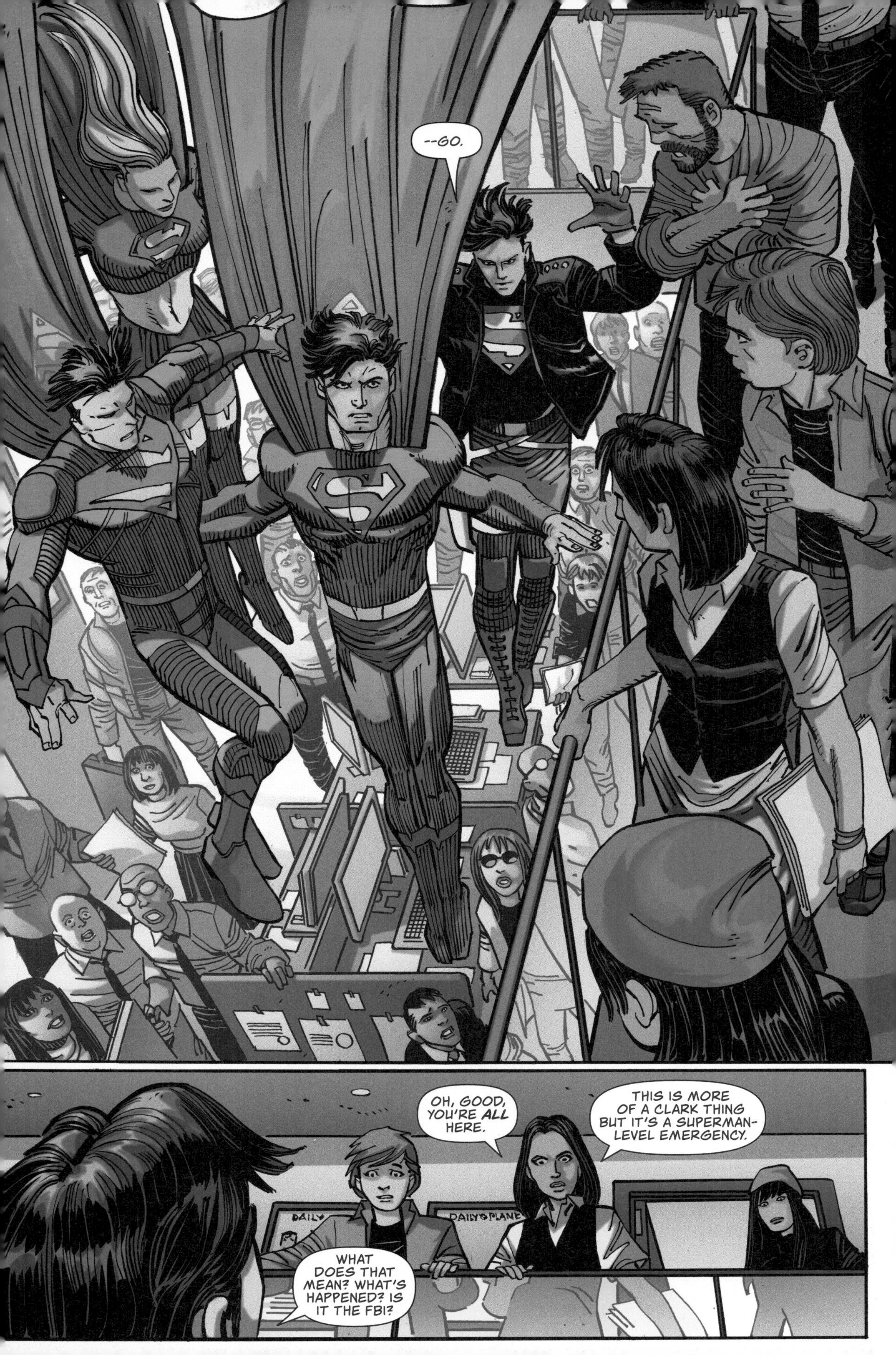
--GO.
OH, GOOD, YOU'RE ALL HERE.
THIS IS MORE OF A CLARK THING BUT IT'S A SUPERMAN-LEVEL EMERGENCY.
WHAT DOES THAT MEAN? WHAT'S HAPPENED? IS IT THE FBI?

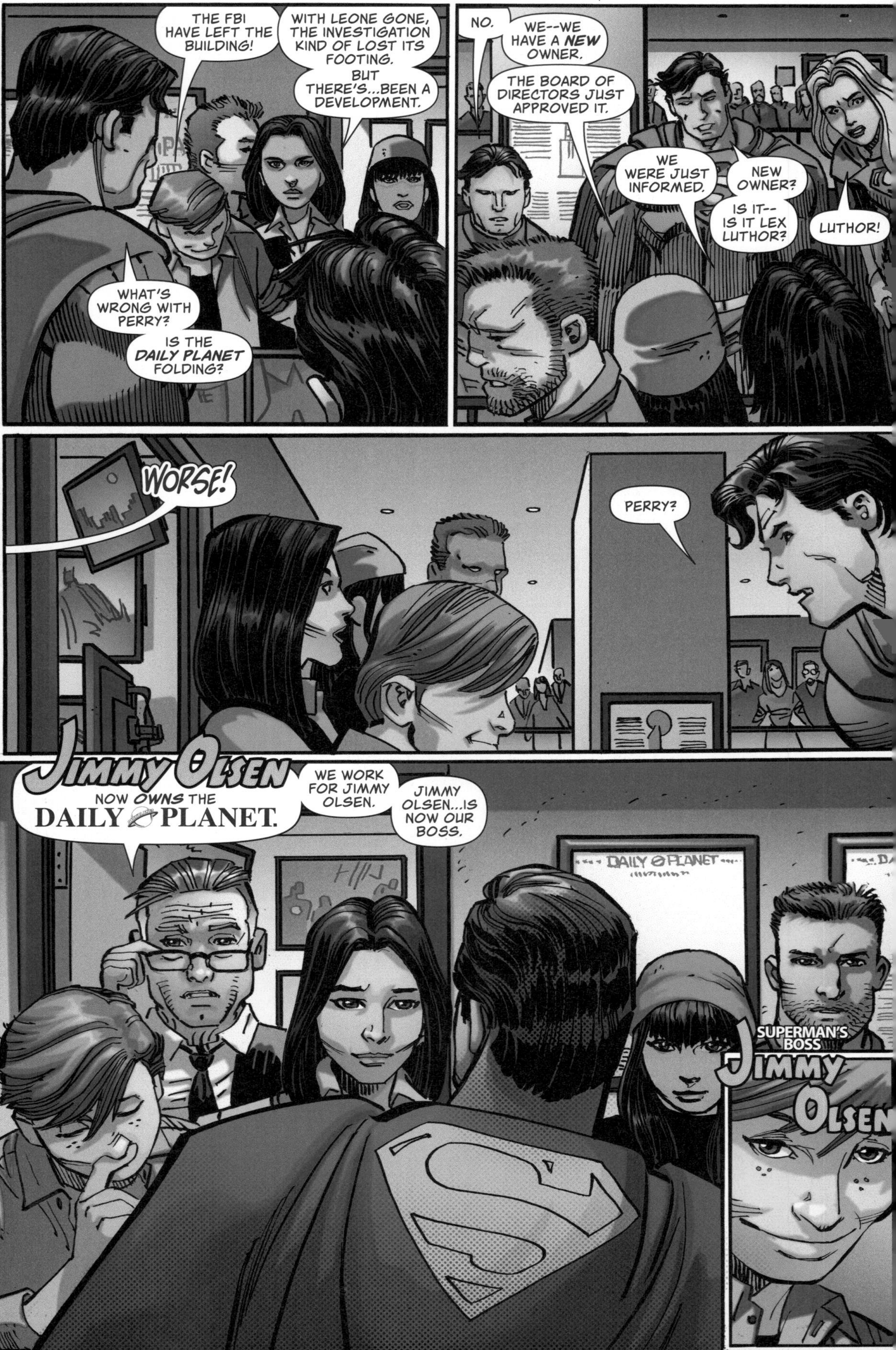
THE FBI HAVE LEFT THE BUILDING!
WITH LEONE GONE, THE INVESTIGATION KIND OF LOST ITS FOOTING.
BUT THERE'S...BEEN A DEVELOPMENT.
WHAT'S WRONG WITH PERRY?
IS THE DAILY PLANET FOLDING?
NO.
WE--WE HAVE A NEW OWNER.
THE BOARD OF DIRECTORS JUST APPROVED IT.
WE WERE JUST INFORMED.
NEW OWNER?
IS IT-- IS IT LEX LUTHOR?
LUTHOR!
WORSE!
PERRY?
JIMMY OLSEN NOW OWNS THE DAILY PLANET.
WE WORK FOR JIMMY OLSEN.
JIMMY OLSEN...IS NOW OUR BOSS.
DAILY PLANET
SUPERMAN'S BOSS JIMMY OLSEN

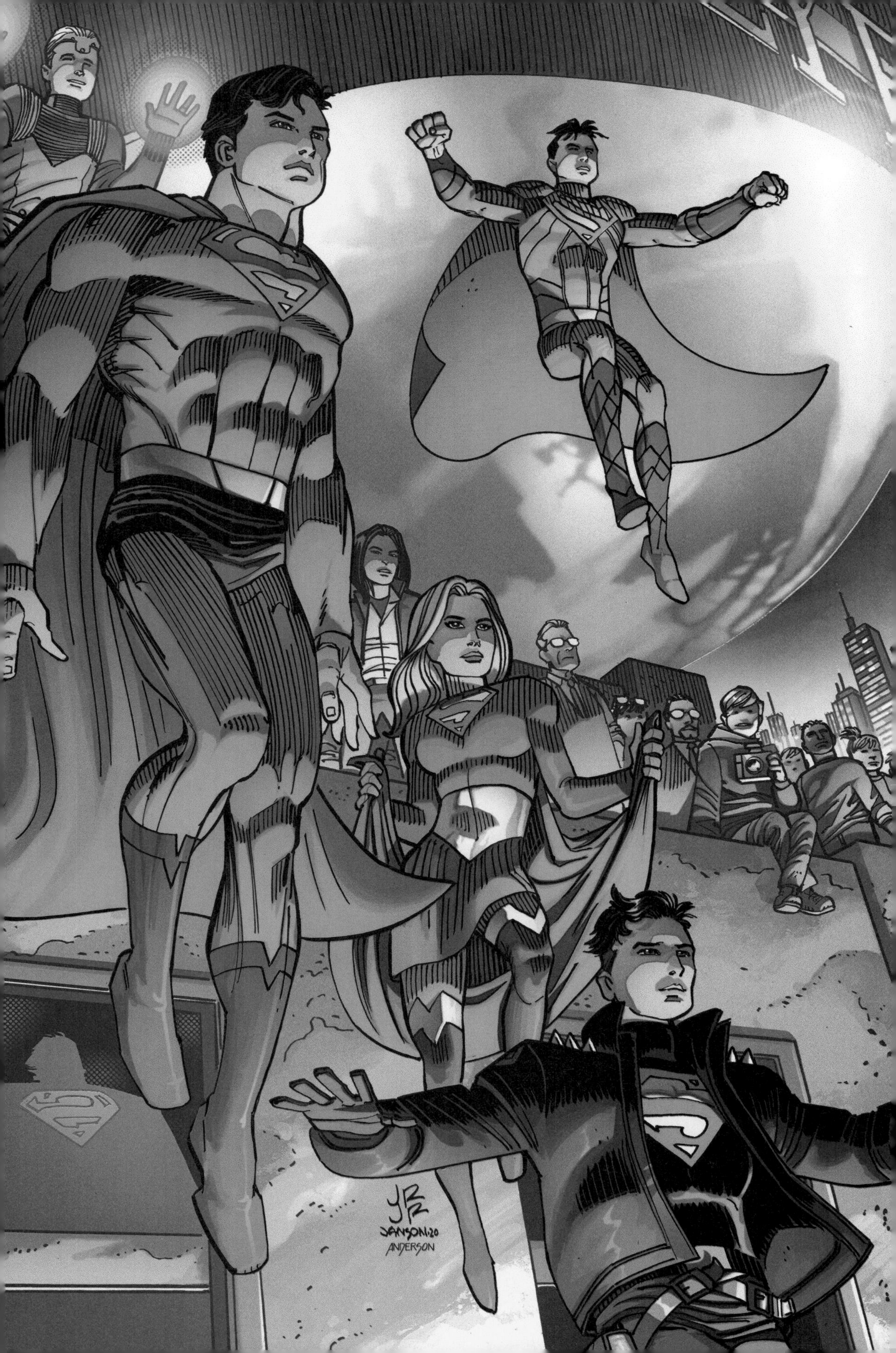
JANSON·20
ANDERSON

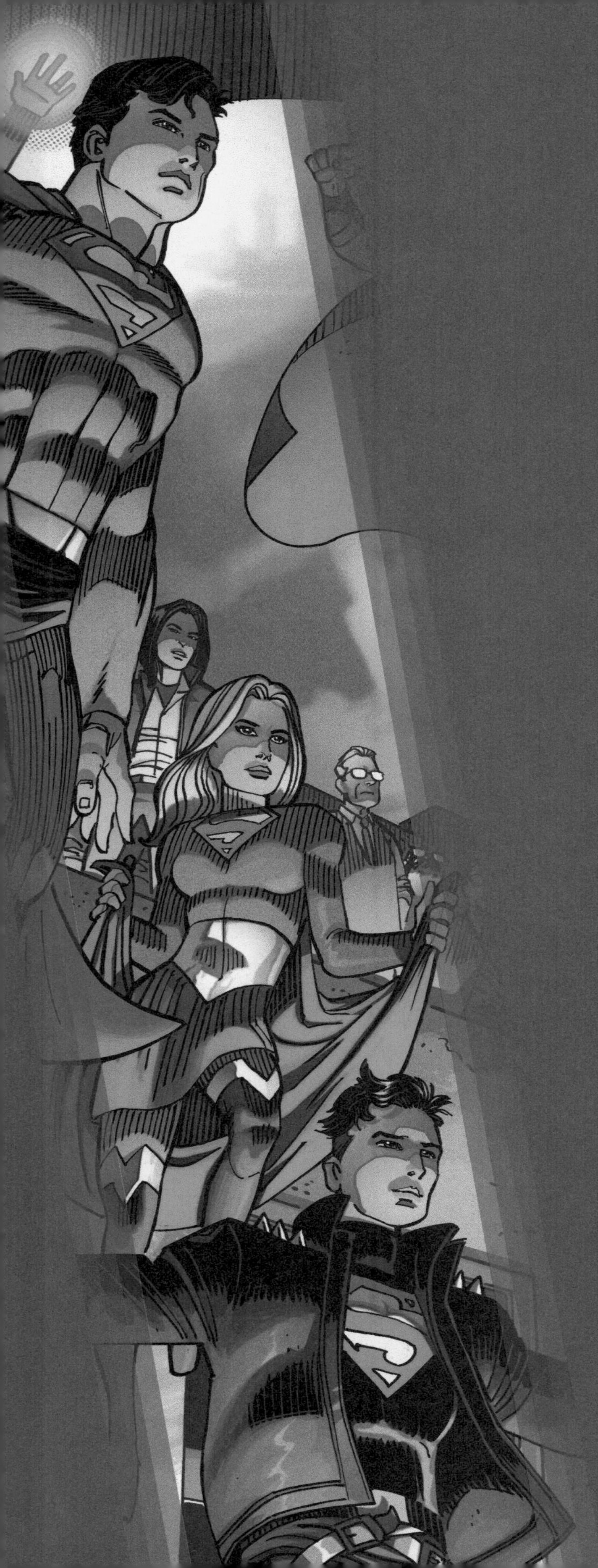

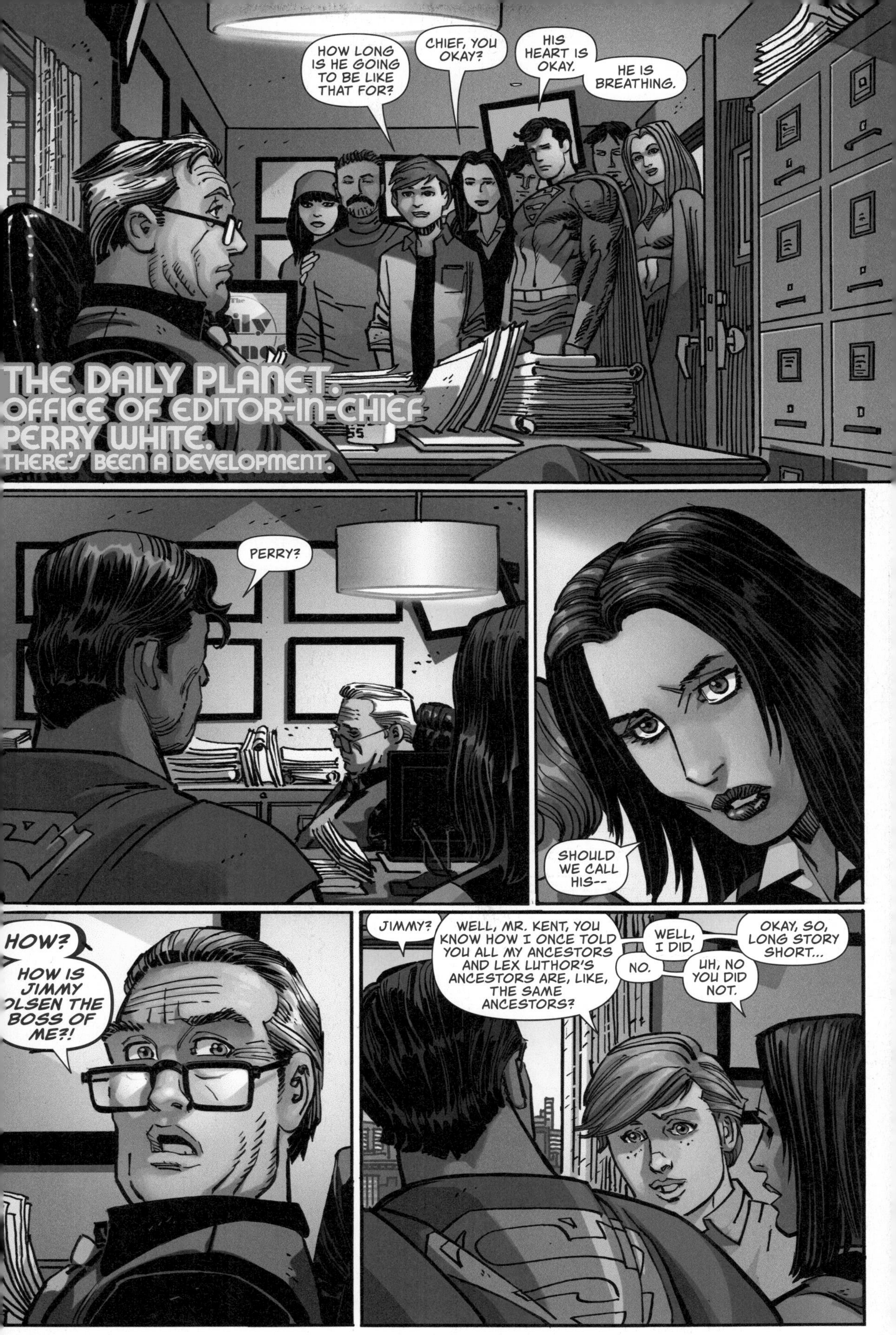
THE DAILY PLANET.
OFFICE OF EDITOR-IN-CHIEF PERRY WHITE.
THERE'S BEEN A DEVELOPMENT.
HOW LONG IS HE GOING TO BE LIKE THAT FOR?
CHIEF, YOU OKAY?
HIS HEART IS OKAY.
HE IS BREATHING.
PERRY?
SHOULD WE CALL HIS--
HOW?
HOW IS JIMMY OLSEN THE BOSS OF ME?!
JIMMY?
WELL, MR. KENT, YOU KNOW HOW I ONCE TOLD YOU ALL MY ANCESTORS AND LEX LUTHOR'S ANCESTORS ARE, LIKE, THE SAME ANCESTORS?
WELL, I DID.
NO.
UH, NO YOU DID NOT.
OKAY, SO, LONG STORY SHORT...

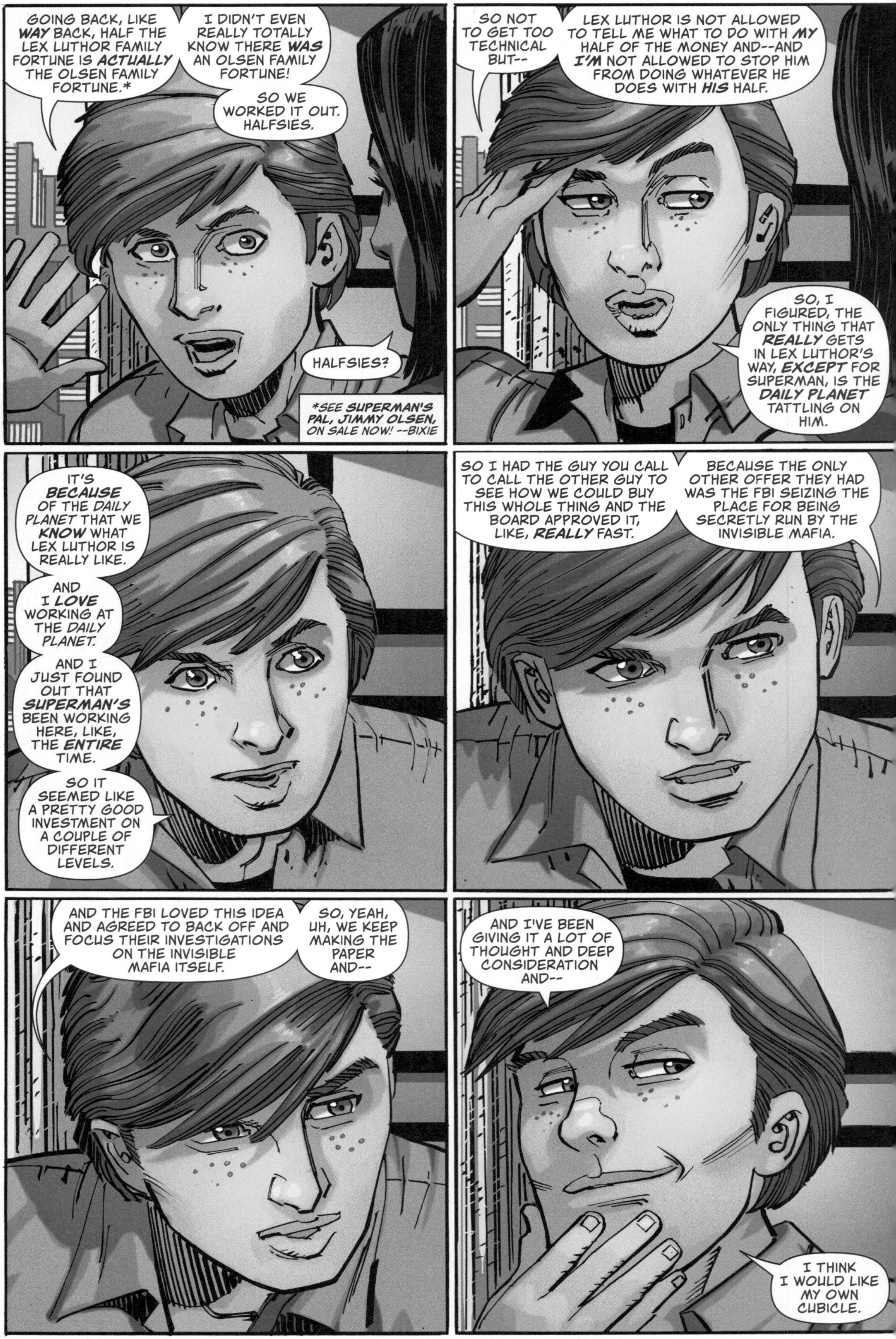
GOING BACK, LIKE WAY BACK, HALF THE LEX LUTHOR FAMILY FORTUNE IS ACTUALLY THE OLSEN FAMILY FORTUNE.*
I DIDN'T EVEN REALLY TOTALLY KNOW THERE WAS AN OLSEN FAMILY FORTUNE!
SO WE WORKED IT OUT. HALFSIES.
HALFSIES?
*SEE SUPERMAN'S PAL, JIMMY OLSEN, ON SALE NOW! --BIXIE
SO NOT TO GET TOO TECHNICAL BUT--
LEX LUTHOR IS NOT ALLOWED TO TELL ME WHAT TO DO WITH MY HALF OF THE MONEY AND--AND I'M NOT ALLOWED TO STOP HIM FROM DOING WHATEVER HE DOES WITH HIS HALF.
SO, I FIGURED, THE ONLY THING THAT REALLY GETS IN LEX LUTHOR'S WAY, EXCEPT FOR SUPERMAN, IS THE DAILY PLANET TATTLING ON HIM.
IT'S BECAUSE OF THE DAILY PLANET THAT WE KNOW WHAT LEX LUTHOR IS REALLY LIKE.
AND I LOVE WORKING AT THE DAILY PLANET.
AND I JUST FOUND OUT THAT SUPERMAN'S BEEN WORKING HERE, LIKE, THE ENTIRE TIME.
SO IT SEEMED LIKE A PRETTY GOOD INVESTMENT ON A COUPLE OF DIFFERENT LEVELS.
SO I HAD THE GUY YOU CALL TO CALL THE OTHER GUY TO SEE HOW WE COULD BUY THIS WHOLE THING AND THE BOARD APPROVED IT, LIKE, REALLY FAST.
BECAUSE THE ONLY OTHER OFFER THEY HAD WAS THE FBI SEIZING THE PLACE FOR BEING SECRETLY RUN BY THE INVISIBLE MAFIA.
AND THE FBI LOVED THIS IDEA AND AGREED TO BACK OFF AND FOCUS THEIR INVESTIGATIONS ON THE INVISIBLE MAFIA ITSELF.
SO, YEAH, UH, WE KEEP MAKING THE PAPER AND--
AND I'VE BEEN GIVING IT A LOT OF THOUGHT AND DEEP CONSIDERATION AND--
I THINK I WOULD LIKE MY OWN CUBICLE.

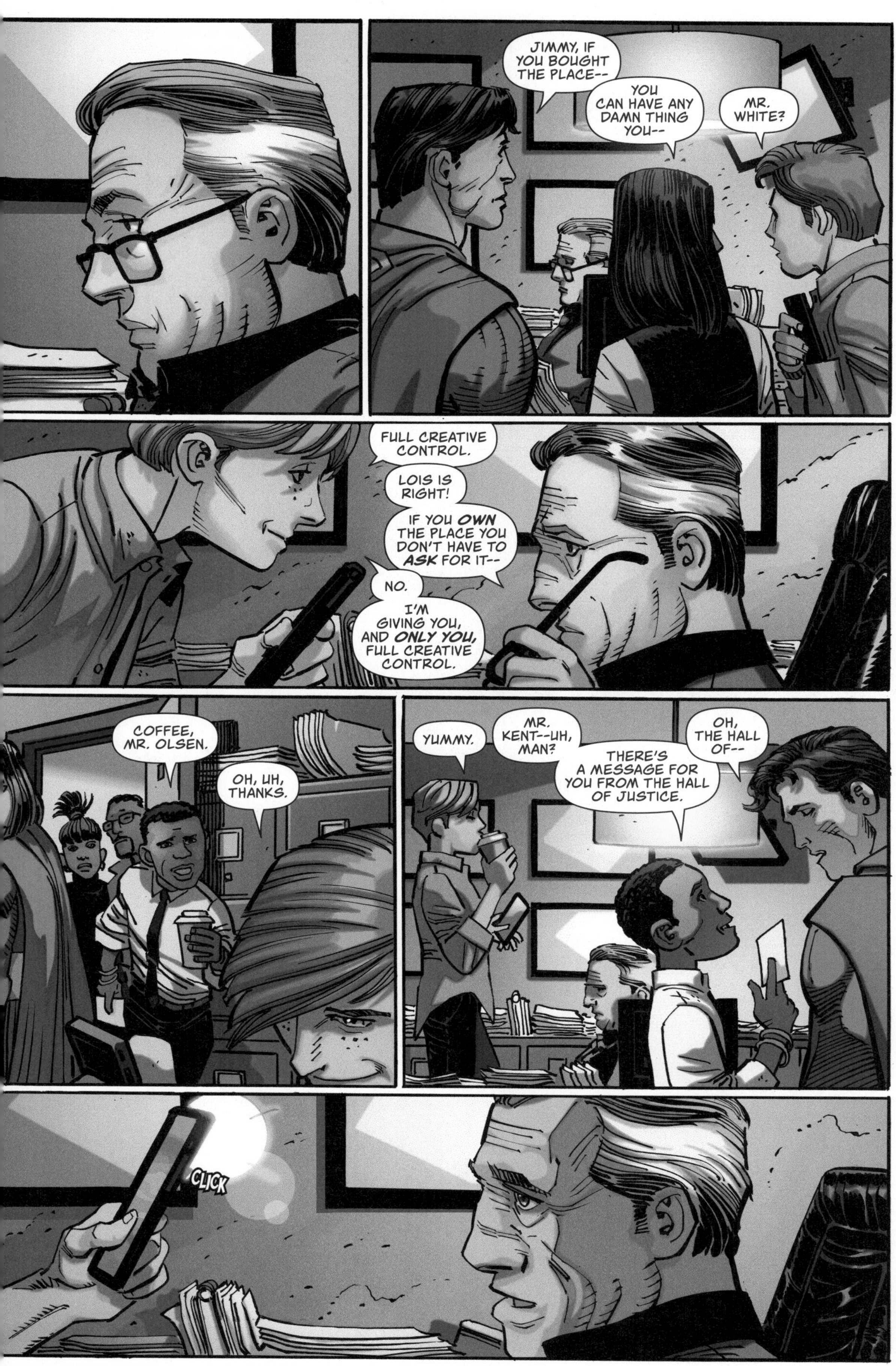
JIMMY, IF YOU BOUGHT THE PLACE--
YOU CAN HAVE ANY DAMN THING YOU--
MR. WHITE?
FULL CREATIVE CONTROL.
LOIS IS RIGHT!
IF YOU OWN THE PLACE YOU DON'T HAVE TO ASK FOR IT--
NO.
I'M GIVING YOU, AND ONLY YOU, FULL CREATIVE CONTROL.
COFFEE, MR. OLSEN.
OH, UH, THANKS.
YUMMY.
MR. KENT--UH, MAN?
THERE'S A MESSAGE FOR YOU FROM THE HALL OF JUSTICE.
OH, THE HALL OF--
CLICK

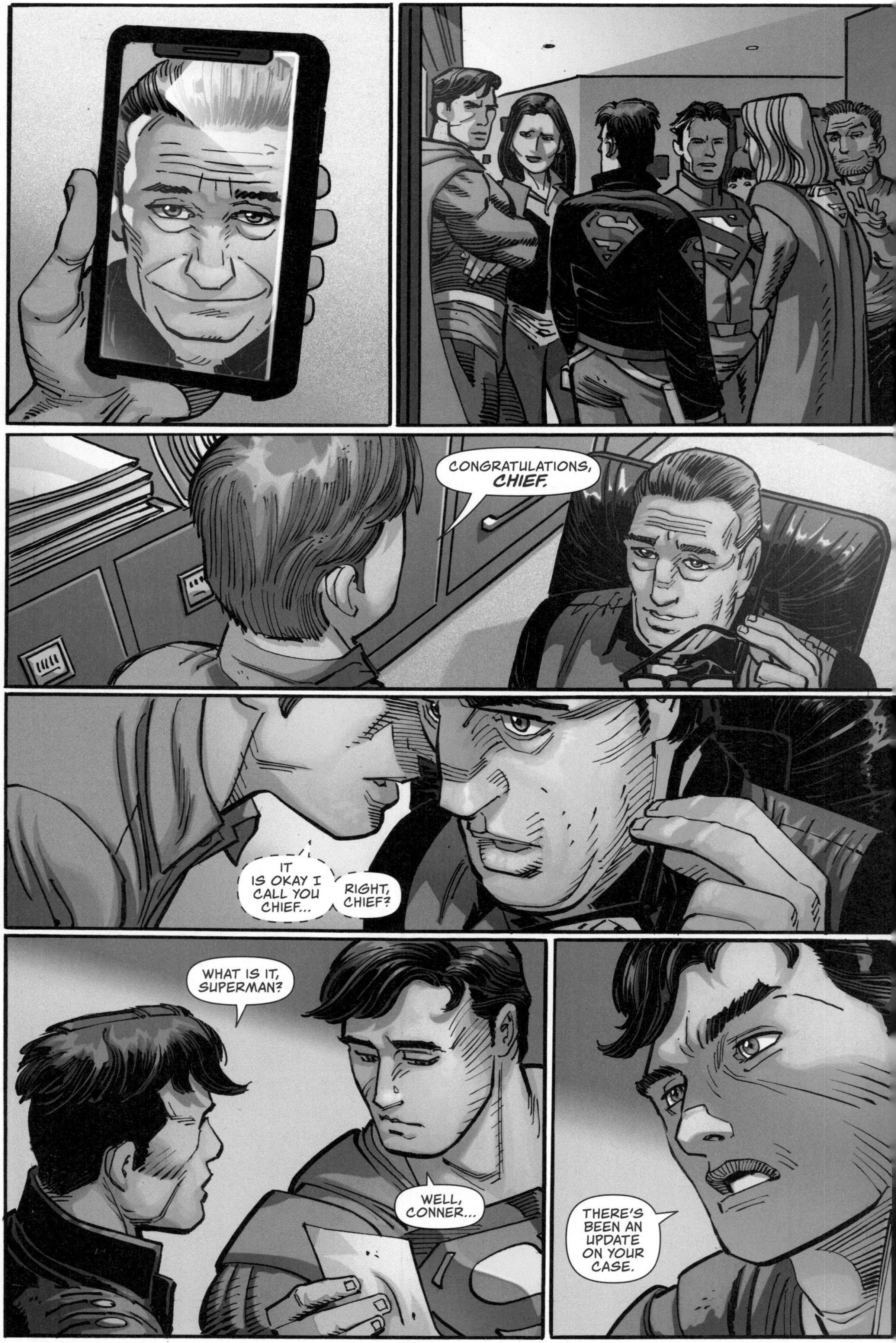
CONGRATULATIONS, CHIEF.
IT IS OKAY I CALL YOU CHIEF...
RIGHT, CHIEF?
WHAT IS IT, SUPERMAN?
WELL, CONNER...
THERE'S BEEN AN UPDATE ON YOUR CASE.

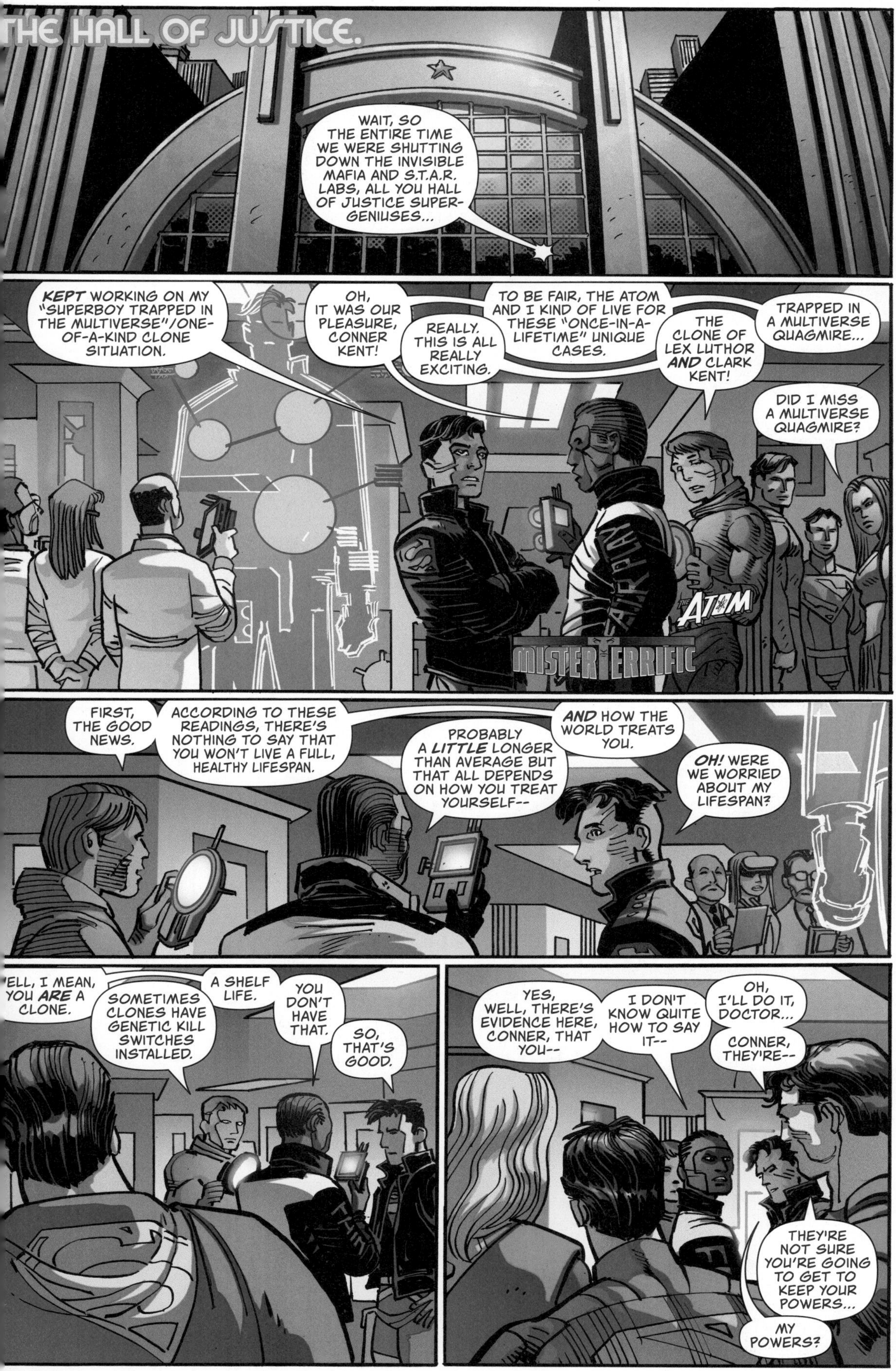
THE HALL OF JUSTICE.
WAIT, SO THE ENTIRE TIME WE WERE SHUTTING DOWN THE INVISIBLE MAFIA AND S.T.A.R. LABS, ALL YOU HALL OF JUSTICE SUPER-GENIUSES...
KEPT WORKING ON MY "SUPERBOY TRAPPED IN THE MULTIVERSE"/ONE-OF-A-KIND CLONE SITUATION.
OH, IT WAS OUR PLEASURE, CONNER KENT!
REALLY. THIS IS ALL REALLY EXCITING.
TO BE FAIR, THE ATOM AND I KIND OF LIVE FOR THESE "ONCE-IN-A-LIFETIME" UNIQUE CASES.
THE CLONE OF LEX LUTHOR AND CLARK KENT!
TRAPPED IN A MULTIVERSE QUAGMIRE...
DID I MISS A MULTIVERSE QUAGMIRE?
THE ATOM
MISTER TERRIFIC
FAIR PLAY
FIRST, THE GOOD NEWS.
ACCORDING TO THESE READINGS, THERE'S NOTHING TO SAY THAT YOU WON'T LIVE A FULL, HEALTHY LIFESPAN.
PROBABLY A LITTLE LONGER THAN AVERAGE BUT THAT ALL DEPENDS ON HOW YOU TREAT YOURSELF--
AND HOW THE WORLD TREATS YOU.
OH! WERE WE WORRIED ABOUT MY LIFESPAN?
ELL, I MEAN, YOU ARE A CLONE.
SOMETIMES CLONES HAVE GENETIC KILL SWITCHES INSTALLED.
A SHELF LIFE.
YOU DON'T HAVE THAT.
SO, THAT'S GOOD.
YES, WELL, THERE'S EVIDENCE HERE, CONNER, THAT YOU--
I DON'T KNOW QUITE HOW TO SAY IT--
OH, I'LL DO IT, DOCTOR...
CONNER, THEY'RE--
THEY'RE NOT SURE YOU'RE GOING TO GET TO KEEP YOUR POWERS...
MY POWERS?

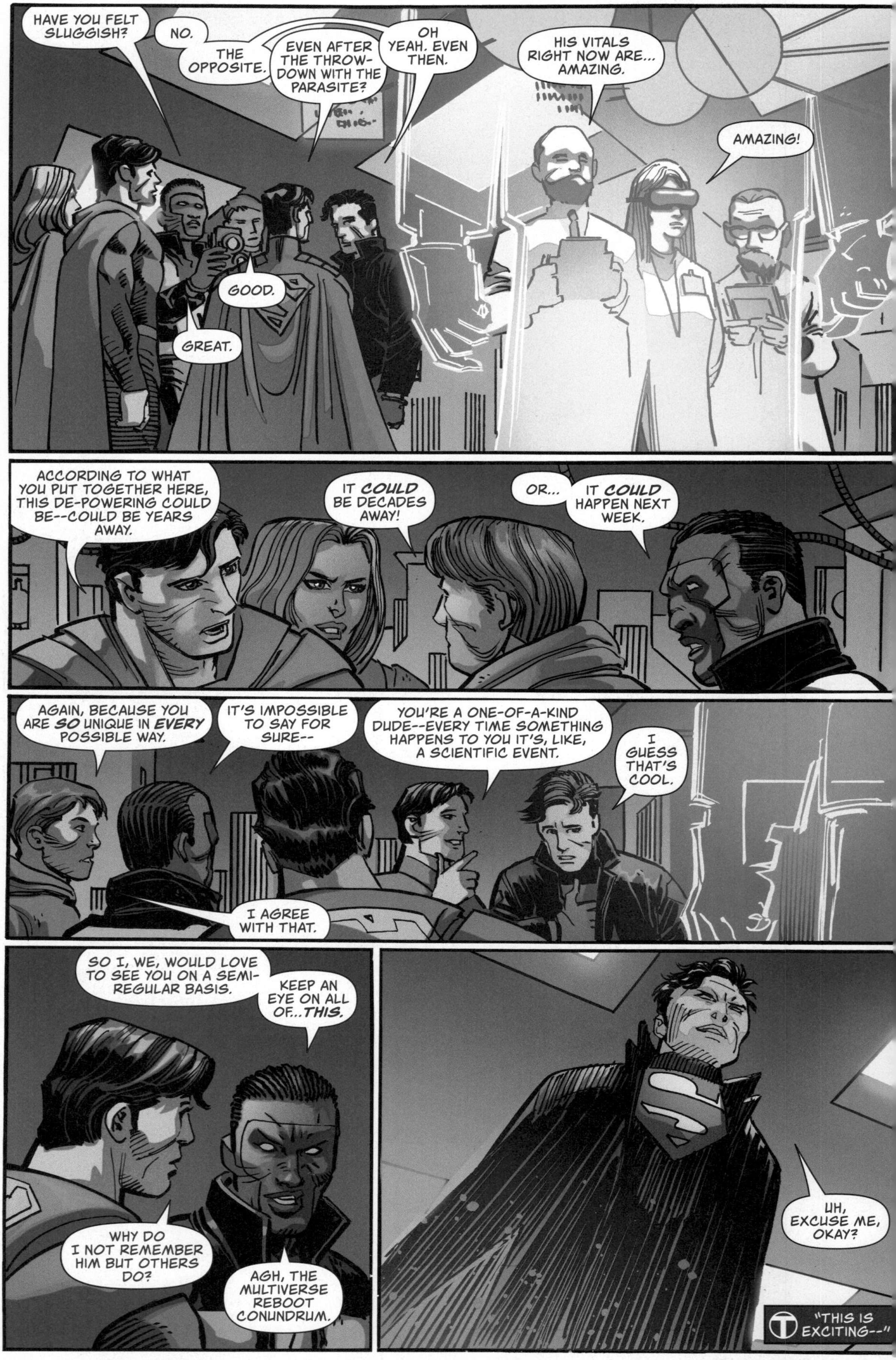
HAVE YOU FELT SLUGGISH?
NO.
THE OPPOSITE.
EVEN AFTER THE THROW-DOWN WITH THE PARASITE?
OH YEAH. EVEN THEN.
HIS VITALS RIGHT NOW ARE... AMAZING.
AMAZING!
GOOD.
GREAT.
ACCORDING TO WHAT YOU PUT TOGETHER HERE, THIS DE-POWERING COULD BE--COULD BE YEARS AWAY.
IT *COULD* BE DECADES AWAY!
OR...
IT *COULD* HAPPEN NEXT WEEK.
AGAIN, BECAUSE YOU ARE *SO* UNIQUE IN *EVERY* POSSIBLE WAY.
IT'S IMPOSSIBLE TO SAY FOR SURE--
YOU'RE A ONE-OF-A-KIND DUDE--EVERY TIME SOMETHING HAPPENS TO YOU IT'S, LIKE, A SCIENTIFIC EVENT.
I GUESS THAT'S COOL.
I AGREE WITH THAT.
SO I, WE, WOULD LOVE TO SEE YOU ON A SEMI-REGULAR BASIS.
KEEP AN EYE ON ALL OF...*THIS.*
WHY DO I NOT REMEMBER HIM BUT OTHERS DO?
AGH, THE MULTIVERSE REBOOT CONUNDRUM.
UH, EXCUSE ME, OKAY?
"THIS IS EXCITING--"

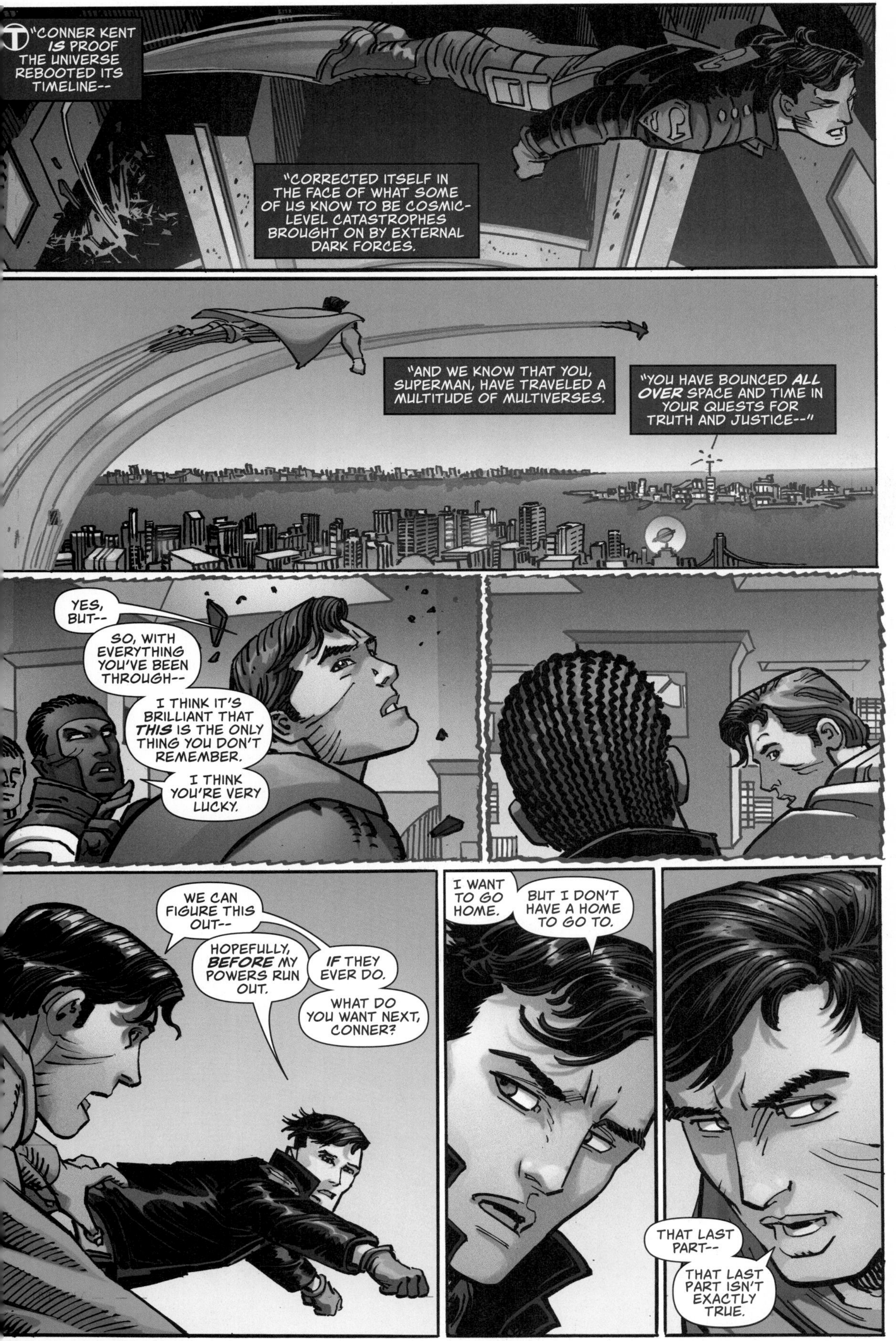
"CONNER KENT IS PROOF THE UNIVERSE REBOOTED ITS TIMELINE--
"CORRECTED ITSELF IN THE FACE OF WHAT SOME OF US KNOW TO BE COSMIC-LEVEL CATASTROPHES BROUGHT ON BY EXTERNAL DARK FORCES.
"AND WE KNOW THAT YOU, SUPERMAN, HAVE TRAVELED A MULTITUDE OF MULTIVERSES.
"YOU HAVE BOUNCED ALL OVER SPACE AND TIME IN YOUR QUESTS FOR TRUTH AND JUSTICE--"
YES, BUT--
SO, WITH EVERYTHING YOU'VE BEEN THROUGH--
I THINK IT'S BRILLIANT THAT THIS IS THE ONLY THING YOU DON'T REMEMBER.
I THINK YOU'RE VERY LUCKY.
WE CAN FIGURE THIS OUT--
HOPEFULLY, BEFORE MY POWERS RUN OUT.
IF THEY EVER DO.
WHAT DO YOU WANT NEXT, CONNER?
I WANT TO GO HOME.
BUT I DON'T HAVE A HOME TO GO TO.
THAT LAST PART--
THAT LAST PART ISN'T EXACTLY TRUE.

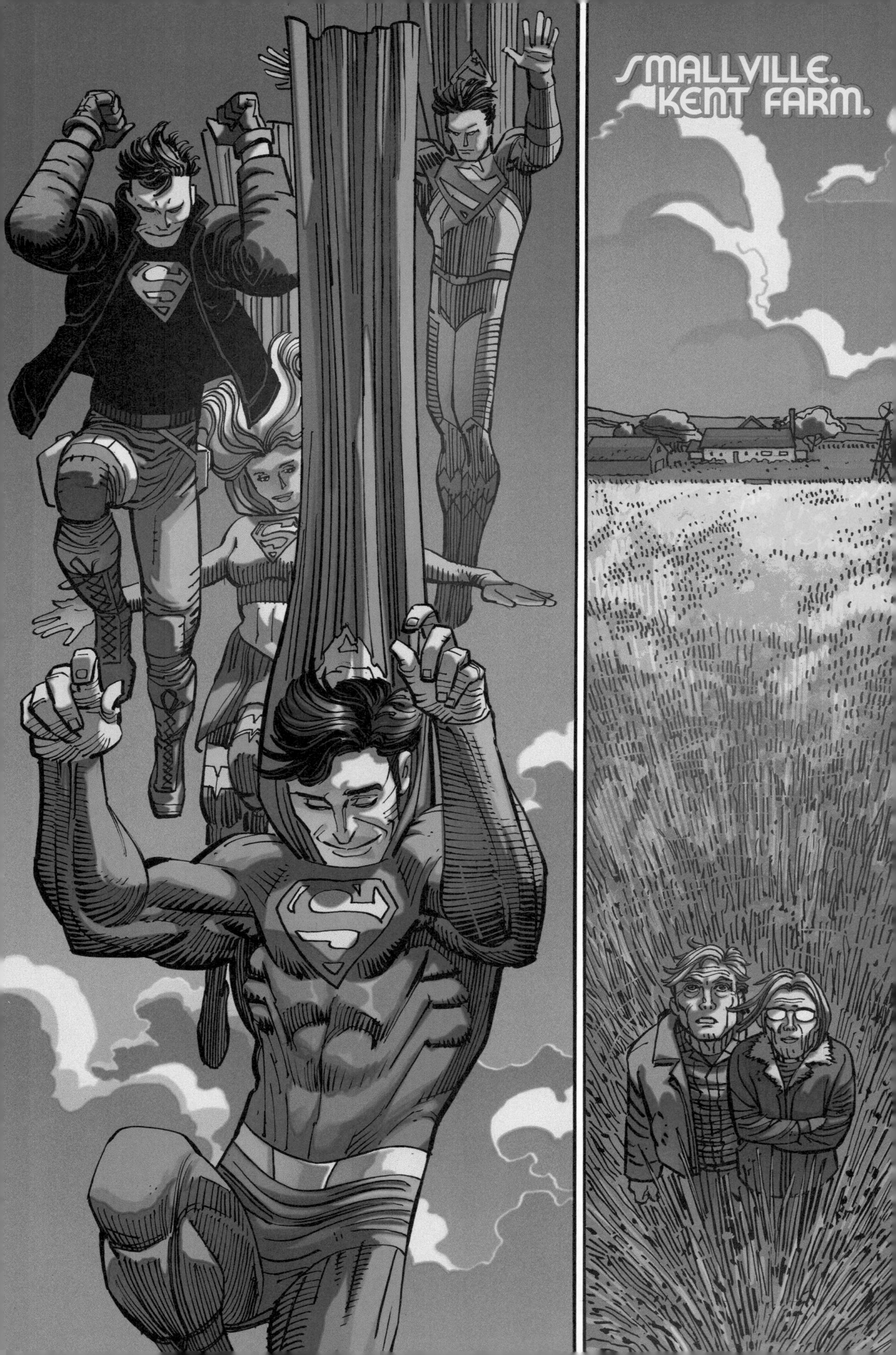
SMALLVILLE.
KENT FARM.

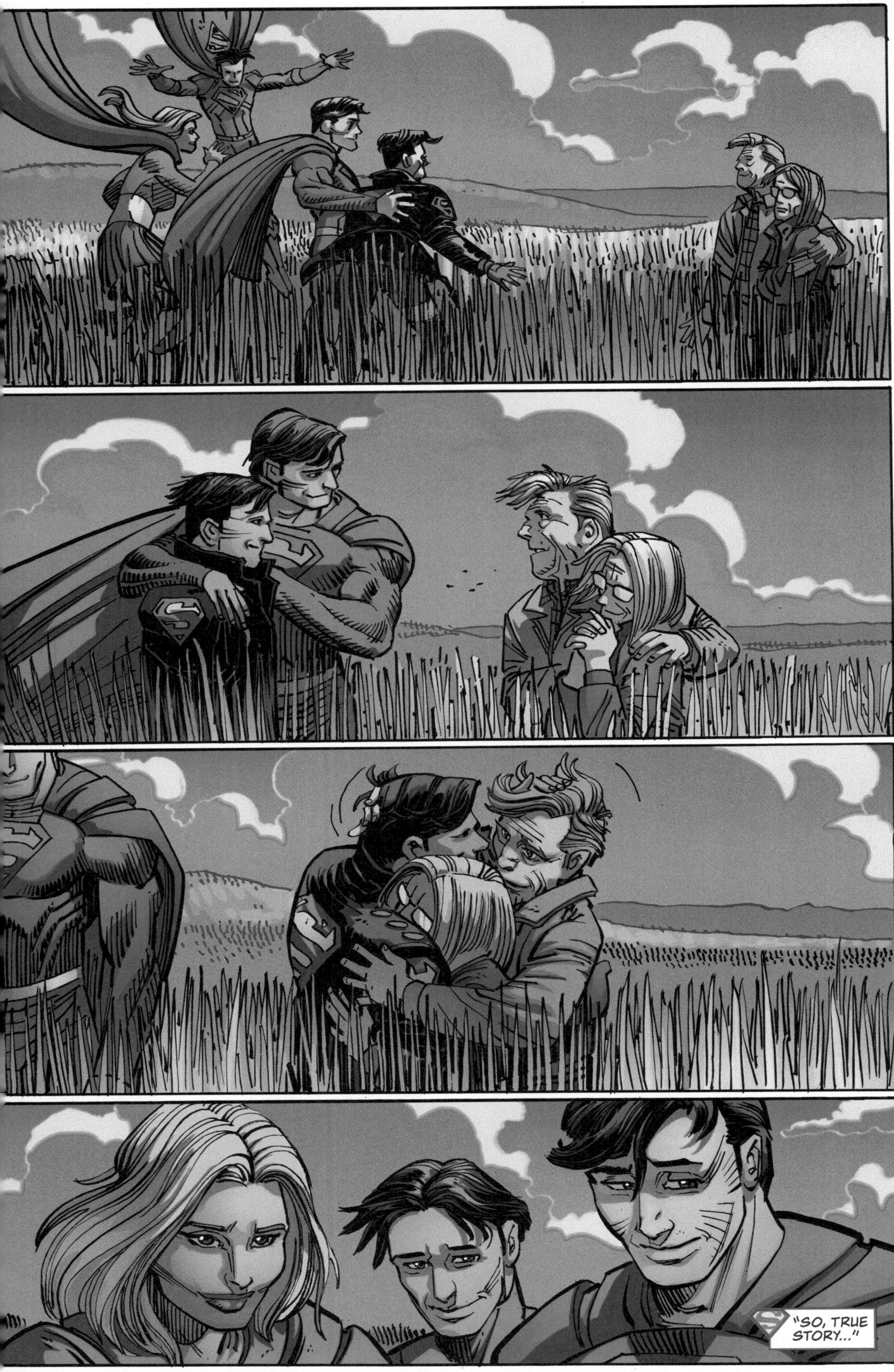
"SO, TRUE STORY..."

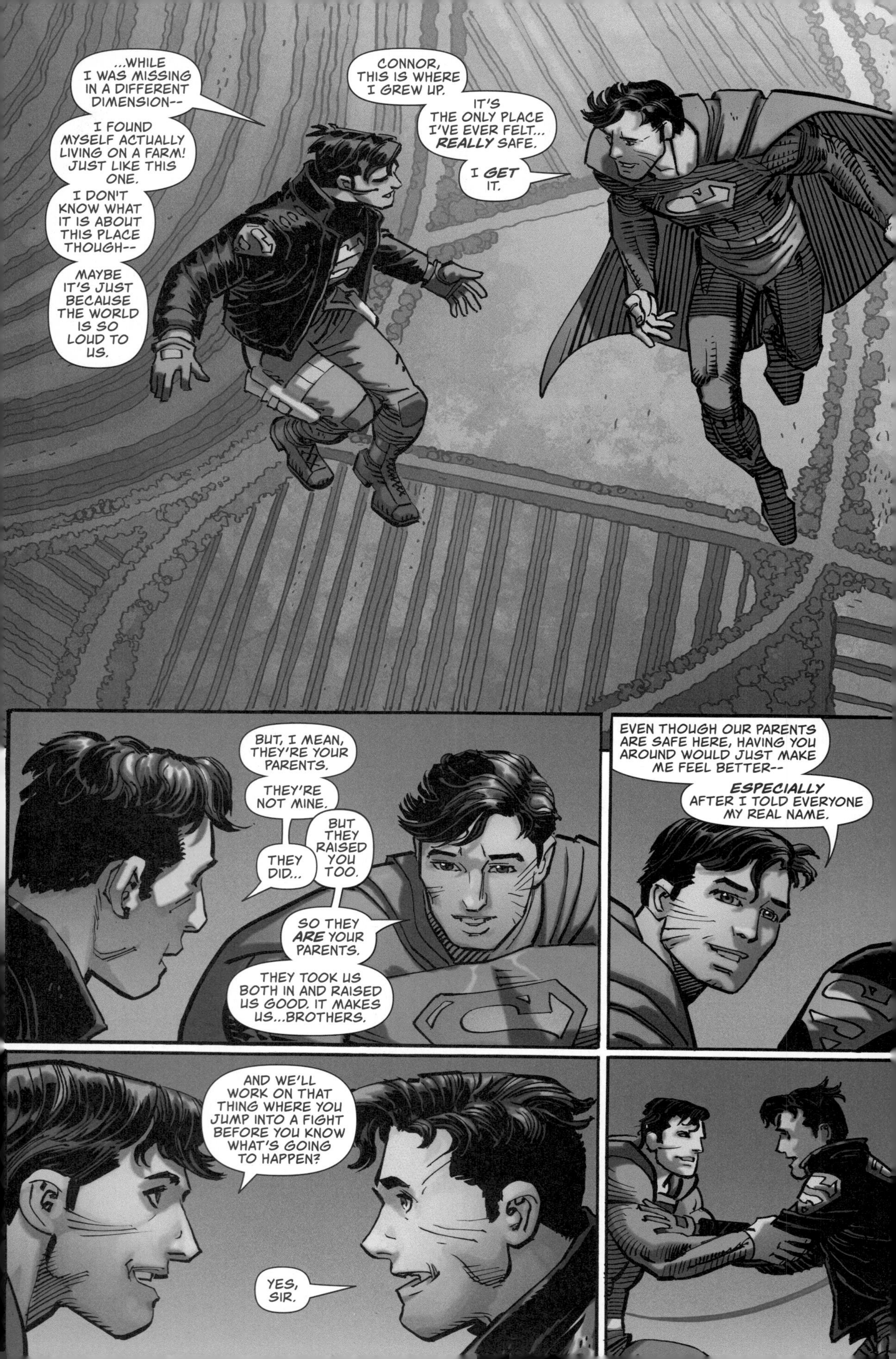

...WHILE I WAS MISSING IN A DIFFERENT DIMENSION--
I FOUND MYSELF ACTUALLY LIVING ON A FARM! JUST LIKE THIS ONE.
I DON'T KNOW WHAT IT IS ABOUT THIS PLACE THOUGH--
MAYBE IT'S JUST BECAUSE THE WORLD IS SO LOUD TO US.
CONNOR, THIS IS WHERE I GREW UP.
IT'S THE ONLY PLACE I'VE EVER FELT... REALLY SAFE.
I GET IT.
BUT, I MEAN, THEY'RE YOUR PARENTS.
THEY'RE NOT MINE.
THEY DID...
BUT THEY RAISED YOU TOO.
SO THEY ARE YOUR PARENTS.
THEY TOOK US BOTH IN AND RAISED US GOOD. IT MAKES US...BROTHERS.
EVEN THOUGH OUR PARENTS ARE SAFE HERE, HAVING YOU AROUND WOULD JUST MAKE ME FEEL BETTER--
ESPECIALLY AFTER I TOLD EVERYONE MY REAL NAME.
AND WE'LL WORK ON THAT THING WHERE YOU JUMP INTO A FIGHT BEFORE YOU KNOW WHAT'S GOING TO HAPPEN?
YES, SIR.

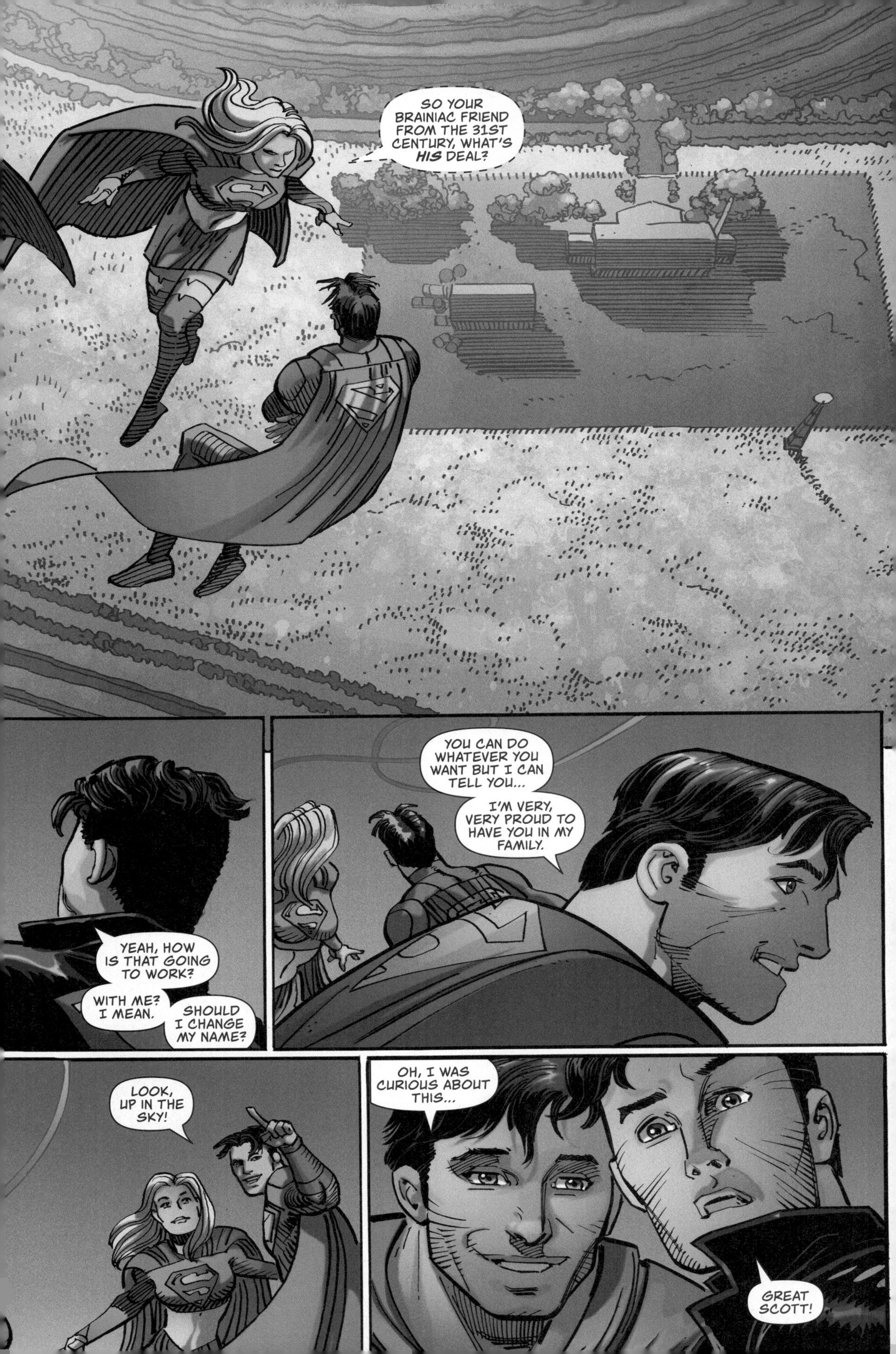
SO YOUR BRAINIAC FRIEND FROM THE 31ST CENTURY, WHAT'S **HIS** DEAL?
YEAH, HOW IS THAT GOING TO WORK?
WITH ME? I MEAN.
SHOULD I CHANGE MY NAME?
YOU CAN DO WHATEVER YOU WANT BUT I CAN TELL YOU...
I'M VERY, VERY PROUD TO HAVE YOU IN MY FAMILY.
LOOK, UP IN THE SKY!
OH, I WAS CURIOUS ABOUT THIS...
GREAT SCOTT!

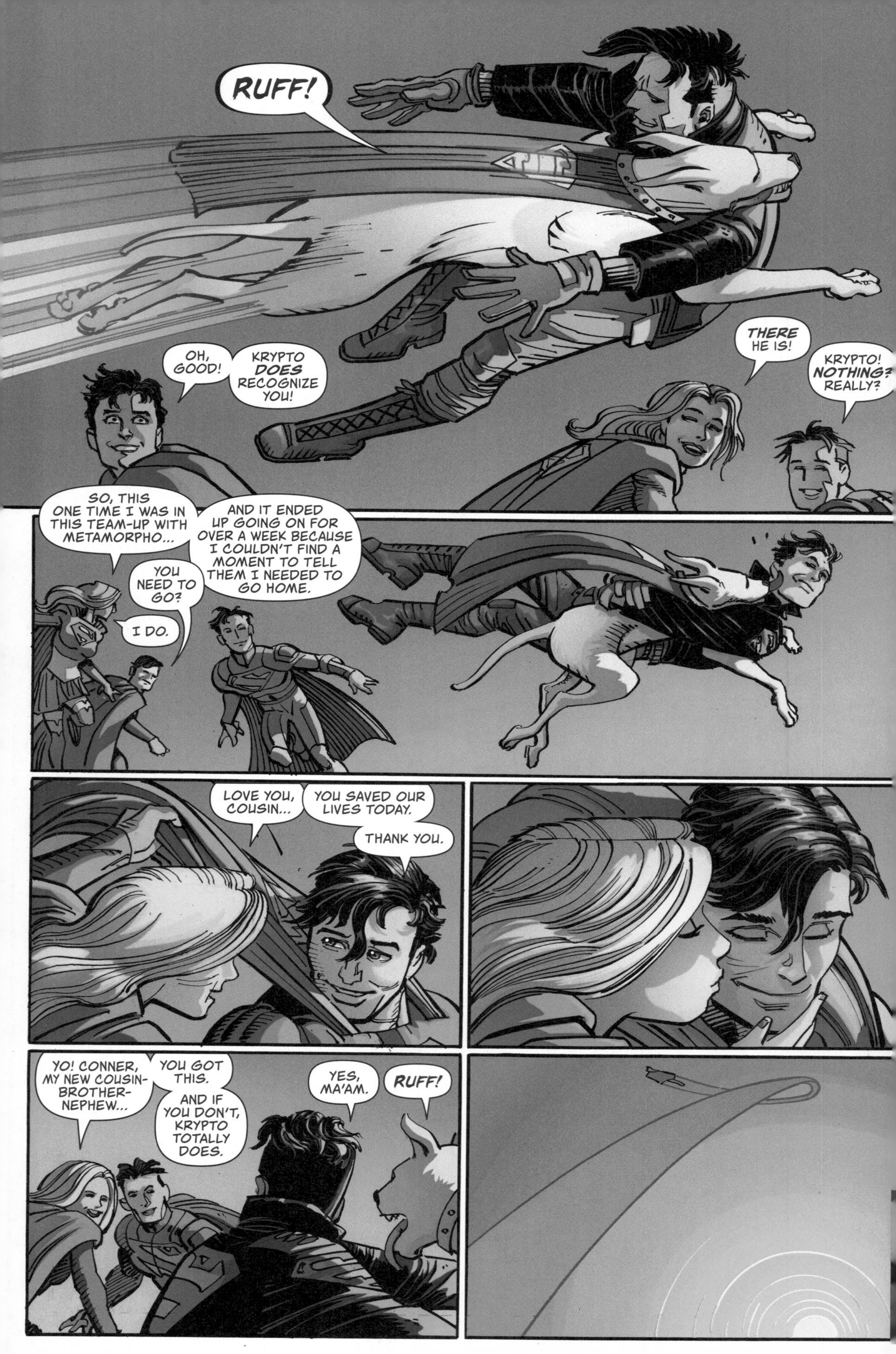
RUFF!
OH, GOOD!
KRYPTO DOES RECOGNIZE YOU!
THERE HE IS!
KRYPTO! NOTHING? REALLY?
SO, THIS ONE TIME I WAS IN THIS TEAM-UP WITH METAMORPHO...
AND IT ENDED UP GOING ON FOR OVER A WEEK BECAUSE I COULDN'T FIND A MOMENT TO TELL THEM I NEEDED TO GO HOME.
YOU NEED TO GO?
I DO.
LOVE YOU, COUSIN...
YOU SAVED OUR LIVES TODAY.
THANK YOU.
YO! CONNER, MY NEW COUSIN-BROTHER-NEPHEW...
YOU GOT THIS.
AND IF YOU DON'T, KRYPTO TOTALLY DOES.
YES, MA'AM.
RUFF!

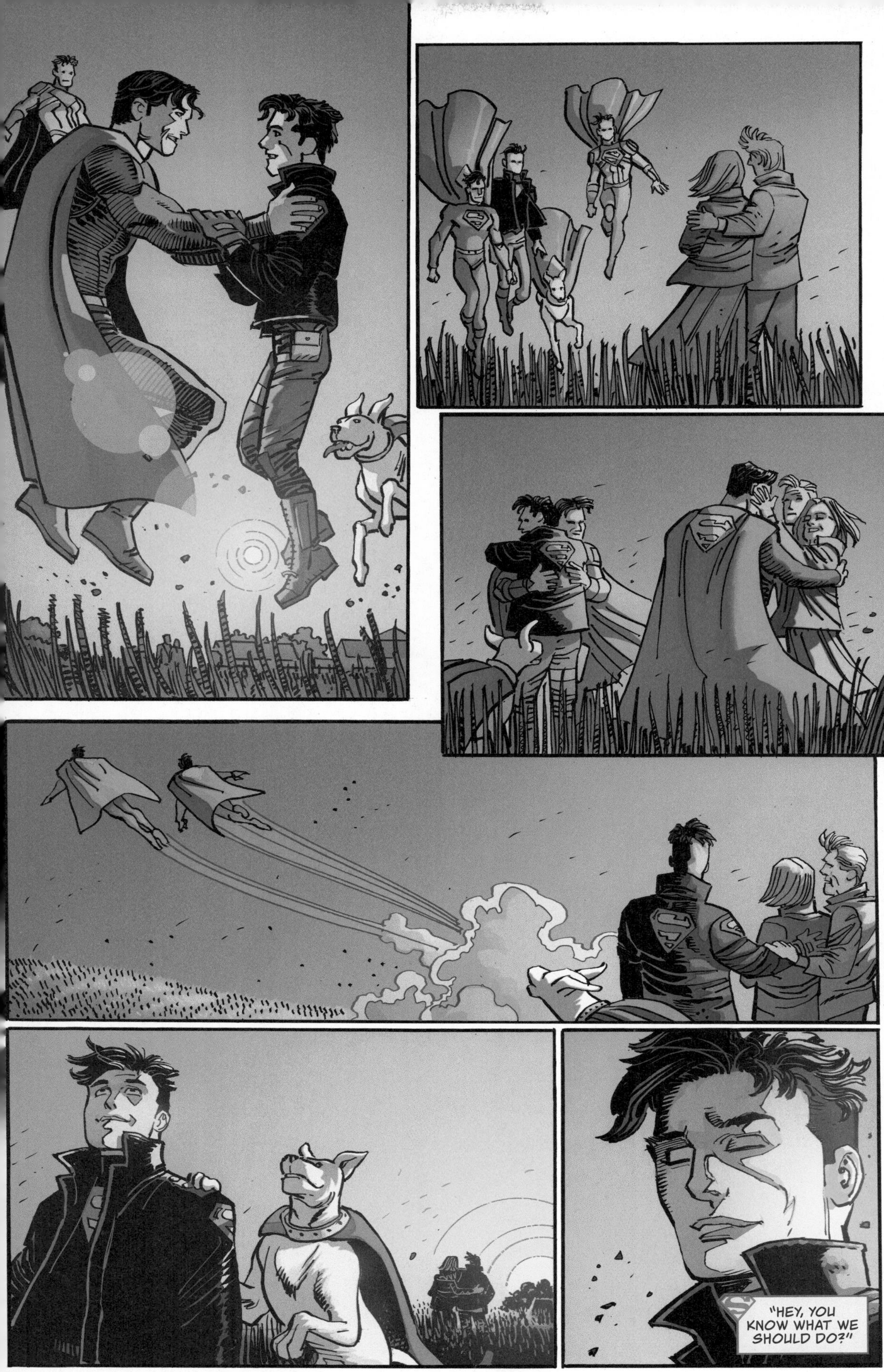
"HEY, YOU KNOW WHAT WE SHOULD DO?"

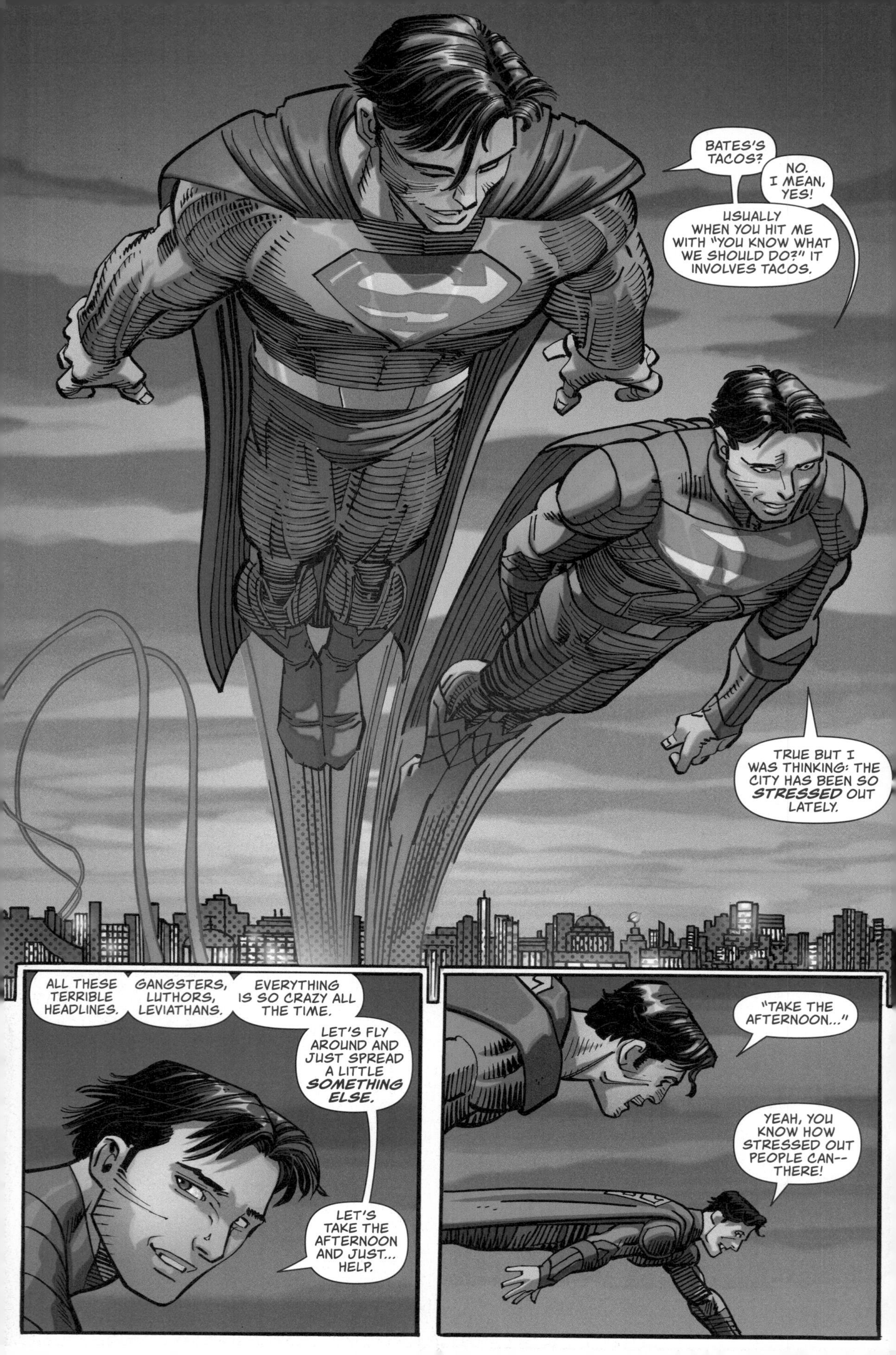
BATES'S TACOS?
USUALLY WHEN YOU HIT ME WITH "YOU KNOW WHAT WE SHOULD DO?" IT INVOLVES TACOS.
NO. I MEAN, YES!
TRUE BUT I WAS THINKING: THE CITY HAS BEEN SO STRESSED OUT LATELY.
ALL THESE TERRIBLE HEADLINES.
GANGSTERS, LUTHORS, LEVIATHANS.
EVERYTHING IS SO CRAZY ALL THE TIME.
LET'S FLY AROUND AND JUST SPREAD A LITTLE SOMETHING ELSE.
LET'S TAKE THE AFTERNOON AND JUST... HELP.
"TAKE THE AFTERNOON..."
YEAH, YOU KNOW HOW STRESSED OUT PEOPLE CAN-- THERE!

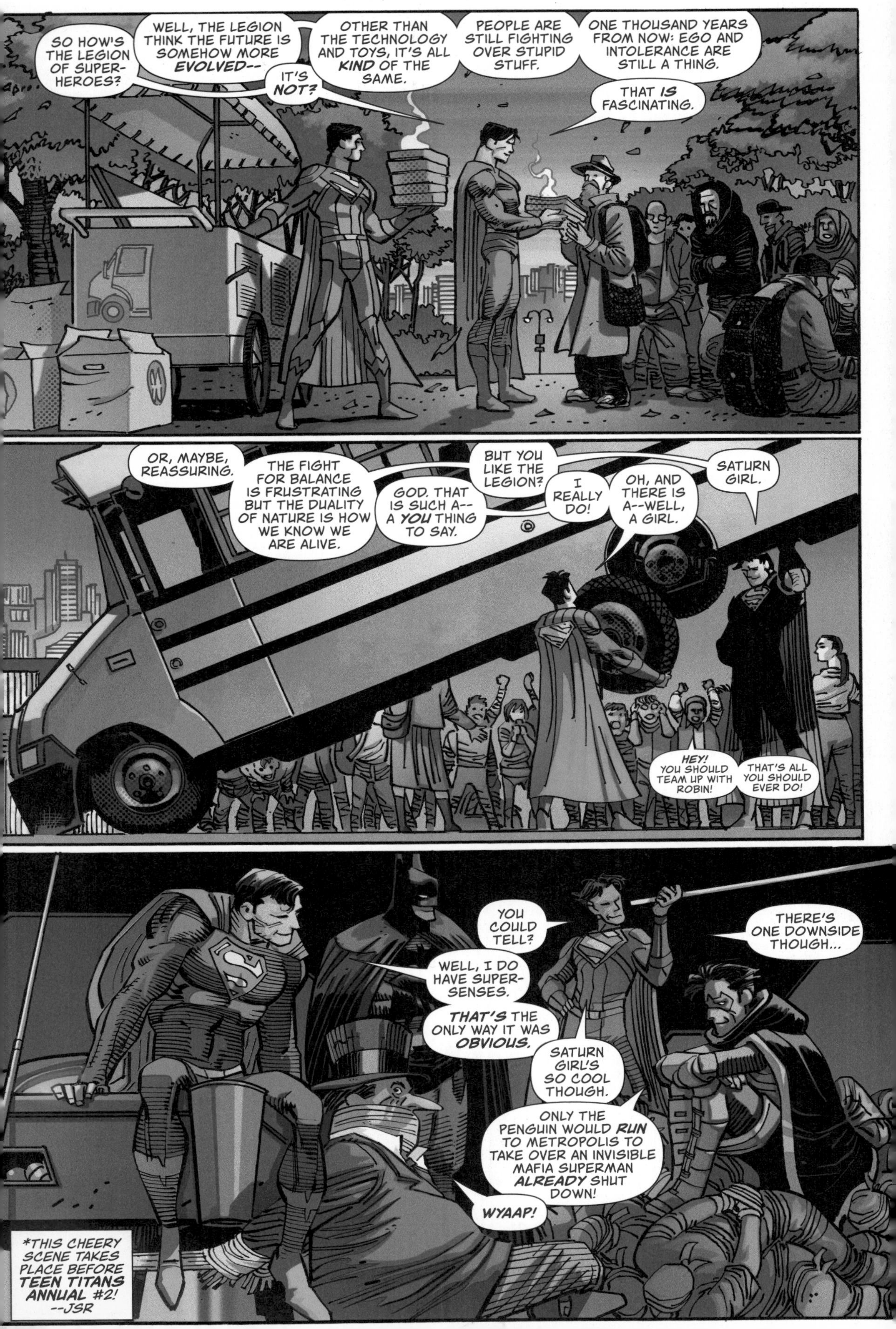

SO HOW'S THE LEGION OF SUPER-HEROES?
WELL, THE LEGION THINK THE FUTURE IS SOMEHOW MORE EVOLVED--
IT'S NOT?
OTHER THAN THE TECHNOLOGY AND TOYS, IT'S ALL KIND OF THE SAME.
PEOPLE ARE STILL FIGHTING OVER STUPID STUFF.
ONE THOUSAND YEARS FROM NOW: EGO AND INTOLERANCE ARE STILL A THING.
THAT IS FASCINATING.
OR, MAYBE, REASSURING.
THE FIGHT FOR BALANCE IS FRUSTRATING BUT THE DUALITY OF NATURE IS HOW WE KNOW WE ARE ALIVE.
GOD. THAT IS SUCH A-- A YOU THING TO SAY.
BUT YOU LIKE THE LEGION?
I REALLY DO!
OH, AND THERE IS A--WELL, A GIRL.
SATURN GIRL.
HEY! YOU SHOULD TEAM UP WITH ROBIN!
THAT'S ALL YOU SHOULD EVER DO!
YOU COULD TELL?
WELL, I DO HAVE SUPER-SENSES.
THAT'S THE ONLY WAY IT WAS OBVIOUS.
THERE'S ONE DOWNSIDE THOUGH...
SATURN GIRL'S SO COOL THOUGH.
ONLY THE PENGUIN WOULD RUN TO METROPOLIS TO TAKE OVER AN INVISIBLE MAFIA SUPERMAN ALREADY SHUT DOWN!
WYAAP!
*THIS CHEERY SCENE TAKES PLACE BEFORE TEEN TITANS ANNUAL #2! --JSR

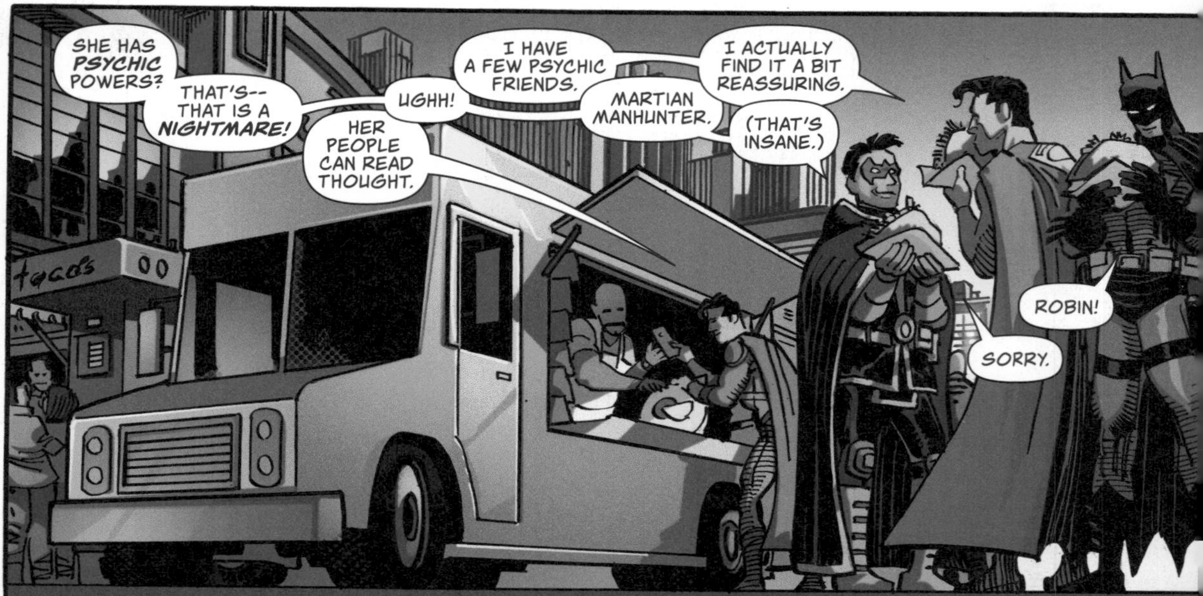
SHE HAS PSYCHIC POWERS?
THAT'S-- THAT IS A NIGHTMARE!
UGHH!
HER PEOPLE CAN READ THOUGHT.
I HAVE A FEW PSYCHIC FRIENDS.
MARTIAN MANHUNTER.
I ACTUALLY FIND IT A BIT REASSURING.
(THAT'S INSANE.)
ROBIN!
SORRY.

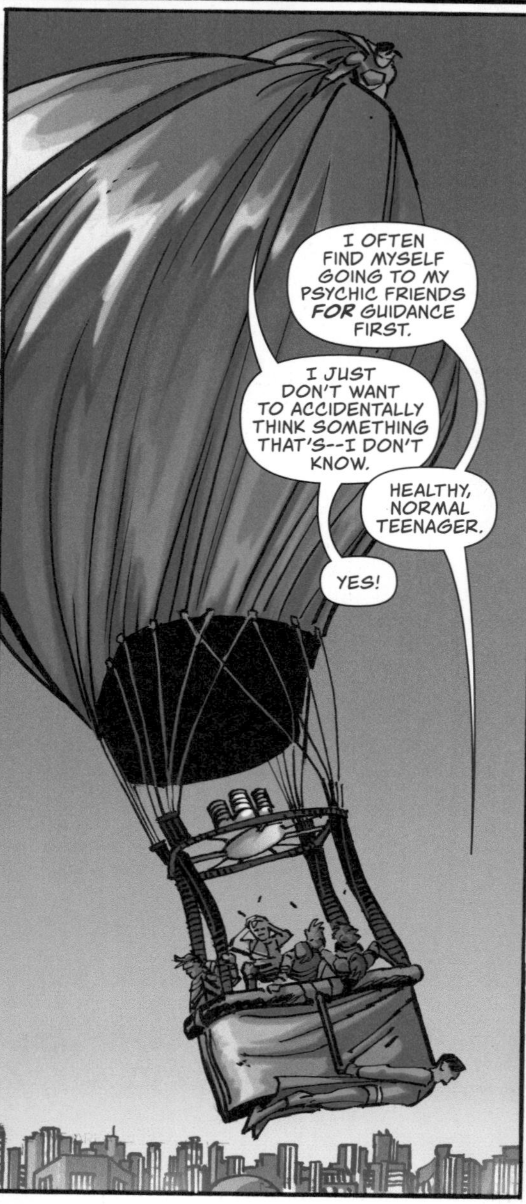
I OFTEN FIND MYSELF GOING TO MY PSYCHIC FRIENDS FOR GUIDANCE FIRST.
I JUST DON'T WANT TO ACCIDENTALLY THINK SOMETHING THAT'S--I DON'T KNOW.
HEALTHY, NORMAL TEENAGER.
YES!

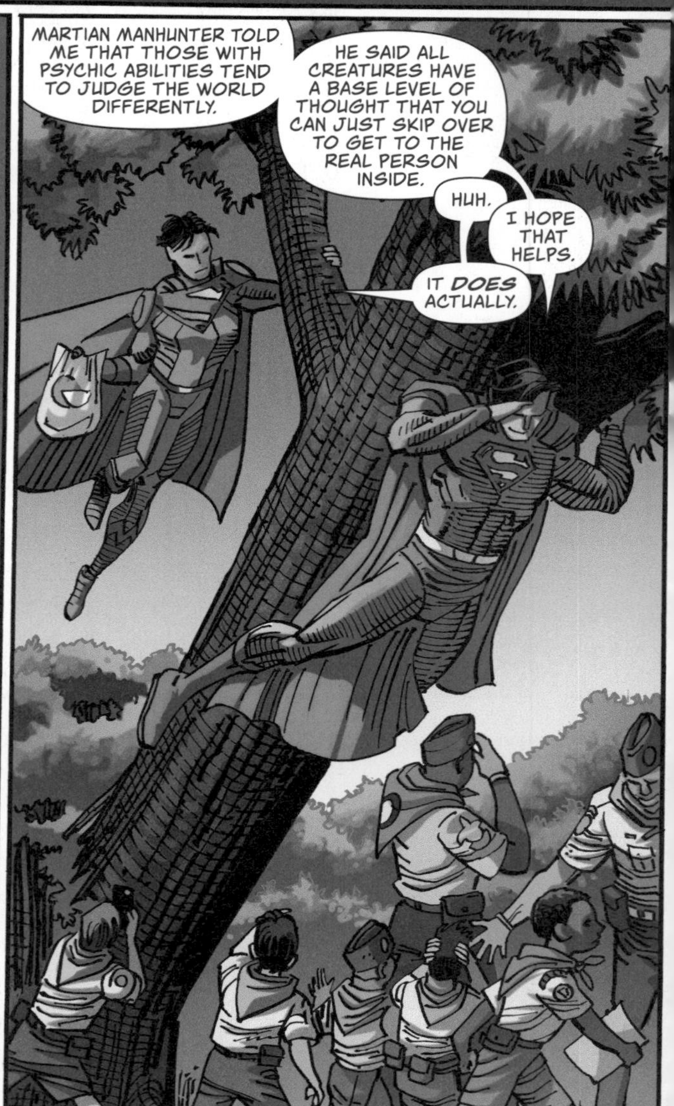
MARTIAN MANHUNTER TOLD ME THAT THOSE WITH PSYCHIC ABILITIES TEND TO JUDGE THE WORLD DIFFERENTLY.
HE SAID ALL CREATURES HAVE A BASE LEVEL OF THOUGHT THAT YOU CAN JUST SKIP OVER TO GET TO THE REAL PERSON INSIDE.
HUH.
I HOPE THAT HELPS.
IT DOES ACTUALLY.

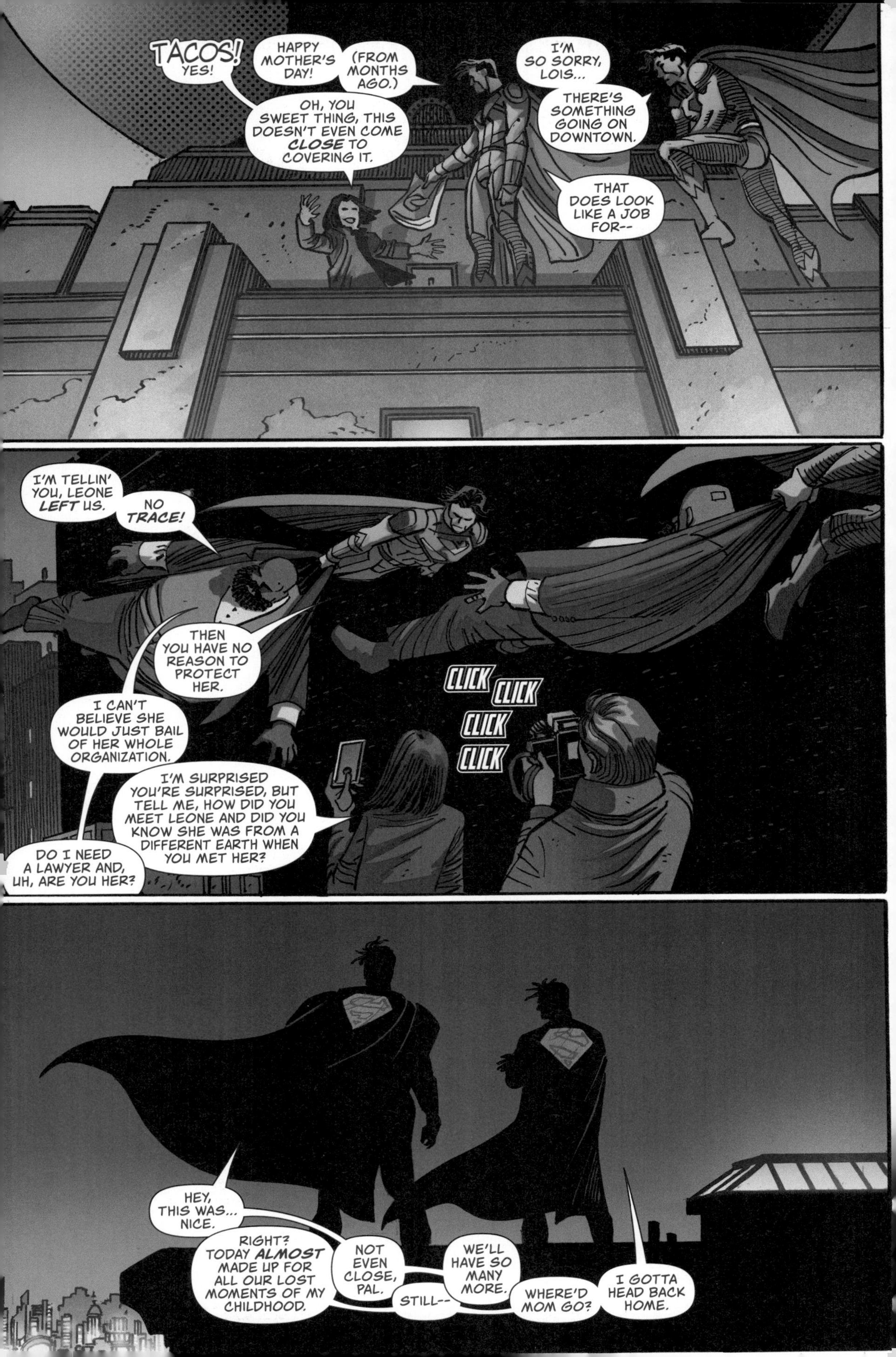

TACOS! YES!
HAPPY MOTHER'S DAY!
(FROM MONTHS AGO.)
OH, YOU SWEET THING, THIS DOESN'T EVEN COME CLOSE TO COVERING IT.
I'M SO SORRY, LOIS...
THERE'S SOMETHING GOING ON DOWNTOWN.
THAT DOES LOOK LIKE A JOB FOR--
I'M TELLIN' YOU, LEONE LEFT US.
NO TRACE!
THEN YOU HAVE NO REASON TO PROTECT HER.
I CAN'T BELIEVE SHE WOULD JUST BAIL OF HER WHOLE ORGANIZATION.
I'M SURPRISED YOU'RE SURPRISED, BUT TELL ME, HOW DID YOU MEET LEONE AND DID YOU KNOW SHE WAS FROM A DIFFERENT EARTH WHEN YOU MET HER?
DO I NEED A LAWYER AND, UH, ARE YOU HER?
CLICK
CLICK
CLICK
CLICK
HEY, THIS WAS... NICE.
RIGHT? TODAY ALMOST MADE UP FOR ALL OUR LOST MOMENTS OF MY CHILDHOOD.
NOT EVEN CLOSE, PAL.
STILL--
WE'LL HAVE SO MANY MORE.
WHERE'D MOM GO?
I GOTTA HEAD BACK HOME.

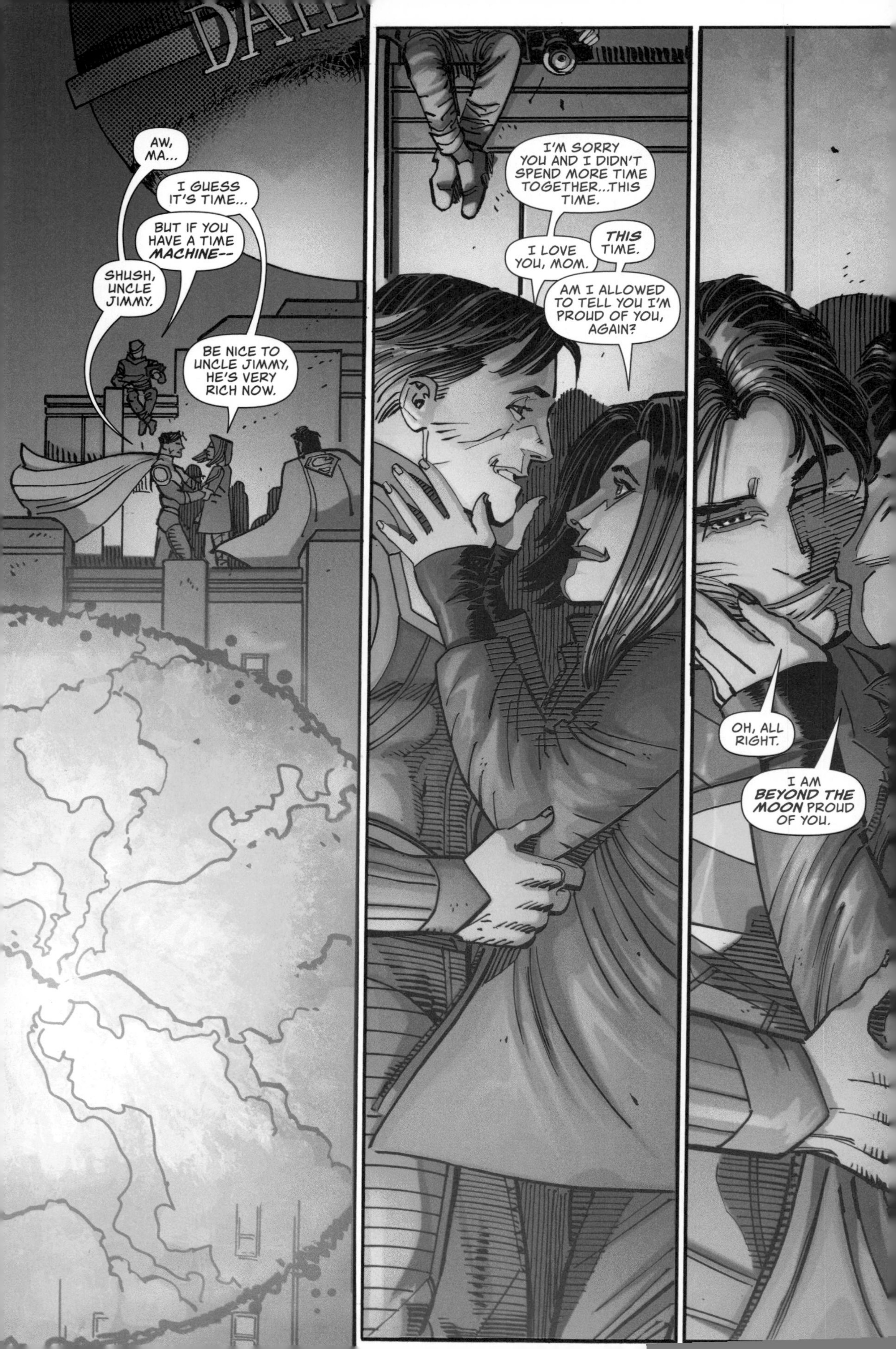
AW, MA...
I GUESS IT'S TIME...
BUT IF YOU HAVE A TIME MACHINE--
SHUSH, UNCLE JIMMY.
BE NICE TO UNCLE JIMMY, HE'S VERY RICH NOW.
I'M SORRY YOU AND I DIDN'T SPEND MORE TIME TOGETHER...THIS TIME.
I LOVE YOU, MOM.
THIS TIME.
AM I ALLOWED TO TELL YOU I'M PROUD OF YOU, AGAIN?
OH, ALL RIGHT.
I AM BEYOND THE MOON PROUD OF YOU.

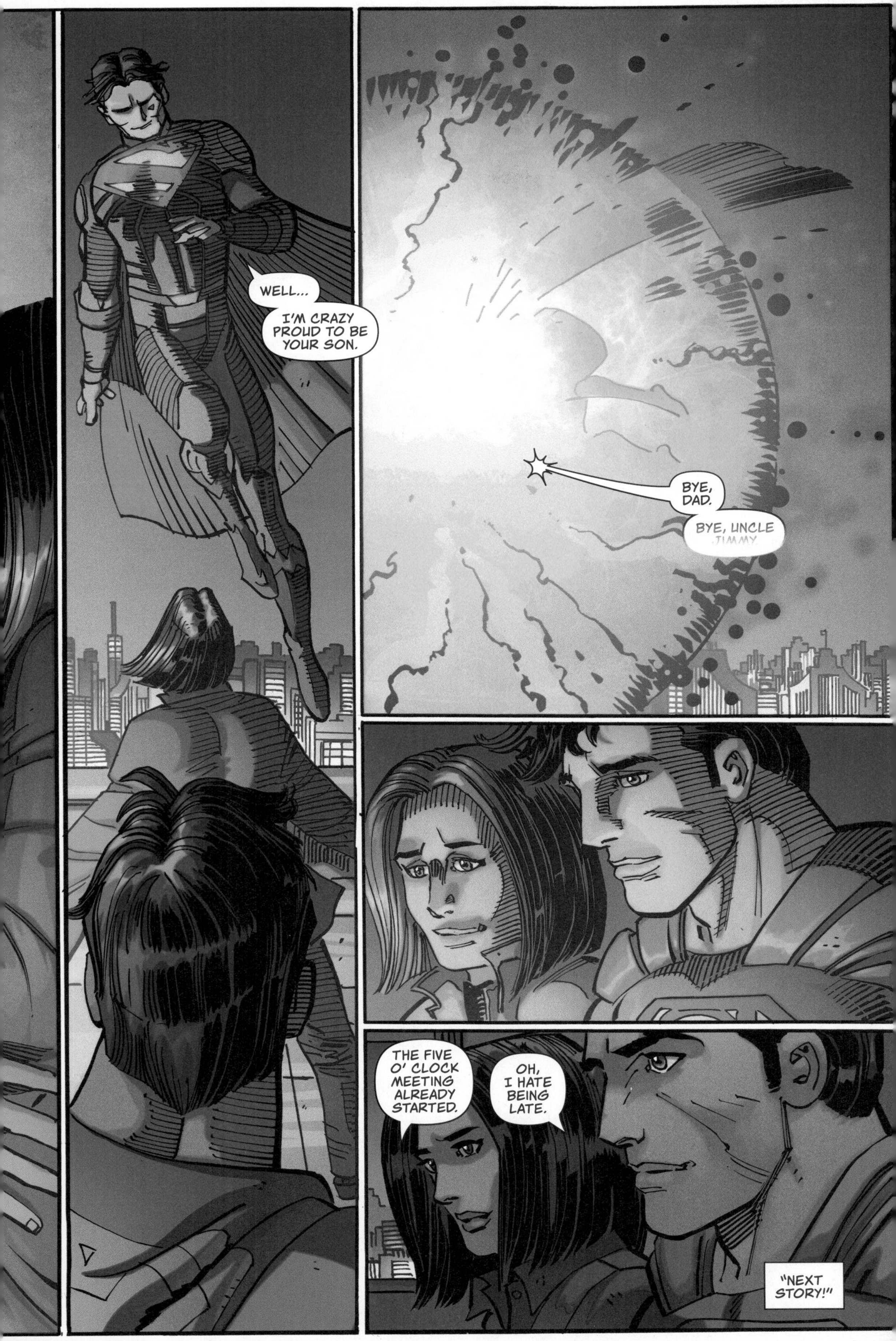
WELL...
I'M CRAZY PROUD TO BE YOUR SON.
BYE, DAD.
BYE, UNCLE JIMMY.
THE FIVE O' CLOCK MEETING ALREADY STARTED.
OH, I HATE BEING LATE.
"NEXT STORY!"

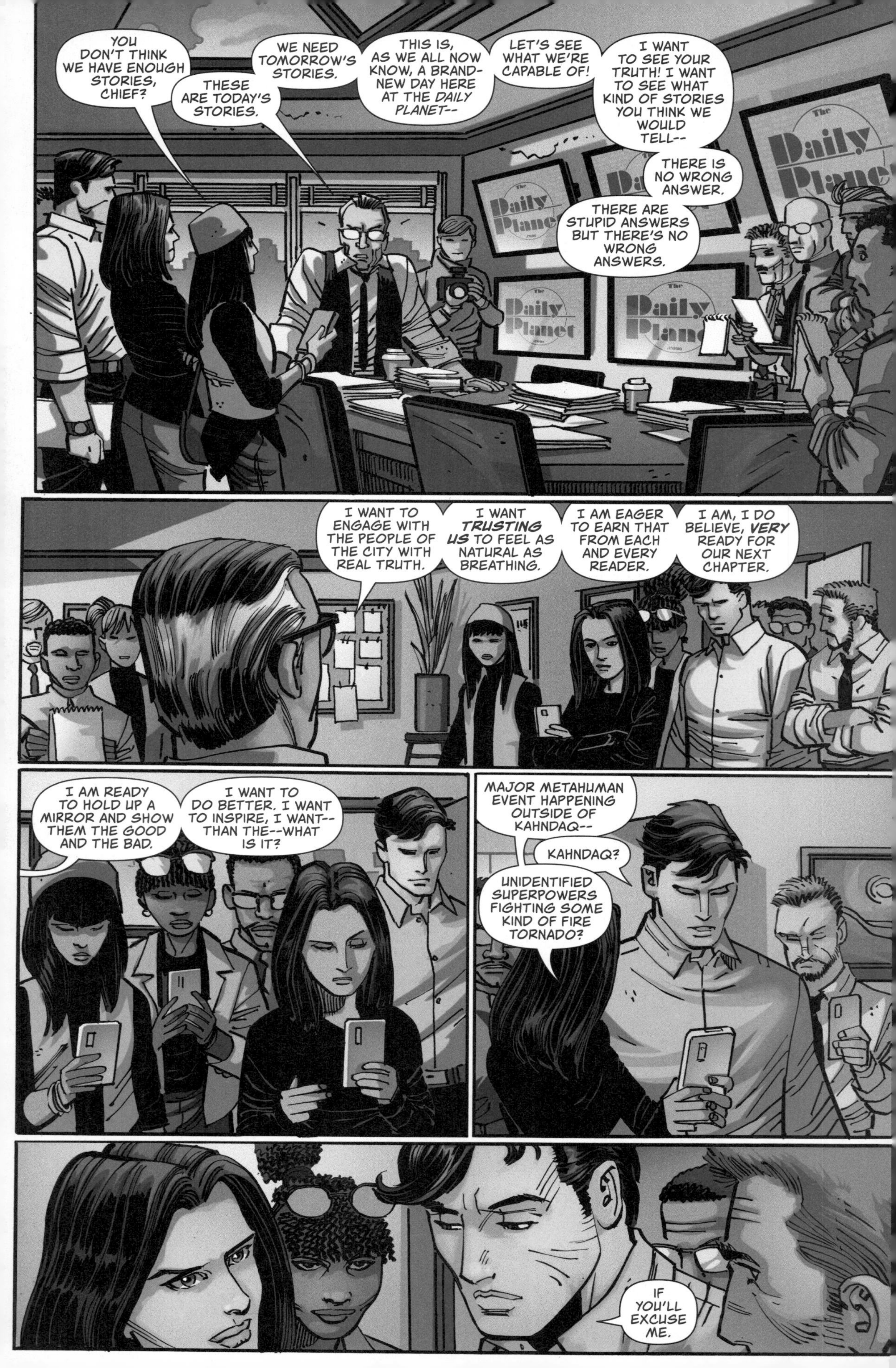
YOU DON'T THINK WE HAVE ENOUGH STORIES, CHIEF?
THESE ARE TODAY'S STORIES.
WE NEED TOMORROW'S STORIES.
THIS IS, AS WE ALL NOW KNOW, A BRAND-NEW DAY HERE AT THE *DAILY PLANET*--
LET'S SEE WHAT WE'RE CAPABLE OF!
I WANT TO SEE YOUR TRUTH! I WANT TO SEE WHAT KIND OF STORIES YOU THINK WE WOULD TELL--
THERE IS NO WRONG ANSWER.
THERE ARE STUPID ANSWERS BUT THERE'S NO WRONG ANSWERS.
I WANT TO ENGAGE WITH THE PEOPLE OF THE CITY WITH REAL TRUTH.
I WANT ***TRUSTING US*** TO FEEL AS NATURAL AS BREATHING.
I AM EAGER TO EARN THAT FROM EACH AND EVERY READER.
I AM, I DO BELIEVE, ***VERY*** READY FOR OUR NEXT CHAPTER.
I AM READY TO HOLD UP A MIRROR AND SHOW THEM THE GOOD AND THE BAD.
I WANT TO DO BETTER. I WANT TO INSPIRE, I WANT-- THAN THE--WHAT IS IT?
MAJOR METAHUMAN EVENT HAPPENING OUTSIDE OF KAHNDAQ--
KAHNDAQ?
UNIDENTIFIED SUPERPOWERS FIGHTING SOME KIND OF FIRE TORNADO?
IF YOU'LL EXCUSE ME.

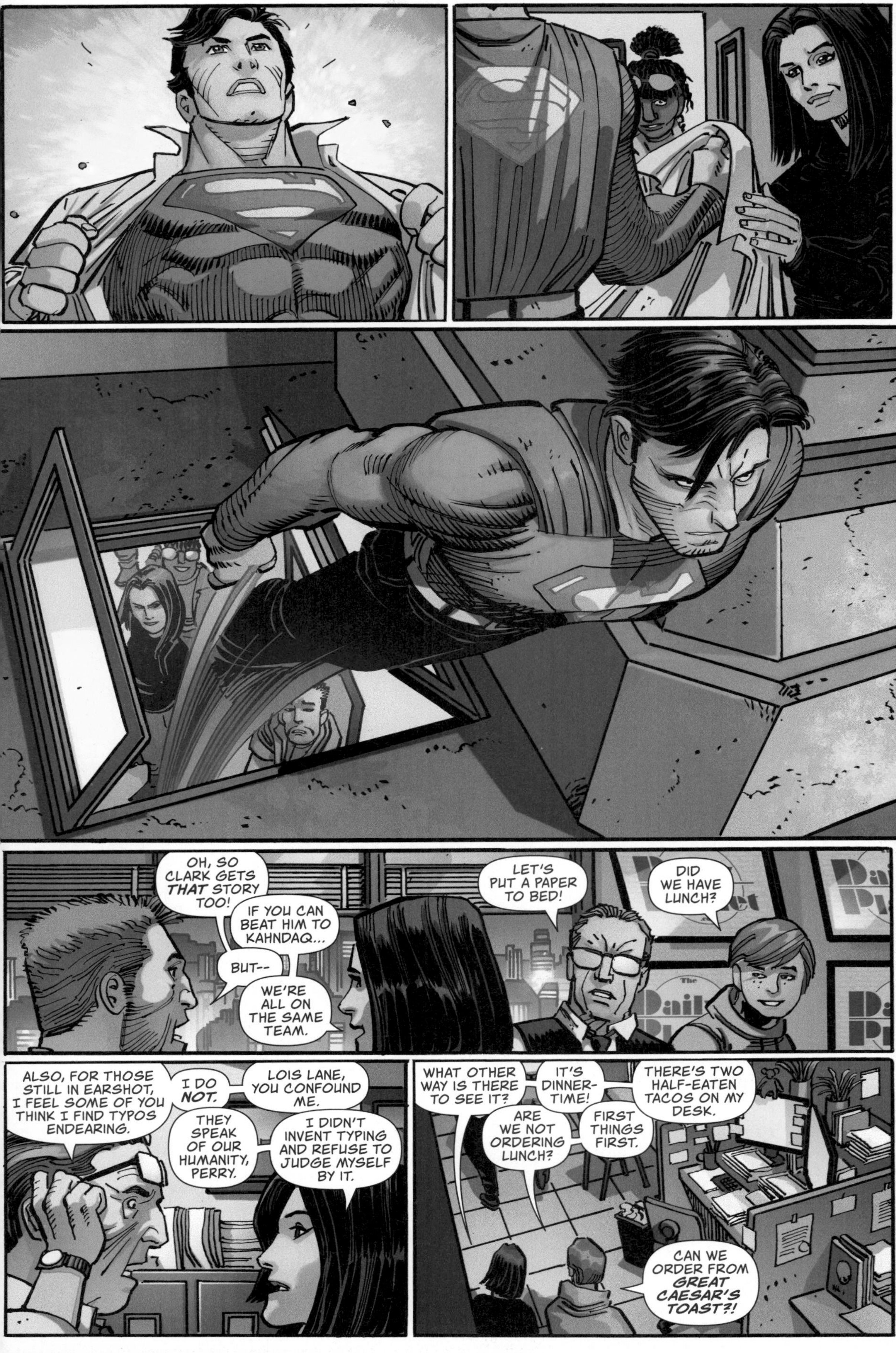
OH, SO CLARK GETS *THAT* STORY TOO!
IF YOU CAN BEAT HIM TO KAHNDAQ...
BUT--
WE'RE ALL ON THE SAME TEAM.
LET'S PUT A PAPER TO BED!
DID WE HAVE LUNCH?
ALSO, FOR THOSE STILL IN EARSHOT, I FEEL SOME OF YOU THINK I FIND TYPOS ENDEARING.
I DO *NOT.*
LOIS LANE, YOU CONFOUND ME.
THEY SPEAK OF OUR HUMANITY, PERRY.
I DIDN'T INVENT TYPING AND REFUSE TO JUDGE MYSELF BY IT.
WHAT OTHER WAY IS THERE TO SEE IT?
IT'S DINNER-TIME!
THERE'S TWO HALF-EATEN TACOS ON MY DESK.
ARE WE NOT ORDERING LUNCH?
FIRST THINGS FIRST.
CAN WE ORDER FROM *GREAT CAESAR'S TOAST?!*

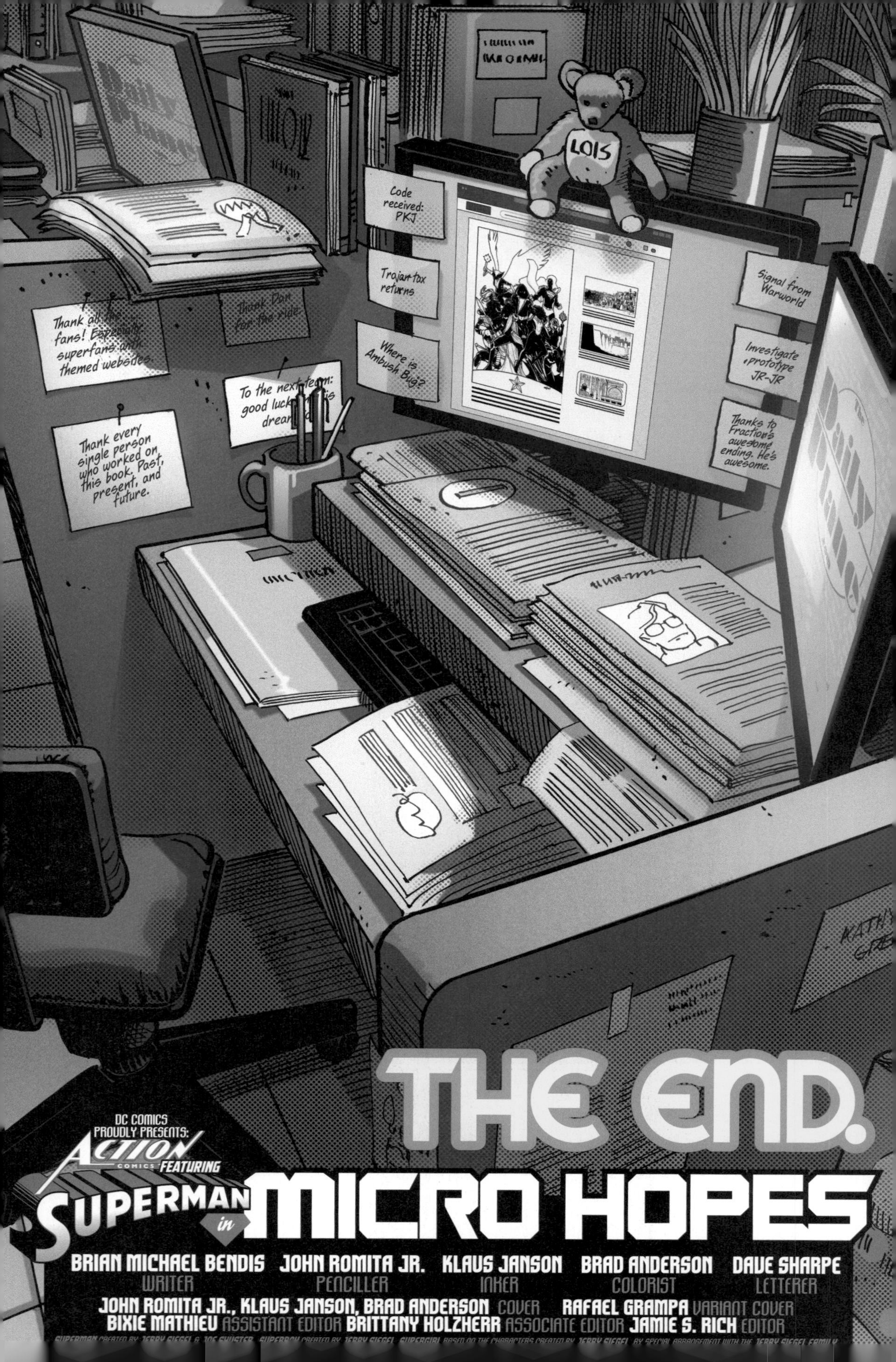
LOIS
Code received: PKJ
Trojan tax returns
Where is Ambush Bug?
Signal from Warworld
Investigate prototype JR-JR
Thanks to Fraction's awesome ending. He's awesome.
Thank all the fans! Especially superfans with themed websites.
Thank Dan for the ride.
To the next team: good luck ... dream
Thank every single person who worked on this book. Past, present, and future.
THE END.
DC COMICS PROUDLY PRESENTS:
ACTION COMICS FEATURING
SUPERMAN in MICRO HOPES
BRIAN MICHAEL BENDIS WRITER
JOHN ROMITA JR. PENCILLER
KLAUS JANSON INKER
BRAD ANDERSON COLORIST
DAVE SHARPE LETTERER
JOHN ROMITA JR., KLAUS JANSON, BRAD ANDERSON COVER
RAFAEL GRAMPA VARIANT COVER
BIXIE MATHIEU ASSISTANT EDITOR
BRITTANY HOLZHERR ASSOCIATE EDITOR
JAMIE S. RICH EDITOR
SUPERMAN CREATED BY JERRY SIEGEL & JOE SHUSTER. SUPERBOY CREATED BY JERRY SIEGEL. SUPERGIRL BASED ON THE CHARACTERS CREATED BY JERRY SIEGEL. BY SPECIAL ARRANGEMENT WITH THE JERRY SIEGEL FAMILY

VARIANT COVER
AND DESIGN GALLERY

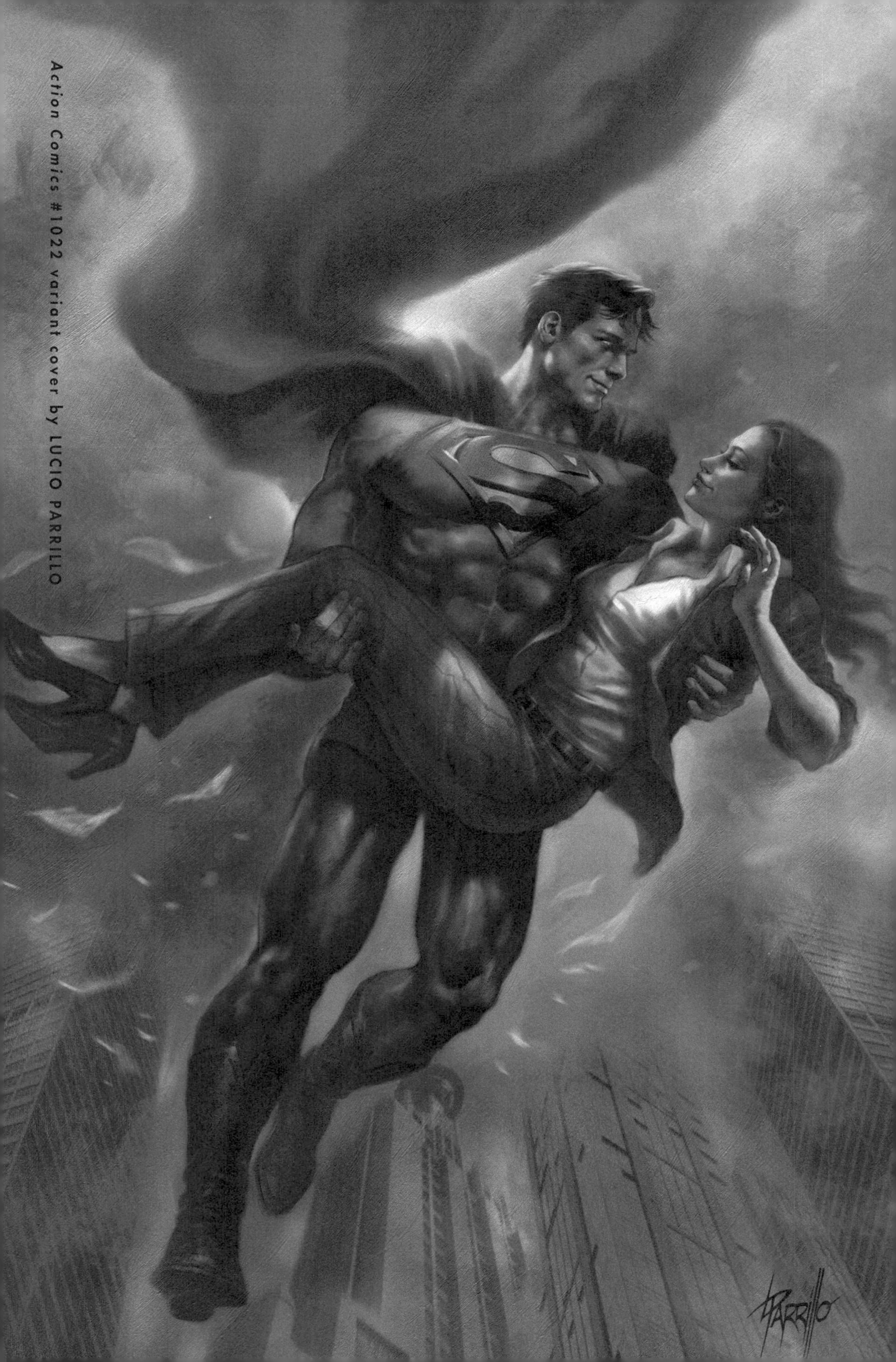
PARRILLO
Action Comics #1022 variant cover by LUCIO PARRILLO

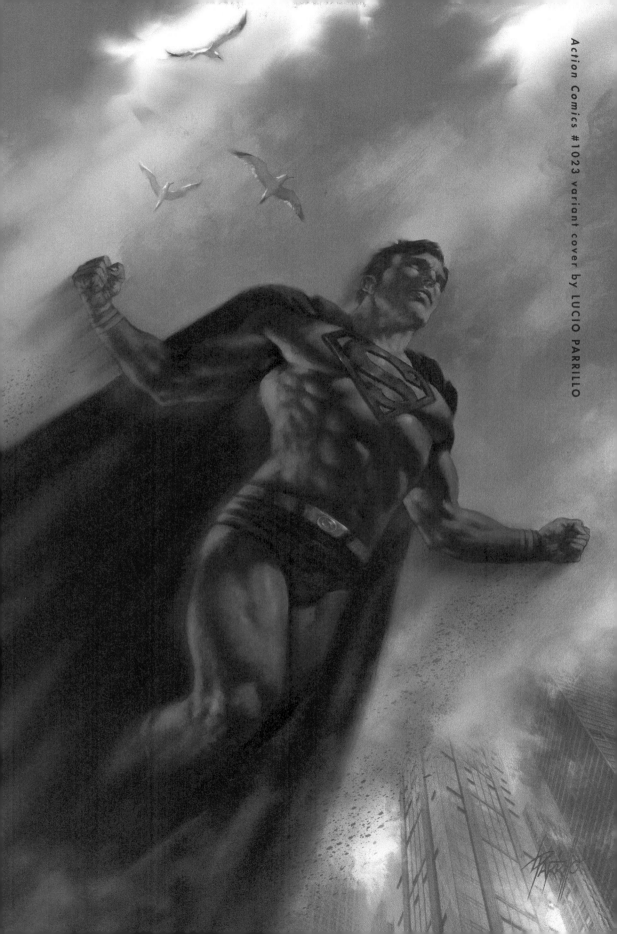

Action Comics #1023 variant cover by LUCIO PARRILLO

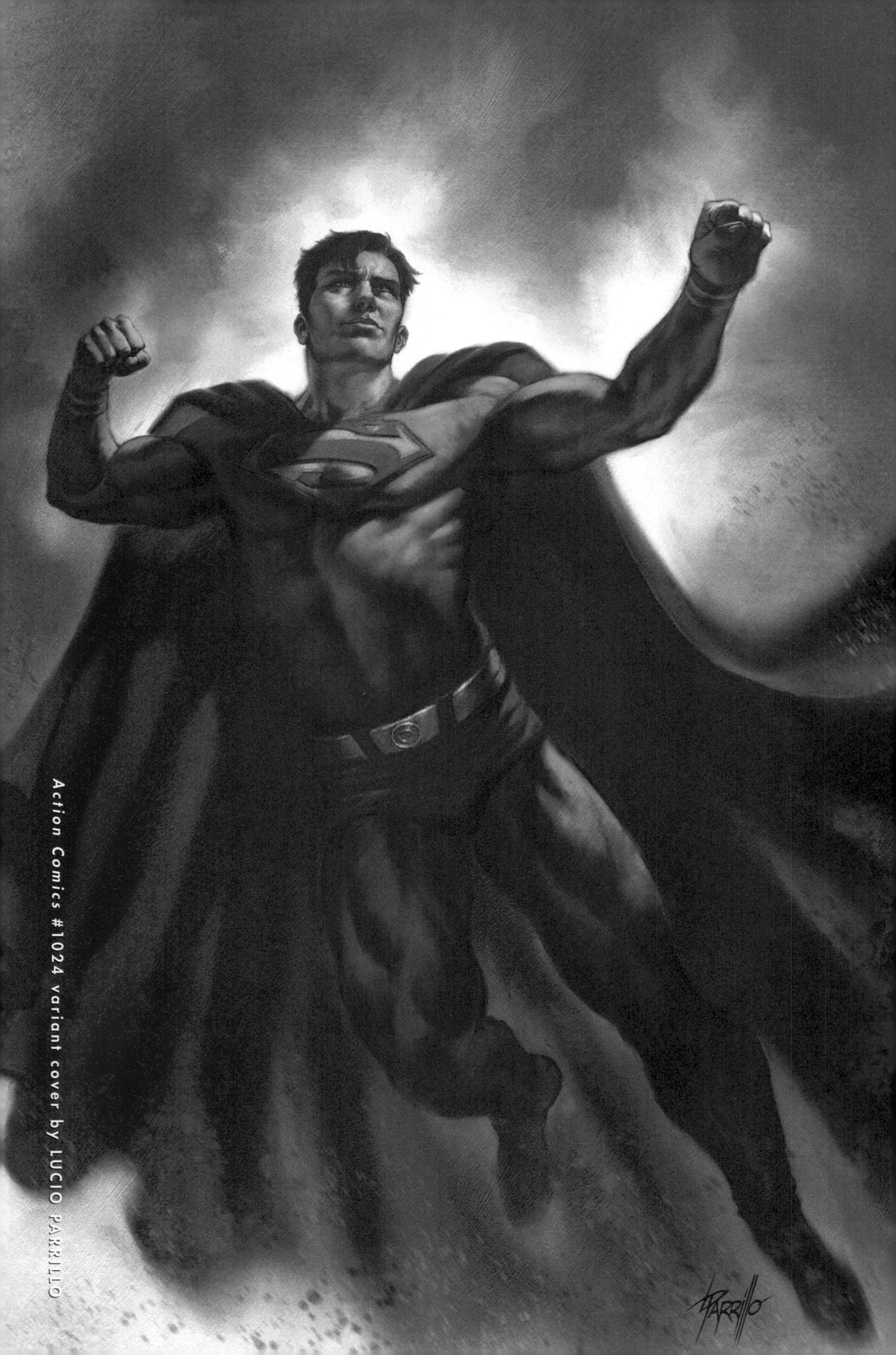

Action Comics #1024 variant cover by LUCIO PARRILLO

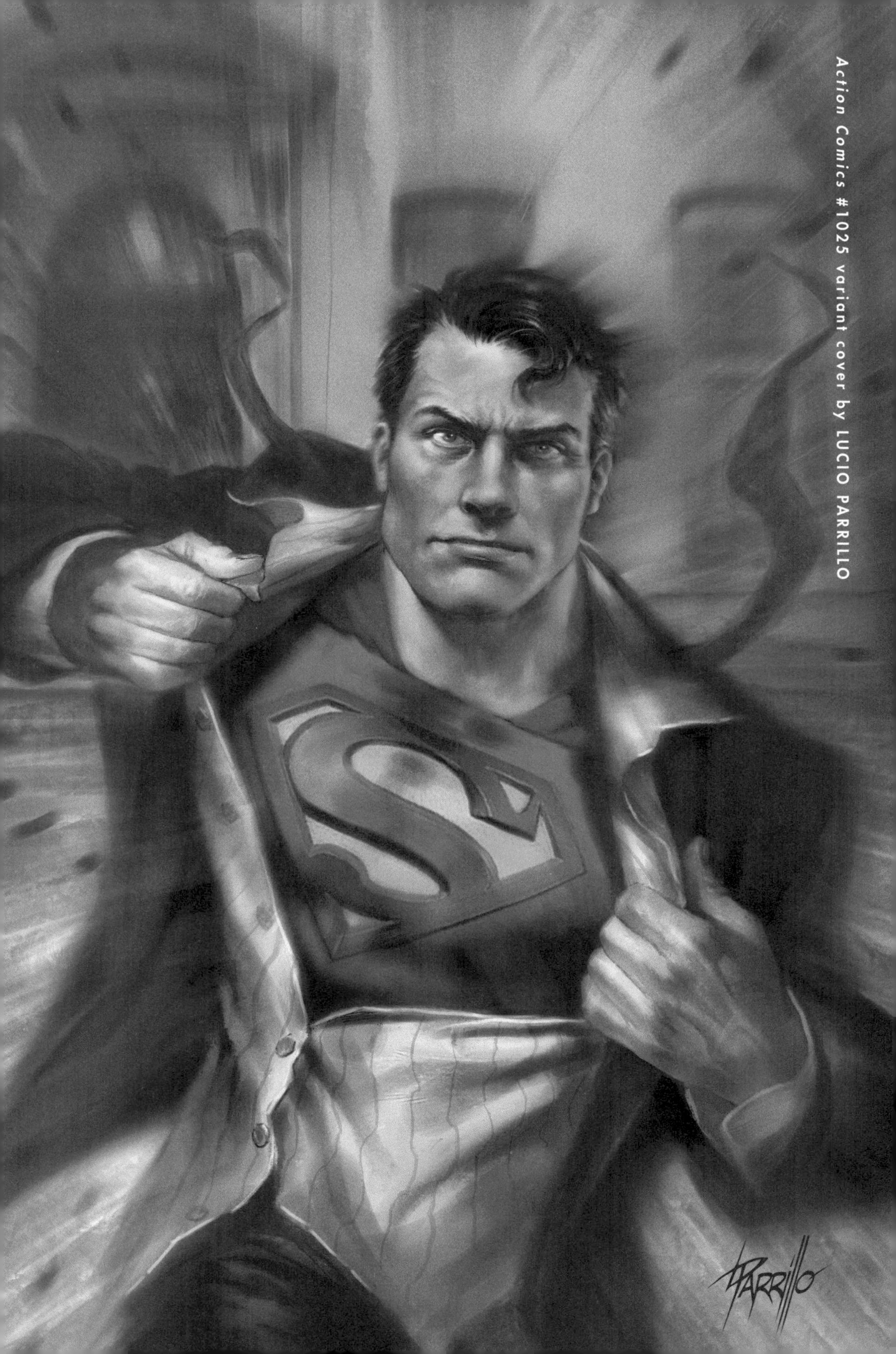

Action Comics #1025 variant cover by LUCIO PARRILLO

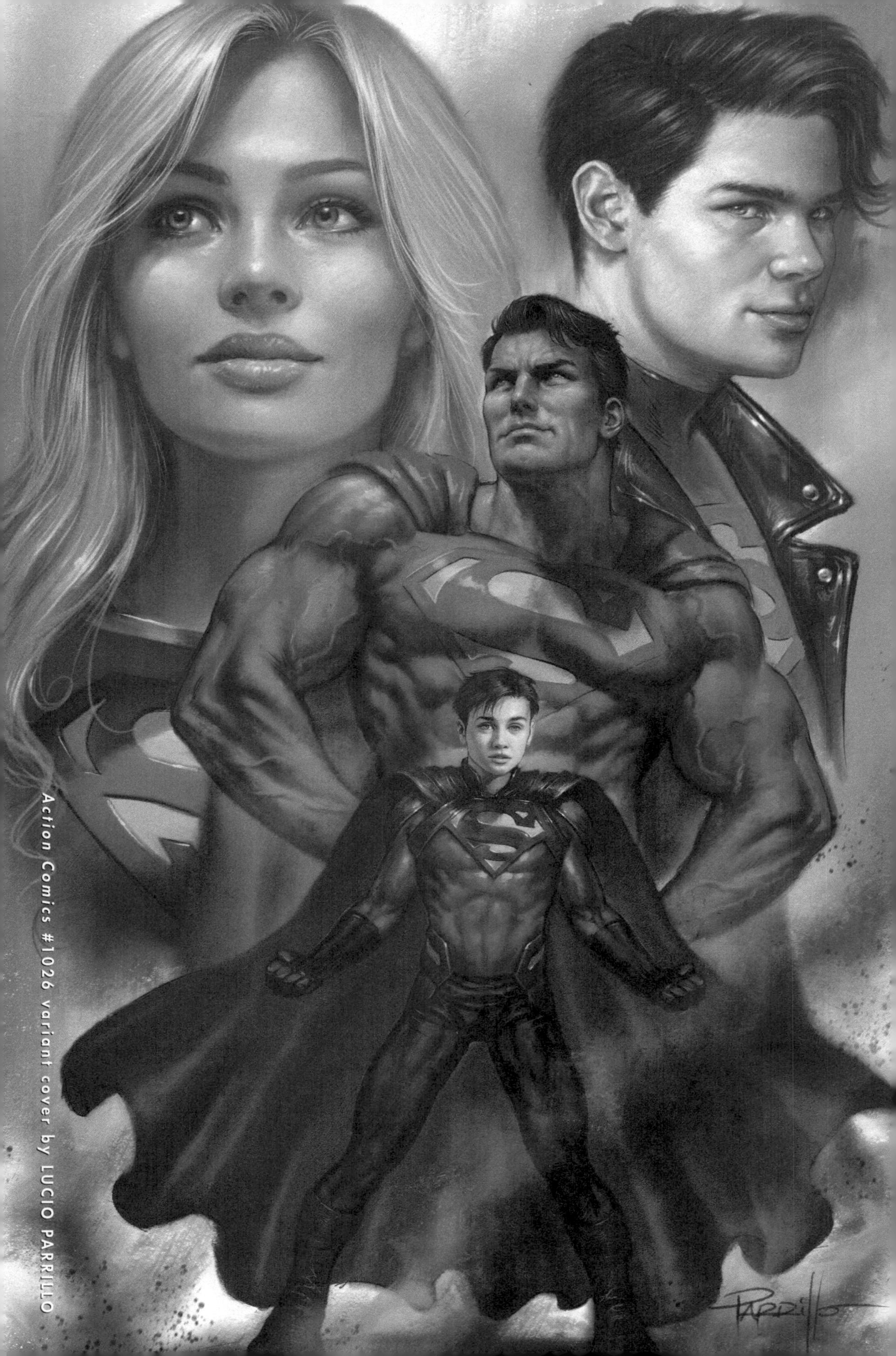

Action Comics #1026 variant cover by LUCIO PARRILLO

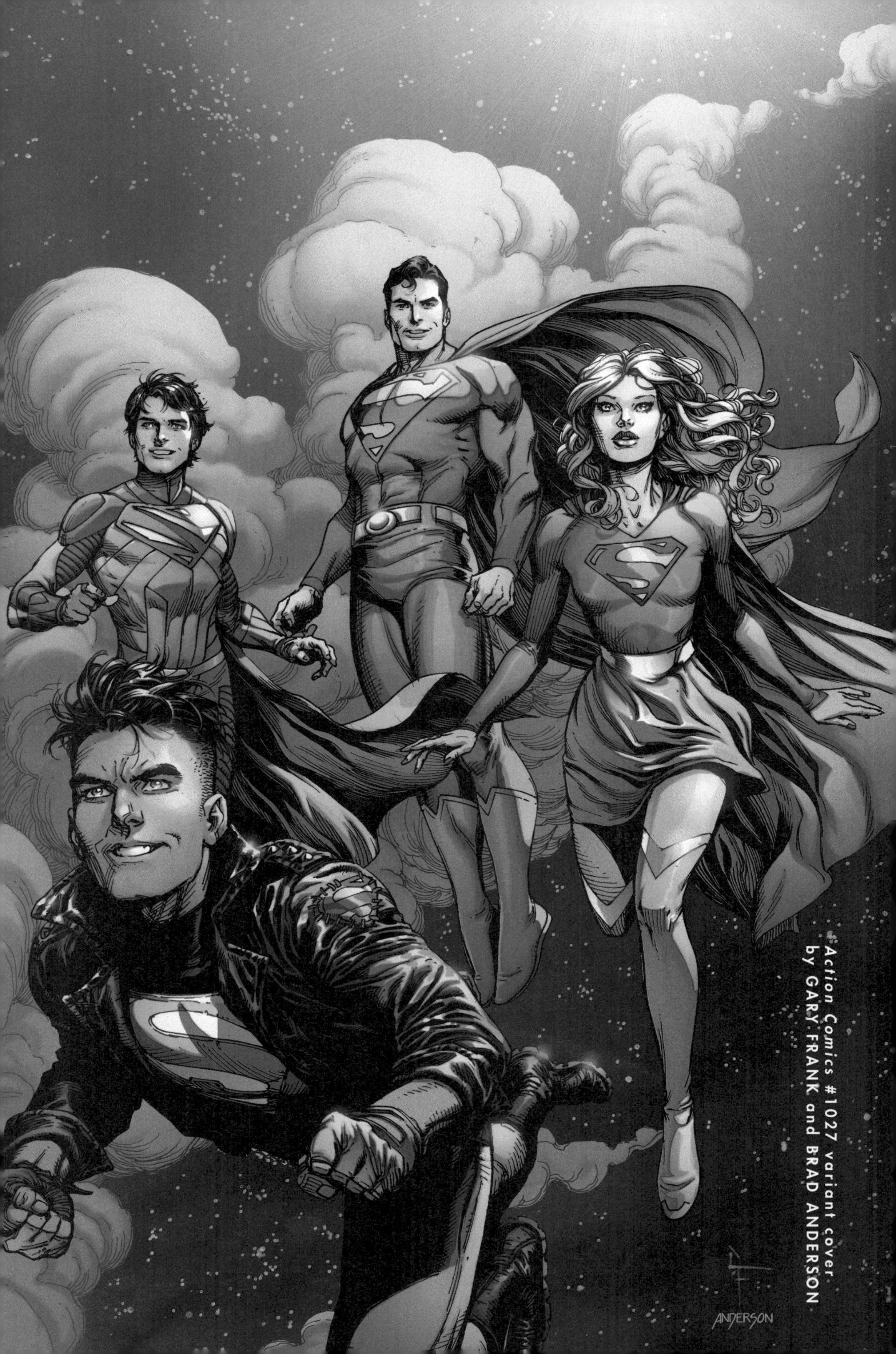
ANDERSON

*Action Comics* #1027 variant cover
by GARY FRANK and BRAD ANDERSON

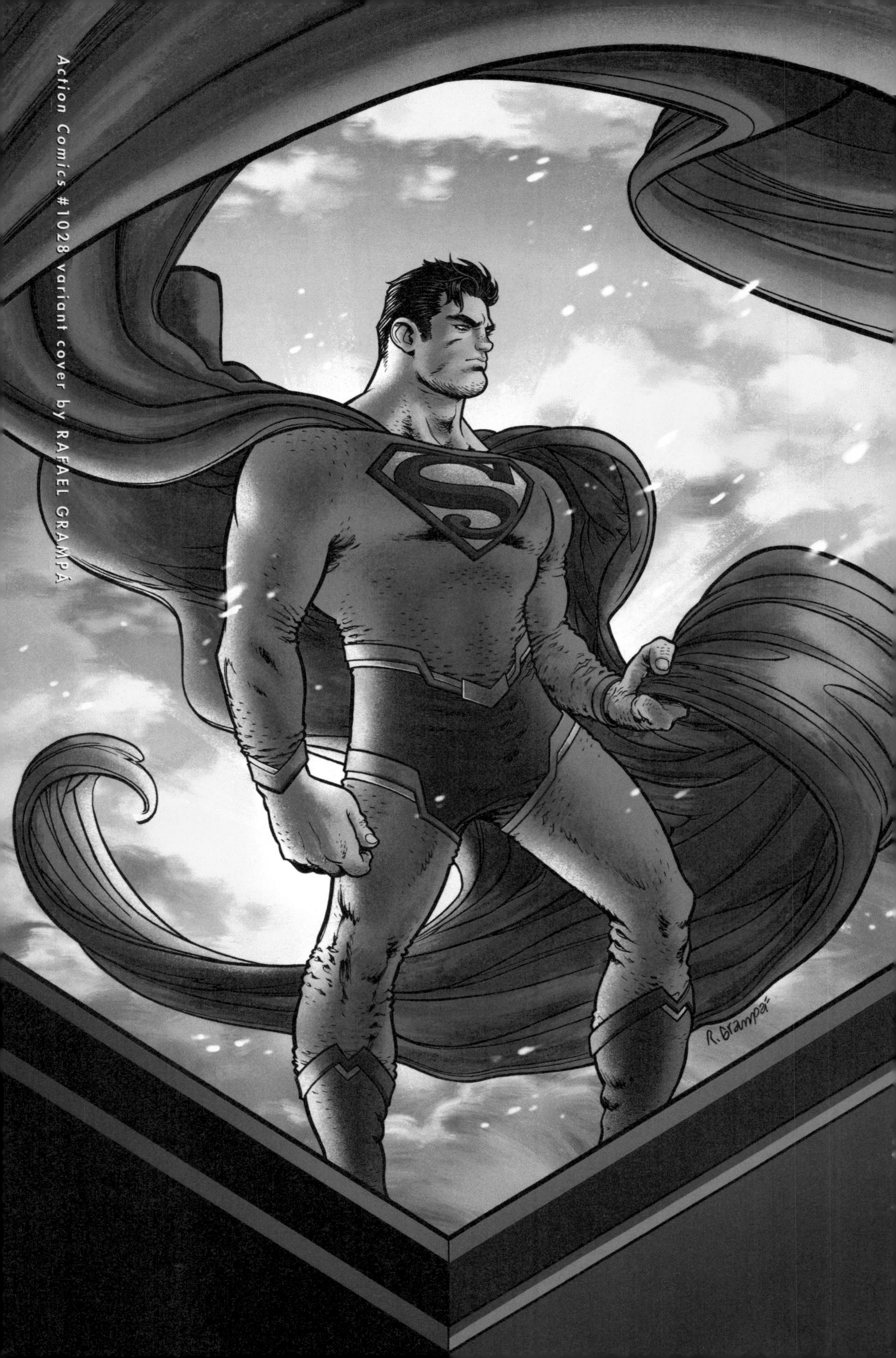
R. Grampá
Action Comics #1028 variant cover by RAFAEL GRAMPÁ